The Relationships
Among the Gospels

An Interdisciplinary Dialogue

The Relationships Among the Gospels

An Interdisciplinary Dialogue

Edited by
William O. Walker, Jr.

Contributors
Albert C. Outler, Albert B. Lord, George Kennedy,
Lou H. Silberman, Roland Mushat Frye, Charles
H. Talbert, Wayne A. Meeks, James A. Sanders,
William R. Farmer, Leander E. Keck, Reginald H.
Fuller, Joseph A. Fitzmyer, S.J., Joseph B. Tyson

Trinity University Press • San Antonio

Trinity University
Monograph Series in Religion

Volume Five

Grateful acknowledgment is extended to the publishers for permission to quote from the following works: Kurt Aland, ed., *Synopsis of the Four Gospels*, Greek-English Edition of the Synopsis Quattuor Evangeliorum with the Text of the Revised Standard Version (Stuttgart: United Bible Societies, 1972), transliteration of pp. 113–14; Charles W. Kennedy, *Early English Christian Poetry Translated into Alliterative Verse; with Critical Commentary* (London: Hollis & Carter, 1952); *Serbocroatian Heroic Songs*, coll. Milman Parry, vol. 2, *Novi Pazar: Serbocroatian Texts*, ed. Albert Bates Lord (Belgrade: The Serbian Academy of Sciences/Cambridge, Mass.: Harvard University Press, 1953); Roman Jakobson and Marc Szeftel, "The Vseslav Epos," reproduced by permission of the American Folklore Society from *Russian Epic Studies*, ed. Roman Jakobson and Ernest J. Simmons, Memoirs of the American Folklore Society 42:30, 1949.

This volume is based on proceedings of the Colloquy on the Relationships among the Gospels, sponsored by Trinity University and the Southwest Commission on Religious Studies and held at Trinity University, San Antonio, Texas, May 26–29, 1977. The Colloquy was made possible by grants from the Henry Luce Foundation, Inc., New York, and the National Endowment for the Humanities. The findings, conclusions, etc. of this Colloquy do not necessarily represent the view of the Endowment or the Luce Foundation.

Participants in the Colloquy Seminars

SEMINAR ON ORAL TRADITIONAL LITERATURE AND THE GOSPELS

Principal: Albert B. Lord (Harvard University)
Respondent: Charles H. Talbert (Wake Forest University)
Seminar Leader: Leander E. Keck (Emory University)

Paul J. Achtemeier (Union Theological Seminary in Virginia)
George N. Boyd (Trinity University)
Bruce Corley (Southwestern Baptist Theological Seminary)
Virgil P. Howard (Southern Methodist University)
Anitra Bingham Kolenkow (Graduate Theological Union)
Thomas H. Olbricht (Abilene Christian University)
Albert C. Outler (Southern Methodist University)
Wayne G. Rollins (Assumption College)

SEMINAR ON CLASSICS AND THE GOSPELS

Principal: George Kennedy (The University of North Carolina at Chapel Hill)
Respondent: Wayne A. Meeks (Yale University)
Seminar Leader: Reginald H. Fuller (The Protestant Episcopal Theological Seminary of Virginia)

William S. Babcock (Southern Methodist University)
David L. Barr (Wright State University)
M. Eugene Boring (Phillips University)
Earle McMillan (Abilene Christian University)
Bernard Orchard, O.S.B. (Ealing Abbey)
Sheldon V. Shirts (Phillips University)
Philip L. Shuler (University of Dallas)
James W. Thompson (The University of Texas in Austin)
Herold Weiss (St. Mary's College)

v

SEMINAR ON JUDAIC STUDIES AND THE GOSPELS

Principal: Lou H. Silberman (Vanderbilt University)
Respondent: James A. Sanders (Union Theological Seminary in New York)*
Seminar Leader: Joseph A. Fitzmyer, S.J. (The Catholic University of America)

John A. Bailey (University of Michigan)
Arthur J. Bellinzoni, Jr. (Wells College)
Lamar Cope (Carroll College)
F. Lamar Cribbs (Methodist Church, Rocky Ford, Colorado)
Francisco O. Garcia-Treto (Trinity University)
Allan J. McNicol (The University of Texas in Austin)
E. P. Sanders (McMaster University)
Ronald D. Worden (Friends Bible College)

SEMINAR ON LITERARY CRITICISM AND THE GOSPELS

Principal: Roland Mushat Frye (University of Pennsylvania)
Respondent: William R. Farmer (Southern Methodist University)
Seminar Leader: Joseph B. Tyson (Southern Methodist University)

Elizabeth Carey (Principia College)
Charles Thomas Davis, III (Appalachian State University)
Henry Gustafson (United Theological Seminary of the Twin Cities)
Lonnie D. Kliever (Southern Methodist University)
Daniel Wm. O'Connor (St. Lawrence University)
Reuben J. Swanson (Western Carolina University)
J. D. Thomas (Abilene Christian University)

*Now of Claremont Graduate School.

Acknowledgments

The Colloquy on the Relationships among the Gospels and this volume, which is based upon the Colloquy, would never have been possible without the cooperation, encouragement, and support of a great number of people, many of whom must remain unnamed because of limitations of space.

Trinity University co-sponsored, provided facilities, and secured funding for the Colloquy. J. Norman Parmer, Vice President for Academic Affairs, George N. Boyd, Dean of the Faculty of Humanities, and Gail E. Myers, formerly Dean of the College of Arts and Sciences and now Dean of the Faculty of Communications and Arts, were particularly helpful in making the project a success. Various individuals in the Development Office, the Office of Public Relations, the Office of Governmental Affairs, the Office of Research Grants, the Office of Student Housing, I. T. T. Building Services, and A. R. A. Food Services also contributed in many significant ways to the Colloquy and/or the volume. The Academic Leave Committee recommended an academic leave for me during the 1977 fall semester, and this made it possible for me to devote full time to the editing of materials for the volume. The Department of Religion, under the leadership first of Guy H. Ranson and later of R. Douglas Brackenridge, supported the project from the beginning and allowed me a reduced teaching load during the 1978 spring semester in order that I might complete the task of editing the volume. The assistance of two skilled and conscientious typists, Virginia A. Olmo and Cynthia A. Narciso, was invaluable. The many and varied contributions of my student secretary, Joan M. Lambert, before and particularly during the Colloquy, are here noted with sincere gratitude; in many respects, she was really the one who made the Colloquy "happen" as smoothly as it did.

The Henry Luce Foundation, Inc., and the National Endowment for the Humanities provided the funds that made possible the Colloquy at Trinity University. The Southwest Commission on Religious Studies lent its name and support as co-sponsor of the Colloquy. The members of the Steering Committee gave generously of their time and energy in planning the numerous details of the Colloquy, and they should be recognized by name. They were: Paul J. Achtemeier, Professor of New Testament at Union Theological Seminary in Virginia; William R. Farmer, Professor of New Testament at Perkins School of Theology,

Southern Methodist University; Joseph A. Fitzmyer, S.J., Professor of New Testament at The Catholic University of America; Reginald H. Fuller, Professor of New Testament at The Protestant Episcopal Theological Seminary of Virginia; Leander E. Keck, Professor of New Testament at Candler School of Theology, Emory University; and Joseph B. Tyson, Professor of Religious Studies at Southern Methodist University, who was co-convener of the Committee with me and deserves particular thanks for his valuable contributions. John H. Hayes, editor of the Trinity University Monograph Series in Religion, agreed to include this volume in the series, and his cooperation from the beginning has been greatly appreciated.

Finally, I take this opportunity to express my profound respect and gratitude to Joe W. Nicholson, Director, and Lois Boyd, Editor, of Trinity University Press. They encouraged and supported the project from the start, assisted in the planning and holding of the Colloquy, and have provided enthusiastic, patient, and professional counsel and assistance at every stage of the editing and publishing of this volume.

W. O. W., Jr.
February, 1978

Contents

Contributors

KEYNOTE SPEAKER

Albert C. Outler
Research Professor of Theology
Perkins School of Theology
Southern Methodist University

PRINCIPALS

Albert B. Lord
Arthur Kingsley Porter Professor of Slavic and Comparative
    Literature
Harvard University

George Kennedy
Paddison Professor of Classics
The University of North Carolina at Chapel Hill

Lou H. Silberman
Professor of Jewish Literature and Thought
Vanderbilt University

Roland Mushat Frye
Professor of English Literature
University of Pennsylvania

RESPONDENTS

Charles H. Talbert
Professor of Religion
Wake Forest University

Wayne A. Meeks
Professor of Religious Studies
Yale University

James A. Sanders
Elizabeth Hay Bechtel Professor of Intertestamental and
    Biblical Studies
School of Theology at Claremont
Claremont Graduate School

William R. Farmer
Professor of New Testament
Perkins School of Theology
Southern Methodist University

SEMINAR LEADERS

Leander E. Keck
Professor of New Testament
Candler School of Theology
Emory University

Reginald H. Fuller
Professor of New Testament
The Protestant Episcopal Theological Seminary of Virginia

Joseph A. Fitzmyer, S.J.
Professor of New Testament
The Catholic University of America

Joseph B. Tyson
Professor of Religious Studies
Southern Methodist University

EDITOR OF VOLUME

William O. Walker, Jr.
Professor of Religion
Trinity University

The Relationships
Among the Gospels

An Interdisciplinary Dialogue

Introduction: The Colloquy on the Relationships among the Gospels

William O. Walker, Jr.

Background

Critical scholarship is dependent almost exclusively upon a group of early Christian writings known as "gospels" for historical data regarding the life and activity of Jesus of Nazareth. A plurality of gospels has survived, and the various gospels do not present identical portrayals of Jesus. It would seem, then, that a cogent picture of the chronological and literary relationships among the gospels is a prerequisite for understanding the origins and early development of the Christian movement: Do the gospels represent separate and independent accounts? Do they rely upon a common source or sources? Are they dependent upon one another for some or all of their contents, and, if so, in what chronological sequence do they stand?

These questions become particularly acute in the case of the so-called "Synoptic Gospels," Matthew, Mark, and Luke. Even a superficial reading of these gospels discloses striking similarities of content, sequence, and, indeed, wording at many points. In the judgment of most modern New Testament scholars, these similarities point almost certainly to some type of literary relationship, direct and/or indirect, among the three; that is, they are dependent either upon one another or upon a common source or sources or upon both. On the other hand, the differences

1

among these gospels—differences also of content, sequence, and wording—suggest that the relationship is more complex than might at first be supposed. The so-called "Synoptic Problem," which has troubled New Testament scholars for more than a century, is the problem of accounting for both the similarities and the differences.

Until quite recently, there has been a general consensus among most critical scholars in the field that Mark was the earliest of the gospels, that it served as a major source for both Matthew and Luke, and that Matthew and Luke also made extensive use of another common source, no longer extant, usually referred to as "Q" (from the German *Quelle*, meaning "source").[1] Such scholars characteristically have regarded the fourth gospel, John, as a late, theologically motivated writing, possessing little historically reliable material, although some have suggested that the author of John may have known and used one or more of the Synoptics.

In recent years, however, the so-called "Two-Document" or "Two-Source Hypothesis" (i.e., Mark and "Q") has been seriously challenged from various quarters, and an increasing number of scholars is now arguing both for the elimination of the "Q" theory and for the priority of Matthew or perhaps even Luke.[2] At the same time, there has been new interest in the provenance, date, sources, and historical reliability of John, as well as in other, "noncanonical" gospels and their relationship to the four

---

[1] The classic statement of this view in English is Burnett Hillman Streeter, *The Four Gospels: A Study of Origins Treating of the Manuscript Tradition, Sources, Authorship, & Dates*, rev. ed. (London: Macmillan and Co., Limited, 1936). Streeter and others have also believed that Matthew and Luke each had its own special source, sometimes known, respectively, as "M" and "L." For an illuminating discussion of the symbol, "Q," see Harvey K. McArthur, "The Origin of the 'Q' Symbol," *The Expository Times*, 88 (1977), 119–120.

[2] The most thoroughgoing and systematic challenge to the Two-Source Hypothesis has come from William R. Farmer, who argues for the elimination of "Q" and for the priority of Matthew; see esp. his *The Synoptic Problem: A Critical Analysis* (New York: The Macmillan Company/London: Collier-Macmillan Limited, 1964); this book has now appeared in a very slightly revised edition (Dillsboro, N.C.: Western North Carolina Press, Inc., 1976). Other scholars, both before and since Farmer's initial publication on the subject, have argued for one or both of the same points, and Farmer himself continues his research and publication in the area. For the most significant attempt to demonstrate Lucan priority, see Robert L. Lindsey, *A New Approach to the Synoptic Gospels* (Jerusalem: Dugwith Publishers, 1971).

2

gospels of the New Testament.[3] In short, the critical consensus regarding gospel relationships now appears to have been shaken, if not shattered. The leading, though not the only, challenge to the Two-Source Hypothesis, with its view of Marcan priority and the "Q" theory, comes from a form of the "Griesbach Hypothesis," which holds that Matthew was the earliest gospel, that Luke depended heavily upon Matthew, and that Mark represents a later abbreviated and conflated version of the two.[4] Many believe that an impasse has now been reached, with confidence in the Two-Source Hypothesis weakened but no other hypothesis successful in replacing it. Thus, an attempt to break this impasse by a renewed examination of the relationships among the gospels would seem to be both appropriate and timely.

In its study of early Christian literature and history, modern New Testament scholarship has relied extensively upon critical tools, methods, and insights developed in other academic disciplines, such as history (including history of religions), literary criticism, linguistics, philosophy, classics, folklore, comparative literature, anthropology, and psychology. A unique concept, however, led to the Colloquy on the Relationships among the Gospels at Trinity University in San Antonio, Texas, on May 26–29, 1977. The concept was that a small number of internationally known and respected scholars from certain of these other dis-

---

[3]Perhaps the single most important and suggestive work dealing with these aspects of the Gospel of John is C. H. Dodd, *Historical Tradition in the Fourth Gospel* (Cambridge: Cambridge University Press, 1963). Interest in the non-canonical gospels has been stimulated by the publication of the so-called "Gospel of Thomas" and other materials discovered in 1946 near the modern city of Nag Hammadi in Upper Egypt; see, most recently, James M. Robinson, gen. ed., *The Nag Hammadi Library in English* (New York, Hagerstown, San Francisco, and London: Harper & Row, Publishers, 1977); for a popular treatment, see John Dart, *The Laughing Savior: The Discovery and Significance of the Nag Hammadi Gnostic Library* (New York, Hagerstown, San Francisco, and London: Harper & Row, Publishers, 1976).

[4]The name comes from Johann Jakob Griesbach (1745–1812). Griesbach assumed Luke's use of Matthew but never discussed the relationship between the two. "Contemporary advocates of the Griesbach hypothesis have been obliged to explain the relationship of Luke to Matthew and in other ways develop a more convincing explanation of this hypothesis" (William R. Farmer, "Modern Developments of Griesbach's Hypothesis," *New Testament Studies*, 23 [1977], 275). For a helpful summary of a number of proposed solutions to the Synoptic Problem, see George Wesley Buchanan, "Current Synoptic Studies: Orchard, the Griesbach Hypothesis, and Other Alternatives," *Religion in Life*, 46 (1977), 415–425.

ciplines be invited to apply their knowledge and expertise *directly* to an exploration of the relationships among the gospels and that this be done in dialogue with a select group of New Testament experts and other interested academicians. Presumably, such scholars would have encountered similar or analogous problems in their own respective areas of study, and it could be expected that their experience, perspectives, and insights would be of interest and help to those working in the field of gospel studies. Such an interdisciplinary approach to the problem had not previously been attempted, and, since the specialists in the field had thus far been unable to solve the problem, this approach appeared to offer one possible way of breaking the current impasse and moving the discussion in constructive directions.

It was not expected that any definitive answers would emerge from the Colloquy or that the Colloquy would solve the problem of gospel relationships. It was only expected that the Colloquy would stimulate renewed interest in the problem on the part of New Testament scholars, that it would provide relevant and helpful data and insights from other disciplines, that it would suggest a partial agenda for continuing research into the problem, and that, in these ways, it would result in significant progress toward clarifying the relationships among the gospels. It should go without saying that there was absolutely no presupposition or hope by the Steering Committee that the results of the Colloquy would strengthen or weaken any particular scholarly hypothesis or perspective. All that was asked and expected of the participants was that they be open to whatever possibilities might emerge in the course of the Colloquy.

Leander E. Keck's opening comments at the first meeting of the Seminar on Oral Traditional Literature and the Gospels, which was also the first seminar meeting of the Colloquy, expressed the hopes and expectations of the Steering Committee as it planned the Colloquy:

I assume that we all take the genre of this occasion seriously. It is a scholars' "colloquy," that is, a structured setting in which colleagues talk together and learn from one another. I take it that a colloquy is not a debate, nor a trial, whether by ordeal or by jury, nor an oral exam, nor a negotiating session. It is a conversation, in which we talk to one another and, indeed, may find ourselves saying and thinking things that we have not said or thought before and that we may not want to defend until dark, but that we might want to test, to experiment with. In other

4

words, I hope we forget the tape recorder and feel free to think and speak on the edge of our competence and probably beyond. I suspect that the conversation will go nowhere if we merely exegete in public the positions we already hold.

Of course, this occasion is also called a "seminar," and this, I take it, means that our conversation is serious, that it is focused, and that we expect to learn as we proceed.

I also take the timing of this occasion seriously—not just the nine o'clock in the morning, but with reference to Mr. Farmer's recent article in *New Testament Studies*, where he observes that we are between eras. The Griesbach Hypothesis has not established itself, and at the same time the dominance of the Two-Source Theory is eroded. This is a good time, I think, to ascertain the extent to which colleagues in related disciplines might help us forward.[5]

Members of the Southwest Seminar on Gospel Studies began informal conversations regarding the Colloquy in the spring of 1974.[6] It was assumed that the Colloquy would, in some sense, serve as a sequel to the Festival on the Gospels, held at Pittsburgh Theological Seminary in 1970, although on a much smaller scale and with a more narrowly specified topic.[7] Trinity University and the Southwest Commission on Religious Studies agreed to co-sponsor the Colloquy, and Trinity University secured funding for it from the Henry Luce Foundation, Inc., and the National Endowment for the Humanities. By the end of 1974, formation of a Steering Committee had been completed.

During the next two years, the Steering Committee met on four occasions, carried on extensive communication by mail and telephone, made basic decisions regarding the general nature and format of the Colloquy, and selected the various participants. Before the middle of 1976, the Keynote Speaker, the four "Prin-

[5] The reference is to Farmer, "Modern Developments of Griesbach's Hypothesis," 275–295. References to the seminar discussions and to what was said during the Panel Discussion and at the concluding banquet will not be documented. All of the Colloquy sessions were recorded on audio tape, and these tapes are preserved in my possession.

[6] The Southwest Seminar on Gospel Studies meets approximately seven times each year at Perkins School of Theology, Southern Methodist University, in Dallas, Texas, to discuss research being carried on by its members. Membership in the spring of 1974 included William R. Farmer, Joseph B. Tyson, and me; all of us were to become members of the Steering Committee for the Colloquy.

[7] Papers and reports from the Festival on the Gospels were published as *Jesus and Man's Hope*, vol. 1 ed. David G. Buttrick, vol. 2 ed. Donald G. Miller and Dikran Y. Hadidian, 2 vols., Perspective Books (Pittsburgh: Pittsburgh Theological Seminary, 1970–1971).

cipals" from outside the field of New Testament studies, and the four "Respondents" from within the field had been selected and were at work on their Colloquy presentations. By early 1977, approximately forty other scholars, most of them New Testament specialists, had been selected and assigned to the four working seminars whose meetings were to constitute most of the Colloquy sessions.

It had been assumed that, since neither the Keynote Speaker nor any of the four Principals was known as an expert in the field of early Christian literature or history, none of them would be identified with any particular "school" of thought regarding the relationships among the gospels. Rather, on the basis of his own knowledge, experience, and expertise, each would present his views regarding the nature of the problem and his suggestions for dealing with it. In the case of the Respondents, however, since they were selected from within the field of New Testament studies, there was something of a conscious and deliberate attempt to secure a balance of viewpoints and perspectives.

The Colloquy convened on the evening of Thursday, May 26, 1977. At the opening session, a senior scholar, distinguished by his breadth of knowledge, experience, and reputation, delivered the Keynote Address, in which he identified certain of the key issues involved in the problem of gospel relationships, sketched something of the relevant history of the discussion, and emphasized the potential importance of the Colloquy. On the following three days, each of the four working seminars met, under the leadership of a member of the Steering Committee, for a total of approximately five hours, during which it discussed topics suggested by one of the principal papers and its response. The papers and responses had been distributed to all participants prior to the Colloquy, and the Principals and Respondents participated actively in the seminar sessions. A Panel Discussion on Saturday evening, involving the Keynote Speaker and the four Principals, and a concluding banquet on Sunday, at which the Keynote Speaker and the Principals delivered brief summary remarks, provided additional opportunities for these "outsiders" to reflect upon the problem of the relationships among the gospels. All sessions of the Colloquy were preserved on audio tape.

During the summer following the Colloquy, the Keynote Speaker, the four Principals, and the four Respondents revised their Colloquy presentations for publication in this volume. In addition, each of the four Seminar Leaders prepared a paper, 6 in which he (1) summarized the primary points in his seminar's discussions (audio tapes of the discussions were provided for his use); (2) assessed the contribution toward resolving the problem of gospel relationships made by the principal paper, the response, and the seminar discussion in his particular area; and (3) identified specific items suggested by the paper, the response, and the discussion that he believed should be placed on the agenda for future gospel studies. All of this material was then edited and has been approved by the various authors for publication in its present form. It should be emphasized that, although this volume is based upon the Colloquy on the Relationships among the Gospels, it is by no means to be understood as representing merely the "proceedings" of this Colloquy.

Impressions of the Colloquy

A realistic assessment of the results of the Colloquy is difficult, if not impossible, for at least two reasons. In the first place, the results will inevitably be viewed differently by each of the approximately fifty-five participants. Some will have had their previously held assumptions and opinions strengthened, and these assumptions and opinions will themselves have differed widely; others will have had them weakened. Some will have come away with new perspectives and viewpoints, others with new questions and problems. Thus, it would be misleading to speak of any general consensus or conclusion that emerged from the Colloquy, for there was none. In the second place, and perhaps even more importantly, the true significance of the Colloquy will be seen only in retrospect. In his concluding remarks at the Colloquy's final session, Albert C. Outler recognized the Colloquy as the scholarly gathering "that will stand in the succession of ones that we have already started,"[8] but he insisted: "It is *very* clear that it must not be the last." One measure of the Colloquy's success will be whether there are further such gatherings and whether they recognizably stand in the succession of this Colloquy. Another, and perhaps more important, measure will be the extent

[8]The reference is to the Pittsburgh Festival on the Gospels (see n. 7 above) and the Griesbach Bicentennial Colloquium at Münster in 1976. One of the papers prepared for the Colloquium has been published: Farmer, "Modern Developments of Griesbach's Hypothesis"; others are scheduled to be published by Cambridge University Press under the editorship of Bernard Orchard and Thomas R. W. Longstaff.

to which individual scholars and groups of scholars, both those who were in attendance at the Colloquy and those whose participation will have been limited to a reading of this volume, include as items on their own research agendas the many data and suggestions that, as Outler observed, have been "piled on our plate" as the result of the Colloquy. Outler's comment is apposite: "My guess is that two weeks from now, two months from now, two years from now, the impact of this experience will be more in evidence for each one of us than it is now. This is the way it should be."

No two participants in the Colloquy would compile exactly the same list of points that received significant attention and that may influence gospel studies in the future. As I took part in the Colloquy sessions, however, and particularly as I have studied the audio tapes of these sessions and edited the materials in this volume, certain impressions have become clear in my own mind.

In the first place, despite the designation of the gathering as a "Colloquy on the Relationships among the *Gospels*," virtually no attention was devoted to the Gospel of John or the noncanonical gospels, either in the principal papers and responses or in the seminar discussions. In fact, the meeting was essentially a "Colloquy on the Relationships among the *Synoptic* Gospels" or even a "Colloquy on the *Synoptic Problem*." Given the makeup of the Colloquy and the present state of gospel studies, this may have been inevitable, but the Steering Committee had quite early rejected the title, "Colloquy on the Synoptic Problem," in favor of "Colloquy on the Relationships among the Gospels," with the hope that Johannine and perhaps apocryphal materials would be included and that other aspects of gospel relationships than the source question would be considered. There were suggestions, particularly in the Seminar on Literary Criticism and the Gospels, that the Fourth Gospel and the noncanonical gospels, as well as the Apostolic Fathers and the Apologists, "might shed light on the relationships among the gospels" (p. 340), but even here it appeared that the primary interest was in the light that these writings might shed on the Synoptic Problem. The larger question, then, of *the relationships among the gospels* remains an item of unfinished business (or rather untouched, so far as the Colloquy was concerned), which belongs on the agenda of gospel studies.

In the second place, some of the participants apparently were startled to discover that the question of gospel sources seemed

8

much less pressing to scholars in other disciplines than to many New Testament specialists. Albert B. Lord, for example, expressed surprise that the Synoptic Problem "should have agitated New Testament scholars so deeply" (p. 115). Lou H. Silberman suggested "the need to withdraw, at least temporarily, from our preoccupation with questions of chronology and literary relationships" (p. 218), and he was supported at this point by James A. Sanders (p. 231). Roland Mushat Frye radically questioned the prevailing assumptions and methods of New Testament form and redaction criticism, calling for the application to the various gospels of "the readily available techniques of secular literary-historical criticism" as a means of "bringing the character of Jesus to life literarily" (p. 302). Even George Kennedy, in answer to the question as to "whether an understanding of sources makes a significant difference" in the interpretation of ancient documents, asserted that, while "the general answer to this question seems to be affirmative," nevertheless "the relative importance of identifying the sources varies from case to case" (p. 127). None of the principals dismissed the problem, however, and all of them, either directly or indirectly, suggested possible ways of dealing with it.

In the third place, there was significant, though by no means unanimous, agreement that the solution to the problem of gospel relationships may be considerably more complex than most New Testament scholars have assumed. Kennedy spoke most directly to this point when he observed: "The inability of New Testament scholars over a period of two hundred years to agree on the history of the composition of the gospels, despite a general agreement that there are signs of a literary relationship, suggests that the true relationship may be very complex" (p. 153). Reference was made on various occasions to the statement of E.P. Sanders:

> I rather suspect that when and if a new view of the Synoptic problem becomes accepted, it will be more flexible and complicated than the tidy two-document hypothesis. With all due respect for scientific preference for the simpler view, the evidence seems to require a more complicated one.[9]

In this volume, Reginald H. Fuller's paper presses this point most strongly (pp. 173–176), but even Frye, who rather cautious-

[9]E. P. Sanders, *The Tendencies of the Synoptic Tradition*, Society for New Testament Studies Monograph Series 9 (Cambridge: Cambridge University Press, 1969), 279.

ly argued for the Griesbach Hypothesis, acknowledged that "arguments for synchronic and overlapping developments" may "ultimately prove to be convincing" (p. 286).

One aspect of the possible complexity of the problem relates to the role of oral tradition, not only in the pre-gospel stage but also after the appearance of one or more written gospels. Lord suggested that the problem of the relationships among the gospels is not a "literary" problem at all in the usual sense of the term (i.e., documentary) but rather an "oral traditional" problem: the Synoptic Gospels represent three independent versions of "oral traditional literature."[10] Silberman also stressed the essentially oral character of Jewish and early Christian narrative, and Kennedy pointed out that "memory of oral teaching, especially if the teaching was heard repeatedly, could be retained with considerable integrity over an extended period of time" (p. 152). Again, the point is pressed by Fuller, who speaks of "cross-fertilization" among the various gospels "from ongoing oral tradition" (p. 173). On the other hand, Charles H. Talbert insisted that the problem of gospel relationships be seen as essentially a literary or documentary problem. A further aspect of the complexity was introduced by Kennedy's suggestions regarding note-taking as a likely intermediate stage between oral tradition and finished gospels (pp. 148–51). It appeared that most participants in the Colloquy were inclined to give this suggestion serious consideration.

In the fourth place, it is difficult to determine whether the Colloquy resulted in any weakening of the case for Marcan priority and/or strengthening of that for Matthean priority. Frye concluded that he "would accept the Griesbach explanation as, overall, the most credible of the linear hypotheses" (p. 284). Kennedy proposed that Matthew (in *Aramaic!*) was the earliest of the gospels but that Mark may have preceded and influenced the *Greek* version of Matthew. Lord found Marcan priority unlikely at various points and, at times, suggested that the *traditions* found in Matthew might be earlier than those in Luke and/or Mark, but, for him, this did not imply the priority of Matthew as a *document* or its use by either Luke or Mark. On the other

---

[10] Cf. J. M. Rist, *On the Independence of Matthew and Mark*, Society for New Testament Studies Monograph Series 32 (Cambridge: Cambridge University Press, 1978). Rist, a classicist, denies a direct literary relationship between Matthew and Mark, suggesting that the two depend upon a common oral tradition.

hand, Joseph A. Fitzmyer insists "that the Colloquy in no way contributed to any alleged 'eroding' of the dominance of the Two-Source Theory" (p. 257): "Nothing was said that could not easily be fitted into the modified form of the Two-Source Theory that is used by what was called at the Colloquy 'the establishment' among modern New Testament scholars." Fitzmyer does go on to say, however: "By the same token, I should have to admit that nothing was said either that could not be fitted into the efforts of those who are seeking to resurrect the Griesbach Hypothesis" (p. 257). Keck suggests that "the greater the role of oral tradition in early Christianity, the less viable the Griesbach Hypothesis becomes, because this hypothesis forces the whole discussion into strictly literary terms" (p. 120–21). Joseph B. Tyson may be closest to the overall "sense" of the Colloquy when he observes: "Most of the participants in the seminar [i.e., the Seminar on Literary Criticism and the Gospels] concluded that the Griesbach theory had now achieved a position of respectability, that it is at least a possible solution" (p. 340–41). Tyson also suggests "the situation now appears to be one in which there are no certainties and few probabilities regarding relationships among the gospels" (p. 341). Similarly, Fuller concludes that "we are entering into a period of great 'fluidity' so far as acceptable views regarding the relationships among the gospels and other introductory matters are concerned" and "that a pluralism of viewpoints is perfectly respectable in this as in many other matters and indeed is the only viable possibility for today" (p. 192). Surely, the Colloquy has contributed in some meaure to this "fluidity."

In the fifth place, the possibility that the problem of Synoptic sources is finally insoluble may turn out to be the most significant and far-reaching suggestion made at the Colloquy. Frye, for example, acknowledged that, "in the present state of the evidence," he would "have to choose a Scottish verdict of *non liquet* for all of the sequential arguments regarding the relationships among the Synoptic Gospels" (p. 284), and his concluding statement on the subject is one of caution:

I do not come away from my analysis with a feeling of certainty regarding the source relationships. We do not have preserved from the first century the kinds and extent of evidence that render certainty possible in other literary-historical contexts. Perhaps such evidence may yet come to light, or perhaps new methods of approaching the present evidence may make demonstration possible. Perhaps too the arguments for synchronic and overlapping developments . . . will ultimately prove

11

to be convincing. We shall see: *Veritas filia temporis*. In the meantime, I have more confidence in the Griesbach explanation than I have in the alternatives among the hypotheses of linear development. (p. 286)

It was Outler, however, who expressed his reservations at this point most forcefully. In the course of the Panel Discussion with the four Principals, he said:

> I regard this whole problem as *formally* insoluble. Methodologically, I do not share the optimism with which Professor Lord ended his paper on that hopeful note that it is not solved now but could be. I know how many of my colleagues live by the faith that one of these days we'll get the hang of this and we'll get it done right. I do not myself know how it could so be done.[11]

Of course, Outler by no means called for a cessation of attempts to clarify the relationships among the gospels; rather, he spoke of "the challenge, excitement, and reward" of such studies, insisting only that "the important thing, both to avoid frustration on the one hand and misunderstanding on the other, is to acknowledge the limits within which one is working." Nevertheless, Fuller suggests in his paper that solving the Synoptic Problem, "at the present juncture, seems both impossible and unnecessary" (p. 176), "that a universally acceptable solution of the Synoptic Problem will not be found and [as quoted above] that a pluralism of viewpoints is perfectly respectable in this as in many other matters and indeed is the only viable possibility for today" (p. 192). On the other hand, William R. Farmer stated at several points in the Seminar on Literary Criticism and the Gospels that there is sufficient "hard but tacit" evidence to convince scholars that the Griesbach Hypothesis is the most likely solution to the Synoptic Problem, "provided that an effective way to present it can be found and provided that prejudice against the Griesbach Hypothesis can be further reduced" (p. 340). It is important to solve the Synoptic Problem if it can be solved, but even if a solution to this particular problem remains elusive, past and continuing explorations of the relationships among the gospels will be well worth the time and effort devoted to them, for the

---

[11]The original version of Lord's paper, prepared for the Colloquy, ended with the sentences: "The reality is infinitely complex. But I firmly believe that we can and will eventually discover the full truth." These sentences do not appear in the revised version, published in this volume. One can only wonder whether the course of the Colloquy itself may have somehow dampened Lord's earlier optimism.

"spin-off" effects of such explorations are that the more we investigate gospel relationships, the more we learn about the gospels, and this is all to the good.[12]

In the sixth place, a more general matter that received some attention at the Colloquy was the alleged "scepticism" that characterizes much contemporary study of the New Testament. During the Panel Discussion, Lord commented that he had encountered no higher a degree of scepticism among New Testament scholars than among professionals in the areas of his own expertise. Kennedy saw the matter somewhat differently, however, suggesting two possible reasons for such scepticism: (1) a sense of needing to be particularly "scientific" or "objective" (he spoke of "super-scientific scepticism") in order to justify the status of religious studies as an academic discipline and its legitimate role within the liberal arts curriculum of a college or university; and (2) the almost inevitable fact that concentration on a relatively small body of material (i.e., the New Testament or even the gospels as opposed to, say, the great mass of classical literature) tends to produce a "microscopic" approach that seeks to expose and explore every possible problem in the literature. In his paper, Kennedy had insisted that " 'scientific' scepticism can easily be carried too far" and, in a masterpiece of understatement, that "ancient traditions have sometimes been confirmed by archaeology; ancient writers sometimes meant what they said and occasionally even knew what they were talking about" (p. 126). His phrase, "scepticism about scepticism" (p. 126) became almost a slogan at some points during the Colloquy. Specifically, Kennedy called for more confidence in what he termed the *testimonia* or external evidence regarding the composition of the gospels, particularly that preserved by Eusebius. In a suggestive and provocative reversal of terminology, Frye called for *more* scepticism regarding what he labeled the "disintegrating" assumptions and methods of form and redaction criticism, together with *less* scepticism regarding the gospels themselves as literary works. The urgings of Kennedy and Frye at this point parallel a continuing debate within the New Testament guild itself, and the debate will not soon end. It is perhaps significant, however, that Fuller finds in Kennedy's suggestions regarding

[12]My colleague, George N. Boyd, suggests the American and Soviet space programs as a partial analogy. Whatever one may think about the value of the space program *per se*, it must be recognized that the "spin-off" effects of the program in such areas as electronics and medical technology have been enormous.

note-taking as an intermediate stage in the process of gospel composition a possible basis for overcoming "the excessive scepticism of which Kennedy not unjustly complains" (p. 179).

Finally, the Colloquy emphasized once again the value, importance, and even necessity of an interdisciplinary context for gospel studies. During the Colloquy, Outler repeatedly stressed this point, as he spoke of "gospel studies linked to church history and to rabbinical history, together with . . . the disciplines of oral literature, classics (and especially classics as they illuminate Greco-Roman history from Augustus to Septimius or Decius or Diocletian or Constantine), and of literary criticism." One aspect of this interdisciplinary context that received considerable attention, particularly in the Seminar on Classics and the Gospels, had to do with certain questions of a more or less "sociological" nature regarding early Christianity: the sociology of early Christian rhetoric, the function of early Christian ("sectarian") literature, and the institutionalization of transmission in early Christianity. Research in these and related areas is still in its infancy at best, and such research is crucial to a more adequate understanding of the gospels. It can best, and perhaps only, be carried on in an interdisciplinary context. The more fully the world in which the gospels were produced is known, the more clearly will the gospels themselves and the processes of their composition be understood. There is much that New Testament scholars need to learn about this world from specialists in related disciplines. Furthermore, what gospel critics have learned from other disciplines needs constantly to be tested and revised in the light of new data, new insights, new tools and methods that are developing within these disciplines.

Conclusion

The gathering of scholars at Trinity University on May 26–29, 1977, was designated a "Colloquy on the Relationships among the Gospels." This volume is entitled, *The Relationships among the Gospels: An Interdisciplinary Dialogue.* In his concluding remarks at the final session of the Colloquy, Silberman spoke eloquently of the relationship between a "colloquy" and a "dialogue," and his remarks suggest the appropriateness of the term "dialogue," as applied both, in retrospect, to the Colloquy and to this volume:

14

... dialogues are not things that are planned, that are built in. A dialogue happens. A colloquy is a place where a dialogue may happen, or it may not happen. It may occur because of the openness of the participants, but there is no guarantee that it need occur. There has been a particular and, I think, a special quality about our meeting together on these several days. There has been that kind of openness, that kind of readiness, that kind of willingness to have something happen to us, as individuals and as a group, to allow ourselves to be illuminated, to allow ourselves to be irritated, to allow ourselves to be bemused, to allow ourselves suddenly to see something from a new perspective, to understand it anew in a new way, as it opens up for us and grows for us . . . in a particular fashion.

Along similar lines, Outler summarized his own impressions of the Colloquy and its importance for gospel studies:

... if education is like inquiry, if it is immersion in the pleasures of the mind and the spirit, then I submit that we, all of us, surely have had an experience of that sort in these last few days. I was thinking this morning in our last seminar . . . that a whole semester of seminars like that and the entire curriculum would be reordered, and my guess is that something like this has happened to us all. . . . My point is that what has happened in our midst is itself an augury, a good augury, of life and spirit and prospect and promise in New Testament studies and in inter-disciplinary studies between New Testament people and church historians and folklorists and rabbinists and literary critics and classicists. This is an experience that corresponds to what most of us have defined as education and what too few of us have experienced as education. . . . Most of us are going away feeling that the job has not been finished, but that every one of us has now an agenda that is not only richer but significantly different from the one we brought. And this is the most important point. . . . This [colloquy] has been worth the time and effort and difficulty, primarily because it illustrates once again that people with strong minds, good tools, and imagination and vision have learned and have not had other people notice that they have learned. Ecumenical discussions are always ruined if somebody changes his mind and somebody else calls attention to this fact, because at that point someone . . . "back-edits" his convictions. . . . In short, this does seem to me to be the colloquy that will stand in the succession of the ones that we have already started. It is *very* clear that it must not be the last. It's been one of the best, and I'm very grateful to have been involved in it and to have had the pleasure of being with every one of you, for it has been a useful experience in every case.

The "colloquy" became a "dialogue," and the "dialogue" is now shared with the larger public.

"Gospel Studies" in Transition
Albert C. Outler

"Keynote addresses," as I understand the genre, have two essential functions, whatever else may also be hoped for from them.[1] One is to indicate the overall significance of a given occasion: why it matters that this particular company has gathered in this place at this time. The other is to comment on the *status quaestionis* of our theme and its implied agenda: what it is that we have come together to try to do. Two obvious perils threaten any such attempt: banality on the one hand and presumption on the other. Banality may be unavoidable, but in our case one feels partially safeguarded against presumption because of the Colloquy's interdisciplinary design. All of us are more nearly amateurs in such a motley group than we might otherwise suppose ourselves to be if we were only clusters of fellow specialists. As a church historian, I feel much less an "outsider" among New Testament experts when there are also classicists among us, *and* folklorists, *and* rabbinists, *and* literary critics. And yet I also feel rather more "at home," since there are so many overlapping borders between our several "fields."

This interdisciplinary format and process is, therefore, one of this Colloquy's most significant features. It will help underscore the multi-faceted character of gospel studies and exhibit the many horizons of inquiry that open out from them in various

---

[1] Albert C. Outler delivered the Keynote Address for the Colloquy on the Relationships among the Gospels. It was decided that this address should not be re-written as an introduction to the present volume; thus it is here published essentially as it was delivered [Editor's note].

directions. This suggests that collaboration, in its most literal sense, will be our most appropriate style of work. Almost certainly, such collaboration will generate its own brand of Babel, given the obvious differences in our respective procedures, jargons, and scoring systems. But just as certainly, it will enrich our discussions and leave us with fresh grist for further ruminations. Over a long academic career, I have profited more fruitfully from collaborations of this sort than from my formal interchanges with fellow specialists. And the papers and responses that we have had prepared for us strengthen my expectations that this Colloquy could rank with the best.

Another significant aspect of our meeting is this actual place and region where we are gathered. Here we are, in a part of America somewhat more famous, in popular stereotypes, for other sorts of pioneering than those of critical biblical scholarship. Moreover, we meet under the auspices of a rather special private university, which, although it has no graduate theological faculty, boasts a splendid record of faithfulness to the study of religion as one of the liberal arts. What this means, of course, is that the academic "diaspora" in theological America is more extensive than our stereotypes have recognized, that scholarly vision and initiative are wherever you find them; and this, obviously, is as it should be. Thus, each of us has his/her own reason to be truly grateful to Trinity University for its hospitality, to the Henry Luce Foundation and the National Endowment for the Humanities for their generosity, to the Steering Committee for its uncommon imagination and efficiency, and to the Southwest Commission on Religious Studies for its endorsement of the Colloquy.

But most of all the Colloquy is significant because of its topic and its implied expectations. These reflect the fact (or what I take to be a fact) that a century-old consensus in the liberal Protestant tradition of gospel studies (with respect to dating, order, provenance, literary interdependence, etc.) has somehow, almost unexpectedly, become problematic all over again. This is why "a renewed attempt to clarify the relationships among the gospels *is* appropriate and timely," as the Steering Committee has reminded us in its brochure.[2] The least we can infer from this is that the tide of dissent from the academic conventions in which most of us were indoctrinated has now reached a level where it has to be taken seriously. I can envisage some interesting con-

[2] Brochure prepared and distributed prior to the Colloquy on the Relationships among the Gospels (1976). Emphasis mine.

sequences for new experiments in "New Testament Introductions," synopses of the *four* gospels, and even in "Canon and Hermeneutics." The old frontiers between "New Testament," early church history, classics, oral tradition, Judaic studies, literary criticism, etc., now clearly need redrawing in ways that could be unprecedented. This is why I view this Colloquy as standing in the succession of events, such as the Pittsburgh Festival on the Gospels (1970)[3] and the Griesbach Bicentennial Colloquium in Münster (1976).[4] Even as a veteran from an older generation, who will not live to see the outworkings of these new developments, I find it all very exciting. For those of you who will have to carry the job forward, I should hope it excites you, too, though I think it might well seem daunting to those who have taken some measure of the difficulties involved.

A mildly obtrusive sign of these times is that the Old Dissent (i.e., William R. Farmer, David L. Dungan, E. P. Sanders, Thomas R. W. Longstaff, Bernard Orchard, *et al.*) has lately been reinforced (on one front at least) by John A. T. Robinson's provocative *Redating the New Testament*.[5] With all due allowance for Robinson's penchant for fireworks (one remembers the flash-and-fizzle of *Honest to God*),[6] this new assault of his on time-honored conventions of New Testament chronology is a sort of ticking bomb that had better be defused quickly (if it can be), or we could find ourselves with a whole new agenda on our hands, and this will involve not only the New Testament people but early church historians as well (what with Robinson's hypotheses about the Didache, Barnabas, etc.). This is to admit that, flaws and all, Robinson's overall argument holds up plausibly enough so that, even when it is not wholly convincing, it cannot simply be dismissed out of hand, and it will bear critical comparison with

---

[3]The papers and reports of this Festival on the Gospels were published as *Jesus and Man's Hope*, vol. 1 ed. David G. Buttrick, vol. 2 ed. Donald G. Miller and Dikran Y. Hadidian, 2 vols., Perspective Books (Pittsburgh: Pittsburgh Theological Seminary, 1970–1971).

[4]One of the papers prepared for this Colloquium has been published: William R. Farmer, "Modern Developments of Griesbach's Hypothesis," *New Testament Studies*, 23 (1977), 275–295; others are scheduled to be published by Cambridge University Press under the editorship of Bernard Orchard and Thomas R. W. Longstaff.

[5]John A. T. Robinson, *Redating the New Testament* (Philadelphia: The Westminster Press, 1976).

[6]John A. T. Robinson, *Honest to God* (Philadelphia: The Westminster Press, 1963).

the now "standard" *Einleitungen*, at least on points of chronology and sequence.[7] The least that this can mean, methodologically, is that in New Testament "introductions" equally ingenious conjectures can produce widely discrepant results, depending on different presuppositions. Let us not single out Robinson's book as a paradigm; it is much more a signal of the fading of the special set of cultural presuppositions of the Enlightenment that guided the first pioneers in what has since come to be "the critical tradition" (e.g., Richard Simon, Johann August Ernesti, Johann Salomo Semler, David Friedrich Strauss, Ferdinand Christian Baur, Ludwig Feuerbach, Heinrich Julius Holtzmann, *et al.*) It is in this new *post*-Enlightenment context that we must now try to redefine the present *status quaestionis* of the study of the gospels.

One of the starting points in such a redefinition is a reconsideration of the history of liberal Protestant New Testament studies and their basic derivations from Enlightenment attitudes toward religion: e.g., its pervasive anti-institutionalism and its own special views of *"development"* (from "apostolic" to "catholic" Christianity). When Immanuel Kant in 1784 defined "enlightenment" as "liberation from all self-accepted tutelage," one of his prime targets was the tutelage of the institutional church (and always in the background the papal church).[8] When Johann Jakob Griesbach in 1790 summarized "tradition" in two pages,[9] it was chiefly to discredit it. Theories of Marcan priority (from as early as Gottlob Christian Storr and Johann Gottfried Herder) have all appealed to historical-literary analysis for justification, but it was never coincidental that these theories also served to extend the claims of "intellectual freedom" from ecclesiastical tradition.

This cleavage between tradition and criticism appeared in microcosm in the long forgotten quarrel between Johann August

[7]E.g., Werner Georg Kümmel, *Introduction to the New Testament*, rev. ed., trans. Howard Clark Kee (Nashville and New York: Abingdon Press, 1975); and Norman Perrin, *The New Testament: An Introduction: Proclamation and Parenesis, Myth and History* (New York: Harcourt Brace Jovanovich, Inc., 1974).

[8]Immanuel Kant, "Beantwortung der Frage: Was ist Aufklärung?," *Berlinische Monatsschrift*, 4 (1784), 481–494; for an English translation, see, e.g., Carl J. Friedrich, ed., *The Philosophy of Kant: Immanuel Kant's Moral and Political Writings*, The Modern Library (New York: Random House, Inc., 1949), 132–139.

[9]Jo. Jacob Griesbach, *Opuscula Academica*, ed. Jo. Phillippus Gabler, 2 vols. (Jena: Sumtibus et Typis Fr. Grommanni, 1825), 2: 359–360.

Ernesti and Johann Sebastian Bach in Leipzig in 1734 and the following years, a quarrel that has been recalled for us lately by Jan Chiapusso,[10] Robert Stevenson[11] and Paul S. Minear.[12] The formal issues between these two epochal figures were jurisdictional and temperamental, but the substantive issues were rooted in their divergent hermeneutics. Bach was settled in an older global tradition preoccupied, first and foremost, with "the hearing of faith" (and with music's contribution to such a hearing). Ernesti was a pioneer in a new hermeneutic based on the premise that "the Scriptures are to be investigated by the same rule as other books."[13] He was certainly not indifferent to "the hearing of faith," but he was convinced that such hearings would be saved from superstition only if they had been properly validated by historical-literary criticism. Ernesti's triumph over Bach now seems to have been inevitable; his then startling theses have long since become our commonplaces. The tragedy was the radical disjunctions that set two such disparate geniuses at irreconcilable odds. No thanks to Ernesti, Bach was rescued by Felix Mendelssohn for the world of music, and Ernesti's place is now chiefly in the encyclopedias and the histories of hermeneutics. But why should not "The Passion According to St. Matthew" also have a place in these histories and for that matter in New Testament "introductions"?

Historical-literary criticism brought with it immense gains and opened up many exciting prospects. It seemed plausible in those halcyon days, for example, that if the chronology of the New Testament could ever be worked out (accurately intermeshed with the history and literature of the first two centuries before and after Christ), a more credible account of the *Christian ori-*

[10]Jan Chiapusso, *Bach's World* (Bloomington and London: Indiana University Press, 1968), 262–272.

[11]Robert Stevenson, "Bach's Quarrel With the Rector of St. Thomas' School," *Anglican Theological Review*, 33 (1951), 219–230.

[12]Paul S. Minear, "J. S. Bach and J. A. Ernesti: A Case Study in Exegetical and Theological Conflict," in *Our Common History as Christians: Essays in Honor of Albert C. Outler*, ed. John Deschner, Leroy T. Howe, and Klaus Penzel (New York: Oxford University Press, 1975), 131–155.

[13]Of his *Institutio Interpretis Novi Testamenti* (Leipzig, 1761; English translation, Edinburgh, 1834) C. F. Georg Heinrici could say that "his work denotes a turning-point in the development of theological science"; see G. Heinrici, "Ernesti, Johann August," in *The New Schaff-Herzog Encyclopedia of Religious Knowledge*, ed. Samuel Macauley Jackson, 12 vols. and Index (New York and London: Funk and Wagnalls Company, 1908–1914), 4:170.

gins and development might be constructed, which, in its turn, would support liberal views with respect to the contemporary religious situation. This was ventured, in an exemplary fashion, by Adolf Harnack in his *Geschichte der altchristlichen Littera-tur.*[14] Conversely, it was further assumed that if a credible scheme of *Christian origins and development* could be delin-eated, in terms of literary forms and editorial ideas, this would reinforce the new historical hypotheses regarding dating and sequence. This was one of the chief aims of "form criticism," as in Rudolf Bultmann's *Die Geschichte der synoptischen Tradi-tion.*[15] For a hopeful while, it looked as if all this might indeed work out. And yet, here we are, with the problems of dating and sequence back "up in the air" again and the crucial problem of *Christian origins and development* far from stabilized.

Moreover, there are also the old questions about literary inter-dependence still around to plague us. As if in succession, source criticism *and* form *and* redaction *and* genre criticism have all contributed mightily to the heroic effort to reconstruct the inner history of the Gospel texts and the theological perspectives of the Evangelists. But the validity of these reconstructions always turns, at least in part, on presuppositions about the meaning of such notions as "primitive," "derivative," "interdependent," etc. Most of us understand now that all such terms carry their own special freight of ideology as well as their more objective philological and other implications. But folklorists and literary critics will tell us that in the transmission of traditions "primi-tive" does not always and necessarily mean "early." As a church historian, I still must acknowledge that the dating and sequence of the materials in the "Apostolic Constitutions" or the dating and character of the Muratorian Fragment, etc., are mired inex-tricably in conjecture, though some conjectures are a good deal better than others.

From all this, I have concluded that the ratio of conjecture to hard data in the historical-literary study of the gospels is higher than most critical historians would find acceptable. This fact (if

[14]Adolf Harnack, *Geschichte der altchristlichen Litteratur bis Eusebius*, 2 vols. in 4 (Leipzig: J. C. Hinrichs, 1893–1904).

[15]Rudolf Bultmann, *Die Geschichte der synoptischen Tradition*, Forschungen zur Religion und Literatur des Alten und Neuen Testaments, n. F. 12 (Göttingen: Vandenhoeck & Ruprecht, 1921); English translation of 2d ed. (1931) with correc-tions and additions from 1962 supplement: *The History of the Synoptic Tradition*, trans. John Marsh, rev. ed. (New York and Evanston: Harper & Row, Pub-lishers, Inc., 1968).

it be a fact) warrants no counsel of despair nor any greater historiographical scepticism than goes with the morality of historical "knowledge" in general. But it does suggest an emphatic methodological modesty regarding the limits of historical-literary analysis of the New Testament as a "science" in its own right.[16] The aims of historical reconstruction had best not include the hope of pre-emptive certainty. They had better be more concerned with credible narration and stable etiologies (taking all public evidence into account and then mixing this with whatever it takes to produce a plausible conjecture). The best history is that which yields the most intelligible "perspectives" on significant slices of historical experience (which is what we mean by the terms "epoch," "period," etc.). The aims of such reconstructions do not include narratives that are *wholly* verifiable (a rare if not nonexistent achievement). What may be hoped for is etiological insight, which is *not* the same thing as a set of strict cause-effect equations. No critical historian will flinch from ingenious conjecture. The decisive factor for him/her, however, will be the *ratio* of unavoidable conjecture to public data and their interweaving with his/her own metahistorical presuppositions.[17]

Thus it is that I welcome the reopening of old questions, which, as I have said, this Colloquy asks of us. None of us *knows* that the now reigning wisdoms in gospel studies have been finally discredited. It is only that they have become "destabilized," to use a current political metaphor. There will, of course, be scant gain in any alternative "rush to judgment," from one monopolistic view to another. The "Two-Document" Hypothesis is under attack; it will also be defended. But even if it were surrendered, the Griesbach Hypothesis is not the only possible alternative. Some of us think that there is something to be said for the *canonical* order, not on the basis of any ecclesiastical authority but because this order might turn out to exhibit a functional logic that was at work in the minds of the canon-makers. This, of

[16]Cf. W. B. Gallie, *Philosophy and the Historical Understanding* (New York: Schocken Books, 1964); and R. G. Collingwood, *The Idea of History* (Oxford: The Clarendon Press, 1946). See also Albert C. Outler, "Theodosius' Horse; Reflections on the Predicament of the Church Historian," *Church History*, 34 (1965), 251–261.

[17]Martin Buber seems to me to have understood this better than most in his *Moses* (Oxford: East & West Library, 1946); reissued as *Moses: The Revelation and the Covenant*, 1st Harper Torchbook ed. (New York: Harper & Brothers, Publishers, Inc., 1958).

course, is a main concern of what is now called "canon criticism."[18] Clearly, the genius of our Colloquy, in my hopes for it, is not its prospect of any neat consensus, on the one hand, nor the dangers of confused and fruitless disputation, on the other. Its test will be the gracefulness with which we come to terms with the irreducible pluralism of our views. That most of us bring strong predilections to these discussions goes without saying. But if many of us leave with these pre-views wholly intact, our gathering will scarcely have been worth the trouble.

From the beginning, one of the crucial issues in gospel studies (and I have already alluded to it) has been this business of *Christian origins and development*: this is to say, the identity and continuity of the Christian message and praxis during the course of its "Hellenization," in the ante-Nicene church. The generality of liberal Protestants has tended to view this movement from "apostolic" to "catholic" Christianity as retrograde.[19] What was partially ignored here was the axial influence in this development of the schism between Christianity and Judaism (however and whenever it occurred, by what stages, and with what results).

[18]James A. Sanders and William R. Farmer prefer the phrase "canonical criticism," in consonance with "historical criticism," "structural criticism," etc.; to me, "canon criticism" seems a better analogue to "form criticism," "redaction criticism," "genre criticism," etc. Cf. Sanders, "Adaptable for Life: The Nature and Function of Canon," in *Magnalia Dei: The Mighty Acts of God: Essays on the Bible and Archaeology in Memory of G. Ernest Wright*, ed. Frank Moore Cross, Werner E. Lemke, and Patrick D. Miller, Jr. (Garden City, N.J.: Doubleday & Company, Inc., 1976), 531–560; Farmer, "Matthew and the Bible: An Essay in Canonical Criticism," *Lexington Theological Quarterly*, 11 (1976), 57–66, 71; David L. Dungan, "The New Testament Canon in Recent Study," *Interpretation*, 29 (1975), 339–351; Albert C. Sundberg, Jr., "The Bible Canon and the Christian Doctrine of Inspiration," *Interpretation*, 29 (1975), 352–371; Hans von Campenhausen, *The Formation of the Christian Bible*, trans. J. A. Baker (Philadelphia: Fortress Press, 1972); etc. Much of this discussion seems preoccupied with the *limits* of the Old and New Testament canons; what appears more interesting to me is the yet underdeveloped inquiry regarding the *beginnings* of the New Testament. The question as to when the canon was "closed" (if it ever was) is a relic of Catholic-Protestant polemics; the question that interests me is why *all* the canonical lists that we have begin with four gospels.

[19]See Adolph Harnack, *History of Dogma*, trans. Neil Buchanan, Dover ed., 7 vols. in 4 (New York: Dover Publications, Inc., 1961), 1:1–40 ("Prolegomena to the Discipline of the History of Dogma") and 1:41–136 ("The Presuppositions of the History of Dogma"). The work was first published in German beginning in 1885, but the English translation is based on the 3rd edition of 1893. See also Thomas F. Torrance, *The Doctrine of Grace in the Apostolic Fathers* (Edinburgh: Oliver and Boyd, 1948), v: "the misunderstanding of the Gospel which took place as early as the second century with the consequent relapse into non-

Ignoring or playing down this schism has prompted liberal criticism to underemphasize the question of the "gospels" ("canonical" and "apocryphal") as "etiologies" for different Christian groups, in their different regions and different stages of development, vis-à-vis Judaism on the one hand and Hellenism on the other. Only when this line of inquiry is more fully completed, by Jewish and Christian historians *together*, will we be able to get much further with the crucial questions as to why the gospels were set at the head of every "canon," why *our four* were selected (and then placed in various sequences), and, most importantly, how these gospels *functioned* in the process of the development of "catholic Christianity."

From both Paul and Acts one gathers that the hostilities between the Pharisees and the disciples of Jesus had broken out immediately after Pentecost (along with various tensions between the "Judaizers" and the "Hellenizers" amongst the disciples). In both accounts, however, the troubles seem to reflect a family quarrel (cf., e.g., Galatians 3; Romans 9–11; Acts 4:1–8:4). In the Gospels of Matthew and John and in the so-called "Epistle of Barnabas," however, the atmosphere is different. There, some sort of irreparable breach seems already *fait accompli*. Given such a breach, it was urgent for the Christians to reassert and vindicate their claim to their Jewish heritage. This reassertion and claim appear in Matthew and John. In the Gospel of Mark, we have a Jewish Jesus who fulfilled the Messianic hope but one who also transcended the need for a holy homeland. In the Gospel of Luke, Jesus is portrayed as the universal savior (as also in Acts 17), whose mission inaugurated a new Covenant Community, inclusive of the *ethnē* without excluding the Jews. Now, how and by what stages had these processes of alienation and reidentification taken place? St. Paul's contribution to them had been superseded, since the Pauline *Sitz im Leben* had been radically altered after the final excommunication and schism.

From the Jewish side, especially the Pharisees, the rejection

---

Christian ideas, has resulted in a doctrine that is largely unbiblical . . ."; and Samuel Laeuchli, *The Language of Faith: An Introduction to the Semantic Dilemma of the Early Church* (London: Epworth Press, 1962), 94: ". . . there is no such thing as 'Christian language' between A.D. 100 and 180." The most extreme version of this thesis appears in Martin Werner, *The Formation of Christian Dogma: An Historical Study of its Problem*, trans. S. G. F. Brandon, Beacon Paperback ed. (Boston: Beacon Press, 1965).

25

of the Christian messianic kerygma (proclamation) would have been reflex. Ellis Rivkin recently suggested (in a small-group discussion) that the Christians had been designated as *minim* ("heretics") within the first decade after Pentecost. If this were the case, the Christians would have had to move quickly with their own alternative process of institutionalization, since their original intention had been to remain loosely within the institutions of Judaism. This accelerated institutionalization would presumably have included written "gospels," and this, in turn, would illuminate Robinson's point about the New Testament's alleged silence regarding "the destruction of Jerusalem" (70 C.E.)[20]

On the other hand, such a view fails to explain why Paul seems never to have regarded himself as a *min*, or as excommunicated. Conversely, it ignores the fact that intelligent Romans, from Tacitus to Septimius Severus, seem consistently to have confounded Jews and Christians as if they could be lumped together in Roman law.[21] The Tannaim were certainly clear about the distinction, as we can see from the Javneian "Benedictions." There, the "Nazarenes" are excommunicated and the hostilities that had set church and synagogue at enmity have taken an irreparable turn.[22] This, in turn, suggests that written gospels (in their variety) were called forth by this new *Sitz im Leben* in which various Christian groups found themselves: now finally expelled from their original Jewish matrix.

Given some such situation and also the metahistorical emphases of Pauline Christianity, written gospels would have had as *one* of their functions the legitimation of the claims of the main Christian subgroups to their respective stakes in a "common gospel" that was rooted in the Old Testament. The Jewish Christians claimed a rightful share in the Old Testament heritage. The Christians in the Diaspora (in a place like Rome, for

[20]See Robinson, *Redating the New Testament*, esp. 13–30.

[21]There are no exceptions that I know of, and the Septimian edict is especially striking, indiscriminately lumping together the Jews and the Christians as late as A.D. 202; see W. H. C. Frend, *Martyrdom and Persecution in the Early Church: A Study of a Conflict from the Maccabees to Donatus*, Anchor Books ed. (Garden City, N.Y.: Doubleday & Company, Inc., 1967), 239–240 and notes.

[22]Cf., e.g., Kaufman Kohler, "Christianity in Its Relation to Judaism," in *The Jewish Encyclopedia: A Descriptive Record of the History, Religion, Literature, and Customs of the Jewish People from the Earliest Times to the Present Day*, ed. Isidore Singer *et al.*, new ed., 12 vols. (New York and London: Funk and Wagnalls Company, 1925), 4:53.

example) needed a sense of "belonging," apart from Jerusalem. Gentile Christians needed an etiology for their professions of faith in the God of Abraham, Isaac, and Jacob, apart from circumcision and the ceremonial law. Finally, there was a claim that Torah had been transfigured and personalized in the Logos-Christos. Thus the canonical shape of the four gospels (not a *diatessaron!*). After the gospels would come the Pauline corpus as a centerpiece. Finally (as in the Old Testament canon) there would be a sort of Christian miscellany added to round out the lot.[23] What matters most here, I suggest, is that the canon-makers had no paramount concern for dating or sequence and also that they seem not to have posed the questions of literary interdependence in the fashion that we might have, had we been in their place.

They were persuaded, even before Augustine,[24] that Matthew stood first among these four documents that linked them with the Old Testament heritage and yet also differentiated them from what Judaism had become. The theory of Marcan priority has always rested on a very different presupposition: viz., that, on several levels, Mark is the most "primitive" of the four. By the same token, Griesbach's thesis that Mark recapitulates Matthew and Luke has its own particular editorial concerns: viz., the de-emphasis of "tradition" and, equally, of the Petrine primacy. None of the theories about sequence that I know, however, really comes to grips with the obvious anomaly that Luke-Acts should ever have been separated from each other by a fourth *gospel*! The least that this can mean is that the canon-makers had com-

[23]This roughed-out model of the shape of the canon would still hold even if Sundberg's thesis that the Muratorian Canon is an Eastern list of approved books dating from the fourth century were confirmed; see Albert C. Sundberg, Jr., "Canon Muratori: A Fourth-Century List," *Harvard Theological Review*, 66 (1973), 1–41; cf. his "The Bible Canon and the Christian Doctrine of Inspiration," 360–364. As of now, the thesis seems to me more ingenious than convincing.

[24]Griesbach's comment that "Primus, quod sciamus, Augustinus, Marcum tanquam pedissequum et breviatorem subsecutum esse Matthaeum iudicavit" (Griesbach cites Augustine's *De consensu Evangeliorum* [sic: *Evangelistarum*], 1, 2) ignores the fact that Eusebius cites the canonical order from Origen, and even if the dubious contention that Origen had no concept of a New Testament canon were allowed (see R. P. C. Hanson, *Origen's Doctrine of Tradition* [London: S. P. C. K., 1954], 140), Eusebius' list is secure and antedates Augustine's by more than a full half century at least. Cf. Griesbach, *Opuscula Academica*, 2:359. Griesbach's essay has recently been translated into English (but not yet published) by Bernard Orchard.

pelling reasons to lead off any Christian canon with as many *gospels* as they were prepared to accept. But why? If, on whatever grounds, the "canon" were "reopened" (e.g., to consider the inclusion of "Thomas" as a *fifth* "gospel"), what canonical principles would apply and *why*?

Happily, it is no part of my duty to preempt our forthcoming discussions by anticipating their outcome. I would, however, be remiss if I did not broach a concluding question that will be hovering over our gathering: To what *meta*historical ends are our historical-literary analyses aimed, given the fact that we *are* engaged in metahistorical judgments, willy-nilly? Surely, a partial answer is that all these historical-literary inquiries are themselves auxiliary to the yet more ultimate issue of the New Testament's function in our concerns to divine and to participate in the self-revealing Holy in human history and in life.

A full generation ago, Erich Auerbach tried to remind us that there is more in the import and impact of the New Testament than can be gathered in by our dating games and such: "whatever kind of movement it may be which the New Testament writings introduced into phenomenal observation, the essential point is this: the deep subsurface layers, which were static for the observers of classical antiquity, began to move."[25] Has the time come, or is it in sight, when Ernesti's world and Bach's world can be integrated into one world in which the gospel history becomes a transparency of the Numen and the Numen in turn has acquired a Name and nature: "Jesus Christ, . . . the power of God and the wisdom of God"? For, as à Kempis put it quaintly long ago: "he who through grace may have the inner eye of his soul opened unto a soothfast beholding of the Gospels of Christ, shall find in them . . . true spiritual food for the soul."[26]

Our agenda, then, must also be theological as well as whatever else it may and ought to be. The time is long past when New

[25] Erich Auerbach, *Mimesis: The Representation of Reality in Western Literature*, trans. Willard Trask, Anchor Books ed. (Garden City, N.Y.: Doubleday & Company, Inc., 1957), 39; cf. also page 40: "A scene like Peter's denial fits no antique genre" [not even the closing paragraphs of Plato's *Apology*]; and, on the radical differences between the intentions of St. Mark on the one side and those of Tacitus and Petronius on the other, page 42: "Without any effort on his part, as it were, and purely through the inner movement of what he relates, the story [of Peter] becomes visually concrete," and all his readers are "urged and indeed required to take sides for or against it."

[26] Thomas à Kempis, *De Imitatione Christi* 1.1, in the Richard Whiford translation (1556) as reprinted (Mt. Vernon, N.Y.: The Peter Pauper Press, 1947).

Testament scholarship can confine itself to the linear ideologies of the Enlightenment or tamely acquiesce in its prevailing animus against the *fides historica*. But are we not also still heirs of that great liberal tradition, rooted in the Platonic awareness that the truth surpasses all our synthetic propositions, that delights in *dialogue* as much as it dreads *dogmatism*? If so, then our discussions will aim at a high level of precision and rigor, and yet we will be eager to match this with as high a degree of grace in dialogue. What less could fulfill our sponsors' rightful hopes? What else would be so richly rewarding in these hours and days that we shall have together?

1
ORAL TRADITIONAL LITERATURE and the GOSPELS

The Gospels as Oral Traditional Literature

Albert B. Lord

SOME THEORETICAL OBSERVATIONS

Oral History and Oral Traditional Literature

One must, from the outset, distinguish between oral history and oral traditional literature.[1] Oral history concerns itself with the various accounts that people give of an event, a person, or a series of happenings. Each individual tells of what occurred in a different way from every other individual. Each saw something different, each heard something different, and each had somewhat different motivation or bias in interpreting what he or she saw and heard. There is no prescribed form that oral history must use. It is typically in prose not verse, and it typically follows or attempts to follow what happened or what was thought to have happened. For example, when in the course of collecting epic, ballad, and lyric songs in Yugoslavia we recorded conver-

---

[1] The classic work on oral history is Jan Vansina, *Oral Tradition: A Study in Historical Methodology*, trans. H. M. Wright (Chicago: Aldine Publishing Company, 1965). See also Eduard Nielsen, *Oral Tradition: A Modern Problem in Old Testament Introduction*, Studies in Biblical Theology 11 (London: SCM Press Ltd, 1954); Walter E. Rast, *Tradition History and the Old Testament*, Guides to Biblical Scholarship, Old Testament Series (Philadelphia: Fortress Press, 1972).

sations with informants (singers and others), we asked them about their lives, and they recounted both what they remembered about people, places, and happenings in their own experience and things they had heard.[2] This was oral history.

On the other hand, oral traditional literature is expressed in the well-defined forms and genres with which we are familiar from written literature. Indeed most of these forms and genres originated in oral literature. In oral literature we find prose narrative, in all its subdivisions from the simplest anecdote through legend and saga to the complex *Märchen*, all of them highly developed forms before they were first written down. In oral literature we also find verse narrative, ballad, epic, and historical song. Most of these forms had their ultimate origins in very ancient times, and they retain narrative patterns from those times even to the present day. Some scholars, myself among them, believe that a significant body of epic tales, for example, is of mythic origin and that they and ballad were associated with ritual. Their verse form and stanzaic arrangements would seem to support this view. If this is true, then historical songs are later and derive from epic or ballad, in part by a process of demythologizing. In other words, stories about gods, such as are found in *Enuma Elish*[3] or the *Theogony* of Hesiod,[4] set the basic patterns. Semi-gods, such as Gilgamesh,[5] Achilles, or

[2]For information on the Milman Parry Collection of Oral Literature at Harvard University, see Albert B. Lord, *The Singer of Tales*, Harvard Studies in Comparative Literature 24 (Cambridge, Mass.: Harvard University Press, 1960), 3–12; *The Making of Homeric Verse: The Collected Papers of Milman Parry*, ed. Adam Parry (Oxford: The Clarendon Press, 1971), ix–lxii, 376–390, 437–478; and *Serbocroatian Heroic Songs*, coll. Milman Parry, vol. 1, *Novi Pazar: English Translations*, ed. and trans. Albert Bates Lord (Cambridge, Mass.: Harvard University Press/Belgrade: The Serbian Academy of Sciences, 1954), 3–45.

[3]James B. Pritchard, ed., *Ancient Near Eastern Texts Relating to the Old Testament*, 2d ed. (Princeton: Princeton University Press, 1955), 60–72; or Alexander Heidel, *The Babylonian Genesis: The Story of Creation*, 1st Phoenix ed. (Chicago and London: The University of Chicago Press, 1963).

[4]*Hesiod, the Homeric Hymns and Homerica*. With an English translation by Hugh G. Evelyn-White, rev. D. L. Page, The Loeb Classical Library (Cambridge, Mass.: Harvard University Press/London: William Heinemann Ltd, 1936), 78–155.

[5]Pritchard, ed., *Ancient Near Eastern Texts Relating to the Old Testament*, 72–99; or Alexander Heidel, *The Gilgamesh Epic and Old Testament Parallels*, 1st Phoenix ed. (Chicago and London: The University of Chicago Press, 1963).

34

Hercules,[6] then took their place and also introduced new problems, such as whether these part-god, part-man creations were mortal or not. When full-fledged mortals, such as Odysseus or Marko Kraljević the Serbian hero,[7] became associated with the patterns, there were other changes, including the performance of supernatural deeds by human heroes, the diminishing of supernatural opponents to natural dimensions, and finally the development of a completely natural story. History could and did then enter the stories—more or less accurate human history told in the verse forms that stemmed from the cosmic history and deeds of supernatural or preternatural beings.

In addition to the mythic patterns in the sacred realm, to use Mircea Eliade's distinction,[8] there are profane traditional narrative patterns that may be derived from the traditional anecdote. Such profane narrative patterns might be illustrated by local stories, like those of a blood feud between neighbors arising from sheep stealing.[9] They are not relevant to the subject of this paper. Local traditional anecdotes about miracle workers fall into the sacred category, of course.

I have used examples above from poetic texts, but the points could be illustrated from prose myth and saga as well. In ancient Irish lore, for instance, there were stories of supernatural beings, the Tuatha Dé Danann (the Tribes of the Goddess Danann), of such a semi-supernatural figure as Cúchulainn, or of the human Fergus mac Roich in the Táin Bó Cuailnge.[10]

Whether the progression from supernatural to semi-supernatural to human is correct—and I do not mean to imply in the specific examples quoted above that the progression is neces-

[6] The most accessible account of his life and adventures is in Apollodorus, *The Library*. With an English translation by Sir James George Frazer, 2 vols., The Loeb Classical Library (Cambridge, Mass.: Harvard University Press/London: William Heinemann Ltd, 1921), 1:167–273.

[7] *The Ballads of Marko Kraljević*, trans. D. H. Low (Cambridge: Cambridge University Press, 1922), reprinted (New York: Greenwood Press, 1968).

[8] Mircea Eliade, *The Sacred and the Profane: The Nature of Religion*, trans. Willard R. Trask, 1st Harper Torchbook ed., The Cloister Library (New York: Harper & Brothers, Publishers, Inc., 1961).

[9] For examples, see any collection of Montenegrin epic songs, e.g., Radovan Zogović, *Crnogorske epske pjesme raznih vremena. Antologija* (Titograd: Grafički zavod, 1970).

[10] *The Táin*, translated from the Irish epic Táin Bó Cuailnge by Thomas Kinsella (London and New York: Oxford University Press, 1970), ix–xvi.

sarily from one to the next—a tradition of epic or saga literature would for generations have included stories of all three kinds
of creatures.

On the first level, that of divine beings, one of the basic narratives tells of the parentage and birth of the great god (e.g.,
Marduk in *Enuma Elish* or Zeus in Hesiod's *Theogony*) and
of his encounter with the cosmic dragon (Ti'amat, Typhoeus)
and the subsequent establishment of order and organization in
the universe. This mythic and cosmic dragon-slaying pattern
pervades all later traditional dragon-slaying stories. Much of
the significance of the narrative is that it sets forth the special
parentage, special upbringing, and special attributes of the
divine figure who brings order out of chaos. It is the beginning
of the "biography" of the great god, and it establishes a pattern.
The pattern is: 1) special parentage (divine), 2) special birth,
3) special upbringing or training, 4) special attributes, weapons,
etc., 5) special opponent, 6) combat, 7) disposition of defeated opponent, establishment of order, including place of our hero in
this order. This is a typical narrative pattern for one of the
dragon-slayer types. It is a mythic pattern, because a) its actors
are gods, b) its telling is an act of effective magic, eternally re-
establishing order in a chaotic world. We know that *Enuma
Elish*, for example, was recited as a regular part of the ritual
of the New Year's Festival at Babylon.[11]

The mythic pattern most relevant to the New Testament, however, is that of the dying and resurrected god. While the myth
of the establishment of order stresses the birth of the god and
his ascendance to power, the myth of the dying and resurrected
god stresses his death. Also involved here is the idea of the scapegoat and of sacrifice.

All such accounts that tell part or even all of the life story of
a divine being in verse or prose genres are to be regarded as
oral traditional literature rather than oral history. The two cate-
gories are not always mutually exclusive, however. Oral history
is sometimes incorporated into oral traditional literature. The
telling of recent events by someone who is also an active narrator
of the oral traditional literature of a culture tends to follow the
patterns of traditional story. The "facts" may well fit the tradi-

[11] Pritchard, ed., *Ancient Near Eastern Texts Relating to the Old Testament*,
332 ("Temple Program for the New Year's Festival at Babylon"): ". . . the
urigallu-priest of the temple Ekua shall recite (while lifting his hand?) to the
god Bel the (composition entitled) *Enūma eliš*."

tional elements, in which case there is little or no distortion. Thus oral history sometimes may be manifested in part in oral traditional literature. On occasion, however, "facts" may unconsciously be created to fill places in the traditional narrative pattern. If, for example, it were not historically true that the boy Jesus astounded the teachers in the temple, the creation of this story would have been necessary in the tradition to fill an important place in the account of the early life of such a figure as Jesus. While these "facts" may not be true in a more limited view of history, they carry a larger truth that fits properly the special milieu of the narrative. They come to constitute history on a different, some believe, higher level.

One of the earmarks of an oral traditional narrative is its textual fluidity, which is to say, because it has no fixed original it is constantly being repeated without concern for word-for-word retelling of a set, established text.[12] In oral traditional literature "transmission" is in reality composition of the same story by someone else in the tradition, i.e., by another traditional narrator. Each such narrator, using the phrases and devices picked up from others, develops his or her own usage of lines and half-lines, clusters and passages, but always within the parameters of the tradition. The narrator does not memorize a text, no matter how stable, from someone else. One is not concerned with transmission of text, but with transmission a) of the art of composition and b) of the story itself.

One might say that an oral literary tradition consists of stories or various kinds of non-narrative elements that are in suspension, potential actions (performances) to be realized. In practice each teller has some elements, narrative and non-narrative, more or less pre-formed in his or her mind. These are the compositional "themes" of the traditional narrator or composer. It is perfectly understandable that the compositional themes of one teller in a small closed group are sometimes similar to, and for short runs even occasionally identical with, those of another.

One might ask whether a *fixed* unwritten or oral original is possible. In my experience, it is possible for short forms in oral tradition, such as incantations, riddles, proverbs, or sayings, to be comparatively stable, if not actually "fixed." In narrative, particularly longer narrative, of course, an oral fixed text is impossible, although, as I have said, some shorter parts of the

[12] See Lord, *The Singer of Tales*, 99–123.

narrative may attain a fair degree of fixity in the retellings of a given storyteller or of narrators in a closed group, without conscious memorization. The comparative fixing of short forms or passages appears in oral traditional literature but not in oral history as I have defined it, where, generally speaking, form is not of the essence.

Before turning to the problems of the interrelationship of the gospels, I must make one further differentiation. It is one that emerges clearly from the material of the gospels and is recognized by scholars, but it is important for the analysis of oral traditional literature. Narrative must be distinguished from non-narrative. The main difference is obvious, but it has to be said: non-narrative materials are not bound by a given order, whereas narrative sequences are so bound, at least within limits.

If the gospels, all or any of them, in whole or in part, are oral traditional narratives, they must belong to a tradition of oral life story or biography. Such a tradition argues the existence of both tellers and audience as well as of stories told. From the Old Testament we can see a repeated pattern of life stories of significant figures, and we can assume that these stories were told to an interested audience. Because the stories are of the leaders of Israel, both priestly and secular, we can also assume that these stories were told by certain members of the priestly or ruling class to the Israelites for cultic purposes. The story of Jesus would fit into such a tradition, but it would, of course, be a life story of the leader of another religious group, albeit a splinter one, told to members of this group for cultic purposes.

To be considered traditional, the story must be one that has persisted for several generations. The story of a recent personage can also be regarded as traditional if the essential story pattern is one that has been used by storytellers in the given culture for a long time.

Before embarking on a further discussion of mythic patterns, it would be appropriate to say a few words about the question of whether the gospels are themselves myth. If one defines myth as "sacred narrative in the full truth and efficaciousness of which people believe," then the New Testament gospels are four versions of the Christian myth, in the very best sense of this word. This is the definition of myth to which I subscribe. Some prefer, wrongly I believe, to define myth as fiction rather than historical fact. Such a definition raises many questions, but mainly that of the historicity of the events in Jesus' life as told in the gospels.

38

I cannot discuss the problems of historicity, but it is important to understand the way in which story patterns, be they mythic or secular, function in oral traditional narrative, especially when an oral tradition undertakes to relate the events of its present or immediate past. Traditional narrators tend to tell what happened in terms of already existent patterns of story. Since the already existing patterns allow for many multiforms and are the result of oft repeated human experience, including spiritual experience, it is not difficult to adjust another special case to the flexibly interpreted story patterns. A pattern, such as special parentage and birth, special childhood, initiatory testing, special deeds and death, is helpful rather than restrictive in narrating reality. The fact that the Entry into Jerusalem, for example, fits an element of a mythic pattern does not necessarily mean, however, that the event did not take place. On the contrary, I assume that it did take place, since I do not know otherwise, and that it was an incident that traditional narrators chose to include, partly at least because its essence had a counterpart in other stories and was similar to the essence of an element in an existing story pattern. In other words, when I say that an incident in the gospel narrative of Jesus' life fits in a mythic pattern, there is no implication at all that this incident never happened. There is rather an implication that traditional narrators chose to remember and relate this incident because an incident of similar essence occurred in other traditional stories known to them and their predecessors. That its essence was consonant with an element in a traditional mythic (i.e., sacred) pattern adds a dimension of spiritual weight to the incident, but it does not deny (nor does it confirm, for that matter) the historicity of the incident.

Life Story: Mythic Patterns and Their Realization in Oral Traditional Narrative

The traditional pattern of the life of the hero includes: 1) birth, 2) precocious childhood, 3) transition to maturity, 4) marriage, 5) deeds, 6) death. Each of these elements itself has sub-elements, and both elements and sub-elements exist in a variety of multiforms.

In their normal tellings, oral traditional narratives about individuals, whether in verse or prose, only rarely include a single account that begins with birth and ends with death. Most commonly, the separate elements or incidents in the life of the hero form individual poems or sagas. Thus, there are songs of the birth of Marko Kraljević, of his marriage, of this or that incident in his "life," and of his death.[13] There is no "life song" of Marko Kraljević or, to the best of my knowledge, of any other South Slavic hero. In Old Irish saga the life of Cúchulainn is told in separate stories—e.g.: "How Cúchulainn was Begotten," "Cúchulainn's Courtship of Emer and his Training in Arms with Scáthach," "The Death of Aife's One Son" (How Cúchulainn killed his own son), "The Cattle Raid of Cuailnge," "The Death of Cúchulainn," and others—all independent tales that together would form a life of Cúchulainn.[14] Collectors and editors put them together to form cycles, but no teller sat down to recount Cúchulainn's life nor any singer that of Marko Kraljević.

One of the reasons for this is that the several narratives cluster around the "transitional" points in the man's life: his birth, his childhood or growing up, his initiation into manhood, his marriage, his mature deeds, and his death.[15] Such stories would be appropriate to tell as models at similar times of crisis in the life of the audience or to retell on anniversaries of the birth or death of a great figure (although I confess I know of no evidence for this in the case of either Marko or Cúchulainn). Thus, indeed, are composite stories of Jesus' birth told at Christmastime and of his death and resurrection at Easter.

On the other hand, *Enuma Elish* and Hesiod's *Theogony* are connected narratives, which extend from cosmic beginning through the ascent to power of Marduk and Zeus respectively and the establishment of their divine rules. They correspond roughly to the Hebrew Pentateuch, for both the Pentateuch and *Enuma Elish* end with the establishment of seats of worship and rules pertaining to worship.

The story of Gilgamesh, like that of Marko, is told in separate songs covering a single incident or grouping several incidents together. The central epic is the history of his life with Enkidu and the effect of the latter's death on the hero. In short, the epic is concerned not with the whole life story of the hero but with

---

[13] *The Ballads of Marko Kraljević*, trans. Low, 174–178.

[14] These are actual titles taken from Kinsella's translation (see note 10 above).

[15] For more on this subject see Arnold van Gennep, *The Rites of Passage*, trans. Monika B. Vizedom and Gabrielle L. Caffee (Chicago: The University of Chicago Press, 1960).

the problem that arises when a semi-divine hero faces the prospect of his own death.

Many, if not all, of those cases where we have a traditional narrative of a given hero's full life are the result of some kind of compilation and arranging of the traditional elements listed above. Sometimes there are both the full account and the separate parts. For example, we have in the *Iliad* the account of Achilles' wrath and its consequences for the Achaeans and himself (part of Achilles' "life story," if you will), and we also have other events of his life in Apollodorus' *Library*[16] and in Quintus of Smyrna's *Posthomerica*,[17] although, it is true, not as a connected *Vita*.

Although singers know separate songs about the birth, various deeds, and death of a hero, they can, however, join several of these songs in a number of ways. One way is by flashback. In *The Wedding of Smailagić Meho*, for example, the story of Meho's birth and precocious childhood (incidentally, very reminiscent of Old Testament birth stories) is told by the young man's uncle in flashback.[18] In "The Captivity of Djulić Ibrahim," the tale of the hero's wedding and capture is related by the hero himself to a newly arrived prisoner.[19] In this way one segment of a life is included in the account of another segment of a life. There are also songs that reach linearly from the birth of the hero through his precocious childhood to his first major adult deed, such as the Bulgarian "Tri narečnici," which covers the period from birth to dragon slaying.[20] Another example is the story of Zeus in the *Theogony*, which reaches from birth to Typhoeus and beyond.

---

[16] Apollodorus, *The Library*, Loeb 2:69–75; 2:185–241.

[17] Quintus Smyrnaeus, *The War at Troy: What Homer Didn't Tell*, trans. Frederick M. Combellack (Norman: University of Oklahoma Press, 1968).

[18] *The Wedding of Smailagić Meho*, by Avdo Medjedović, in *Serbo-Croatian Heroic Songs*, coll. Milman Parry, vol. 3, *The Wedding of Smailagić Meho* by Avdo Medjedović, trans. Albert B. Lord and David E. Bynum (Cambridge, Mass.: Harvard University Press, 1974). The text of the original, edited by David E. Bynum, who also translated the conversations with the singer in vol. 3, can be found in *Serbo-Croatian Heroic Songs*, coll. Millman Parry, vol. 4, *Ženidba Smailagina Sina* by Avdo Medjedović, ed. David E. Bynum with Albert B. Lord (Cambridge, Mass.: Center for the Study of Oral Literature, 1974).

[19] *Serbocroatian Heroic Songs*, 1:90–113.

[20] *B'lgarsko narodno tvorčestvo*, vol. 1, ed. Ivan Burin (Sofija: B'lgarski pisatel, 1961), 116–123 ("Krali Marko i tri narečnici").

The Finnish tradition offers another instructive example of methods of joining incidents.[21] The separate songs that went into Elias Lönnrot's compilation of the *Kalevala* were sometimes actually sung by singers in small groups of varying composition. In the practice of a given singer, songs a, b, and c, for example, might usually be sung together in that order. Another singer might never sing them together, and still another might group them differently. Lönnrot justified his own compilation by pointing to the fact that he was only doing what the traditional singers themselves regularly did.[22]

Is Fullness of Telling A Sign of Later Date?

Since the Gospels of Mark and John begin only with the advent of John the Baptist and Jesus' baptism, we might ask whether the absence or presence of a narrative of Jesus' birth and early years has any implications regarding the relationship between the two pairs of gospels. Is fullness a sign of a later date and, therefore, of dependence of Matthew and Luke on Mark, to speak only of the Synoptic Gospels? The answer is that, if we are dealing with oral traditional literature, it is not *necessarily* true that the longer text is later than the shorter, although it may be.

A parallel to this situation is to be found in the texts in the Parry Collection that tell of the return of a long absent hero.[23] Most of these texts begin with the hero in prison in enemy country who learns of affairs at home and begins to shout in order to gain the attention of the jailer and eventually to bargain for his release. A number of texts, however, begin with the details of the capture of the hero on his wedding night or on the morning after his wedding and of his imprisonment. Given the nature of

---

[21] Elias Lönnrot, comp., *The Kalevala, or Poems of the Kaleva District*, trans. Francis Peabody Magoun, Jr. (Cambridge, Mass.: Harvard University Press, 1963); Elias Lönnrot, comp., *The Old Kalevala and Certain Antecedents*, trans. Francis Peabody Magoun, Jr. (Cambridge, Mass.: Harvard University Press, 1969).

[22] Dominico Comparetti, *The Traditional Poetry of the Finns*, trans. Isabella M. Anderton, with an Introduction by Andrew Lang (London and New York: Longmans, Green and Company, 1898).

[23] See Lord, *The Singer of Tales*, 242–259 (Appendix III, "Return Songs") and 260–265 (Appendix IV, "Return-Rescue Songs"), for a survey of some of these texts.

oral traditional composition and transmission, it is impossible to say for sure that the latter group of texts is either later or earlier than the former.

When confronted by several texts of the same story, the best and surest thing that one can do is simply to describe each text, noting that one is fuller than another or longer than another. It does not in any way necessarily follow that the shortest is the oldest and the longest the latest or that the crudest is the oldest and the most polished the latest. It may be, but it is not necessarily so.

Envisage, if you will, a tradition of return songs that open with the prisoner shouting in his dungeon. A singer, who knows a song about the capture of a hero on his wedding night, at one time began his return story with the narrative of an attack and capture. Other singers continued to tell the return story without a preceding account of capture. In this case, therefore, there are texts without the capture that are later than texts with it. But *if* what I supposed were true, namely, that the story of the capture was used to introduce an already existing return song, then the *tradition* of the return song *without* the story of capture is older than the *tradition* of it with the narrative of capture. Any given text, however, might be either older or younger than any other given text.

In the preceding paragraph I supposed that the story of capture was used by some singer at some time to introduce a return song and that some other singers followed suit while some, who may well never have heard any of the other group, did not. The picture is somewhat simplistic, but let it stand. Let us suppose, on the other hand, that there was a tradition of telling the return story that began with an account of the capture of the hero on his wedding night; in short, that the longer form was primary. This might well be true, if the capture on the wedding night after the consummation of the marriage would account for the presence of a son, like Telemachus in the *Odyssey*, who would play a role later in the story. Let us suppose also that there were return songs in which the son played no role. His birth would, therefore, be irrelevant, and sometime, one might imagine, some teller omitted it from the story. In this case the tradition of the fuller telling would have been older than that of the shorter account, but this does not mean that any given text of the longer account is necessarily older than any given text of the shorter account.

I am not arguing here for the priority of either the shorter form as seen in Mark or of the longer form as seen, for example, in Luke, whose birth tradition fits so well with the later role of John the Baptist in the gospels. I am simply saying that the presence or absence of the material at the beginning of the Gospels of Matthew and Luke does not *in itself* constitute an indication of the comparative age of any given text.

The account of the birth of the hero may constitute a separate story or, in a sung epic tradition, a separate song. It is possible that in a number of cases such separate songs or episodes are additions to songs already in existence dealing with the main contributions of the hero. In the case of the gospels, for example, according to this view, the story of Jesus' birth and early years might have been added to the account of his ministry and his passion. In other words, the tradition built on or added to a core, consisting of the events and sayings of the ministry of Jesus and of his passion. Note that I am saying that the story is added to existing oral accounts, not that Matthew and Luke added episodes to an already existing Mark (or John). If this is oral traditional literature, we do not know who actually made the changes reflected now in Matthew and Luke or, put differently, in the tradition of which Matthew and Luke are a part. Thus, when I say that the stories of the birth and upbringing of Jesus may well have been added to accounts of the ministry and passion, I am saying that at some time someone added an element to an already existing element. At this moment the versions (only one at first) with the story of the birth were later than those without it. However, versions without it continued to be told, and versions without the birth story that were told after the addition of the story of the birth in other versions would actually be later than versions with it. In short, while the tradition found in the versions with the story of the birth may be later than the tradition found in those without it, any given text of the story without the birth story might well be later than any given text with the story. All we can say is that Matthew and Luke reflect or belong to traditions that may be later than the tradition or traditions reflected by Mark and John.

THE LIFE STORY: THE PATTERNS OF THE GOSPELS

In this part of the essay I wish to examine several of the sections of the Synoptic Gospels that accord with elements in   44 patterns encountered in oral traditional literary lives or segments of lives. The sections as they are found in the gospels will be discussed both as separate units and as parts of a whole. The main sections to be considered are: 1) Birth, 2) Precocious Childhood, 3) Investiture, 4) Death of the Substitute, and 5) Death and Resurrection. These sections do not include the major deeds of the mature hero, which in Jesus' case would be the events and teachings of his ministry. There are several reasons for this omission. First, some of Jesus' major deeds are considered in detail in the next part of this essay, though from a different point of view. Second, Jesus' deeds are not like the deeds of most mythic heroes but are *sui generis*: the actions and words of the miracle worker and teacher. From the point of view of oral traditional literature, each of the miracle stories is an anecdote, a brief narrative in itself, and the *logia* are related to traditional wisdom literature. As such they have been studied and classified by Martin Dibelius[24] and Rudolph Bultmann.[25] Many of them are multiforms of one another; i.e., the essential idea of the narrative or saying appears in several different forms. Obviously the miracles and teachings are of vast importance in the gospels, but I have concentrated in this section on the mythic patterns in the account of Jesus' life.

The Birth Stories

Oral traditional literature abounds in stories of the birth of a hero. Heroes have extraordinary powers and do extraordinary things. Tradition accounts for this in part on the basis of a hero's extraordinary birth. It is understandable, therefore, that the parentage of the hero is of primary significance. There are several ways in which parentage may be indicated and emphasized. One way is by listing the pairs in a family tree: in short, a genealogy. Zeus' genealogy is set forth in the *Theogony* of Hesiod, where Zeus traces his line to the union of Earth and Sky. Another way of presenting the parentage of a hero is less pretentious: simply naming father and mother, (e.g., Achilles, son of Peleus and Thetis) or saying, for example, that the hero was two-thirds god and one-third man, as was Gilgamesh, whose mother was the

---

[24]Martin Dibelius, *From Tradition to Gospel*, trans. Bertram Lee Woolf (New York: Charles Scribner's Sons, 1934).

[25]Rudolf Bultmann, *The History of the Synoptic Tradition*, trans. John Marsh, rev. ed. (New York and Evanston: Harper & Row, Publishers, Inc., 1968).

goddess Ninsun. Finally, one can in traditional narrative tell of the miraculous birth of the hero. The Gospels of Matthew and Luke use all these ways of indicating the parentage of Jesus, for all were traditional in Hebrew lore as well as in that of other ancient Near Eastern cultures. Jesus' genealogy is traced to Abraham (Matthew) and to Adam (Luke). He was of the house of David, and he was the son of God and the son of man.

The Miraculous Birth. In order to understand properly the traditional character of the accounts of Jesus' birth in the gospels, one must turn to the tradition of birth stories found in the Old Testament and elsewhere, especially in the ancient Near East. The first miraculous birth in the Old Testament (excluding the creation of Adam and Eve, which, of course, is not a birth) is that of *Isaac*, son of Abraham and born of Sarah in her old age (Genesis 15:1–21:21). It is noteworthy that Isaac has a half-brother, *Ishmael*, son of Hagar. We are also told of a special incident in his boyhood, namely, his father's near sacrifice of the son (Genesis 22:1–19), and we are told of his special marriage with Rebekah (Genesis 24). From Isaac's life we can see a pattern emerging: miraculous birth—"brother"—special marriage.

The next miraculous birth, miraculous because Rebekah was barren, is that of Isaac and Rebekah's sons *Jacob* and *Esau* (Genesis 25:19–34). Clearly the "brother" element is there again, and again we are told of a special marriage, that of Jacob with Rachel (Genesis 29:1–30). Moreover, both here and in the case of Ishmael there is an affinity of the "brother" with the wild and the wilderness (note Ishmael's birth in the wilderness and Esau's hairiness), and the brothers separate from each another (Genesis 25:19–34; 27:1–28:5).

The third miraculous birth in the series is that of *Joseph*, son of Jacob and Rachel, who was also barren (Genesis 30:22–24).

These three were among the traditional birth stories known to Matthew and Luke or their sources.

It would be well to look first at the central core, the actual birth of Jesus, in Matthew and Luke since it and the genealogy are the most obvious common elements in the two birth stories. In distinction from the Old Testament tradition as set forth above, Jesus was born not of a patriarchal couple in old age but of an as yet unmarried virgin, and thus he was an incarnation of the Holy Spirit by human birth. In the telling of this, however, the accounts of the two Evangelists are clearly independent. Matthew 1:18–25 is Joseph-oriented. Joseph finds his betrothed with child and is about to divorce her secretly, when an angel appears to him in a dream and explains that the child is of the Holy Spirit. When Joseph awakes, he follows instructions and marries Mary, "but knew her not until she had borne a son; and he called his name Jesus." On the other hand, Luke's account (1:26–2:7) is Mary-oriented and, of course, much fuller than Matthew's. The angel appears to Mary, who is betrothed to Joseph, to announce the future. Mary visits Elizabeth, John is born, and Joseph goes to Bethlehem with his pregnant wife to be enrolled. There Jesus is born. Except for a common concern with the betrothal and the virginal conception, the stories seem quite independent of each another.

In addition to 1) the miraculous birth itself and 2) the existence of a second child (John in Luke's account), there is another element in the gospel tradition of Jesus' birth that has a parallel in the traditional narrative literature of the Old Testament. The story of the birth of Isaac clearly includes an annunciation, in fact two annunciations. In Genesis 17:15–21 God tells Abraham that Sarah will conceive and bear a son who shall be named Isaac. Genesis 18:1–15 contains the multiform of this annunciation in the tale of the three men who visit Abraham's tent at midday. It is worthy of note that an annunciation is found also in the story of the birth of Ishmael. In Genesis 16:7–14 the angel of the Lord appears to Hagar in the wilderness and says: "I will so greatly multiply your descendants that they cannot be numbered for multitude . . . Behold, you are with child, and shall bear a son; you shall call his name Ishmael; because the LORD has given heed to your affliction." It should be noted that in the first case God speaks to Abraham, the husband, not to Sarah. Matthew follows this tradition. In the second case the angel appears to Hagar, the mother, to announce the birth of the "wilderness child," Ishmael. It is clear that Luke's account of the annunciation to Zechariah of the birth of John follows the first pattern, and the annunciation to Mary echoes the second. The associations with the "wilderness child" and the "hero" are here reversed. Which tradition has primacy? Perhaps Matthew.

Genealogy. Matthew's account of Jesus' birth is preceded by a traditional type of genealogy, i.e., a genealogy like those found in the Old Testament. Of course, a genealogy is also found in Luke (3:23–38), but this genealogy differs from the one in Matthew in that: 1) it is placed between Jesus' baptism and his temptation in the wilderness, and 2) it goes backward from Jesus to Joseph and ultimately to "Adam, the son of God," unlike the genealogy in Matthew, which begins with Abraham and moves forward through David and Joseph to Jesus. The placing of the genealogy at the beginning of the gospel rather than after the baptism *seems* to be primary.[26]

Herod and the Flight into Egypt. Matthew includes another very traditional element, namely, the attempt of Herod to kill the child and the child's escape and survival (chapter 2). Examples of this traditional tale are so numerous and so well known that it seems superfluous to go into detail. Suffice it to say that here are to be found the many exposed children whose existence threatens a father or ruler and who are saved and brought up by others: Oedipus, Cyrus, Moses, even Zeus.[27] Matthew's Gospel incorporates into the account of Jesus' birth a succession story that entails an unsuccessful attempt to eliminate the successor and that ends with the god's attainment of power and reign. The example of Zeus in the *Theogony* of Hesiod is pertinent. It is to be noted that genealogy is of the essence of this pattern and that this pattern is congenial to history and historical absorption because of its concern with lineality and with time. Hence the case for the primacy of the genealogy in Matthew over that in Luke is strengthened. The historical genealogy from Abraham suits the myth of succession. The orientation of Matthew towards the father, Joseph, and towards Herod, the ruler, is also understandable in this setting. In this pattern Jesus is looked on as the King of Heaven and Earth.

The Traditional Pairs: Jesus and John in Luke. The tradi-

[26] On the other hand, a genealogy is a form of catalogue that is common in oral traditional literature and does not require writing for its composition. Matthew's tradition is more concerned with history and with the connection of Jesus' family with the Patriarchs, and his genealogy fits the beginning of a record with such concerns. The genealogy in Luke also seems to indicate the opening of a new narrative division, i.e., the traditional account of the ministry, with which the birth story has become associated. At this moment, when Jesus' role as the Christ is about to unfold, a genealogy that traces his ancestry back beyond the Patriarchs to Adam is particularly pertinent. It reinforces the voice at the baptism: "Thou art my beloved son; with thee I am well pleased." It is natural that genealogies of Jesus became part of the traditional lore about him and that both Matthew and Luke drew from what they had heard. The reverse genealogy in Luke stresses the divinity of Christ, as does the story of his birth and early years. It could not be better placed than where it is in Luke.

[27] For Oedipus see Sophocles, *Oedipus the King* 1120–1185. For Cyrus see Herodotus, 1.107–113. For Moses see Exodus 2:1–10. For Zeus see Hesiod, *Theogony* 463–491.

tional pairs that we have noted in the stories of the lives of Old Testament figures form one of the links between these stories and that of Jesus and John the Baptist. Beginning with Cain and Abel (Genesis 4:1–16), one notes that one of the members of these pairs is killed or otherwise eliminated, while the other is the main hero. The pairs are brothers or half-brothers (or simply friends, as in the case of David and Jonathan later in the Old Testament), but only one of the two survives.

Insofar as the role of John the Baptist is concerned, only the Gospel of Luke, as has been noted, has a full narrative of his birth, connecting it with the birth of Jesus (1:5–80). This is a beautifully elaborated account of two clearly traditional elements, namely, the birth of John and the birth of Jesus. These are also traditional elements that belong together, if our appeal to the pattern that "began" with Cain and Abel is the proper one, as I believe it is. Luke's story of the birth of Jesus and of John reflects the pattern that centers on a pair of figures, one divine and one human, the latter of whom dies in the place of the former, a fact that leads the remaining member of the pair to attempt to determine whether he also is to die. In short, the pattern is that of Gilgamesh and Enkidu and of many others, including Cain and Abel, Isaac and Ishmael, and Jacob and Esau. One member of the pair is associated with animals and/or has animal characteristics and with the wilderness. He is killed or eliminated. In Genesis 16:12 we read of Ishmael whom Hagar bore to Abraham, "He shall be a wild ass of a man, his hand against every man and every man's hand against him; and he shall dwell over against all his kinsmen." This was said by an angel of the Lord to Hagar at a spring in the wilderness when she was fleeing from Sarah. In this example the birth of Ishmael occurs before the birth of Isaac. Although the next pair, Jacob and Esau, were twins, Esau, the hairy one, was born first, and Jacob clung to Esau's heel. "When the boys grew up, Esau was a skilful hunter, a man of the field, while Jacob was a quiet man, dwelling in tents" (Genesis 25:27). Enkidu was created after Gilgamesh as a companion for him. Enkidu has the hairy characteristics and the association with the wild that characterize both Ishmael and Esau, but his role vis-à-vis Gilgamesh is different from theirs vis-à-vis Isaac and Jacob. In a literal sense Ishmael and Esau are forerunners of Isaac and Jacob. Here, however, the analogy seems to end.

49   *Celestial Phenomena and Visitors.* Both Matthew and Luke

tell of the visit of a group of people who saw an unusual celestial phenomenon and came to see the newborn child (Matthew 2:1–12; Luke 2:8–20). Matthew's visitors are the Wise Men, Luke's the Shepherds. The Wise Men play an important part in the story in Matthew. They inform Herod of the possible threat to his kingdom, and this results in the flight to Egypt, the slaughter of the innocents, and the return of the Holy Family from Egypt.

In a Bulgarian song of the birth and childhood of Marko Kraljević (Bulgarian, Krali Marko) soothsayers foretell at his birth that he will "crush his father's bones." His father, King Vukašin, in response to this threat casts him into the River Vardar in a chest, whence he is rescued by a young shepherd who brings the baby home to his (the shepherd's) mother and father, by whom Marko is brought up.[28]

Compared to the Wise Men, the Shepherds seem to play no role in the story at all, but Luke's tradition is, nevertheless, aware of celestial phenomena and the visit of a group foretelling the greatness of the child. Since it plays no integral part in the story, however, I am led tentatively to conclude that the narrative of the Shepherds is subsequent in the tradition to that of the Wise Men and that it is a vestigial multiform of that visit of Magi from the East. This conclusion suggests primacy *on this point* to the tradition represented by Matthew compared to that represented by Luke.[29] This does not necessarily mean, however, that the Gospel of Matthew is older than the Gospel of Luke or that Matthew's version of other episodes is older than Luke's. Thus far, only in the Wise Men/Shepherds episode and perhaps in the genealogies does there seem to be any possibility of determining primacy, and such determination might be in favor of Matthew's *tradition* (not necessarily Matthew's *Gospel*).

Precocious Childhood

If there are two traditional patterns involved, one in Matthew and one in Luke, what are the expectations for each with respect to incidents after the birth complex? The Matthew pattern so far is: genealogy—birth—flight and return. The Luke pattern so far is: birth of companion (John the Baptist)—birth of hero (Jesus). In both cases we would expect the next element in the

[28] See note 20 above.

[29] Bultmann's comments on Luke 2:1–20 (*The History of the Synoptic Tradition*, 297–299) are informative but inconclusive.

pattern to be precocious childhood. It is not in Matthew, which leaps forward to the initiation: baptism and testing of power in the temptation by Satan. Luke alone fills the slot in the traditional pattern with incidents in Jesus' precocious childhood, which indicate his special character, his divinity.

Precocious childhood is a mark of the figure who is at least partly divine or of supernatural origin. Sometimes his precocity is shown by the fact that he has occult knowledge and is a wizard, as in the Russian epic of Volx Vseslav'evič, who was the son of a princess and a snake and later became savior of his people.[30] The pattern takes many outward forms, but its ultimate meaning is that a person of divine origin early exhibits characteristics of the power of this origin and in due time saves his people. In view of the significance of precocious childhood as an element in the traditional pattern, it is surprising that this is found only in Luke.

In the childhood anecdotes about the boy destined to become king in spite of all the present king's efforts to destroy him, there is often to be found a reference to a rather unusual kind of precocity. As he grows up the child kills or maims or otherwise mistreats his playfellows. Examples can be cited from the *History* of Herodotus (life of Cyrus the Great),[31] the Finnish *Kalevala* (Kullervo),[32] the Armenian *David of Sassoun*,[33] a Bulgarian song of Krali Marko,[34] and elsewhere. Such anecdotes are told of Jesus in apocryphal texts[35] and reflected, for example, in the English ballad "The Bitter Withy."[36] It is not surprising that the scriptural canon rejected such stories, but their existence shows that the mythic tradition was clearly at work at that

[30] For a translation and full discussion of this Russian Epic see Roman Jakobson and Marc Szeftel, "The Vseslav Epos," in *Russian Epic Studies*, ed. Roman Jakobson and Ernest J. Simmons, Memoirs of the American Folklore Society 42 (Philadelphia: American Folklore Society, 1949), 13–86.

[31] Herodotus, 1.114.

[32] Lönnrot, comp., *The Kalevala*, 223–227 (Poem 31).

[33] *Daredevils of Sassoun: The Armenian National Epic*, trans. Leon Surmelian (Denver: Alan Swallow, 1964), 120–121.

[34] See note 20 above.

[35] See Oscar Cullmann, "Infancy Gospels," trans. A. J. B. Higgins, in Edgar Hennecke, *New Testament Apocrypha*, ed. Wilhelm Schneemelcher, English trans. ed. R. McL. Wilson, 2 vols. (Philadelphia: The Westminster Press, 1963–1965), 1:363–417. It is to be noted that in these stories Jesus brings back to life the boys who have been killed.

[36] MacEdward Leach, ed., *The Ballad Book* (New York: Harper & Brothers, Publishers, Inc., 1955), 689–690. For the history of the ballad, see Gordon Hall

time on the life of Jesus. They would have been suitable in Matthew, with its story of the "exposed infant," because such incidents were indications of extraordinary powers before the identity of the child was made manifest. Could it be that the element of "precocious childhood" is missing in Matthew because it was suppressed at some point? This is possible, but we cannot be sure. There is no vestige of any sort of the "precocious childhood" element in Matthew. If the mythic pattern were operative there, I should have expected some sign of this important kind of incident.

Investiture

Matthew starts with the birth of a child whose existence threatens the king, who tries unsuccessfully to destroy the child. The "exposed child" pattern is completed with the element of "investiture" or assumption of the child's rightful place and power. Expectations are that the child will eventually replace the king. This element, or vestiges of it, is present in Matthew in a number of multiforms on more than one level. History tells us that Jesus did not become King of Judea after Herod's death. The mythic pattern must be changed, if it is still operative. In short, some vestige of an investiture must be present to fulfill the pattern, or else it is no longer felt as a force in the narrative. Such a vestige is first found in an anticipatory way in the words of the Holy Spirit at the time of Jesus' baptism, "This is my beloved Son." Jesus' Triumphal Entry into Jerusalem could also be such a vestige. But it is to be noted that it can be this *only in Matthew*, because only there is found the attempt to destroy the child. The Entry into Jerusalem is found, however, in all the gospels. Should we infer that it is primary in Matthew or at least in his tradition and picked up by other tellers from this tradition? Possibly. Finally, can it be that investiture is to be discerned also in the Transfiguration and in the affirmations of the Crucifixion and Resurrection? Very probably. In sum, the pattern is completed in duplicate, probably triplicate as well, and possibly more. Such repetition, in traditional terms, emphasizes the significance in the gospels of the element of Jesus' assumption of power and his restoration to his rightful place.

Gerould, "The Ballad of the Bitter Withy," *Publications of the Modern Language Association of America*, 23 (1908), 141–167; and Phillips Barry, "The Bridge of Sunbeams," *The Journal of American Folklore*, 37 (1914), 79–89.

The Beheading of John the Baptist and the Death of the Substitute

Just as the epic of Gilgamesh, interestingly enough, does not begin with the birth of the hero but with the need for a companion and the creation of the man of the wilds, Enkidu, so Luke begins his Gospel with the birth of John the Baptist, the man of the wilderness, and the lives of the two cousins are intertwined at their birth in Luke's account. The story of the beheading of John the Baptist is not told in Luke, however, although it is mentioned (Luke 9:9), but only in Matthew and Mark, whose texts here are quite similar (Matthew 14:3–12; Mark 6:17–29). It is natural to ask why the account of John's death is thus distributed among the gospels. Luke is John the Baptist's book, as it were. Having devoted much time to the birth of John, Luke might be expected also to have an account of his death.

The beheading of John the Baptist, especially as told fully in Matthew and Mark, would also be more appropriate in Luke because it represents the "death of the substitute" in a mythic pattern. In this pattern a pair of heroes, one mortal and the other divine or partly divine, defies the gods, one male and another female, including the goddess of love (Ishtar), and for their insolence the mortal member of the pair is killed as a substitute for his friend. The story of Herod, Herodias, and Salome fits the pattern for it is they whom John the Baptist defies, and we have already suggested that John be viewed as the mortal member of the Jesus-John pair. Tradition has a fondness for duplication, and one would expect that the death of John the Baptist, which is viable as a historical element in Matthew and Mark, would be welcomed in Luke as an element in the mythic pattern. While its absence in Luke is puzzling, one might infer that the death and resurrection of Jesus were so dominant in Luke that the death of John was reduced to a vestigial reference.

In the Gilgamesh epic defiance is also expressed by Gilgamesh in the triumphal procession of the friends before the citizens and deities of Uruk after the slaying of Humbaba. Jesus' Triumphal Entry into Jerusalem, which is perhaps the key event of that portion of his life story between his Temptation by Satan and the Last Supper and which begins the account of his death and resurrection, thus plays the same role as Gilgamesh's triumph. In other words, by this deed, as a culmination of much else, Jesus brings down the wrath of the priests and elders and thus sets in motion the forces that will kill him.

Death and Resurrection

Up to the account of the arrest and crucifixion of Jesus, the mythic pattern behind the life story narrative in the gospels has included the parentage, birth, upbringing, testing, acquiring of comrades, and proving of the miraculous power of the dragon-slaying hero. Only the actual combat with the dragon and all that this entails (e.g., special weapons) is missing. The dragon-slaying myth, as seen in *Enuma Elish* and in Hesiod's *Theogony*, is also a myth of the establishment of cosmic order and of the succession of divine kingship.[37] We now turn from this pattern to stories of the death of the hero, myths of the dying and returning god, and other similar traditional material.

Dragon-slayers such as Marduk and Zeus were great gods, supreme gods in fact, and one would not expect to find stories of their deaths. In epic and saga, however, we do find narratives of the death of some dragon-slaying heroes, such as Heracles, Siegfried, Beowulf, Cúchulainn, and Roland, none of whom is a god, although several of them are either half gods or have some divine connections.[38] The mortal portion of partly divine figures has always been a cause of difficulty for such anomalous heroes. One thinks of Gilgamesh, Sarpedon the son of Zeus,[39] Achilles the son of Thetis in the *Iliad*, and many others. Jesus himself

[37] An excellent compendium and study of combat myths is Joseph E. Fontenrose, *Python: A Study of Delphic Myth and its Origins* (Berkeley: University of California Press, 1959). See also C. Scott Littleton, "The 'Kingship of Heaven' Theme," in *Myth and Law Among the Indo-Europeans: Studies in Indo-European Comparative Mythology*, ed. Jaan Puhvel, Publications of the UCLA Center for the Study of Comparative Folklore and Mythology 1 (Berkeley: University of California Press, 1970), 83–121.

[38] For Heracles see Apollodorus, *The Library*, Loeb 1:269–273. For Siegfried see *Das Nibelungenlied*, ed. Karl Bartsch, 6th ed., Deutsche Classiker der Mittelalters 3 (Leipzig: F. A. Brockhaus, 1886), 152–184. For Beowulf see Fr. Klaeber, ed., *Beowulf and the Flight at Finnsburg: Edited, with Introduction, Bibliography, Notes, Glossary, and Appendices*, 3d ed. with First and Second Supplements (Boston: D. C. Heath and Company, 1950), 96–106. For Cúchulainn see *The Táin*, trans. Kinsella, xv. The story of Cúchulainn's death is found in Tom Peete Cross and Clark Harris Slover, eds., *Ancient Irish Tales*, with rev. Bibliography by Charles W. Dunn (New York: Barnes and Noble, 1969), 333–340. For Roland see *La Chanson de Roland, publiée d'après le manuscrit d'Oxford et traduite par Joseph Bédier* (Paris: L'édition d'art, H. Piazza, 1922), 185–201.

[39] One of the most extraordinary and moving passages in the *Iliad* describes the death of Sarpedon at the hands of Patroclus. Zeus' anguish is presented in a

(as Jesus, not as the Christ) falls into this category. Another element that several of these dying semi-gods have in common is that they are betrayed; i.e., their deaths are the result of betrayal. Siegfried, for example, is treacherously slain by Hagen, and Roland and all his men are betrayed by Ganelon into the hands of the Saracen forces. Finally, some of these heroes are entirely or almost entirely bereft of the companions whom they have or have acquired. One is reminded of Siegfried, Roland, and Beowulf. There is, then, a cluster of elements around such heroes' deaths that would include both betrayal, often by someone close, and loss of companions. Both Jesus' betrayal by Judas, one of the Twelve, as is pointed out in the gospels, and his desertion by his disciples are in keeping with this mythic cluster.

The deaths of this class of heroes are final. Neither Siegfried nor Beowulf returns from the dead, nor does Achilles or Roland. Even Heracles does not return, although he is apotheosized, just as indeed Roland is taken to heaven by the angels. Old Testament parallels would be Enoch, who "walked with God; and he was not, for God took him" (Genesis 5:24), and Elijah, who "went up by a whirlwind into heaven" (2 Kings 2:11b).

The closest mythic parallel to the gospel narratives of the death and resurrection is clearly that of the dying deity of vegetation myths, who returns annually from the underworld.[40] The best known of these myths concerns the Babylonian Tammuz,[41] Adonis[42] and Persephone[43] of Greek myth, and Telepinus in

---

conversation with Hera, showing how gods feel when they cannot save their half-mortal offspring. See Homer, *Iliad* 16.419–507.

[40] The classic work here is Sir James George Frazer, *The Golden Bough: A Study in Magic and Religion*, 3d ed., 12 vols. (London: Macmillan and Co. Ltd, 1911–1915), which is available in a one-volume abridged edition (New York: The Macmillan Company, 1922). A useful book on this subject is Theodor H. Gaster, *Thespis: Ritual, Myth, and Drama in the Ancient Near East*, 1st Harper Torchbook ed., The Academy Library (New York: Harper & Row, Publishers, Inc., 1966).

[41] Information on Tammuz is scanty, but see G. R. Levy, *The Sword from the Rock: An Investigation into the Origins of Epic Literature and the Development of the Hero* (London: Faber and Faber, 1953), 50–56, 121–122; Gaster, *Thespis*, e.g., 31–32, 47, 176, 324; and Pierre Grimal, ed., *Larousse World Mythology*, trans. Patricia Beardsworth (New York: G. P. Putnam's Sons, 1965), 94. See Ezekiel 8:14–15.

[42] Apollodorus, *The Library*, Loeb 2:84–89.

[43] Apollodorus, *The Library*, Loeb 1:35–41. The prime source is the Homeric "Hymn to Demeter," in *Hesiod, the Homeric Hymns and Homerica*, 289–325.

Hittite myth.[44] In Hesiod's *Theogony* Persephone is a daughter of Zeus, a sky and weather deity, and in the Hittite myth Telepinus is son of the sky or storm god. Note that both are offspring of gods. Adonis and, presumably, his older Semitic equivalent Tammuz were killed and brought back from the world of the dead by the goddess of love, Aphrodite or Ishtar. Tammuz is mentioned by Ezekiel (8:14): "Then he brought me to the entrance of the north gate of the house of the LORD; and behold, there sat women weeping for Tammuz." He is also found in the Gilgamesh epic: "For Tammuz, the lover of thy youth, Thou hast ordained wailing year after year" (Tablet VI, lines 46 and 47). While Tammuz and Adonis were killed and brought back, both Persephone and Telepinus disappeared and returned. It would be too daring to see in the devotion of the women at the Crucifixion any vestige of the love that brought Tammuz and Adonis back from the dead, but the disappearance of Jesus' body from the tomb and his reappearance to the women and later to the disciples are consonant with the myth as represented by Persephone and Telepinus, who disappear, are sought for, and return. During their absence devastation reigns, and the orderly processes of nature are disrupted. All of this fits well the account of Jesus' death and resurrection in the gospels. Lastly, the return of the dying god of the vegetation myth is characterized by new life, abundance, an effulgence of glory, a new beginning. This element of glorification in many forms is part of the pattern. Also related to it is the fact that the returned god or hero is frequently not recognized by those he had left behind when he disappeared and has to prove his identity.[45] The shining brightness of the Risen Lord and his need to assure the disciples that it is really he may be thought of as multiforms of these mythic elements.

One of the elements of the combat myth that, in oral tradition itself, facilitated a merging of the god in the combat myth with the dying god was the part of the narrative telling how the dragon-slayer, usually a sky or storm god, was temporarily defeated

[44]Pritchard, ed., *Ancient Near Eastern Texts Relating to the Old Testament*, 126–128.

[45]The classic example of absence-devastation-return is Achilles in the *Iliad* and that of return-recognition is Odysseus in the *Odyssey*. For a discussion of details see Lord, *The Singer of Tales*, 158–197. The Roman historian Livy's account of the death of Romulus and his reported return and appearance to a certain Proculus Julius is not without interest; see Livy, 1.16.

but regained his power, usually with outside help, and was eventually victorious. In Nonnos' *Dionysiaca* there is an account of how Typhoeus stole Zeus' symbols of strength, which were eventually restored to him by Cadmus, after which Zeus went on to kill the primeval, cosmic foe.[46] In a Hittite myth the storm god also is deprived of his strength by a dragon figure called Illuyankas. When his stolen members have been returned by his half-mortal son, the storm god overcomes Illuyankas. In the ensuing battle the god's son willingly sacrifices himself on his father's behalf.[47] There are other examples of such incidents in the dragon-slaying or combat myth.[48] The great god temporarily loses his power (in the Hittite myth he is vanquished and loses heart and eyes!) and then regains it with outside assistance. Just as the dying god returns with new vigor, even so the god in the dragon-slaying myth who is temporarily *hors de combat* returns invigorated and with new powers.

One wonders whether, in the Synoptic Gospels, Jesus' foretelling of his own Death and Resurrection, followed by the prefiguring of the Resurrection in the Transfiguration, is a vestige of the death and resurrection element of the succession myth. If so, then this prefiguration comes before the Entry into Jerusalem, which may itself be a vestige of the assumption of the kingship, which is later duplicated in its turn at the time of the Trial and the Crucifixion by the proclaiming of Jesus as King of the Jews.

It seems as if in the gospels we are witnessing the formation of a new multiform of a very ancient myth of ever-renewed life, namely, the promise of eternal life through death. The succession myth, the myth of divine kingship, modulates in the gospels, through the vestige of a temporary defeat, into the myth of the dying and resurrected god, who is also a king or son of a king.

Almost all the elements that we have been regarding as mythically significant are present in all three Synoptic Gospels. In all four gospels Jesus is betrayed by Judas, abandoned by his disciples, mocked as a scapegoat, crucified, entombed, and resur-

---

[46] Nonnos, *Dionysiaca*. With an English translation by W. H. D. Rouse, with Notes by H. J. Rose and L. R. Lind, 3 vols., The Loeb Classical Library (Cambridge, Mass.: Harvard University Press/London: William Heinemann Ltd, 1940), 1:13–45.

[47] Pritchard, ed., *Ancient Near Eastern Texts Relating to the Old Testament*, 125–126 ("The Myth of Illuyankas").

[48] See Fontenrose, *Python*, 11, 268, and elsewhere.

rected to meet again with the living. Mark alone is defective in that he does not tell of the risen Christ's meeting anyone. One should remark that the Transfiguration is missing in John, a fact that may be an indication of this gospel's lesser involvement than the others with mythic patterning (at least with the mythic patterns under scrutiny here).

Summary

To pursue the mythic elements in the gospels more fully would be a greater task than I can undertake in this essay. To summarize: In their early chapters Matthew and Luke show the presence of at least two ancient mythic narrative patterns, but both patterns are to some extent imperfectly realized in each gospel. Just as an element of precocious childhood would be appropriate in Matthew but is not found there, so the element of the beheading of John the Baptist, as told in Matthew, would be appropriate in Luke but is not found there, at least not in full (John's death is mentioned). From the analysis of these story patterns, therefore, it becomes clear that, on the whole, Matthew and Luke represent independent traditions.

Beginning with the baptism and temptation, the basic elements of the mythic patterns seem to be found in all four gospels. This sharing indicates the traditional character of the narratives. In general, however, the individual treatments of the several elements point to the independence of each gospel rather than to the primacy of any one.

PARALLEL SEQUENCES AND VERBAL CORRESPONDENCES

Parallel Sequences

General Comments on Sequence. The oral traditional composer works with fairly distinct units of various shapes and sizes. These units are not the same as the elements of story pattern discussed in the preceding section and should not be confused with them. One can see from the charts that follow in this section of my essay that the units with which we are now concerned are the discrete episodes of the gospels, which frequently have parallels in more than one gospel. The boundaries of the several units are often set by comparison of one gospel with another. Instead of

58

following the divisions in such excellent works as Kurt Aland's *Synopsis of the Four Gospels*,[49] I have made my own pericope divisions, partly because I feel that the texts with which one is working must themselves make known their inner segmentation. It is the sequence of such units that receives our attention here. Oral traditional composers think in terms of blocks and series of blocks of tradition. The "catalogue," i.e., the listing of units in sequence, is one of the most characteristic structural devices in oral composition.[50]

As we observe the sequences in the Synoptic Gospels, the pattern that we see most often repeated is either a sequence found in all three gospels or a sequence shared by two of the three. In the latter cases either there may be a blank in the third gospel or, equally if not more frequently, the correspondences in the third gospel may be scattered at random, or so it seems, in this gospel. What do these patterns mean? This is one of the basic questions in the relationships among the gospels, perhaps indeed *the* basic question. There are really two questions here: a) what is the significance of the correspondences of sequence (note that it is of sequence, not necessarily of text!)? and b) what is the meaning of the scattered and fragmented references in the third text? Both questions are important. The fragmentation would seem to indicate that the third gospel does not recognize the passage in the other two as a unit but does know the elements of the passage, either separately or as part of a different grouping or passage. On the other hand, the correspondences in two or more of the gospels are an indication that the relevant passage was recognized as a unit by more than one of the gospel writers. One would be tempted to conclude that the relationship among the gospels was one of written documents were it not for two decisive phenomena. First, there are many instances where elements of a sequence are scattered sporadically in one or more gospels. Second, there is less verbal correspondence than I would expect in a manuscript tradition. I find it unusual for a writer to choose passages from several documentary sources as if from a

[49] Kurt Aland, ed., *Synopsis of the Four Gospels*. Greek-English Edition of the Synopsis Quattuor Evangeliorum with the Text of the Revised Standard Version (London and New York: United Bible Societies, 1972).

[50] The most famous catalogue is that of the ships in the *Iliad*. The *Song of Roland* has many such catalogues. The South Slavic songs show the way in which singers in a pure oral tradition vary catalogues. But the principle of listing extends far beyond such obvious catalogues.

buffet. The sporadic nature of the positioning of some of the elements seems more likely to be an indication of an oral traditional relationship among the texts.

Baptism and Temptation. With the entrance of John the Baptist into all four of the gospels, the problem of interrelationship takes on a new and different aspect. We now encounter textual similarities and differences, but the question remains, whether the relationship is one of manuscript or of oral traditional composition.

The elements that tell of John's appearance, preaching, and baptizing prior to the Baptism of Jesus are the following:

Matthew (3:1–12)	*Mark (1:2–8)*	*Luke (3:1–17)*
A John appeared preaching in the wilderness of Judea (3:1)	C "The voice of one crying in the wilderness" (1:2–3)	A John preaching in the wilderness (3:1–2)
B "Repent, for the kingdom of heaven is at hand." (3:2)	A John appeared preaching in the wilderness (1:4a)	B Preaching baptism for repentance (3:3)
C "The voice of one crying in the wilderness" (3:3)	B Preaching a baptism of repentance (1:4b)	C "The voice of one crying in the wilderness" (3:4–6)
D Description of John (3:4)	E People of Judea and Jerusalem went to him and were baptized (1:5)	———————
E People of Judea and Jerusalem went to him and were baptized (3:5–6)	D Description of John (1:6)	———————
F "You brood of vipers" (3:7–10)	———————	F "You brood of vipers" (3:7–9)
———————	———————	(H elaboration of F) "What shall we do?" (3:10–14)
G "He who is coming after me is mightier than I" (3:11–12)	G "After me comes he who is mightier than I" (1:7–8)	G "He who comes is mightier than I" (3:15–17)

60

		[I	Herod imprisons John (3:18–20)
_____	_____	J	Jesus baptized (3:21–22)
_____	_____	K	Genealogy (3:23–38)]

ABCDEFG　　　　　CABEDG　　　　　ABCF(H)G

From the above chart, it would appear that there was a story about John's preaching that contained seven elements, A–G, four of which (B,C,F, and G) centered around quotations. Luke and Matthew agree on the order, but D and E, which are concerned not with quotations but rather with the description of John (D) and the fact that people came from Judea and Jerusalem to be baptized (E), are not found in Luke.

In Mark the order of ABC and of DE is changed, i.e., to CAB and to ED. Such changes of order are typical in oral tradition but not easy of explanation in manuscript tradition.[51] It might be argued that the order in Matthew and Luke (ABC), or at least in the tradition they represent, is primary because it seems "logical" to depict John appearing in the wilderness before the quotation from Isaiah, but this "logic" is debatable. I could defend the dramatic effectiveness of the quotation followed by the appearance of John in the wilderness. The same arguments can be used in discussing DE/ED, although in this case, I must confess, the order DE does seem more appropriate. Luke's over-all text is longer than Matthew's, in spite of the fact that DE are not in Luke. Luke's length is explained by the elaborate placing of the appearance of John in time and history and by the inclusion of the question of the multitude, "What then shall we do?," and

[51] See, e.g., Bruce M. Metzger, *The New Testament: Its Background, Growth, and Content* (New York and Nashville: Abingdon Press, 1965), 81: "When the sections of Mark and Luke differ in sequence, Matthew agrees with Mark; but when the sections of Mark and Matthew differ in sequence, Luke agrees with Mark. Furthermore, Matthew and Luke never agree in sequence against Mark." This does not seem to hold true with respect to the appearance of John the Baptist (and the Baptism of Jesus) in the Synoptic Gospels. Whether one takes the ABC of Matthew and Luke as against the CAB of Mark or assigns ABC to Mark and CAB to Matthew and Luke, Mark varies in sequence from both Matthew and Luke, who agree with one another. This sequence seems clearly to be an exception to Metzger's statement, which would appear to need some modification.

its answer. The indications may be that the story as told by Matthew presents the general form of the tradition, the order of which was changed by Mark's tradition and expanded by that of Luke.

With respect to the story of John the Baptist, the Gospel of John does not follow the pattern of the other three but is distinctive (John 1:6–34). The Fourth Gospel exhibits some knowledge of the traditional story, however, especially in the quotations of G ("He who comes after me ranks before me, for he was before me"), C ("The voice of one crying in the wilderness"), and G in still another form ("even he who comes after me, the thong of whose sandal I am not worthy to untie").

The actual Baptism of Jesus is told simply and briefly and has only three elements.

Matthew (3:13–17)	*Mark (1:9–11)*	*Luke (3:21–22)*
A Jesus came from Galilee to the Jordan to be baptized by John. (3:13)	A Jesus came from Nazareth of Galilee and was baptized in the Jordan. (1:9)	A When the people had been baptized and Jesus also had been baptized. (3:21)
B John tried to prevent him. (3:14–15)		
C When Jesus went up from the water, the Heavens opened, the Spirit of God descended as a dove and a voice said: "This is my beloved son." (3:16–17)	C Same (1:10–11), except voice said: "Thou art my beloved son."	C The heavens opened, the Holy Spirit descended as a dove, and a voice said, "Thou art my beloved son." (3:22)

C contains the real substance of the episode and is common to all three Synoptic Gospels in somewhat similar form. Matthew, however, is different from the other two not only in B, but also in its use of the third person in C. It would seem, then, that Mark and Luke may represent one tradition, characterized by the absence of B and the use of the second person in C, and Matthew another. As might be expected, the Gospel of John is different. I find it, frankly, impossible to say whether Mark or Luke has primacy in the tradition represented by that pair and equally impossible to say whether Mark-Luke or Matthew "came first."

As one proceeds from section to section trying to find a possible reason or reasons for the primacy of one of the Synoptic Gospels over the other two, one begins to wonder whether one may be dealing with the kind of oral tradition to which the question of primacy, a question formed in the crucible of manuscript or fixed text tradition, is not applicable in the same way as it is in dealing with literary tradition.

In Matthew's account of the Temptation (4:1–11) we have the following sequence:
1) wilderness/hunger (4:1–2)
2) stones/bread (4:3–4)
3) pinnacle of temple (4:5–7)
4) mountain/kingdoms of world (4:8–9)
5) begone/"You shall worship . . ." (4:10–11)

Mark has only two verses: 1:12, "The Spirit immediately drove him out into the wilderness," and 1:13, "And he was in the wilderness forty days, tempted by Satan; and he was with the wild beasts; and the angels ministered to him." These verses of Mark are only the frame of the episode. They seem to me to imply that Mark knew more details, the same sort of fuller story, for example, that is found in Matthew (and Luke), but preferred to tell this episode in Jesus' life briefly, for whatever reason. I find it difficult to see how this element might indicate priority of Mark over Matthew (and Luke), as the Two-Source Theory of Synoptic relationships would ask us to believe.

Luke (4:1–13) is fairly close to Matthew, but he reverses items three and four in the sequence. Thus Luke has:
1) wilderness/hunger (4:1–2)
2) stones/bread (4:3–4)
3) (mountain)/kingdoms of world (4:5–8)
4) pinnacle of temple/"You shall not tempt the Lord your God" (4:9–12)
5) "And when the devil had ended every temptation, he departed" (4:13)

The Temptation is missing in John.

The closeness of the text at certain points in Matthew and Luke is not surprising nor is it inconsistent with the hypothesis that both represent oral traditional texts. The passage abounds in striking statements by both Satan and Jesus; in fact, it consists largely of a series of "punch lines," and such statements are usually kept fairly stable in oral tradition. Thus, close verbal correspondence would be expected. In a series of this sort, tradition tends to produce a progression in importance. Matthew places the stress on worship; Luke places it on temptation. While I feel that Matthew's stress may be the more basic, and, were I pressed, I might be willing to concede that Matthew's tradition on this point has primacy, I should prefer to say that the two texts are simply different. The order is not firmly set or irrevocably established. The very fact that it is possible to have two texts that are different implies the fluidity of a traditional text.

At this point, it seems to me unlikely that Mark was a source for either Matthew or Luke. There are elements that point in the opposite direction, this is to say elements that imply that Mark was aware of some of the same stories told by Matthew and Luke: the tradition of John the Baptist, where he reverses the order of some of the incidents, and the Temptation, which he treats very briefly. With respect to the material as a whole from Jesus' Birth through the Temptation, I think it possible that Matthew's tradition could be older than Luke's. This conclusion is based on my feeling: 1) that the Shepherds might be vestiges of the Wise Men, 2) that the order of the third and fourth items in Luke vis-à-vis that in Matthew was possibly not primary, and 3) that the greater fullness on the part of Luke *might* be secondary. All this is very tentative, however. It seems more likely that the relationship of the gospels is that of three or four men telling the "same" oral traditional story and that the results are both traditional and individualistic within the tradition.

The Sequence Following the Temptation. The task of investigating the relationships among the gospels becomes more complicated as we move into a consideration of Jesus' Ministry.[52] At this juncture, it will be helpful to recall that, generally speaking, there are two kinds of oral traditional literature that are of importance for both the Old and the New Testaments. One is narrative, the other non-narrative. In the gospels, however, one often finds separate narratives (usually, but not necessarily, short ones) treated in an ordered series as though they were non-narrative materials. I refer, of course, to episodes of miraculous healing and other miracles, as well as to the parables.

At this point in the story of Jesus' life his testing is over and he

[52] Because of the exigencies of time and the complexity of the material, I shall deal only with the early part of the Ministry of Jesus.

is ready to begin his Ministry, which is signaled in Matthew (4:12) and Mark (1:14) by the arrest of John and Jesus' coming into Galilee. (The arrest of John had been mentioned slightly earlier in Luke [3:18–20], just before Jesus' Baptism.) Mark's account (1:14–15) is the simpler of the two: "Now after John was arrested, Jesus came into Galilee, preaching the gospel of God, and saying: 'The time is fulfilled, and the kingdom of God is at hand; repent, and believe in the gospel.'"

The fact that Matthew's passage is longer than Mark's might lead one to suppose that Matthew has simply embroidered on Mark, but Matthew's "Repent, for the kingdom of heaven is at hand" is in reality a repetition of the same sentence in Matthew 3:2, where, of course, the words are spoken by John. (In the corresponding passage, Mark 1:4 has no direct quotation, but "John the baptizer appeared in the wilderness, preaching a baptism of repentance for the forgiveness of sins.") Matthew's quotation at 3:2 does not need to depend on Mark, but the opposite might well be true: namely, that Mark's general statement about repentance in 1:4 stems from an acquaintance with the quotation, which was surely well known. It should be noted, however, that Mark and Luke (3:3) both have the same general statement! The "repent" quotation is peculiar to Matthew, where it is used twice, being attributed to John in 3:2 and to Jesus in 4:17. Mark uses a much modified form of it at 1:15. I see no necessary dependence one way or another between Matthew 4:12–17 and Mark 1:14–15.

The section in the Synoptic Gospels that follows the Temptation consists primarily of the Calling of the Disciples and of the Sermon on the Mount (Matthew) or on the Plain (Luke). The latter is identifiable in both Matthew and Luke by the Beatitudes at the beginning (Matthew 5:3–12; Luke 6:20–23) and by its close, the "house built on a rock" passage (Matthew 7:24–27; Luke 6:47–49). Thus, the Sermon clearly forms a discrete unit in the teller's mind, having its own beginning and end. It also has a frame. It is immediately preceded in both Matthew and Luke by an element concerned with: a) the calling of Jesus' disciples (Matthew 4:18–22; Luke 6:12–16) and b) the gathering of a large number of people (Matthew 4:23–25; Luke 6:17–19). It is followed in both gospels by the incident of the healing of the centurion's servant (Matthew 8:5–13; Luke 7:1–10), which, however, is separated from it in Matthew by another incident, that of the healing of a leper (Matthew 8:1–4).

65 Matthew 4:18–22 (the Calling of the Disciples) is almost ver-

batim the same as Mark 1:16–20. Luke 5:1–11 tells a quite different story, which, however, exhibits some awareness of the story told in Matthew and Mark. John's account of Calling the Disciples (1:35–51) is quite different, but it should be noted that, like the others, it places the calling of Simon Peter and his brother Andrew first. In Luke, the passage telling of the Calling of the Disciples is separated from the Temptations by other material, some of which *follows* the Calling in Matthew and Mark. It will be helpful to schematize the order of the various elements from the Call of Disciples in Matthew and Mark through Luke's account of the Call to the Healing of the Centurion's Servant and to designate these elements as "Complex I":

Complex I

Matthew	*Mark*	*Luke*
A Calling disciples to follow him (4:18–22)	A Calling disciples to follow him (1:16–20)	_____
B He went about Galilee teaching in synagogues, preaching the gospel and healing; his fame spread, and people assembled. Seeing crowd, he went up on Mount. (4:23–5:1)	B Went to Capernaum on Sabbath, entered synagogue and taught (1:21)	B Same as Mark (4:31–32)
	B¹ Taught with authority, not as the scribes. (1:22)	_____
_____	C Healing an unclean spirit. (1:23–28)	C Same (4:33–37)
_____	D Simon's mother-in-law healed (1:29–31)	D Same (4:38–44)
_____	_____	A Calling disciples to follow him (5:1–11)
E The Sermon on the Mount (5:2–7:27)	_____	_____
B¹ When Jesus finished, the crowd was astonished, for	_____	_____

he taught with
authority, not as
the scribes.
(7:28–29)

F Healing a leper (8:1–4)	F Same (verbally close, with addition at end) (1:32–45)	F Luke 5:12–16
G Healing centurion's servant (8:5–13)	_____	[G Luke 7:1–10; cf. John 4:46–53]
D Simon's mother-in-law healed (8:14–17)		

ABEB¹FGD   ABB¹CDF   BCDAF(G)

In this complex, Mark and Luke use the same five elements
of story, ABCDF, but they differ in the placing of A. Matthew
knows and uses four of the elements, ABDF, agreeing with Mark
on the placement of A, but reversing D and F. He adds two important elements not in Mark and Luke in this complex, namely,
E (the Sermon) and G (the Centurion's Servant), both of which,
however, are found elsewhere in Luke. It seems logical that A
(Calling the Disciples) should begin this sequence. (In traditional
heroic patterns, the gathering of a retinue occurs in this position.)[53] The order of CDF, however, is not fixed by logical or
narrative necessity, and it is easy enough to insert other material
into this order. This is a fundamental principle in oral composition
and transmission of non-narrative complexes, as has already been
noted. In this case the elements are narrative, but their order is
not governed by a larger narrative of which they form a part. The

---

[53] In some oral traditional epics the young hero acquires a group of companions
with whom he embarks on adventures. One finds this in the *Odyssey* when
Telemachus sets out with a crew his own age to visit Pylos and Sparta. It is
frequent in Slavic epic. One of its earliest examples is the *bylina* of Volx
Vseslav'evič; see Jakobson and Szeftel, "The Vseslav Epos," 13–86, for Russian
text, English translation, and discussion. The pertinent lines (52–57) are trans-
lated by Jakobson and Szeftel (page 30):
  And when Volx was twelve years old,
  He started to pick a retinue for himself;
  He picked a retinue for three years,
  He picked a retinue of seven thousand;
  Volx himself is fifteen years old,
  And all his retinue is fifteen each.

Sermon on the Mount and the episode of the Centurion's Servant are not found in Mark, but they do occur in Luke. The Centurion's Servant occurs also in John, but, as might be expected, the story in Luke is closer to Matthew than to John. In order to understand the positioning of the episodes in Luke (and perhaps also in John) it will be necessary to examine the sequence further on in Luke. Thus, we must continue the parallel analysis.

"Calling the Disciples" has two or three steps.[54] The first relates the calling of Simon Peter and Andrew, then of James and John, sons of Zebedee, which takes place by the boats. The account in John (1:35–51) is considerably different and does not take place by the boats. Here, Jesus calls Andrew and Simon Peter on one day; then, on the next day, in Galilee, he calls Philip and Nathanael. This step ("Calling A"), the essence of which is the calling of four disciples, the first two of whom are Andrew and Simon Peter, is readily distinguishable from the next step, which I shall call "B." "Calling A" is found in all four gospels, but it is associated with the Sermon on the Mount only in Matthew. In Mark and Luke it is associated with a group of healing miracles, a series which also occurs, at least in part, after the Sermon in Matthew. In John "Calling A" is followed by the first "sign," the marriage at Cana in Galilee.

"Calling B," the second step, is really the naming and commissioning of the Twelve. It is found in all the gospels except John and always follows "Calling A," but after a considerable interval. It is associated with the Sermon on the Mount (Plain) only in Luke, where it leads into the Sermon (Luke 6:12–16). It is preceded by a series of elements (H through L; see chart of "Complex II" below), which are paralleled in both Matthew and Mark, with the following exceptions: 1) the series is preceded in Matthew by a group of episodes found later in Mark and Luke (one of which is not found in Mark at all), and 2) there is an insertion between J and K in Matthew. In Matthew (10:1–4), "Calling B" is followed by Jesus' speech of instruction to the Twelve (the remainder of chapter 10). Its associations in Mark (3:13–19) are somewhat different, although it is led up to by the same series of events or elements that lead up to its counterpart in Luke. These elements reach in essence from "Calling A" to "Calling B" in both Mark and Luke. Here then is an established sequence used by both Mark and Luke and also, but less strictly, by Matthew.

[54] The third step would be the calling of the seventy (see below).

It is to be noted that Luke places "Calling A" awkwardly and uses "Calling B" to introduce the Sermon on the Mount (Plain), in spite of the fact that "Calling B" is most logically followed immediately by the commissioning of the disciples. For this reason it is difficult for me to defend Luke's *tradition* of the sequence of these passages as primary. Mark clearly belongs to the *same tradition* as Luke, at least with respect to this material, but he presents a somewhat more coherent series up to the Sermon on the Mount (which he omits). Before examining the material that follows "Calling B" in Mark, it will be useful to study the associations of the second element in the frame around the Sermon on the Mount (the first element was Calling, both A and B), namely, the gathering of a large number of people.

Matthew 4:23–5:1 tells that Jesus went about all Galilee teaching in the synagogues and preaching and healing. People from many places brought the sick to him, and crowds followed him. He went up on the mountain, and his disciples came to him and he spoke to them. Luke 6:17–20 tells that Jesus, who had gone up into the hills to pray all night and had called his disciples the next day and chosen the Twelve (6:12–16), came down to the level ground and a multitude came from all around to hear him and to be healed. Then he spoke to them. These are the two immediate settings for the Sermon. They are the passages that come between Calling and Sermon in Matthew and Luke. The key idea in them is that people flocked to Jesus to be healed and thus the crowds were formed. With this introduction to the Sermon it is not strange, but completely fitting, that the elements that follow the Sermon are examples of miraculous healing.

Mark, who (as I have said above) follows along with Luke from "Calling A" to "Calling B," reverses the order of "Calling B" and the gathering of a multitude, as these are set forth in Luke, first telling of the gathering of the multitude and then relating the calling of the Twelve. These two sequences in Mark and Luke (ABCDF of "Complex I" above and H through N of "Complex II" below) appear to me to be excellent examples of two oral versions of an oral traditional sequence. The language is not exactly the same, there is at least one typical expansion (of the gathering of the multitude), and there are two cases of metathesis.

Matthew places the Sermon with its introductory assembling of the multitude after "Calling A" and then follows the same sequence as do Mark and Luke up to 12:14, with two insertions

(8:18–34 and 9:18–11:30). On the surface, these two insertions have only sporadic relations to Mark and Luke, yet one of the correspondences is "Calling B," which begins chapter 10 in Matthew. At 12:24 Matthew joins Mark, or vice versa as the case may be, for the final sequence.

Before proceeding, it will be helpful to schematize the elements following "Complex I," beginning with the first Matthean insertion, "Sequence W," and ending with the incident of the Centurion's Servant, and to designate these elements as "Complex II":

Complex II

Matthew	Mark	Luke
W (Matthew's first insertion: 8:18–34)		
H 9:1–8	H 2:1–12	H 5:17–26 Man lowered through roof
I 9:9–13 Calling of Matthew, tax collectors	I 2:13–17 Calling of Levi, tax collectors	I 5:27–32 Calling of Levi, tax collectors
J 9:14–17	J 2:18–22	J 5:33–38 Fasting of John's disciples, new garment, new wine skins
X (Matthew's second insertion: 9:18–11:30)		
M 10:2–4		
K 12:1–8	K 2:23–28	K 6:1–5 Lord of Sabbath
L 12:9–14	L 3:1–6	L 6:6–11 Man with withered hand
	N 3:7–12	
	M 3:13–19	M 6:12–16 The Twelve
N 12:15–16, 17–21		N 6:17–19 Crowds gather, seek to touch him, healing
	Y	

[E 5:2–7:27] ———————— E 6:20–49 Sermon
on Mount (Plain)

G 8:5–10 Cen- ———————— G 7:1–10 Centurion's servant turion's servant;
cf. John 4:46–54

Matthew's first insertion, "Sequence W," can be schematized as follows:

Sequence W

Matthew		Mark	Luke
8:18–20	Foxes have holes	——	9:57–58
8:21–22	Leave dead to bury dead	——	9:59–60
8:23–27	Rebukes the sea	4:36–41	8:22–25
8:28–34	Demoniacs and swine	5:1–20	8:26–39

Matthew 8:18–34 ("Sequence W") has parallels in Luke, although these parallels are found later and are in reverse order (Luke 9:57–60; 8:22–39), and part of the passage is paralleled in Mark (4:35–5:20). This first Matthean insertion has two parts. The first (Matthew 8:18–22) is a "travel" passage, i.e., one that occurs at a juncture where Jesus was going from one place to another. In Matthew, Jesus had just healed Peter's mother-in-law, many possessed with demons had been brought to him that evening, and he had cast out the demons and healed the sick. At the beginning of the passage, Jesus saw great crowds around him and decided to cross over by boat to the other side. There ensues then an episode in which a man, in this case a scribe, says that he wishes to follow Jesus. The incident fits here appropriately, and the adding of one instance in which Jesus asked someone to follow him to another in which a man volunteered is a normal kind of accumulation in oral traditional style. The narrative in Matthew runs along smoothly, easily moving into the episode of crossing the sea and rebuking the waves and, when all have arrived on shore, that of the demoniacs and the swine. The skill of the composer is clearly manifested, and the elements with which he was composing apparently belonged to the traditional stories about Jesus.

Luke used all of the same units as did Matthew, but not in the same positions in Jesus' life. The first passage (Luke 9:57–60) is associated with the beginning of Jesus' journeying to Jerusalem as he realizes that the time of his being delivered up is drawing near. The passage is suitable in both gospels, for the key to its introduction is the statement by someone that he will go with Jesus wherever he goes. It fits well near the beginning of the Ministry as Jesus is recruiting his followers (Matthew), but it has added poignancy as Jesus turns toward Jerusalem and the cross (Luke).

The second part of the first Matthean insertion (8:23–34) also occurs independently in other contexts in both Mark and Luke. Its two episodes are linked by the body of water, which is necessary to both stories. In Mark (4:35–5:20) and Luke (8:22–39), the passage (Rebuking the Waves, plus Demoniacs and Swine) is found after the parables of the sower and of the lamp. What "triggers" this passage is the movement of Jesus and his disciples to cross the sea. In Matthew 8:18, "when Jesus saw great crowds around him, he gave orders to go over to the other side." The fulfillment of this action is delayed by the first passage discussed above, but it is accomplished in the present passage. In Mark, immediately preceding the parables (4:1), Jesus "began to teach beside the sea. And a very large crowd gathered about him, so that he got into a boat and sat in it on the sea; and the whole crowd was beside the sea on the land." There follow then several parables, and in verse 35 we read, "On that day, when evening had come, he said to them, 'Let us go across to the other side.'" With that, the passage now under discussion begins. The circumstances that lead up to the passage are similar in both Matthew and Mark, although they are not in the same position in the two gospels. Matthew used the passage in one place, Mark in another. Luke used it in the same position as Mark, but in Luke its connection with its surroundings is less clear than in the other two gospels. The series of parables beginning with that of the sower is addressed to "a great crowd" (Luke 8:4); in fact, we are told in verse 19 that the crowd was so great that his mother and brothers "could not reach him for the crowd." In Luke 8:22 the passage under discussion begins, "One day he got into a boat with his disciples, and he said to them, 'Let us go across to the other side of the lake.'" Here in Luke, the causal thread between crowd and crossing, both of which are present but separated by time, is not explicit, but the position of the passage remains the same as in Mark. Luke, it would seem, represents a telling that is dependent on one like Mark's (but not necessarily Mark itself,

72

of course). Matthew and Mark seem to use the passage independently of one another.

To sum up thus far, after "Complex I" Matthew proceeds with two passages not found in this same position in Mark and Luke but occurring later in them (these two passages, 8:18–22 and 8:23–34, comprise the first Matthean insertion or "Sequence W" above). As we have seen, these passages appear to be independent entities that can be and are located wherever the teller deems them appropriate.

After "Sequence W," we return briefly to parallel passages in all three gospels in the same position (H through J in "Complex II"). That we are dealing with a separable unit in Matthew 9:1–17 is indicated by the fact that it exists in Mark and Luke as a unit in this same setting but also because it breaks a sequence in a different setting. This is to say, we found in studying the previous passage that Matthew 8:23–34 parallels Mark 4:36–5:20 and Luke 8:22–39. These passages in Mark and Luke are part of a longer sequence in the two gospels, the continuation of which is also paralleled in Matthew after 9:1–17, which we are presently investigating. In short, Matthew 9:1–17 breaks into a longer unit found in all three gospels, although the longer unit is not in the same position in Matthew as in Mark and Luke.

While the first two elements in the longer unit (Rebuking the Sea and the Demoniacs and the Swine) are linked together, they must have a break of some kind after them, because Jesus is required to leave the neighborhood. This creates a vulnerable joint, at which any unit or sequence beginning with crossing back (or going home) would be appropriate. Mark 5:21, the verse that continues the longer sequence in this gospel, reads, "And when Jesus had crossed again in the boat to the other side, a great crowd gathered about him; and he was beside the sea." In the parallel passage, Luke is somewhat less explicit, as he was earlier regarding the connection of the crowd and the crossing, but he is nonetheless clear enough: "Now when Jesus returned, the crowd welcomed him, for they were all waiting for him" (Luke 8:40). The passage beginning in Matthew 9:1–17 opens with similar phraseology: "And getting into a boat he crossed over and came to his own city" (9:1).

Each of these three passages brings Jesus back across the sea after the same set of adventures in all three Synoptics. In Mark and Luke, the passages introduce the healing of Jairus' daughter, the next unit in the longer sequence. This healing in Matthew, however, is found beginning in 9:18, i.e., *after* the passage in Matthew that we are studying. In its place is the healing of the paralytic lowered through the roof. The healing episode after the return in the longer sequence has been postponed by Matthew. The pull of the longer sequence has given way in the return by sea passage to the attraction of a competing sequence, which has its parallels in Mark and Luke at the same position as in Matthew. These parallels also begin with a returning home, which probably led to the confusion, or which perhaps more likely led to Matthew's return to the original sequence before it was interrupted by Matthew 8:18–34.

Thus, Mark 2:1 is similar to Matthew 9:1, but Mark 2:2 contains further information; the two verses in Mark read: "And when he returned to Capernaum after some days, it was reported that he was at home. And many were gathered together, so that there was no longer room for them, not even about the door; and he was preaching the word to them." The difference between Mark 2:1 and Matthew 9:1 is that in the former Jesus is not returning from across the sea. Luke 5:17 ("On one of those days, as he was teaching, there were Pharisees and teachers of the law sitting by, who had come from every village of Galilee and Judea and from Jerusalem; and the power of the Lord was with him to heal.") also indicates a setting for the ensuing incident that is different from a return across the sea. In other words, the unit (Matthew 9:1–17; Mark 2:1–22; Luke 5:17–38) is adapted by Matthew to follow the return crossing of the sea, but since it occurs in Mark and Luke before the crossing over the sea to avoid the crowds, it is adapted to different settings.

Thus, as we have seen, Matthew 9:1–17 interrupts a longer run that begins at Matthew 8:23 and is attested as a viable unit in Mark 4:36 ff. and Luke 8:22 ff., and the passage has been adapted to its new setting by Matthew 9:1. Looked at in another way, of course, one can also argue that Matthew 8:18–34 is an interruption. It leads Matthew into the beginning of a run, which for one reason or another the author sees fit, in turn, to interrupt.

"Complex I," then, is essentially a series of healings, with the exception of the Sermon on the Mount in Matthew. These healings follow after the Calling of the Disciples. Matthew 8:18–22 continues the idea of the calling of followers and the refusing of volunteers who set special conditions. As I said earlier, this fits well at an early point in Jesus' Ministry. The same subject is in-

74

troduced again in Matthew 9:9–13 (Mark 2:13–17 and Luke 5: 27–32), when Jesus calls Matthew (Levi in Mark and Luke), a passage embellished in all three gospels with comments on tax collectors. In Matthew the Calling of the Disciples culminates in chapter 10, when the Apostles are named and commissioned and sent forth. This is paralleled in Mark 3:13–19 and 6:7–13 and in Luke 6:12–16 and 9:1–6. In Mark and Luke the naming and the commissioning and sending forth are separated. It is to be noted that only the somewhat eccentric calling found in Matthew 8: 18–22 occurs in Luke (9:57–60) *after* the naming and commissioning, a fact that, indeed, points out the peculiar character of this passage. This observation also leads one to see that Luke has a duplication of appointing and commissioning and reporting. In both Mark's and Luke's earlier complex of calling, naming, and commissioning (Mark 6:30 ff.; Luke 9:10 ff.), the disciples return and report what they have done. In Luke 10:1–16 (immediately following the "calling" in Luke 9:57–60), Jesus appoints and instructs the seventy, and they report back and are cautioned by Jesus in Luke 10:17–20. The "calling" units can be schematized as follows:

	Matthew	*Mark*	*Luke*
A The "special" disciples called	4:18–22	1:16–20	5:1–11
D^1 "Eccentric" calling	8:18–22	————	9:57–60
B Matthew (Levi) called	9:9	2:13–14	5:27
C c^1 The Twelve named and commissioned	10	3:13–19 6:7–13	6:12–16 9:1–6 9:7–9
	Herod thinks John risen	6:14–29	
c^2 The Twelve report	————	6:30	9:10
D^2 The seventy appointed, commissioned and report	————	————	10:1–20
	AD^1BC^1	ABC^1C^2	$ABC^1C^2D^1D^2$

Luke is complete. Mark lacks D^1 and D^2 (i.e., the seventy "duplication"). Matthew lacks D^2 (the seventy) but has D^1 "displaced" (?), and Matthew also lacks the reporting of the Twelve (C²).

Those who favor the priority of Mark might say that Luke's "the seventy" comes from "Q." Since "Q" is hypothetical, however, I prefer to say that we do not know where Luke heard of the seventy. Structurally it follows the plan of the Twelve, and it thus looks like a duplication of this plan, or, to put it differently, they are both multiforms of the calling, commissioning, and reporting pattern. From the point of view of oral traditional literary techniques, this latter explains the seventy in Luke satisfactorily enough. Oral traditional literature tends to duplicate in multiform those elements or patterns that are significant. The duplication in Luke stresses the importance of the appointing, commissioning, and reporting of the first followers of Jesus— obviously a subject of vital interest to the gospel composers.

The following chart presents the sequence of Matthew's second insertion (9:18–11:30), to be designated as "Sequence X," together with another interlocking sequence beginning with Matthew 8:23–34. The elements in this second sequence are in brackets.

Sequence X

Matthew		Mark	Luke
[8:23–34	Jesus rebukes the sea; Demoniacs and swine]	[4:36–5:20]	[8:22–39]
[9:1–17	Man lowered through roof; calling Matthew, tax collectors, etc.]	2:1–22	5:17–38
[9:18–26	Healing Jairus' daughter and woman with flow of blood]	[5:21–43 (end of chapter)]	[8:40–56 (end of chapter)]
———		[6:1–6a Is not this the carpenter]	———
9:27–31	Healing two blind men (cf. Mt. 20:29–34)	not in Mark (cf. Mk. 10:46–52)	not in Luke (cf. Lk. 18:35–42)

76

9:32–34	Healing dumb demoniac (repeated Mt. 12:22–24)	3:22 (in part)	11:14–15
[9:35–38 (end of chapter)	He went about all cities . . .]	[6:6b]	[_____]
[10 (whole chapter)	The Twelve named and given instructions]	[6:7–13 commissioning of disciples]	[9:1–6 commissioning of disciples]
11:1	After this he went about teaching in the cities,	_____	_____
11:2–19	Messengers from John in prison. Jesus about John	not in Mark, but [cf. Mk. 6:14–29 Herod thinks of John risen; beheading of John told in flashback]	7:18–35, and cf. [Lk. 9:7–9 Herod thinks of John risen.]
11:20–24	"Woe to you, Chorazin"	not in Mark	10:13–15
11:25–27	"No one knows the son except the Father"	not in Mark	10:21–22
11:28–30	"Come to me, all who labor and are heavy laden."	not in Mark	not in Luke
	not in Matthew	[6:30 Apostles' report]	[9:10]

This insertion in Matthew contains various material, beginning with three healings, two of which have counterparts in both Mark and Luke but in later passages. These healings are followed by teachings and instructions to the disciples, as discussed previously when considering the Callings in Matthew, Mark, and Luke.

The second insertion picks up again the sequence that had begun in Matthew 8:23; Mark 4:36; Luke 8:22, which had been interrupted by Matthew 9:1–17; Mark 2:1–22; Luke 5:17–38. The healing of Jairus' daughter and of the woman with a flow of blood continues the earlier sequence after Jesus' return across the sea and ends the story begun when Jesus had crossed over the sea to avoid the crowds. In Matthew, two other healings are then added, that of two blind men (9:27–31) and that of a dumb demoniac (9:32–34). Both of these incidents have parallels later in Matthew itself, and these parallels in their turn have counterparts later in Mark and Luke where, at least in the case of the blind men, they belong to still other sequences! In fact, the healings of the blind men in the gospels are excellent examples of oral traditional multiforms: essentially the same story told in various settings.

In the second sequence (in brackets), there is a passage in Mark (6:1–6a) that is found in neither Matthew nor Luke at this point. In this passage, Jesus' neighbors ask, "Is not this the carpenter?" Jesus says that "a prophet is not without honor, except in his own country," and he marvels at their unbelief. The passage has parallels in Matthew (13:53–58) and in Luke (4:16–30) but not in the same position as in Mark, that is, not as part of this sequence. What has brought this passage into Mark at this place? Jesus has returned across the lake and has healed Jairus' daughter. At the beginning of the immediate passage, Jesus has returned home. Luke puts this incident, much "modified" and "elaborated," immediately after the Temptation and thus within the larger group of passages after the Temptation that includes the Sermon on the Mount (Plain) and the Mission of the Seventy. Luke depicts Jesus, after the Temptation, going about Galilee and the surrounding country and teaching in the synagogues (4:14–15). In the course of this teaching, Jesus comes to Nazareth, and here the passage under discussion is appropriate. Its form in Luke is particularly Lucan, showing Jesus being given the book of the prophet Isaiah to read in the synagogue in Nazareth; his reading:

"The Spirit of the Lord is upon me,
because he has anointed me to preach good news to the poor.
He has sent me to proclaim release to the captives
and recovering of sight to the blind,
to set at liberty those who are oppressed,
to proclaim the acceptable year of the Lord" (Luke 4:18–19);

and proclaiming (verse 21), "Today this scripture has been fulfilled in your hearing." We remember back to Luke's picture of the boy Jesus in the temple. There are echoes also of the Temptation that has just preceded the telling of this incident. Finally, the general discussion of prophets in this passage also makes it a coherent and understandable whole. Mark is enigmatically brief

78

regarding the Temptation, and he has nothing about the boyhood of Jesus. In this passage Mark was certainly not following Luke, nor was Luke following Mark. They are independent of one another, both in the form of the passage and in its placing. The parallel in Matthew (13:53–58) occurs much later, *after* the parables. In form it is similar to Mark, and the setting is also similar: "And when Jesus had finished these parables, he went away from there, and coming to his own country he taught them in their synagogue, so that they were astonished . . ." (verses 53–54). There is no clue here as to why this passage occurs where it does in either Matthew or Mark. As a matter of fact, the passage is moveable and can occur whenever in his early ministry Jesus has returned home after teaching elsewhere and begins to teach in the synagogue in Nazareth. In Matthew the incident in question immediately follows the parables and ends chapter 13. Chapter 14 in Matthew begins with the account of the beheading of John the Baptist, reference to which is also part of this sequence.

The relationship between Luke and Mark in respect to this sequence is comparatively simple. Both know the sequence. Mark, following perfectly acceptable oral traditional associative techniques, adds a passage which is in the "moveable" category and, in another place, elaborates on a passage by recounting in flashback the beheading of John the Baptist, which is a set piece, as we know from Matthew, where it is also found.

There follows then a continuation of the sequence once again, with travel and gathering verses in Matthew and Mark, the naming of the Twelve in Matthew, and the commissioning of the Twelve in all three gospels. After this, Mark and Luke have a reference to Herod, who thinks that the person accomplishing all these deeds must be John the Baptist, whom he has beheaded. Mark adds to this short passage, as it is found in Luke, a narrative account, this time in flashback, of the beheading of John, such as is found (not in flashback) in Matthew, but in a different position. The sequence ends in Mark and Luke with the Apostles reporting their success. This report is missing in Matthew.

In short, without going into further detail, we can say that two sequences that are placed one after the other in Mark and Luke are intertwined in Matthew. The complexity of the relationships among the Synoptic Gospels, as indicated by the foregoing (partial) analysis, itself points to the probable role of oral traditional composition in the formation and recording of these gospels.

In fact, the complexity of the picture that emerges in "Com-

79

plex II" and in the second Matthean insertion ("Sequence X"), where several sequences are imposed on one another, is so great that I wonder whether, in the case of any one of the gospels, one can truthfully say that it was formed by a single author in a manuscript tradition. I can visualize rather that such superimposing and intertwining took place in the composing and recomposing of story elements in oral tradition. This implies that the versions we have were produced by people who were linked to the oral tradition either by actually being a part of it or, perhaps more probably, by being close to it. By this latter, I mean people who heard the traditional stories but did not themselves tell them: for example, a learned or semi-learned person who had heard the tales all his life but never had written the traditional stories or the traditional style.

Whereas Luke goes from the sequence H through N in "Complex II" into the Sermon on the Mount (Plain), Mark leaps forward to the final sequence of this section of the Synoptic Gospels, a sequence shared by Matthew, who, however, inserts some other material (12:33–45). Luke includes parts of the final sequence, but they are scattered in later chapters. This final sequence, to be designated as "Sequence Y," can be schematized as follows:

Sequence Y

Matthew	*Mark*	*Luke*
12:22–29 He cures a blind and dumb demoniac and the Pharisees say: "It is only by Beelzebul, . . . that this man casts out demons."	3:22–27 The scribes from Jerusalem say: "He is possessed of Satan"	11:14–22 He was casting out a demon who was dumb and some said: "He casts out demons by Beelzebul"
12:31–32	3:28–30 He who blasphemes against	12:10

80

	Holy Spirit never has forgiveness	
12:46–50 end of chapter	3:31–35 "Who are my brothers?" end of chapter	8:19–21

Although the correspondences here between Matthew and Luke are not consecutive, those between Matthew and Mark are, but "Sequence Y" is found considerably later in Matthew (Chapter 12) than in Mark (Chapter 3).

After the Sermon Luke ends this section with a sequence of his own (7:11–8:3), which in part, however, has reflections considerably later in Matthew and Mark. This sequence, to be designated as "Sequence Z," can be schematized as follows:

Sequence Z

Matthew	*Mark*	*Luke*
————	————	7:11–17 Raising young man from dead (cf. Lazarus in John 11:1–44)
11:2–19	————	7:18–35 Jesus about John
26:6–13 (just before Passover)	14:3–9	7:36–50 Woman with precious ointment (cf. John 12:1–8, also associated with Passover)
27:55–57	cf. 15:40–41	8:1–3 The women

Parable of the Sower

Matthew	*Mark*	*Luke*
13:1–9	4:1–9	8:4–8

I find it difficult to believe that the sequences I have analyzed in the preceding pages are related to one another through written documents. Specifically, I cannot understand Luke, perhaps the best writer of the three Synoptic Evangelists, completely confusing his alleged "source" Mark (according to the Two-Source Theory) as he seems to do, thus producing an illogical sequence. Moreover, if "Q" were a written document used by Matthew and Luke, I should expect much greater verbal correspondence than there is between Matthew and Luke in those passages that have no equivalent in Mark (for example, in the Healing of the Centurion's Servant). In short, I find the Two-Source Theory inadequate to explain the relationships among the gospels in this significant complex of passages. I believe, however, that the relationships can be explained by the process of oral traditional literary composition, in terms of thematic groupings and association. The complicated picture presented by this section of the three gospels is not at all inconsistent with the concept of three interrelated oral versions of the material. By interrelated I mean that there are sequences shared by all three but not in exactly the same words nor always in the same order.

Comments on Variations in Arrest, Trial, Crucifixion, and Resurrection. Scanning the last three chapters in each of the Synoptics in order to note the variations, one is struck by the fact that greater diversity is found in the Resurrection stories than in the accounts of the Arrest, Trial, and Crucifixion. Differences there are, however, even in the accounts before the Resurrection. Luke clearly presents a version distinct from that of Matthew and Mark. I find it improbable that Luke here had a manuscript of either Matthew or Mark in front of him as he wrote his account. It is not merely a question of the kinds of differences that might be additions to or omissions from another manuscript. More significant, there is little verbal correspondence, even when they tell the same incident. Luke's version, I feel sure, is distinct from Matthew's and Mark's. Those two, however, are very close, although not verbally exact; the sequences are the same and there are no reversals or displacements.

The differences between Matthew and Mark in the narrative from the Arrest through the Crucifixion consist mainly of several elements in Matthew not found in Mark, with a few in Mark not in Matthew. Matthew, for example, reports Judas' asking Jesus at the Last Supper whether the betrayer is he and Jesus' reply, "You have said so" (26:25). John's account (13:25–27) shows Jesus as indicating to the beloved disciple that Judas would be the betrayer. This shows that two versions were current of the disclosure of Judas as the betrayer. It is noteworthy that, just as

82

the tale of the three Wise Men was functional in Matthew and the corresponding narrative of the Shepherd visitors in Luke was not, so the story of how Jesus at the Last Supper pointed out Judas as his betrayer is functional in John but not so in Matthew. In John, Jesus is presented as initiating the final stage of the betrayal: he gives the morsel to Judas, and "Then after the morsel, Satan entered into him. Jesus said to him, 'What you are going to do, do quickly'" (13:27). The account in Matthew hangs in the air.

Similarly, Matthew later tells about: 1) Judas' attempt to return the thirty pieces of silver and 2) the purchasing of the potter's field with the money (27:3–10). In Acts 1:16–20, the story of Judas' death and the purchase of the Field of Blood is also to be found, indicating that Luke presumably knew a version of this narrative, although a quite different one, but he did not include it in his gospel! Finally, Matthew notes that the Pharisees requested Pilate to post a guard at Jesus' tomb lest the disciples steal the body and claim that he had risen (27:62–66). These reports are not in the other Synoptic Gospels.

On the other hand, Mark tells of the enigmatic young man in a loin cloth who ran away at the time of the Arrest of Jesus (14:51–52), and he also remarks that, when Joseph of Arimathea asked Pilate for the body of Jesus, Pilate wondered if Jesus were already dead and asked a centurion to find out (15:44–45).

There are three other short passages found in Matthew and not in Mark. Two are concerned with Pilate. In 27:19, Matthew tells of a dream of Pilate's wife which warns him not "to have anything to do with that righteous man." It is in Matthew alone (27:24–25) that we see Pilate wash his hands and hear him say, "I am innocent of this man's blood, see to it yourselves." The third passage (27:52–53) is a mysterious one. It relates that at the time of the Crucifixion "the tombs also were opened, the bodies of saints who had fallen asleep were raised, and coming out of the tombs after his resurrection they went into the holy city and appeared to many."

The above examples seem to show that Matthew and Mark, while aware of the same basic story of events in Jesus' life from before the Passover through the Crucifixion, each had his own version of it. One can envisage Matthew as adding some of the above passages to Mark's account, but one can equally well conceive of Mark as cutting some of them out of Matthew, e.g., the reference to the dream of Pilate's wife and the mysterious verses about the rising of the dead and their appearance in the city, which he may have thought to be too superstitious. In these circumstances, it is difficult, if not impossible, to say which gospel came first. One strongly suspects that the question of primacy is not a sensible one. Everything points to the complexity of composition that negates the applicability of such a question.

Verbal Correspondences

Paradoxically, because there is less exact verbal correspondence than independent text, it is difficult to understand the relationships among the gospels when the texts are verbally close. Take for example the Parable of the Sower (Matthew 13: 1–9; Mark 4:1–9; Luke 8:4–8):[55]

Matthew 13:1–9	*Mark 4:1–9*	*Luke 8:4–8*
En tę hēmerą ekeinę exelthōn ho Iēsous		
tēs oikias ekathēto para	Kai palin ērxato didaskein para	
tēn thalassan·	tēn thalassan·	
kai synēchthēsan pros auton ochloi polloi,	kai synagetai pros auton ochlos pleistos,	Syniontos de ochlou pollou kai tōn kata polin epiporeuomenōn pros auton
hōste auton eis ploion embanta	hōste auton eis ploion embanta	
kathēsthai,	kathēsthai en tę thalassę,	
kai pas ho ochlos	kai pas ho ochlos pros tēn thalassan	
epi ton aigialon heistēkei.	epi tēs gēs ēsan.	
kai elalēsen	kai edidasken	eipen
autois	autous	
polla en parabolais	en parabolais polla,	dia parabolēs·
legōn·	kai elegen autois en tę didachę autou· akouete.	
idou exēlthen ho speirōn	idou exēlthen ho speirōn	exēlthen ho speirōn
tou speirein.	speirai.	tou speirai ton sporon autou.
kai en tǭ speirein auton	kai egeneto en tǭ speirein	kai en tǭ speirein auton
ha men espesen para tēn	ho men epesen para tēn	ho men epesen para tēn
hodon,	hodon,	hodon kai katepatēthē,
kai elthonta ta pateina	kai ēlthen ta pateina kai	kai ta pateina tou ouranou
katephagen auta. alla de	katephagen auto. kai allo	katephagen auto· kai heteron
epesen epi ta petrōdē	epesen epi to petrōdes	katepesen epi tēn petran,

<hr>

[55] The transliterated Greek text that follows is based on Aland, ed., *Synopsis of the Four Gospels*, 113–114. The English translation is the Revised Standard Version.

hopou ouk eichen gēn pollēn,	hopou ouk eichen gēn pollēn,	
kai eutheōs exaneteilen dia	kai euthus exaneteilen dia	
to mē echein bathos gēs·	to mē echein bathos gēs·	
hēliou de anateilantos	kai hote aneteilen ho hēlios	kai phuen
ekaumatisthē, kai dia to mē	ekaumatisthē, kai dia to mē	exēranthē dia to mē
echein hrizan exēranthē.	echein hrizan exēranthē.	echein ikmada.
alla de epesen epi	kai allo epesen eis	kai heteron epesen en mesǫ
tas akanthas, kai anebēsan	tas akanthas, kai anebēsan	tōn akanthōn, kai
		symphueisai
hai akanthai kai apepnixan	hai akanthai kai synepnixan	hai akanthai apepnixan
auta.	auto,	auto.
	kai karpon ouk edōken.	
alla de epesen epi tēn	kai alla epesen eis tēn	kai heteron epesen eis tēn
gēn	gēn	gēn
tēn kalēn kai	tēn kalēn kai	tēn agathēn kai phuen
edidou karpon,	edidou karpon anabainonta	epoiēsen karpon
	kai	
ho men	auxanomena kai epheren eis	
hekaton, ho de hexēkonta,	triakonta kai en hexēkonta	hekatontaplasiona.
ho de triakonta.	kai en hekaton.	
	kai elegen·	tauta legōn ephōnei·
ho echōn ōta	hos echei ōta	ho echōn ōta
akouetō.	akouein akouetō.	akouein akouetō.

That same day		
Jesus went out	Again	
of the house and sat beside	be began to teach beside	
the sea.	the sea.	
And great crowds	And a very large crowd	And when a great crowd
gathered about him,	gathered about him,	came together and people
		from town after town came
		to him,
so that he got into a boat	so that he got into a boat	
and sat there;	and sat in it on the sea;	
and the whole crowd	and the whole crowd	
stood on the beach.	was beside the sea on the	
	land.	
And he told them many	And he taught them many	he said
things in parables,	things in parables,	in a parable:
saying:	and in his teaching he said	
	to them:	
"A sower went out	"Listen! A sower went out	"A sower went out
to sow. And as he	to sow. And as he	to sow his seed; and as he
sowed, some seeds fell along	sowed, some seed fell along	sowed, some fell along
the path,	the path,	the path, and was trodden
		under foot,
and the birds	and the birds	and the birds of the air
came and devoured them.	came and devoured it.	devoured it.
Other seeds fell on rocky	Other seed fell on rocky	And some fell on the rock;
ground, where they had not	ground, where it had not	

Matthew 13:1-9	*Mark 4:1-9*	*Luke 8:4-8*
much soil, and immediately they sprang up, since they had no depth of soil, but when the sun rose they were scorched; and since they had no root they withered away.	much soil, and immediately it sprang up, since it had no depth of soil; and when the sun rose it was scorched, and since it had no root it withered away.	and as it grew up, it withered away, because it had no moisture.
Other seeds fell upon thorns, and the thorns grew up and choked them.	Other seed fell among thorns and the thorns grew up and choked it, and it yielded no grain.	And some fell among thorns; and the thorns grew with it and choked it.

Other seeds
fell on good soil
and brought forth grain,
 	
          some
a hundredfold, some sixty,
some thirty.
	And other seeds
	fell into good soil
	and brought forth grain,
	growing up and
	increasing and yielding
	thirtyfold and sixtyfold
	and a hundredfold."
	        And he said,
		And some
		fell into good soil
		
		and grew
		         and yielded
		
		a hundredfold."
		       As he said this,
		he called out,

He who has ears, let him hear."	"He who has ears to hear, let him hear."	"He who has ears to hear, let him hear."

It is clear, I believe, that Luke was not copied textually from either Matthew or Mark. On the other hand, how should we see the relationship of these two to one another? They are at times very close, as in 3b, 4, 5, 6, and 7. These verses are almost close enough to have been copied one from the other, "or from the same source," as is frequently said. Were the passage more extensive, such a conclusion would be justified, but in reality these verses are surrounded by verses which are not so closely paralleled verbally in another gospel. There are islands of closeness in lakes (not seas) of divergence rather than the other way around. Still, the problem is a difficult one. If the texts are copied, I am puzzled by the fact that only a few verses are copied consecutively and these not quite exactly: Matthew 13:2, for example, has the plural, *ochloi* ("crowds"), while Mark has the singular, *ochlos* ("crowd"); similarly, Matthew 13:6 has a genitive absolute, *hēliou de anateilantos* ("but when the sun rose"), where Mark 4:6 has a clause, *kai hote aneteilen ho hēlios* ("and when the sun rose"). Small differences, to be sure, but nonetheless not exact copying.

Can we explain these verses and their surrounding divergences in any way other than by copying? Possibly. In oral traditional literature, insofar as I am acquainted with it, some passages may become reasonably stable verbally in the usage of a single narrator or even perhaps of a group of narrators. These are passages that are used frequently, that exhibit special stylistic devices that bind them together, perhaps that contain the especially significant words of an important person in the story. The following, for example, is the beginning of two recordings of the song, "The Captivity of Djulić Ibrahim," by Salih Ugljanin.[56]

Text No. 659	Text No. 667
Jedno jutro teke osamnulo,	Jedno jutro beše osvanulo,
U Zadaru pucaju topovi,	
Dva zajedno, trideset ujedno.	
	Sve se zemlja i planina trese.
Šenluk čini od Zadara bane;	
Ufatijo slugu Radojicu,	Ufatijo uskok Radovana,
Radojicu, tursku pridvoricu,	
Pa ga baci ledenu zindanu.	
Pa kad Rako u zindanu dodje,	Pa kad Rako u tamnicu dodje,
Tuna nadje trideset Turaka,	
I medju nji' Djulić Ibrahima,	
I kraj njega Velagić Selima	I kodj njega Velagić Selima.
I njihovo trides'i dva druga.	
Pa him Rako pomoj naturijo,	Dodje Rako, pa him pomoj dade,
A Turci mu bolje prifatili.	I svi njemu bolje prifatiše.

One morning it had just dawned,	One morning it had dawned,
In Zadar the cannon are booming,	
Two together, thirty at once.	
	The earth and the mountains tremble.
The governor of Zadar is rejoicing;	
He has captured the servant Radojica,	He has captured the renegade Radovan,
Radojica, the Turkish lackey,	
And thrown him into the cold prison.	

---

[56] *Serbocroatian Heroic Songs*, coll. Milman Parry, vol. 2, *Novi Pazar: Serbocroatian Texts*, ed. Albert Bates Lord (Belgrade: The Serbian Academy of Sciences/Cambridge, Mass.: Harvard University Press, 1953), 75 (Text 659, lines 2–15), 83 (Text 667, lines 2–14). English translation mine.

Text No. 659	Text No. 667
When Rako came into the prison,	When Rako came into the dungeon,

There he found thirty Turks,
And among them Djulić Ibrahim,

And next to him Velagić Selim	And by him Velagić Selim.
And his thirty-two comrades.	
Rako gave them greeting,	Rako came in, and gave them greeting,
And the Turks returned it.	And all returned it.

The textual variations are slight, and whole consecutive lines are verbally exactly the same. In short, verbal closeness and even exactness in frequently used or otherwise important or specially bound passages is not unusual in oral traditional composition. Such passages, therefore, are not *necessarily* proof of manuscript tradition. Much further investigation of this phenomenon in oral traditional texts is needed before we have a complete comprehension of it, but we have plenty of material, and some research has already been done.

When one follows the parallel texts on for the remainder of the songs, one finds a configuration of passages like the one above, surrounded by other passages of considerable divergence. In other words, the picture is not unlike that presented by a comparison of the texts of two gospels.

It is worthy to note, of course, that the two song texts above are from the same singer. There is greater divergence between passages from different singers, except that when a singer has been influenced by a published text without actually memorizing the text, the similarities and divergences are more like those that occur between two or more singings of the same song by the same singer. This can be illustrated by the opening of the famous song of "Marko Kraljević and Musa the Highwayman" as published by Vuk Stefanović Karadžić (No. 66, lines 1–12) and as collected from Ilija Mandarić (Parry Text No. 517).[57]

Karadžić	Parry
	Oj! Mili bože, na svem tebi fala!
Vino pije Musa Arbanasa	Vino pije Musa Keserdžija
U Stambolu, u krčmi bijeloj.	

---

[57] Vuk Stefanović Karadžić, *Srpske narodne pjesme*, 4 vols. (Beograd: Prosveta, 1953–1958), 2:389–398. The Parry Text is unpublished. English translation mine.

Kad se Musa nakitijo vina,
Onda poče pijan besjediti:

Kad se Musa napojijo vina,
Onda poče pijan govoriti:
"Mili bože, na svem tebi fala!

"Evo ima devet godinica
      Kako dvorim cara u Stambolu:

Ev' imadę devet godin' dana

Ni izdvorih konja ni oružja,
Ni dolame nove ni polovne:
Al' tako mi moje vjere tvrde,

Ne izdvori' pare ni dinara,
Nit' aljine nove ni polovne.
A tako mi moja vjera tvrda,
I tako me ne rodila majka,
Već kobila neka bedevija,

Odvré' ću se u ravno primorje,
      Zatvoriću skele oko mora
      I drumove okolo primorja.

oj! odvréu se u primorje ravno,

      Oj! Dear God, thanks to you for all things!

Musa the Albanian is drinking wine

Musa the highwayman is drinking wine

In Istanbul in the white tavern;

When Musa had had his fill of wine,
Then, drunk, he began to speak:

When Musa had drunk his fill of wine,
Then, drunk, he began to say:
"Dear God, thanks for all things!

"It is now nine years

It is now nine years of days

That I have been serving the sultan in Istanbul:

I have not been paid a horse or arms,
Nor a coat, new or used:
But by my firm faith,

I have not been paid money or dinars,
Nor clothes, new or used.
But by my firm faith,
And may no mother have borne me,
But a horse, some bedouin mare,

I shall withdraw to the level coastland,

O, I shall withdraw to the level coastland,

I shall close the landing places on the sea
And the roads in the coastland."

The implications of this kind of comparative investigation for the study of the relationship of manuscripts might be far-reaching, and they must be approached with great caution, circumspection, and with deep thought. My main purpose in introducing reference to such research in this essay is to indicate that close textual correspondence is found, at least in occasional passages, between oral traditional versions of a text. It is time now to return to the gospels and to some concluding ideas.

BY WAY OF CONCLUDING REMARKS

This section of my essay could not possibly be headed "Conclusions." The problems are too many and far too complex for one with my limited background in New Testament scholarship to come to anything that might be called conclusions. I have followed two general approaches: 1) I have searched in the gospels for evidence of oral traditional narrative mythic patterns, to see whether such patterns might have played a role in the formation of the gospels; and 2) I have investigated the gospels as variant texts, observing the sequences of their episodes, to determine the presence, if any, of structural characteristics of oral traditional narrative.

With respect to the second approach, I have seen reason to believe that the Synoptic Gospels exhibit certain characteristics of oral traditional literature. *First*, for example, their texts vary from one another to such an extent as to rule out the possibility that, as a whole, one could have been copied from another. In this respect they have the appearance of three oral traditional variants of the same narrative and non-narrative materials. It is true that on occasion the texts are so close that one should not rule out manuscript transmission; hence, it may be that oral tradition has sometimes had written sources affecting the text, not merely in respect to content but also as *text*. *Second*, the sequences of episodes show chiastic variations in arrangement between gospels (AB in one and BA in another), which are also typical of oral traditional literature. This structural principle applies not only to the order of episodes within a sequence but also to the order of larger sequences. *Third*, one finds a marked tendency to elaboration and expansion both of individual episodes and of sequences, which is, again, characteristic of oral traditional composition. For example, an episode told briefly in one gospel may be told at greater length in another; a series of healings or of sayings tends to expand, more healings or sayings being added. *Fourth*, I have noted several instances of duplication of multiforms. This is peculiarly an oral traditional phenomenon. For example, the appointing, commissioning, and reporting of the seventy in Luke bears the hallmark of a duplication of the similar actions or passages concerning the Twelve. I have also indicated the striking multiforms of the healing of blind men. There is enough such evidence to indicate that these gospels are

90

closely related to oral traditional literature, both narrative and non-narrative.

In carrying out these analyses I have attempted to illustrate several methods of approach to the problem of the interrelationships of the gospels. It would require years of fuller and closer research than I have been able to devote to this subject to arrive at reasonably accurate concepts, and it would require an entire book to set forth in any proper way the results of such study. What I have done is only preliminary, and I hope that someday someone may find it worthwhile to pursue this work to its conclusion. My chief evidence has come from primary texts. I have relied little on other writings about the gospels.

As I see it at the moment, the events in Jesus' life, his works and teachings, evoked ties with "sacred" oral traditional narratives and narrative elements that were current in the Near East and in the eastern Mediterranean in the first century A.D. These were stories whose deepest meanings were concerned with: a) establishing order in the world by invoking divine models and divine intervention, and b) assuring, as part of this order, a continuation of life for a humanity that was puzzled by and anxious about its own mortality.

Oral and Independent or Literary and Interdependent? A Response to Albert B. Lord

Charles H. Talbert

In *The Singer of Tales*,[1] Albert B. Lord took up Milman Parry's quest to understand Homer by a study of the living epic tradition of the Yugoslavs. From the evidence of the Yugoslav oral epic song, Lord worked out a theory, which he then applied to the *Iliad* and the *Odyssey*. The theory is basically this. The singer, who is operating in an illiterate society, tells his stories in poetic song, using stock themes and set formulas. In such a setting, the singer is not working from a fixed text that is memorized but rather is composing in the performance. There is stability in the story, but this stability does not include the wording or the unessential parts of the story. Hence, every time the story is told in an oral performance, it is a new composition, which varies in large measure according to the demands of the audience. No two performances of an oral epic are ever textually alike. When such oral epics are written down, it is because someone asks the singer to tell the story so that the words can be written down. In this way a fixed text is established. With writing, there is a change from stability of the essential story, which is the goal of oral tradition, to stability of text, of the exact words of the story. This theory Lord then applied to Homer. There is

[1] Albert B. Lord, *The Singer of Tales*, Harvard Studies in Comparative Literature 24 (Cambridge, Mass.: Harvard University Press, 1960).

no doubt, he says, that the composer of the Homeric poems was an oral poet. In the form in which we have the *Iliad* and the *Odyssey*, however, they are oral dictated texts. The impulse to write these poems did not come from Homer himself but from some outside source. The influence of Lord's thesis has been tremendous in many different areas of study.[2] It is from this perspective that Lord now approaches the canonical gospels. He wishes to see whether they represent three (or four) tellings of the same story in an oral traditional literature.

Lord's essay follows two general approaches: (1) it seeks evidence of oral traditional mythic patterns in the gospels, and (2) it notes the sequences of episodes in an attempt to determine whether they exhibit structural characteristics of oral traditional narrative (p. 90). If the Synoptics do show signs of traditional mythic patterns and of structural traits that are typical of oral traditional narrative, then, Lord believes, the Synoptic Problem can be removed from the literary sphere to the arena of oral traditional literature. My response to Lord's essay will fall into two unequal parts: the longer will focus on the essay's approach as a whole; the shorter will mention a number of individual points within the essay.

Lord's Approach As A Whole

The analysis in Lord's first approach to the canonical gospels leads him to see at least two ancient mythic patterns in the early chapters of Matthew and Luke. From this he concludes that these two gospels represent, on the whole, independent traditions (p. 58). Granting, for the sake of argument, Lord's description of the mythic patterns, I must ask whether the evidence can lead to the conclusion he suggests. It can do so only on the assumption that control by mythic patterns is limited to oral traditional literature. Such control can also be found in the literary biographies, however. Suetonius' *Augustus*, for example, in-

---

[2] Edward R. Haymes, *A Bibliography of Studies Relating to Parry's and Lord's Oral Theory*, Documentation and Planning Series 1 (Cambridge, Mass.: Harvard University Press, 1973). The impact continues; see, e.g., Michael J. Zwettler, *The Oral Tradition of Classical Arabic Poetry* (Columbus: Ohio State University Press, 1977); *Semeia*, 5 (1976), which is devoted to the possibilities of Lord's thesis for the study of the Old Testament (see especially the fine bibliographical essay, "Oral Tradition and the OT: Some Recent Discussion," by Robert C. Culley, pages 1–33).

cludes in the life story of the emperor such features as: reference to a miraculous birth; portents of warning that nature was pregnant with a king for the Roman people, which caused the Senate to decree that no male child born that year should be reared; references to prodigious acts during childhood, such as commanding the frogs to be silent so that none has ever croaked in that place since; prophecies that the boy was being reared to be the savior of his country; and an ex-praetor's oath that he had seen the form of the emperor on its way to heaven. Other literary examples are too numerous to mention. Since mythic patterns are not the exclusive property of oral traditional literature, Lord's argument that the presence of such patterns in the Synoptics is an indication of the oral traditional character of these gospels must be regarded as inconclusive.

Lord's second approach is to look in the Synoptics for the presence of structural characteristics of oral traditional narrative. Four such characteristics are to be found, he believes.

(1) The texts of the gospels "vary from one another to such an extent as to rule out the possibility that, as a whole, one could have been copied from another" (p. 90). From my point of view, however, the divergent wording is no obstacle to our viewing the Synoptic Problem as a literary one. Given the practices of the Hellenistic Age, it is exactly what one should expect. As a control on our view regarding the use of sources in a literary composition in Greco-Roman antiquity, we can take Josephus' *Jewish Antiquities*, a prose narrative from the first century C.E., written in Greek by an author with a Jewish heritage.[3] Though de-

[3]The question to be put to all examples of comparative material that are advanced to assist in solving the Synoptic Problem is: Are the examples really analogous? There must be some boundaries on what is appropriate. Are examples from Medieval times and later as valuable as those from the Hellenistic era? I think not. Thomas R. W. Longstaff's use of materials from a post-Hellenistic period severely limits the persuasive power of his argument (*Evidence of Conflation in Mark? A Study in the Synoptic Problem*, Society of Biblical Literature Dissertation Series 28 [Missoula, Mont.: Scholars Press for The Society of Biblical Literature, 1977]). If he had looked for comparative material from the Hellenistic Age among lives of hero figures told in terms of the same myth employed in the Synoptics, then Philostratus' *Life of Apollonius of Tyana* would have been available. Philostratus says that he used at least four sources: (a) the memoirs of Damis, which furnished his main material; (b) Maximum of Aegae for what Apollonius did in the Cilician city of Aegae; (c) Apollonius' letters; and (d) various accounts of the end of the career of the hero (*Life of Apollonius* 1.2-3). Even if the reliability of Philostratus' claims be discounted, the claims are still valuable for us in that they indicate what he considered would be appropriate in his time.

tails are uncertain, the broad outlines of his usage of sources in the *Antiquities* seems clear.[4] For example, in Books 1–10 Josephus had no other written authority than the Old Testament. When we reach the days of Antiochus Epiphanes, the history comes mainly from I Maccabees. Nicolaus of Damascus seems to have been the main source for Books 15–17, the time of Herod. Examination of Josephus' use of the Jewish Scriptures shows him to be typical of Hellenistic authors, whose practice is ably described by H. St. John Thackeray:

Now, while it was customary for ancient historians to make free and unacknowledged use of the published work of their predecessors, without any sense of what we should call "plagiarism," it was almost a point of honour with them to vary the phraseology.[5]

This means that one would not expect in the Synoptic Gospels the type of wooden copying that Lord assumes must be typical of a literary procedure.

(2) In the gospels "the sequences of episodes show . . . variations in arrangement between gospels . . . , which are also typical of oral traditional literature" (p. 90). My response to this contention is twofold. In the first place, Joseph B. Tyson has shown that the agreement in order among the Synoptics is so high that a literary explanation is necessary.[6] No amount of variation in sequence at lesser levels can offset this overall fact. In the second place, Josephus again offers a control. *Antiquities* 4.8.4–43 (4.196–301) gives us a case where he rearranges the

---

Here, then, is an analogous document that uses a number of sources from different authors (actually three supplementing a fourth, which is basic), which issues in a text that is longer than the primary source, the memoirs of Damis. There is no comfort here for the advocates of the Griesbach Hypothesis.

[4]So, e.g., F. J. Foakes Jackson, *Josephus and the Jews: The Religion and History of the Jews As Explained by Flavius Josephus* (New York: Richard R. Smith, Inc., 1930), reprinted (Grand Rapids: Baker Book House, 1977), 246–258; H. St. John Thackeray, *Josephus: The Man and the Historian*, Hilda Stich Stroock Lectures 1928 (New York: Jewish Institute of Religion, 1929), reprinted with a new introduction by Samuel Sandmel (New York: KTAV Publishing House, Inc., 1967), 58–72; and R. J. H. Shutt, *Studies in Josephus* (London: SPCK, 1961), 12, 85–92. Heinrich Bloch, *Die Quellen des Flavius Josephus in seiner Archäologie* (Wiesbaden: Dr. Martin Sandig OHG, 1968 reprint of 1879 ed.), was not available to me.

[5]Thackeray, *Josephus*, 107.

[6]Joseph B. Tyson, "Sequential Parallelism in the Synoptic Gospels," *New Testament Studies*, 22 (1976), 276–308.

Mosaic code at the same time that he condenses it because of his particular purpose at the moment. In *Antiquities* 15.5.3 (15.127–146) we meet, in a section derived from Nicolaus, a speech of Herod to the Jews on the eve of battle. The same speech is reported in Josephus' earlier *Jewish War* 1.19.4 (1.373–379), presumably from the same source. The content of the two speeches is essentially the same, but the later document's speech is twice the length of the earlier, and its order is different. In *War* the speech falls into two parts, each with an ABCD sequence (earthquake, enemies' destruction, murder of ambassadors, Jewish courage), whereas in *Antiquities* the arrangement is topical: (a) a just war, (b) the implications of the earthquake. Apparently rearrangement was a literary option. Indeed, in *War* I.Preface.5 (1.15) Josephus provides evidence that the usual procedure in writing during his time was rearrangement of previous work, when he objects: "The industrious writer is not one who merely remodels the scheme and arrangement of another's work. . . . "[7] Thus, as in the case of textual variation, one finds the rearrangement of sequence to be characteristic of literary as well as of oral tradition.

(3) In the Synoptics "one finds a marked tendency to elaboration and expansion both of individual episodes and of sequences, which is, again, characteristic of oral traditional composition" (p. 90). Though Lord does not mention it, there is also the opposite tendency to condense or shorten, unless one assumes that the shorter is always the earlier, which Lord does not. Again, the use of Josephus as a control is helpful. On the one hand, Josephus elaborates individual episodes, such as Abraham's sacrifice of Isaac (*Antiquities* 1.13 [1.222–236]; cf. Genesis 22) and expands sequences, as in *Antiquities* 13.3.1–2 (13.62–71), where he adds to the account of I Maccabees a report of how, in the days of Ptolemy Philometer and his wife Cleopatra, Onias, the son of the High Priest, petitioned the sovereigns of Egypt for permission to build a temple at Leontopolis and includes in this report the letter of Onias and the reply authorizing the project. On the other hand, Josephus shortens individual units, such as the description of Elijah's visit to Sinai (*Antiquities* 8.13.7 [8.349–352]; cf. I Kings 19:8–18) and of Elijah's ascent to heav-

[7] Translation from *Josephus*. With an English translation by H. St. J. Thackeray, Ralph Marcus, Allen Wikgren, and L. H. Feldman, 9 vols., The Loeb Classical Library (Cambridge, Mass.: Harvard University Press/London: William Heinemann Ltd, 1926–1965), 2:9.

en (*Antiquities* 9.2.2. [9.28]), and omits passages in his sources that do not fit his purposes (e.g., Exodus 4:24–26, the circumcision of the son of Moses by Zipporah, or Exodus 32's scandal of the golden calf). From the evidence supplied by Josephus, therefore, it would seem that this third trait also is characteristic of the literary tradition of the Mediterranean world and is not the exclusive property of oral tradition.

(4) In the Synoptic Gospels one finds "several instances of duplication of multiforms," such as the mission of the seventy alongside the mission of the Twelve, which "is peculiarly an oral traditional phenomenon" (p. 90). From the late first century B.C.E. the *Aeneid* of Virgil offers a control. In the *Aeneid* we find material that Lord would call duplication of multiforms. Juno laments her lack of power in two places, twice we meet banquets on the shore, there are repeated prophecies of Roman greatness, and in two different places Ilioneus speaks for Aeneas. Instances could be multiplied indefinitely. Yet these apparent duplications are not signs of the *Aeneid*'s being oral traditional literature. The *Aeneid* was a literary piece. In actuality, these repetitions are consciously created correspondences, designed to further the author's overall plan, which includes the parallelism of the halves, Books 7–12 corresponding to Books 1–6.[8] Once again, the phenomenon that seemed to Lord to point to an oral setting for the gospels is also found to be characteristic of the literary tradition of antiquity.

In addition to these four traits found in the Synoptics and believed by Lord to be uniquely characteristic of oral traditional literature, there is an anomaly in the gospels that also points in the same direction. Lord says: "I find it unusual for a writer to choose passages from several documentary sources as if from a buffet" (pp. 59–60). "Several" means two (e.g., Mark and "Q," as in the Two-Source theory). Once again I must demur, and I do so on the basis of two controls. (a) Josephus furnishes the first control. In Book 13 of *Antiquities* two sources, I Maccabees and another relating to Syrian history, have been amalgamated in alternate blocks. A patch from Maccabees is followed by a patch from an unknown work. A formula referring the reader to another source of information on Syrian history occurs

[8] See George E. Duckworth, *Structural Patterns and Proportions in Vergil's Aeneid: A Study in Mathematical Composition* (Ann Arbor: University of Michigan Press, 1962).

at the point where the narrative of Maccabees is resumed.[9] (b) A second control is found in Arrian, *Anabasis of Alexander*, Book I, Preface, which reads:

> Wherever Ptolemy son of Lagus and Aristobulus son of Aristobulus have agreed in their histories of Alexander son of Philip, I record their story as quite accurate; where they disagree I have chosen what I feel to be more likely and also better worth the narrating . . . Parts, however, of the records of others, such as appeared to me worthy of narration and not wholly untrustworthy, I have included as so much tradition about Alexander.[10]

In Mediterranean antiquity an author could select from several sources and alternate them in patches or blocks without any hesitation. Such a procedure, in and of itself, by no means necessarily points to oral traditional literature.

In conclusion, the first part of this response has attempted to show that all of the types of evidence cited by Lord as pointing to the Synoptics being oral traditional literature are also found in the literary tradition of Greco-Roman antiquity. Lord's case, I believe, has not been made.

Individual Points

There are a number of minor points in Lord's essay that require comment.

(1) New Testament scholars need to hear Lord's statement that when "an incident in the gospel narrative of Jesus' life fits in a mythic pattern, there is no implication at all that this incident never happened" (p. 39). Alan Dundes agrees,[11] citing Francis Lee Utley's tongue-in-cheek application of the pattern to the biography of Abraham Lincoln with the result that Lincoln's

[9] Thackeray, *Josephus*, 63.

[10] *Arrian*. With an English translation by E. Iliff Robson, 2 vols., The Loeb Classical Library (London: William Heinemann Ltd/New York: G. P. Putnam's Sons, 1929–1933), 1:3. This passage cannot be taken as support for the Griesbach Hypothesis for at least two reasons: (a) "Where they disagree I have chosen what I feel to be the more likely . . ." Arrian's work was not just a synthesis of what his two main sources had in common. (b) "Parts . . . of the records of others . . . I have included . . ." Arrian's work was not an abbreviation but was likely a longer work than either of his two primary sources.

[11] Alan Dundes, *The Hero Pattern and the Life of Jesus*, Protocol of the Twentyfifth Colloquy of the Center for Hermeneutical Studies in Hellenistic and Modern Culture (Berkeley, Calif.: The Center for Hermeneutical Studies in Hellenistic and Modern Culture, 1977), 10.

life fits the pattern almost totally.[12] This is helpful for New Testament scholars who, following D. F. Strauss, often think that whenever the story of Jesus in the gospels is described in terms of a mythic pattern this is a clear denial of its historicity.

(2) Speaking of two or more texts of the same story that vary in length, Lord says: "It does not in any way necessarily follow that the shortest is the oldest and the longest the latest or that the crudest is the oldest and the most polished the latest. It may be, but it is not necessarily so" (p. 43). It must be noted, however, that this statement is made within the context of Lord's belief that the gospels are oral traditional literature, and it may not be taken as an aid to those who are working with the gospels as literary documents.

(3) I am puzzled by the various references to "primacy" in Lord's essay. At one point he states, "One strongly suspects that the question of primacy is not a sensible one" (p. 84). Yet at several places he attempts to assert the primacy of one gospel tradition over another (e.g., pp. 47, 52, 64). This seems out of place in the context of oral traditional literature. It is even more suspect when, for example, the basis for Matthean primacy in the birth narratives is the claim that the visit of the Shepherds in Luke is a vestigial multiform of the visit of the Magi in Matthew. More likely is the view that Luke is using an alternative myth, one associated with the Jewish belief that the Messiah would either be a shepherd or be associated with shepherds. In my judgment, Lord's statements about primacy may not be taken as an aid to those working on the gospels as literary documents.

(4) Lord cites examples from the Yugoslav epics to show that in oral tradition some passages may become reasonably stable verbally (pp. 87–89). This, he says, is evidence that verbal closeness is not necessarily proof of manuscript tradition. Yet he notes that the two texts cited are from the same singer. "There is greater divergence," he notes, "between passages from different singers." The exception is "when a singer has been influenced by a published text without actually memorizing the text." Here "the similarities and differences are more like those that occur between two or more singings of the same song by the same singer" (p. 88). This exception suggests the possible situation

[12] Francis Lee Utley, *Lincoln Wasn't There or Lord Raglan's Hero*, CEA Chap Book, Supplement to CEA Critic 22, no. 9 (Washington: College English Association, 1965).

in the composition of the Synoptics. Even if the gospels are literary texts, the use of other gospels by an Evangelist need not be conceived as slavish copying. The Evangelist has been influenced by these other gospels like an oral singer who has not memorized a text that is written. This fits with the procedure noted earlier in this response about the tendency to vary the language of one's sources.

(5) Lord says: "In their normal tellings, oral traditional narratives about individuals . . . only rarely include a single account that begins with birth and ends with death. Most commonly, the separate elements or incidents in the life of the hero form individual poems or sagas" (pp. 39–40). This fact would seem to point to the inappropriateness of oral traditional literature as a model for understanding the gospels, which encompass the whole life story of Jesus. An oral traditional model would appear much more relevant in discussing the pre-gospel collections than the gospels themselves.[13]

In conclusion, the second part of this response has reinforced the line of argument in the first part. The Synoptics do not seem readily to fit the category of oral traditional literature.

Conclusion

Christianity emerged in a Mediterranean culture that was not illiterate. Education was widespread.[14] Books were produced on

[13] If studies in oral tradition could contribute to our understanding of the Gospel materials in such a way as to make possible the rewriting of Rudolf Bultmann's *The History of the Synoptic Tradition* (trans. John Marsh, rev. ed [New York and Evanston: Harper and Row, Publishers, Inc., 1968]), this would be a major contribution. Some beginnings have been made; see, e.g., Ernest L. Abel, "The Psychology of Memory and Rumor Transmission and Their Bearing on Theories of Oral Transmission in Early Christianity," *The Journal of Religion*, 51 (1971), 270–281; Gordon W. Allport and Leo Postman, *The Psychology of Rumor* (New York: Henry Holt and Company, 1947); Tamotsu Shibutani, *Improvised News: A Sociological Study of Rumor* (Indianapolis: The Bobbs-Merrill Company, 1966); Jan Vansina, *Oral Tradition: A Study in Historical Methodology*, trans. H. M. Wright (Chicago: Aldine Publishing Company, 1965). Do studies in oral traditional literature have anything to add to beginnings such as these made by various disciplines? If so, I for one should greatly appreciate any and all help available. I do not think these studies will be of any significance in solving the Synoptic Problem, however.

[14] See, e.g., W. W. Tarn, *Hellenistic Civilisation*, 3d ed. rev. Tarn and G. T. Griffith, Meridian printing (Cleveland and New York: The World Publishing Company, 1961), 268–298.

a scale theretofore unknown. A large reading public consumed prose written with a rhetorical cast. The author of such prose, though often using written sources, would not be a mere scissors-and-paste person. F. J. Foakes Jackson's remarks about Josephus apply equally to the larger scene: "As we saw in his treatment of . . . sources, his individuality, for both good and ill, appears in everything he touches. . . . "[15] At the same time, such an author as Josephus could claim neither to have added to nor to have diminished the records he used.[16] This, it seems to me, is the context for understanding the Synoptic Problem.

[15] Foakes Jackson, *Josephus and the Jews*, 257.
[16] Josephus, *Jewish Antiquities* 1. Preface.3 (1.17); 10.10.6 (10.218).

Oral Traditional Literature and the Gospels: The Seminar

Leander E. Keck

We should doubtless be nearer to a "solution" of the problem of the relationships among the gospels if we knew precisely what a gospel was or, more precisely, what sort of an event the writing of a gospel was and what a gospel "did" in the communities in which it was produced.[1] When the earliest of our gospels was first read in a Christian congregation, for example, did the hearers regard it as an interesting and perhaps even useful variation of what they already knew, somewhat the way concert-goers are intrigued by the way popular gospel songs are used in Charles Ives' music? Did Christian hearers know the plot of the whole before it was written, or did they know only an assortment of bits and pieces, so that hearing a continuous account of Jesus' words and deeds was an unprecedented event? Did the earliest hearers of the gospels resist the idea of writing the material?

[1] Various dimensions of this question emerged during the first session of the Colloquy's Seminar on Oral Traditional Literature but were not explored subsequently. For example: If we knew what a gospel "did" we might be able to correlate the differences among the gospels with the different early Christian constituencies. We might also understand why one gospel was not deemed competent to "do" what had to be done and it was felt that another should be written. We might also understand Tatian better: Was he grappling with this issue when he replaced multiple, diverse gospels with one account, whose function might be controlled more easily than that of four (or more) texts?

Did the Evangelists intend that their texts be read in Christian worship (and how much?), so that they actually designed them for this function, or is this something that Christians later found useful to do with them?[2] Since the gospels (in whatever sequence) were used (on whatever occasions) within communities in which traditions about Jesus continued to circulate orally, how did the texts and the oral traditions interact? How did the existence side by side of orally transmitted traditions and written texts of these same traditions affect the *Sitz im Leben* for other traditions and subsequent texts? If the traditions were common property of the community but the gospels were products of individuals (if that *is* what they were!), how much freedom did the Evangelists have in ordering, phrasing, and composing their material?

Although post-Enlightenment criticism has provided an ample volume of "answers" to such questions, the fact is that in these rather elemental matters we simply do not know the correct answers. Indeed, this whole scholarly phenomenon confirms "Sandmel's Law" that "where the evidence is minimal, the explanations will be multiple."[3] To the extent that we do not know what "happened" when a gospel was written, we do not really know what a gospel was; all we know is what a gospel came to be. Our knowledge, or what passes for knowledge, is *ex post facto*; it is subject to no field investigation in which we can see the gospel-making process occurring. We must infer what the gospels were from what they became (i.e., from their later functions both in the church and in scholarly investigation).

Our inferring can be enriched and guided, however, by attending to other phenomena that are somewhat analogous. Specifically, studies in oral traditional literature might provide certain analogues to the gospel-phenomenon, even though such analogues would by no means offer complete parallels. In any case, this was the rationale for inviting Albert B. Lord, an eminent specialist in oral traditional literature, to participate in the Colloquy on the Relationships among the Gospels and for constituting a Seminar on Oral Traditional Literature and the Gospels

[2] The theory that the gospels were shaped by the synagogue lectionary, which they were designed to complement, has not established itself because it has not been demonstrated that the sort of lectionary required for the theory actually existed in contemporary Judaism.

[3] Samuel Sandmel, *The First Christian Century in Judaism and Christianity: Certainties and Uncertainties* (New York: Oxford University Press, 1969), 8. Sandmel calls this a "rule-of-thumb."

as a part of the Colloquy. Those who planned the Colloquy were not the first to see the import of Lord's work for the Gospels; Erhardt Güttgemanns, for example, has raised provocative questions about New Testament form criticism by relying, in part, on Lord's studies.[4] What Güttgemanns learned from Lord is that one must not naively assume that there is a simple continuity between oral transmission, collecting aggregates of oral traditions, and producing texts of these traditions and aggregates, as though writing the material down did not mark something new in the process. The same conclusion might be reached on the basis of linguistic theory, but Lord's insights derived in large part from something that New Testament students cannot do: field investigation, in which he studied the transition from the oral to the written. Furthermore, Lord not only brings a knowledge of comparative literature and tradition to bear on our questions, but as a classicist he has studied Homer from the perspective of oral literature. Probably no other scholar is as well equipped as he to deal with precisely our concerns about the nature of oral transmission and the significance of the transition from oral to written form.

Because he had not previously applied his craft to the study of the gospels, Lord could do what professional students of the New Testament cannot do but often wish they could: read the texts as though they had just discovered them, with no staked-out positions to defend. Lord was not beholden to any scholarly "orthodoxy" or "heresy" in New Testament studies, as such orthodoxy or heresy might pertain to oral tradition. In short, the seminar provided a probably unprecedented opportunity for New Testament students to test what they think they know about oral tradition and the gospels. None of "us" would have read the gospels the way Lord did. Nonetheless, his openness, no less than his expertise, invited all of us to think on and beyond the frontiers of what we already "knew."

Background for the Seminar

Of course, the seminar did not occur in a vacuum. Thus it will be useful, before discussing what happened in the seminar, to

---

[4] Erhardt Güttgemanns, *Offene Fragen zur Formgeschichte des Evangeliums. Eine methodologische Skizze der Grundlagenproblematik der Form- und Redaktionsgeschichte*, Beiträge zur Evangelische Theologie, Theologische Abhandlungen 54 (Munich: Chr. Kaiser Verlag, 1970).

note certain elements in the common understanding of the oral tradition behind the gospels, as derived from classical form criticism, and then to call attention to two previous attempts to use studies in oral tradition to illumine the gospel traditions.

Form Criticism and the Oral Tradition. Implicit in the virtually unchallenged reign of form criticism among New Testament students is the importance of the oral tradition behind (and alongside) the gospels. For example, the Pittsburgh Festival on the Gospels in 1970 did not find it necessary to deal with the phenomenon of oral transmission; apparently this could simply be taken for granted.[5] (E. Bolaji Idowu, whose paper on "The Relation of the Gospels to African Culture and Religion" might have been expected to comment on such matters, bypassed the topic entirely.)[6] Even the rather strident title of an article by Howard M. Teeple, "The Oral Tradition that Never Existed," is misleading, for Teeple does not deny the oral tradition as such but only the claim that it all began with Jesus,[7] a point that seems to be directed mostly against Harald Riesenfeld and Birger Gerhardsson.[8] They had argued that the Jesus-traditions were carefully formulated by Jesus himself, who, like the rabbis, then taught his disciples to memorize his sayings so that they could be transmitted faithfully. Virtually no one has accepted this argument.[9]

Four of the prevailing assumptions about the oral tradition

[5] The papers and reports of the Festival were published under the title, *Jesus and Man's Hope*, vol. 1 ed. David G. Buttrick, vol. 2 ed. Donald G. Miller and Dikran Y. Hadidian, 2 vols., Perspective Books (Pittsburgh: Pittsburgh Theological Seminary, 1970–1971).

[6] E. Bolaji Idowu, "The Relation of the Gospels to African Culture and Religion," in *Jesus and Man's Hope*, 2:263–272.

[7] Howard M. Teeple, "The Oral Tradition That Never Existed," *Journal of Biblical Literature*, 89 (1970), 56–68.

[8] Harald Riesenfeld, "The Gospel Tradition and Its Beginnings," in *The Gospel Tradition*, trans. E. Margaret Rowley and Robert A. Kraft (Philadelphia: Fortress Press, 1970), 1–29; originally published in monograph form (London: A. R. Mowbray & Co. Limited, 1961); Birger Gerhardsson, *Memory and Manuscript: Oral Tradition and Written Transmission in Rabbinic Judaism and Early Christianity*, trans. E. J. Sharpe, Acta Seminarii Neotestamentici Upsaliensis 22 (Lund: C. W. K. Gleerup/ Copenhagen: Ejnar Munksgaard, 1961); *Tradition and Transmission in Early Christianity*, trans. E. J. Sharpe, Coniectanea Neotestamentica 20 (Lund: C. W. K. Gleerup/ Copenhagen: Ejnar Munksgaard, 1964).

[9] For a trenchant critique, see Morton Smith, "A Comparison of Early Christian and Early Rabbinic Tradition," *Journal of Biblical Literature*, 82 (1963), 169–176.

106

and the gospels are important for our purposes. First, form critics accepted virtually without discussion the Two-Source Hypothesis. Mark was the creator of the "gospel-form," and before Mark there was no continuous account of Jesus' words and deeds but only various aggregates of traditions (e.g., miracle stories, parables, and a rudimentary passion story) and "Q."

Second, form critics assumed that apart from (and prior to) these aggregates, the traditions of Jesus' words and deeds circulated independently as individual units. From this body of more or less free-floating material, teachers and preachers would draw as needed. When Mark created the gospel-form he had no "historical outline" to go by;[10] rather, he was guided by a theological perspective (e.g., the "Messianic Secret" or the kerygma). Moreover, the theological horizon was not even that of the earliest church in Jerusalem but that of the (later) Hellenistic (Gentile) church.

Third, form critics extended the quest for the *Sitz im Leben* (an essentially sociological category) of the traditions about Jesus to the history of Christology. Having learned from Wilhelm Bousset how the kerygma of the Hellenistic Gentile church differed from that of the primitive Palestinian church,[11] form critics correlated individual traditions with their appropriate stages in the church's historical and theological development. Furthermore, for Rudolf Bultmann, the more closely a given bit of tradition could be correlated with a stage in the church's theology/ Christology as reconstructed by Bousset, the more likely it was that the tradition was not only shaped by the church at this stage but that it was also created by the church.[12] This concern for the historical question, with its attendant emphasis on *Gemeindebildung*, caused many Anglo-Saxon scholars to recoil from form criticism and to deny that the community created Jesus-

[10] C. H. Dodd's attempt to argue the contrary has not been accepted even by British scholars; see his "The Framework of the Gospel Narrative" (1932), reprinted in his *New Testament Studies* (Manchester: Manchester University Press, 1953), 1–11. For a critique, see D. E. Nineham, "The Order of Events in St. Mark's Gospel—an examination of Dr. Dodd's Hypothesis," in *Studies in the Gospels: Essays in Memory of R. H. Lightfoot*, ed. D. E. Nineham (Oxford: Basil Blackwell, 1955), 223–239.

[11] Wilhelm Bousset, *Kyrios Christos: A History of the Belief in Christ from the Beginnings of Christianity to Irenaeus*, trans. John E. Steely (Nashville and New York: Abingdon Press, 1970), originally published in German in 1913.

[12] Rudolf Bultmann, *The History of the Synoptic Tradition*, trans. John Marsh, rev. ed. (New York and Evanston: Harper & Row, Publishers, Inc., 1968).

traditions that it handed on along with earlier, genuine material from Jesus himself.

Fourth, form critics saw the writing of gospels, while a momentous event in retrospect, as essentially incidental to the whole process of transmission of the Jesus-traditions. With Huck's *Synopse* before them, they traced the fate of an item in the tradition from Mark to his successors and sometimes through later text traditions. Then it was inferred that the post-Marcan process had gone on before Mark as well. In other words, the view of oral transmission was based largely on observation about editorial work and scribal activity. Thus it was shown, for example, that names of persons and places often appear late in the process, as do other details such as motivations for individuals. This phenomenon cast doubt on such particular details found already in Mark and "Q." It was concluded that the earliest form of the tradition existed almost totally without names or indications of time and circumstance. The more detailed the material, the later it was assumed to be and hence the less reliable historically with regard to Jesus (but all the more reliable as a primary reflex of the community's beliefs). One spoke of the tendencies of the tradition, and even of laws of transmission. Jewish traditions and folk tales were appealed to as parallels.[13]

Oral Tradition's Challenge to Form Critical Assumptions. Prior to the Colloquy on the Relationships among the Gospels,

[13] E. P. Sanders has called attention to the fact that evidence was used selectively (e.g., details drop out as well as appear) and has argued that the conclusions derived were escalated improperly into "laws of oral transmission" that were declared to be in accord with folklore studies; see his *The Tendencies of the Synoptic Tradition*, Society for New Testament Studies Monograph Series 9 (Cambridge: Cambridge University Press, 1969). Sanders too works with the assumption that literary phenomena can be used as a basis for inferring developments in oral transmission, although he is aware of the problem of doing so.

The whole discussion of "laws of oral transmission" needs to be traced in detail and clarified. Lord did not appear to know of any such "laws"! According to Thorlief Boman (see note 14 below), Hermann Gunkel (the pioneer of Old Testament form criticism) relied on an article by Axel Olrik, "Epische Gesetze der Volksdichtung," *Zeitschrift für deutsches Altertum*, 51 (1909), 1–12, as did Bultmann, who misconstrued its title (Boman, 17–18). Olrik did not really deal with laws of transmission but with aesthetic rules of style and composition. Later, he clarified the matter and pointed out that the "rules of composition" are useful only to distinguish folk poetry from conscious artistry (*Kunstdichtung*) and are of no use at all in detecting the relative age of the various materials. An English translation by Jeanne P. Steager and Alan Dundes of Olrik's article appears in Alan Dundes, ed., *The Study of Folklore* (Englewood Cliffs, N.J.: Prentice-Hall, Inc., 1965), 129–141.

these widely held views of the form critics were challenged especially by the studies of Thorlief Boman and Erhardt Güttgemanns, both of whom appealed to studies in oral tradition to support their challenge.

Boman's *Die Jesus-Überlieferung im Lichte der neueren Volkskunde*[14] is weakened by the fact that it tries to deliver more than the title promises. Instead of keeping to his thesis that there are two types of Jesus materials in early Christianity, the kerygmatic and the narrational (pp. 42–47), and exploring the latter in the light of folklore studies, he deals also with the Son of Man, the religious parties in Corinth, and the role of Stephenite refugees in Alexandria, finally adding three articles previously published elsewhere. Moreover, his discussion as a whole is burdened by a generally uncritical use of Acts and is weakened by the claim that John Mark was commissioned by Peter to write the Second Gospel in Jerusalem and that this gospel is simply the written form of what Peter had recited for years (p. 40). Boman's book is somewhat like a "bargain basement counter," onto which the author has loaded a great variety of opinions about early Christianity. The contents need to be sorted out, and we do not have to buy everything.

In the first place, Boman is convinced that the idea of the community as the bearer of oral tradition is derived from Romanticism's image of the people (*Volk*), which folklore study has disproved.[15] "Folklore (*Volkskunde*) teaches us unambiguously that the community neither created nor transmitted Jesus' words" (pp. 10 and 112). Boman does not conclude that everything transmitted is accurate[16] or that the community has no role at all in transmission. Rather, he claims that folklore studies distinguish active from passive roles: only the individual narrators play

---

[14] Thorlief Boman, *Die Jesus-Überlieferung im Lichte der neueren Volkskunde* (Göttingen: Vandenhoeck & Ruprecht, 1967). The page numbers in parentheses refer to this edition.

[15] Although Boman relies heavily on Scandinavian folklore studies, the work of James H. Delargy (O'Duilearga) is also prominent; see James H. Delargy, "The Gaelic Story Teller, with Some Notes on Gaelic Folk Tales," *Proceedings of the British Academy*, 31 (1945), 177–221; reprinted as monograph (London: G. Cumberlege, 1947).

[16] Boman never really accounts for the presence of non-genuine sayings, whose existence he admits in principle. He seems more bent on discrediting other attempts to account for their presence; e.g., he argues that one cannot trace them to early Christian prophets because prophets did not coin sayings, nor would disciples have done so.

active roles, selecting, shaping, and reciting the tradition; the community has a passive role that checks what is recited (p. 10) and expects certain things from the narrator, who responds to these expectations (pp. 112–113). Still, the tradition itself is always borne by individuals, just as it originates with individuals (p. 29). Repeatedly, therefore, Boman rejects Bultmann's idea of *Gemeindebildung*. Of course, one can ask whether he rightly understood Bultmann, just as one can ask whether Bultmann's interest in the historical question did not lead him to use the word *Gemeindebildung* primarily to mean "non-genuine."

In the second place, Boman insists on the basis of folklore studies that the *Sitz im Leben* itself neither changes nor generates oral tradition; the modifying factors lie in the changed cultural situation to which the narrator adapts the material (pp. 112–113). He also claims that the various types of traditions cannot be correlated with types of transmitting groups, as though hunting stories were transmitted only by hunters, cultic materials only by priests, etc. (p. 21). Such correlations are appropriate at the point where the traditions originate, but, once formed, these traditions circulate independently. Usage is not the same as transmission of tradition; nothing is transmitted by usage alone. To transmit oral tradition is to hand on memorized content (p. 41).

In the third place, Boman denies that individual incidents and words of historical persons are transmitted as isolated units; they are transmitted only in a context in which the person of the hero is central. "Form critically, the picture of the person is the starting point of the legend (*Sage*), not individual words, deeds, and experiences" (p. 21). "The hero is the center of the legend" (p. 35). Stories and sayings are indeed told as individual items by eyewitnesses, but this is memory, and memory is not tradition. Tradition about a historical person presupposes a first narrator who forms an account of the hero out of the individual items that people remembered and told separately. According to Boman, from the correct observation that the framework of Mark was not transmitted by eyewitnesses Karl Ludwig Schmidt drew the wrong conclusion: that originally there was no continuous account at all. Actually, no historical legend ever emerged out of individual items that circulated for decades independently (p. 31).

In the fourth place, Boman maintains that tellers of folk materials knew their materials by heart and faithfully repeated them, 110 a phenomenon quite different from the transmission of rumor. Hermann Gunkel was right in speaking of a class of storytellers, as was Martin Dibelius in postulating an analogous group in early Christianity. Dibelius erred, however, in restricting their repertoires to miracle stories and tales (p. 32). In the light of folklore studies, it appears that the Synoptic tradition was transmitted by particular persons in the circle of interested hearers and that the repertoires of the tellers reflect not the diverse social situations in the communities' life but the capacities and tastes of the narrators. In short, there is only one *Sitz im Leben*: the narrator and his hearers. Nothing can be inferred from the forms and contents of the traditions about various *Sitze im Leben* of the church (pp. 36–37 and 42). (Similarly, the Old Testament prophets had used a range of forms in the same *Sitz im Leben*: prophetic preaching.) Moreover, this single *Sitz im Leben* of the Jesus-traditions was not the sermon, as Dibelius claimed, because the sermon used freely formulated kerygmatic statements like 2 Corinthians 8:9 rather than fixed oral traditions in the hands of narrators (the *hypēretai*), who were subordinate to the apostles and prophets (pp. 42–47).

For Boman, then, "oral tradition" is a discrete body of material that goes from narrator to narrator, not anonymously from group to group. From the outset, oral tradition about historical persons embraces both individual items and an overall picture of the hero. If Mark is the bearer of oral tradition, he did not create a picture of Jesus out of miscellaneous items but rather transmitted a picture of Jesus that was already present in the oral tradition.

Güttgemanns' kaleidescopic book also called for a review of form and redaction critical assumptions.[17] Moreover, he rightly emphasized the sociological dimensions of form criticism (p. 95), the perversion of which is epitomized by the transformation of *Sitz im Leben* into historical context. "Form criticism is thus no aesthetic but a deliberate sociological method" (p. 60).

Reliance upon a sociological perspective as well as upon linguistics, which he calls for, means rejecting classical form criticism's assumptions about the continuity between oral tradition

---

[17] Güttgemanns, *Offene Fragen zur Formgeschichte des Evangeliums*. Interestingly, Güttgemanns' book has not received the attention it deserves. See, however, the appreciative review by William G. Doty: "Fundamental Questions about Literary-Critical Methodology: A Review Article," *Journal of the American Academy of Religion*, 40 (1972), 521–527.

and the writing, editing, and revising of texts that record this tradition. Like Boman, whose work he disdains,[18] Güttgemanns sees that the more redaction criticism emphasizes the literary coherence and theological unity of Mark (i.e., the more Mark is seen to be master of his material after all),[19] the less one can understand the writing of Mark in continuity with the pre-Marcan situation of disconnected traditions, which Güttgemanns explicitly affirms (p. 79). What concerns him is the transition from this pre-Marcan situation to the situation of Mark and the literary history that began with Mark.

Since the initial writing of a gospel created a new genre and was not simply the next step in forming aggregates, Güttgemanns asks whether this genre also rested on oral tradition (p. 79; in his own way, Boman too asked the same question). He rejects an appeal to the kerygma as the basis for the new genre, observing that the kerygma would not produce particular genres. He correctly observes that we are a long way from possessing a form history (a *Formengeschichte* to use Franz Overbeck's term),[20] properly coordinated with a *Redaktionsgeschichte* (p. 231). Güttgemanns grants, like Boman, that a given *Sitz im Leben* does not necessarily correlate with a given form or genre; at the same time, he affirms (as Boman does not) that form criticism has discerned a variety of *Sitze im Leben* for the Jesus-traditions (pp. 81–86). Since the first gospel had its *Sitz im Leben* in the same community as did its antecedent traditions, are we to think that a new *Sitz im Leben* emerged and thus called for the composition of a gospel? We cannot appeal to new factors in the historical context because a *Sitz im Leben* is pre-

[18] He calls Boman's conclusions "Phantasieprodukte," especially the idea that Peter commissioned John Mark to put into writing the tradition he was accustomed to reciting (p. 47, n. 27, and p. 151). I agree. Güttgemanns does not reveal how close Boman is to his own work in other regards, however.

[19] Cf. Bultmann, *The History of the Synoptic Tradition*, 350: "Mark is not sufficiently master of his material to be able to venture on a systematic construction himself."

[20] See W. M. L. de Wette, *Kurze Erklärung der Apostelgeschichte*, 4th ed. rev. and amplified by Franz Overbeck, Kurzgefasstes exegetisches Handbuch zum Neuen Testament 1, 4 (Leipzig: S. Hirzel, 1870). Güttgemanns discusses Overbeck's significance for form criticism as well as for the conception of early Christian literature as a whole (pp. 96–100). See also the instructive study of Overbeck: Johann-Christoph Emmelius, *Tendenzkritik und Formgeschichte. Der Beitrag Franz Overbecks zur Auslegung der Apostelgeschichte im 19. Jahrhundert*, Forschungen zur Kirchen- und Dogmengeschichte 27 (Göttingen: Vandenhoeck & Ruprecht, 1975).

112

cisely not a particular historical occasion but rather a repeated, patterned, typical, social situation across a span of time (my formulation).

As noted above, it is at this point that Güttgemanns appropriated the work of Lord,[21] which he deems fundamental even though the materials are not precisely parallel.[22] Lord's research clarified empirically the shift that occurs when oral tradition becomes oral traditional literature. Now there are only two possibilities: (a) one can regard the gospels as written deposits of what previously had been recited orally by the Evangelist himself (an "oral autograph"), as Boman argues, or (b) one must find a new way to combine the tradition-hypothesis and the Two-Source Theory. Preferring the latter, Güttgemanns contends that Matthew and Luke cannot simultaneously have used a literary technique (editing and revising a text of Mark) and an "oral" technique in composition. Even if they used oral traditions, their use of these traditions differed from that of a bard because they also were using Mark. Insofar as Mark himself used "sources" he too proceeded differently from an oral composer. Thus the emergence of written gospels from oral traditions and aggregates becomes more problematic, not less, in light of the Parry-Lord research.

Seminar Discussions

From the seminar discussions during the Colloquy, two issues appear to be especially important, particularly in light of the literature just noted: (a) What does an expert on oral traditional

[21] Güttgemanns reports that Lord's work precipitated a lively methodological discussion among *Germanisten:* see the literature listed in F. H. Bäuml and D. J. Ward, "Zur mündlichen Ueberlieferung des Nibelungenliedes," *Deutsche Vierteljahrsschrift für Literaturwissenschaft und Geistesgeschichte*, 41 (1967), 352–353, n. 3, and 356–357, n. 20. Bäuml also claims that Lord's work has been confirmed by his own work on the Nibelungenlied. Actually, however, Bäuml applied the principles of Parry and Lord, and this involves something other than (independent) confirmation. In any case, for Güttgemanns, Lord's work has "become to a large extent *the* standard work of comparative literature; it has fundamental significance for that research which is concerned with the transition from the oral to the written tradition" (p. 144).

[22] Güttgemanns points out that Lord faced an analogous issue in terms of the Homeric poems and modern Balkan bards and asks whether there is any other body of material that would allow empirical study in order to gain some objective control. Güttgemanns also summarizes Lord's work as presented by Bäuml (pp. 143–160).

literature understand by "oral tradition," and how does this understanding relate to the prevailing view among students of the gospels? (b) What is the relation between what Lord calls "mythic patterns" and the composition/structure of the Synoptic Gospels?[23]

Oral Tradition. It became evident in the seminar that when gospel critics commonly speak of "oral tradition" and when Lord speaks of "oral traditional literature," the two are not referring to the same thing, even though both have in mind orally transmitted material. Indeed, Lord observed that "oral tradition" begs the question.[24] In the first place, gospels students understand oral tradition primarily as a stage in a process of gospel-making, a phase before the material was written down; moreover, oral tradition sometimes seems to be regarded as whatever was repeated by word-of-mouth within a group or by a group and was repeated often enough that the resultant forms can be treated as "footprints" of the group's life, telling us first of all about the community and secondarily (if at all) about Jesus. The more oral tradition is regarded as the common property of the whole community (viz., a rapidly expanding and ever more heterogeneous family of Christian groups), the harder it becomes to distinguish oral tradition from hearsay. This is clearly reflected in the title of Ernest L. Abel's article, "The Psychology of Memory and Rumor Transmission and Their Bearing on Theories of Oral Transmission in Early Christianity."[25] In this light, perhaps the most revolutionary statement made by Lord was that oral traditional literature is not a phase but a genre, at least

---

[23] Unfortunately, because of a technical malfunction that was not detected at the time, the audio tapes of the second seminar session are almost totally blank. Under the circumstances, I deemed it better not to summarize or report directly on the discussion as such but rather, on the basis of the audible tapes, sparse notes, and my own recollections, to reflect on the significance of certain issues that were raised. The tapes will be retained by the editor of this volume.

[24] Lord was reluctant to use the term "oral tradition" on the grounds that it begs the question of a distinction between "oral history" and "oral traditional literature" (see his discussion of the distinction, pp. 33–39). At times he used the terms "oral narrative" or "oral traditional narrative," but for the most part he spoke of "oral traditional literature" or simply "oral literature" (it should be noted here that "literature" does not necessarily imply "written").

[25] Ernest L. Abel, "The Psychology of Memory and Rumour Transmission and Their Bearing on Theories of Oral Transmission in Early Christianity," *The Journal of Religion*, 51 (1971), 270–281.

in epic poetry and in oral traditional prose narrative.[26] Unfortunately, so many other things came on the agenda that the seminar did not press him on this point.

In the second place, Lord does not envisage oral traditional literature as a shapeless mass of disparate logia, apophthegms, stories, etc., that are transmitted as common property of a community until a demiurgic Evangelist brings order from the chaos. Rather, oral traditional literature is transmitted in patterns that have both stability and variation. Lord pointed out that some stability in sequence, for example, is essential to oral traditional literature. Here, Boman is closer to Lord than is Güttgemanns, whose "open questions" do not include the question of the character of the pre-Marcan situation. It was precisely because Boman sought to differentiate memory from tradition, to distinguish the discerned small individual units from tradition, that he was able to avoid Bultmann's conclusion that, because one can "decompose" the gospels into the many small units, these units must have constituted the pre-literary oral tradition, like a mass of tesserae waiting to become a mosaic.

In the third place, closely linked with this latter view is the notion that the shortest, "purest form" of a tradition (e.g., parable, logion, apophthegm, miracle story) was the original and that transmission tended to deform it rather than preserve or improve it. But the work of Lord suggested to him that there never was any fixed "original" as such, because the singer/teller almost never hears a song or story from only one person and every new telling or singing is an act of composition. Thus the tradition is not so stable that variant wordings are to be taken as evidence of dependence, of a later stage in which "editing" has occurred. Rather, the same narrator may vary the formulation, and variant versions can circulate simultaneously. This is why, when confronted by the Synoptic Gospels, Lord did not ask, Which is the original on which the other two depend? His surprise that "the Synoptic Problem" should have agitated New Testament scholars so deeply was almost as revolutionary as his comment about oral traditional literature being a genre rather than a phase.

Charles H. Talbert's response to Lord reiterated the standard claim of New Testament students: that the phenomena of order

---

[26] As noted, Boman learned much the same thing, though he did not formulate it so clearly.

demand an explanation in terms of literary relationships. This may well be the case. Nonetheless, it was important to see an expert in another discipline look at "our" texts and propose that they represent three independent and parallel accounts. If Lord is correct, then the history of the debate over the Synoptic Problem becomes intelligible: this debate has not succeeded in solving the problem because it has pursued the wrong question for two hundred years; in other words, a great deal of gospel study has been a goose chase. On the other hand, if Talbert is correct, then the question was right, but the study of oral tradition can illumine only the careers of the pre-literary materials, not the relationships among the texts, in which case the Steering Committee for the Colloquy sent Lord on a goose chase.

The key issue, then, is whether the gospels are to be classified as oral traditional literature in Lord's sense or whether the differences outweigh the similarities to such a degree that New Testament students have little to learn from oral traditional literature, however much their general understanding of oral traditional prose narrative may be enhanced by a study of the latter.[27] This twin question is a major legacy of the seminar. Unfortunately, time did not allow the matter to be explored in detail. One aspect was touched on: the fact that oral traditional literature as Lord understands it is characteristic of pre-literate societies. But neither the culture in which early Christianity emerged nor the early Christians themselves were non-literate or analphabetic, whatever their "reading level" might have been. The question then is this: Is what was handed on orally from teacher to teacher (who probably could also read and write) sufficiently analogous to what was recited in pre-literate cultures to be classified as "oral traditional literature?"[28]

If, however, "oral traditional literature" is finally an inappropriate category for designating the gospels, and if New Testament students do not wish to have a private meaning for the phrase "oral tradition," what shall the originally oral materials

---

[27] The question was also raised as to whether the gospels might properly be understood as "oral history" rather than as "oral traditional literature."

[28] When asked the basis on which he would identify particular written materials as "oral traditional literature," Lord spoke of "vestigial elements of mythic patterns" that are "operative" in a text, suggesting that certain "anomalies" in a text (i.e., features that make no sense in the present text but can be understood as "vestiges" of traditional patterns) serve as clues that the materials in question are "oral traditional."

incorporated into the gospels be called? This too is the question.

Mythic Patterns and the Gospels. Lord's comments indicated that the notion of "mythic patterns" combines the results of two lines of investigation. (a) "Pattern" reflects the experience of seeing story elements repeatedly structured into larger wholes in a similar way. When diverse narratives found in different cultures, languages, social systems, and religions nevertheless manifest similar sequences (including metathesis of individual parts), one speaks of a persistent pattern of narration. This use of "pattern" is not to be confused with the phenomenon of a single text, such as Mark's use of the three Passion Predictions. Lord would not call this a "pattern" unless the phenomenon were detected in a range of texts. A pattern is a transcultural structure that persists across a considerable span of time. Thus, when Philipp Vielhauer compared the three-fold acclamation of Jesus as Son of God in Mark to an old Egyptian enthronement festival, he was appealing to a "pattern" in Lord's sense.[29] (b) Lord spoke of these patterns as "mythic" not because their content concerned the gods or demigods, but because the persistence of the pattern suggested meaning that must be linked with "the transcendent" in order to have persisted so long. This use of "mythic" interprets the longevity and vitality of the pattern and must be kept in mind, especially in light of the long history of the "mythological" interpretation of the gospels.

For Lord, the mythic pattern is the bearer of meaning; the details and individual units in the narrative make the meaning pattern concrete. The pattern is older than the parts, which it attracts, and it is borne by the community, though sometimes in what Lord called "a sunken awareness." Such an understanding of mythic patterns might be linked with the Jungian concept of archetypes, but Lord himself did not do so. Nor did he indicate exactly how the community carries the pattern or how it is related to cultic or other ritual activity.

Lord made it clear that to speak of mythic patterns is not to deny a historical base to the narratives. Some events take on "cosmic" significance in the oral tradition. The report of events may be cast into mythic patterns or into a narrative incorporating vestiges of such patterns. For instance, the Trojan war lent it-

---

[29] Philipp Vielhauer, "Erwägungen zur Christologie des Markusevangeliums," in *Zeit und Geschichte. Dankesgabe an Rudolf Bultmann zum 80. Geburtstag,* ed. Erich Dinkler (Tübingen: J. C. B. Mohr [Paul Siebeck], 1964), 155–169, esp. 167.

self to such a process, perhaps because it was an unusually long war, thus fitting the pattern of absence and return, which requires a long time span. As a result, the *Iliad* embodies both memory and mythic patterns.

Sometimes only vestiges of mythic patterns appear. When a particular item in a narrative complex appears to serve little purpose in the narrative, its presence might be a vestige of an older pattern that once called for such an item. Hence Lord asked whether the birth narratives or the story of the death of the Baptist might represent vestigial remains of ancient patterns. If they did, this would not in itself impugn the historical base of the stories, for some coherence between the stories and the pattern must have been perceived, else they would not have been correlated. Of course, David Friedrich Strauss would have gone further: he would have claimed that the pattern generated the story because the story was needed.[30]

The pattern may be disturbed or broken by the demands of another pattern or by other factors, such as the memory of what actually happened. One of the issues identified but not explored in the seminar was: What is strong enough to modify, disturb, or break a mythic pattern? Redaction critics emphasize theological issues, which in turn affected the actual "shape" of a gospel. The question of the relationship between mythic patterns (and their vestiges) and the composition of the gospels as literary wholes needs further investigation.

If the gospels are indeed comparable with oral traditional literature, then Lord's understanding of mythic patterns impinges on our understanding of the gospels at two points. First, his view of mythic patterns inevitably undergirds what was said about oral traditional literature: it has elements in a generally stable sequence, though usually with some variations. A totally unstable sequence, a mass of unordered elements, is not oral traditional literature even if it is handed on by word of mouth. Some patterning orders the material and gives it meaning. Clearly what gospel critics call "kerygma" functions as a mythic pattern, unless, of course, kerygma is reduced to Bultmann's sheer *dass* (*that* God acted in Jesus). Such an assertion, I take it, is not a pattern nor would it generate a particular pattern. Bult-

---

[30] David Friedrich Strauss, *The Life of Jesus Critically Examined*, trans. George Eliot, ed. Peter C. Hodgson, Lives of Jesus Series (Philadelphia: Fortress Press, 1972), originally published in German in 1835.

mann asserts that Mark as a *"phenomenon in the history of literature"* is intelligible only in light of the fact that the church heard its (now present) Lord speak in the tradition,[31] but this conviction/experience could just as easily have evoked a quite different text than Mark and thus does not account for Mark at all. Actually, even Bultmann pointed to a mythic pattern that was more than a *dass*: the Christ myth embedded in passages such as Philippians 2:6–11 and Romans 3:24, and he claimed that Mark's purpose was "the union" of this myth with "the tradition of the story of Jesus."[32] If we are to take this claim seriously, then its import accords with Lord's work, in that the individual traditions about Jesus were already patterned into a "tradition of the story of Jesus" before Mark. In other words, to the extent that the gospels are oral traditional literature, the narrative patterns were not imposed on previously unpatterned bits of tradition; rather, the gospels carried forward and perhaps modified the patterns that had ordered and interpreted the traditions all along.

Second, if Mark did not "compose what he calls the Gospel out of a multiplicity of disparate tradition units"[33] but wove together into a coherent whole various clusters and parts of clusters, which had been patterned previously, then tracing the gospel-making process requires a continuing search for pre-Marcan "sources," including a passion narrative. Such a quest assumes more continuity between Mark and his predecessors than many recent critics have tended to allow. For example, John Dominic Crossan even claims that Mark created "an anti-tradition" of the empty tomb: no appearances but "only the harsh negative of the ET [sic] and the Lord who 'is not here,' " because he was hostile toward Jewish Christianity and Peter.[34] But if the antipathy between Mark and Palestinian Christianity (within which Crossan and other contributors to *The Passion in Mark* believe

---

[31] Bultmann, *The History of the Synoptic Tradition*, 348 (his italics).

[32] Bultmann, *The History of the Synoptic Tradition*, 347.

[33] Cf. Werner H. Kelber, "Conclusion: From Passion Narrative to Gospel," in *The Passion in Mark: Studies on Mark 14–16*, ed. Werner H. Kelber (Philadelphia: Fortress Press, 1976), 158: "Mk's literary achievement is to compose what he calls the Gospel out of disparate tradition units." Here Kelber is speaking for the contributors to the volume, none of whom accepts the idea that Mark inherited a passion story which he expanded.

[34] John Dominic Crossan, "Empty Tomb and Absent Lord (Mark 16:1–8)," in *The Passion in Mark*, ed. Kelber, 152.

Mark was written) was so pervasive, then it is difficult to see why Matthew would have used Mark as a primary source; it is also a mystery why Mark would not have written an epistle instead of sailing under a flag of convenience invented for the occasion: a gospel. Thus he is assumed to have achieved three things simultaneously: create a genre (pattern) without any precedent, gain acceptance for this genre among his public, and attack the belief-structure of this same public by means of the new creation. If this is true, the author of the Second Gospel must have been some first-century Merlin!

Conclusions

What, then, is the import of the seminar's work for the question of the relationships among the gospels? As already noted, any answer to this question depends on how a prior question is answered: Are the gospels to be regarded as oral traditional literature in Lord's sense? Assuming for purposes of discussion that they are, what are the consequences?

First, oral traditional literature, however stable, is apparently not so fixed either in oral transmission or in its subsequent written form that we are justified in pressing for a single original. How do we envisage the initial composition/writing of a gospel? Unless we assume that the bearer of the tradition was also a scribe, we must think of him as dictating the tradition. Lord pointed out, however, that precisely in this process "editing" occurs, because this is a new experience for the narrator, who must adjust his pace, break his rhythms, and forego the responses of his customary hearers. Thus he adapts the material as he proceeds, abbreviating or perhaps even explaining. Only a tape recorder can capture the precise form of oral traditional literature. Moreover, because oral transmission of the material does not cease once it is written, both modes thereafter co-exist and perhaps interact. There is no reason whatever to rule out the idea that a gospel circulated in more than one "version." In other words, Lord has opened the door for a reconsideration of *Ur-Markus*, not in the sense of one diverging antecedent of our Mark but as the possibility of multiple "Marks," none of which was exactly identical with another.

Second, the greater the role of oral tradition in early Christianity, the less viable the Griesbach Hypothesis becomes, because this hypothesis forces the whole discussion into strictly literary terms. Streeter's hypothesis, including its various mutations, can be adapted far more easily to take account of oral tradition than can any hypothesis insisting that the solution lies in a genealogical relation among three documents. Moreover, any strictly literary solution to the Synoptic Problem is frustrated by the fact that we do not have texts for any of the gospels that are so nearly identical with the autographs as to justify adducing variations in wording as clear evidence of dependence. In other words, the phenomenon of textual assimilation frustrates any strictly literary solution.

Third, the Synoptic Problem cannot be solved in isolation from the overall problem of the Jesus-traditions in the churches on the one hand and from the interrelation of all gospels on the other. The essays in *The Passion in Mark*,[35] for instance, have reopened the question of the relation between John and Mark. To include John and the non-canonical gospels in the discussion doubtless complicates the matter. Nonetheless, in this question, Ockham's razor must be used sparingly; the most likely solution is not necessarily the simplest.

Finally, even apart from the contribution of Lord and oral traditional literature, understanding the gospel-making process, the oral transmission that preceded it, and the textual history that followed it requires a working framework of the development of Christianity until Constantine. Unfortunately, no consensus prevails today on how this history is to be reconstructed. Among New Testaments students, at any rate, the inherited tradition from Heitmüller-Bousset[36] has been eroded at many points, but nothing has replaced it. Research has become so specialized that it is extremely doubtful whether any single person can still deal persuasively with all the data, let alone argue with all the alternatives in the secondary literature. Consequently, collaborative work demands more than juxtaposing specialties; it requires an at least loosely cohesive approach, even if this runs the risk of producing a "school." A coherent "school" may be more productive in the long run than a bazaar, where each vendor tries to outbid his/her neighbor by emphasizing the distinc-

---

[35] See note 33.

[36] See, e.g., Wilhelm Heitmüller, "Zum Problem Paulus und Jesus," *Zeitschrift für die neutestamentliche Wissenschaft und die Kunde der älteren Kirche*, 13 (1912), 320–337; Bousset, *Kyrios Christos*.

tive wrinkle in his/her own product. After all, a real "school" has internal diversity and is not to be confused with a cult.

Occasions like the Colloquy on the Relationships among the Gospels help identify colleagues with whom one can work in concert and from whom one can learn, including those outside one's immediate field of specialty, such as Albert B. Lord. Nor is it impossible that gospel studies might contribute something to the study of oral traditional literature as such. The only way to find out is for the conversation to continue.

2
CLASSICS
and the GOSPELS

Classical and Christian Source Criticism

George Kennedy

Prince:	Did Julius Caesar build that place [the Tower] my lord?
Buckingham:	He did, my gracious lord, begin that place Which, since, succeeding ages have re-edified.
Prince:	Is it upon record, or else reported Successively from age to age, he built?
Buckingham:	Upon record, my gracious lord.
Prince:	But say, my lord, it were not register'd, Methinks the truth should live from age to age, As 'twere retail'd to all posterity Even to the general all-ending day.
Gloucester (Aside)	So wise so young, they say, do never live long.

Richard the Third, Act III, scene 1, 69–79

The New Testament, whatever else it may be, is a collection of Greek documents: It deals with things said and done in the first century both of the Roman Empire and of the Christian era, in an area where Greek was the official language. The actors in its pages seek the Kingdom of Heaven, but not solely in the solitude of the desert; they walk and talk in the cities of the world, and those cities were significantly Hellenized. The authors of the documents, known or unknown, demonstrate (in varying degrees) a knowledge of Greek language, literature, rhetoric, and philosophy, sometimes also of Roman law and procedure. The transmission to us of the text of the New Testament, of discussion of it, and of commentary on it, was parallel to and intimately connected with the transmission of other Greek works. It is not unreasonable, therefore, to hope that principles and practices of source criticism or information about methods of composition in one tradition might be of some use in the study of the other.

Indeed, there was no differentiation of the two disciplines until sometime in the nineteenth century when classical scholarship, "per colpa della maledetta specializzazione" as Pasquali put it,[1] shut its eyes to Christian writing and New Testament studies in large part. Cicero tells the story of a similar parting of the ways of philosophy and rhetoric in the time of Socrates[2] and seeks to reconcile them (*De Oratore* 3.59–73). I cannot say that he was permanently successful in bringing them back into a single tradition, but he demonstrates that the eloquent philosopher and the philosophical orator are over-lapping concepts. By the same token, we may take the overlap of Jewish, New Testament, and classical studies as a subject worthy of scrutiny.

Some caveats should be declared from the start. The classical scholar does not have any guild secret discovered since last our disciplines met. What has been learned over the century is that the use of written sources is more complex than it once seemed; that oral transmission is important and is capable of preserving the integrity of a large text for a considerable period of time, but that there was a great deal of note-taking; and that among published texts there were different conventions in different genres. Too great an emphasis on abstract principles of criticism is almost certain to distort the evidence, and the case of each text must be individually examined. It seems equally true that "scientific" scepticism can easily be carried too far. Ancient traditions have sometimes been confirmed by archaeology; ancient writers sometimes meant what they said and occasionally even knew what they were talking about.

Scepticism about scepticism is especially appropriate in the

---

[1] Giorgio Pasquali, *Storia della tradizione e critica del testo*, 2d. ed. (Florence: Felice Le Monnier, 1952), 8.

[2] Cicero, *De Oratore* 3.61: "Hinc discidium illud exstitit quasi linguae atque cordis, absurdum sane et inutile et reprehendendum, ut alii nos sapere, alii dicere docerent."

period from the first century B.C. to the second century of the Christian era, because this is the most learned, best informed, and most securely datable period in history before modern times. A fundamental reason for this is Rome itself: the unity and eventually the security that Roman rule gave, improvements in communication, the consistency of the Roman bureaucracy, and the chronological touchstone that Roman officials provided. Two prominent Romans of the first century B.C., Atticus and Cornelius Nepos, worked out chronological schemes of earlier history, and other writers, such as Cicero in the *Brutus*, show a highly developed interest in and understanding of chronological and prosopographical detail. Scholarship of all sorts bloomed in Varro, Livy, Strabo, Dionysius, Philo, Josephus, the elder Pliny, Plutarch, Suetonius, and others. In all the works of the Roman historian Tacitus, writing in the opening years of the second century, no serious chronological problem can be found. There are events that cannot be absolutely dated, of course, including Tacitus' own birth and death, but the relative chronology is excellent. The New Testament could not have been written at a time of greater literacy, education, or understanding.

In the following sections of this essay, I shall discuss the importance of source criticism in the classicist's work, examine two sets of possible classical analogues to the source criticism of the gospels, discuss conventions of translation and imitation in the Roman world, offer certain observations regarding external sources about the origin of the gospels from the point of view of a reader of Greek texts, and conclude with some thoughts about the overall tendency of the evidence regarding the origin of the gospels. The most relevant topic to be omitted entirely is the composition, transmission, and publication of early Greek oral poetry.

Source Criticism

While preparing this essay, I was faced with the question, whether an understanding of sources makes a significant difference in the classicist's study of ancient literature. The general answer to this question seems to be affirmative, but the relative importance of identifying the sources varies from case to case. In almost any texts written in foreign languages or in distant times or both, there are allusions and implications that we are in danger of missing. To read Virgil without hearing the echoes of Homer or Ennius or Lucretius is to deny ourselves perception of a dimension of Virgil's art that he expected his readers to have. If the author of Matthew expected his readers to be familiar with the language of Mark, we need to know this. If Mark expected his readers to hear the voice of Peter repeating the sayings of Jesus, we need to know this, if we can.

About the time that Mark was published, a young Roman poet named Lucan, nephew of Gallio (the governor of Achaea mentioned in Acts 18:12–17), was compelled by Nero to commit suicide, leaving incomplete the *Pharsalia*, a brilliant and bizarre epic on the subject of the civil war between Caesar and Pompey a hundred years before. The epic repeatedly does violence to historical fact and characterization and occasionally to the order of nature. Was Lucan deliberately flouting authority? Was he careless and stupid? More likely, he was influenced by the sources he used, the conventions of the genre in which he wrote, and what seemed to him the "higher truth" of his poetic inspiration. In the case of Lucan's subject, we are reasonably well informed about what actually happened. Source criticism has a heavier task in those cases where we do not know the facts. What did Socrates say at his trial in 399 B.C.? Plato attributes one speech to him, Xenophon another; there is a story (Cicero, *De Oratore* 1.231) that the orator Lysias wrote and offered him a defense to memorize, a hint in Plato's *Gorgias* (521–522) that he was silent, and various other tidbits can be found. The evidence is inconsistent. It would be good to know what Socrates really said, but it is probably impossible. Perhaps it is as important for us to know how he was perceived by others, how they reacted to his trial, and how their accounts relate to each other; this we can do to some extent.

Classical Analogues to Source Criticism of the Gospels

The ideal classical analogue to the source criticism of the gospels should be from writings of the same genre as that of the gospels or close to it; it should date from approximately the same period as the gospels; and it should deal with the sayings and doings of a teacher who did not leave written work, but whose life story and teachings were at first transmitted orally and then, during the two generations after his death, were reduced to writing by several of his followers. Furthermore, the transmission of this teacher's life story and teachings should at some stage

128

involve translation from one language to another; there should be an aura of uniqueness and inspiration about the text; the product should be of more than academic interest; and it should be intended to perform a practical function among the followers of the teacher. These and other possible requirements each introduce special factors in the use of sources.

There is no perfect classical analogue. Probably the best that we can do is to consider two sets. One is the Socratic literature, which is comparable to the gospels spiritually and, like them, provides the basis for our knowledge of an outstanding personality and lays the foundation for a powerful movement. This literature is distant from the gospels in time and ambience, however. The other set is historical, biographical, and scholarly literature, especially that written in the early Roman empire, which might indicate something about conventions of composition at that time, though in the worldly circumstances of blasé Roman society.

Socrates and the Socratics. It was common for Greek philosophers and other teachers to confine themselves to oral instruction and to leave publication of notes or composition of more elaborate statements of their teachings to their followers. Pythagoras and other early philosophers are probable examples; Socrates is the chief model; Arcesilaus, Carneades, and Epictetus are later instances. Epictetus was teaching a highly refined Stoic morality in Rome and Epirus in the last decades of the first and opening decades of the second century of this era. A record of his discourses is preserved by Flavius Arrianus (Arrian, *Discourses of Epictetus*), who says in his preface that he recorded them for his own use and as literally as possible.[3]

Sources on Pythagoras are very unsatisfactory,[4] and as interesting as a comparison between Pythagoreanism and Christianity might be, it is chiefly Socrates and his followers who must

[3]This has generally been believed, though interpretations of the statement have ranged from a shorthand transcription to a regrouping of remarks delivered on various occasions. Theo W. Wirth, however, has recently reexamined the evidence and bibliography, and he attributes primary creative responsibility to Arrian rather than Epictetus; see his "Arrians Erinnerungen an Epiktet," *Museum Helveticum*, 24 (1967), 149–189 and 197–216. Limited new information in classical studies, as in New Testament studies, puts scholars anxious to make new contributions under often destructive pressures.

[4]See, e.g., W. K. C. Guthrie, *A History of Greek Philosophy*, vol. 1, *The Earlier Presocratics and the Pythagoreans* (Cambridge: Cambridge University Press, 1962), 157–172.

furnish us an analogue for Christian source criticism. The question of sources is here closely connected with the so-called Socratic problem, the search for the historical Socrates. Albert Schweitzer labeled this search more difficult than that for Jesus in that Socrates is known exclusively from "literary men who exercised their creative ability upon his portrait."[5] This is partially balanced by the fact that we know these "literary men" much better than we know the writers of the gospels and thus can better detect their hands at work.

Although Socrates had many followers, among whom a considerable number wrote about him, only four "gospels" of Socrates have survived. The earliest and strangest is the "anti-gospel" according to the comic poet Aristophanes in the *Clouds*, produced in 423 B.C. but preserved only in a partial revision made around 420. It cannot in any way reflect the teaching of the last twenty years of Socrates' life or the circumstances of his execution in 399 B.C., and the portrait of Socrates is very much influenced by Aristophanes' satire of contemporary sophists. Although something can be learned from it about contemporary perceptions of Socrates, it is not a useful analogue for Christian source criticism.

Better are the Socrates according to Xenophon and the Socrates according to Plato. We have an *Apology* by each, a *Symposium* by each, the *Memorabilia* and *Oeconomicus* of Xenophon, and the remaining dialogues of Plato, in twenty-three of which Socrates is a character. Both Xenophon and Plato knew Socrates personally when they were in their teens and twenties and he was in his fifties and sixties. Though probably based on a more profound understanding of Socrates' thought, Plato's portrait is colored by his own philosophical development. Clearly, he regarded this development as Socratic in origin, but in his writing, he does not differentiate the seeds planted by his teacher from his own full bloom. A partial parallel in early Christian literature is the Gospel of John.

To the casual reader it probably would seem that Xenophon and Plato each rely entirely on their own memory or oral reports in presenting Socrates, but some scholars believe that they can see in Xenophon's Socratic writings the influence of Plato's early

[5] Albert Schweitzer, *The Quest of the Historical Jesus: A Critical Study of Its Progress from Reimarus to Wrede*, trans. W. Montgomery, Macmillan Paperbacks ed., with a new introduction by James M. Robinson (New York: The Macmillan Company, 1968), 6, first published in German in 1906.

dialogues.[6] More important, it is clear that notes of Socrates' conversations existed and were drawn on in the composition of works about him. In Plato's *Theatetus* (143a), for example, Euclides of Megara claims to have made notes of Socrates' report of his discussion with Theatetus, to have questioned Socrates about the notes repeatedly, and to have made corrections in them. Similarly, in the *Symposium* (173b), Apollodorus says that he has checked the accuracy of some reports with Socrates himself. Antiphon is said to have memorized the discussion in the *Parmenides*, which was repeated to him many times (126c). Even if some of these statements are intended to lend dramatic verisimilitude rather than to reveal actual sources, they do reflect the practice of note-taking and the memory powers of the time. Apparently, note-taking was common and was not even limited to the intelligentsia: Diogenes Laertius reports (2.122) that Simon the cobbler used to make notes of all that he could remember after Socrates visited his shop and that he ended up with thirty-three "dialogues," which were long preserved. Among later Greeks and Romans, note-taking was a widely established custom. The emperor Augustus "always spoke from notes" even when talking to his wife (Suetonius, *Augustus* 84). An even more extreme example of compulsive note-taking is the elder Pliny's dictation to his secretary of his observations as the ship carried him to his death on the shore beneath erupting Vesuvius in August of A.D. 79 (Pliny the Younger, *Epistles* 6.16). It seemed natural to Epictetus to assume that Socrates himself wrote extensive private notes in developing his ideas (Arrian, *Discourses of Epictetus* 1.32–33), though this seems unlikely to scholars now. On the other hand, Aristotle's writings, as we have them, are not published works but his lecture notes, which he continually revised. In any event, the existence of notes on the preaching of the Apostles would not have surprised a first-century Roman interested in Christianity, and the request for such a record by a Christian group would have been predictable.

The fourth Socrates is that according to Aristotle, born fifteen years after Socrates' death. He spent twenty years, from the age of seventeen to thirty-seven, in the school of Plato, where he

[6] Cf., e.g., Max Treu, "Xenophon von Athen," in *Paulys Realencyclopädie der classischen Altertumswissenschaft*, new ed. begun by Georg Wissowa, continued by Wilhelm Kroll and Karl Mittelhaus, second series, half-vol. 18, ed. Konrat Ziegler (Stuttgart: Alfred Druckenmüller Verlag, 1967), cols. 1872, 1892–1894.

heard a great deal about Socrates and read all of Plato's dialogues and the writings of other Socratics. Eyewitness testimony, oral tradition, unpublished notes, and published works all would have been available to him for construction of a picture of Socrates. Aristotle was not interested in the life or personality of Socrates as such, however. Rather, he occasionally referred to individual aspects of Socrates' teaching as representing stages in the history of philosophy. Although, unlike Plato, his works have few literary pretensions, he recast Socrates' teaching in his own terms as he saw Plato doing.

Each of the four reports of Socrates has enjoyed its day among scholars as the one reliable picture of Socrates. The most recent survey with a claim to authority is that of W. K. C. Guthrie.[7] His judgment, which I find persuasive, is that all four sources have some value, that the primary ingredient in each case, however, is the creative view of the reporter, and that our four main sources on Socrates are consistent with a single, if unusual, personality as seen respectively by a comic poet, a gentleman soldier, a theoretical philosopher, and a scholar of the next generation.

What "Q" has been to much modern source criticism of the gospels, Antisthenes has been to Socratic source criticism: that is, a convenient way to crystallize a tradition not otherwise identifiable. Antisthenes was a real person, a follower first of Gorgias the sophist and then of Socrates and the so-called founder of the Cynic sect.[8] Like others, he wrote dialogues about Socrates, but these writings have perished and little can be attributed to them with certainty. Karl Joël in the nineteenth century and more recently A. H. Chroust developed theories in which Antisthenes' presentation of Socrates was the primary datum in the formation of the literary tradition, with Xenophon borrowing from it and Plato reacting against it.[9] Joël and Chroust have had their followers, but enthusiasm for this particular theory has faded.[10]

[7] Guthrie, *A History of Greek Philosophy*, vol. 3, *The Fifth-Century Enlightenment* (1969), 322–377.

[8] Guthrie, *A History of Greek Philosophy*, 3:304–311.

[9] Karl Joël, *Der echte und der xenophontische Sokrates*, 2 vols. (Berlin: R. Gaertner, 1893–1901); A. H. Chroust, *Socrates, Man and Myth: The Two Socratic Apologies of Xenophon* (London: Routledge and Kegan Paul Ltd., 1957), 198–226.

[10] See F. Caizzi, "Antistene," *Studi Urbinati*, series B, *Letteratura, Storia, Filosofia*, n. s. 38 (1964), 48–99.

As contrasted with this kind of "higher" criticism, a counter-part of a more nearly "fundamentalist" view of the gospels might be found in the thesis of Burnet and Taylor, who maintain that whatever was put in the mouth of Socrates in a Platonic dialogue must be assumed to be substantially what Socrates really said, accurately reported by Plato from notes or memory.[11] Burnet and Taylor argue that there were many alive in Plato's time who knew and remembered Socrates well and that to distort his views, especially his final conversations in prison, would have been "an offence against good taste and an outrage on all natural piety."[12] Guthrie calls this "the argument from outraged propriety"[13] and rejects it, as have most recent students of Plato, on the basis of Plato's conception of his own mission. "The justification . . . in Plato's mind for putting a doctrine into Socrates's mouth was not that the doctrine *tel quel*, in its complete form, had been taught by Socrates, but that it could appear to Plato to be based on one of Socrates's fundamental convictions, and constitute a legitimate projection, explication, and defence of it."[14] There were few easy avenues of expression for outraged propriety in antiquity: no reviews in scholarly journals or newspapers, no letters to the editor, no television talk shows. The only recourse was word of mouth or separate publication of an "answer." Although Aristophanes' picture of Socrates outraged propriety, so far as we know it was not refuted at the time. On the other hand, the published *Apologies* of Plato and of Xenophon at least in part were outraged responses to the execution of Socrates and more particularly to the attack upon him published by Polycrates about 393 B.C., which does not survive.[15] There were probably limits to what could be done in rearranging and reinterpreting material about well-known subjects, but these limits were broad. It would not have outraged propriety among Greek readers had Matthew, for example, regrouped disparate sayings of Jesus to create the Sermon on the Mount, but, after such formulation of an oral tradition of Jesus' sayings, it might have outraged the propriety of some Christians to find those say-

[11] John Burnet, *Plato's Phaedo, Edited with Introduction and Notes* (Oxford: The Clarendon Press, 1911), ix–lvi; A. E. Taylor, *Socrates*, Anchor Books ed. (Garden City, N.Y.: Doubleday & Company, Inc., 1953), 11–36.

[12] Burnet, *Plato's Phaedo*, xii.

[13] Guthrie, *A History of Greek Philosophy*, 3:351.

[14] Guthrie, *A History of Greek Philosophy*, 3:353.

[15] Chroust, *Socrates, Man and Myth*, ch. 4.

ings differently expressed in a new gospel. We are all familiar with modern Christians who feel that the Bible should be left "the way King James wrote it."

Socrates not only published no philosophical writings but, in Plato's *Phaedrus* (274–277), expresses strong disapproval of writing.[16] Distrust of dogmatic philosophical exposition among his followers persisted to the time of Aristotle. When the Socratics ventured to write, they chose primarily the new dialogue form, which affected to reproduce their teacher's method. This opposition to writing may have deterred some followers of Socrates from any publication for a time, as did also the continued hostility to him and to his students in Athens after his execution. Such opposition to publication might be compared to feelings among the followers of Jesus, for many of whom the expectation of the coming of the Kingdom may have created a feeling that writing was impracticable.

Is there any significance in the comparative chronology of the development of the Socratic corpus and of the gospels? Socrates was executed in 399 B.C.. For about six years his followers were disorganized, discouraged, or absent from Athens. Around 393 they began to reappear: the philosopher-orator Isocrates opened a school with some Socratic features; Polycrates published his attack but was met with open replies. Plato returned and founded the Academy around 387. We do not know with certainty the dates of his first dialogues, but the oldest is very likely no earlier than the 380s. The main period of composition of Socratic works and formulation of the tradition about Socrates is the twenty-year span between 387 and 367. Aristotle belongs in the next generation, working in the Academy between 367 and 347, teaching in Athens again and putting his lectures in their present form in the years 335–323. The Socratic sources were completed seventy-five years after Socrates' death. A similar "rhythm" in the development of Christianity, taking A.D. 33 as the date of the Crucifixion, would put the first tentative writing after 39, the major period of representation in the years A.D. 45–65, and the work of a more systematic second generation in the period from around 65 to shortly after A.D. 100. A.D. 45 is too early a date for our extant gospels, but it may indeed approximate the date when the need for written versions of apostolic

[16]For a wider consideration of the relation of Plato to oral culture, see Eric A. Havelock, *Preface to Plato: A History of the Greek Mind* (Cambridge, Mass.: Belknap Press of Harvard University Press, 1963), esp. 3–193.

preaching began to be felt: it is in the reign of Claudius (A.D. 41–54) that Eusebius (*Church History* 2.14–15) dates Peter's journey to Rome, with which he associates the composition of Mark. There are said to be tides in the affairs of men, and some "rhythm" in the statement of the teachings of a master is not unimaginable.

The dialogue form was developed by the followers of Socrates, especially by Plato, as an appropriate expression of Socrates' teaching, just as the gospels were an appropriate reaction to the life and teaching of Jesus. Both forms ostensibly are informal and low-key but capable of great subtlety. Later Greek and Latin dialogues developed conventions that are of interest because they involve the use of sources. One such convention is that of claiming a direct or indirect personal link between the writer of the dialogue and the dramatic occasion of the dialogue, as if to explain where the writer got his information. In the *Apology* (2), for example, Xenophon professes to record what he heard from Hermogenes, for he was widely known to have been absent from Athens at the time; in the case of the *Symposium* (1) he asserts that he was present, which few have believed. Plato presents some dialogues as narrated by intermediaries who had heard them, but in general he did not have to establish the credentials of his knowledge of Socrates, even though it is chronologically impossible for him to have been present at some of the discussions (the dramatic date of the *Protagoras*, for example, seems to be earlier than Plato's birth). Later writers who lacked Plato's established relationship do present their credentials. Cicero regularly follows the convention, both in the case of a historical setting such as *De Oratore* (1.23) and in dialogues with a contemporary setting, such as *Tusculan Disputations* (1.7–8). In the case of the gospels, the question of the authority of the writer strangely is neglected by Matthew and Mark. Only Luke follows the classical convention of beginning with a statement of why he writes. That he does so implies that he is addressing a more Hellenized audience, but his failure to maintain the classicizing tone throughout suggests that he also feels great respect for the language of the Christian sources on which he draws.

Once having established a personal link to the conversation, writers of classical dialogues conventionally obscure their use of written sources. That is, they pretend to know what they know only from what was said to them or in their presence. This convention might be called "Hendrickson's Law" from G. L.

Hendrickson who first pointed it out.[17] In practice there is every reason to believe that writers of dialogues used notes, oral tradition, and, in Cicero's case, published works as the basis for their composition. The dialogue, of course, may reflect real interests on the part of the characters, but these are normally artistically arranged and developed. The author had considerable freedom of treatment. One of the few cases in which dialogues actually seem to follow real conversations closely is the early dialogues of St. Augustine, such as *Against the Academics*, which Augustine claims (1.1.4) to have been taken down at the time in shorthand. Stenography, which had begun by the first century B.C., became common under the Roman empire but was probably practiced mostly by trained slaves and freedmen (cf. Seneca, *Epistles* 90.25). An early reference to its use in Christian circles is in connection with the exegesis of Origen (Eusebius, *Church History* (6.36.1).

The Question of Genre. A convenient transition from examination of the first set of analogues to the second is provided by the question of the use of written sources, including notes, and the conventions of literary genres. Ancient critics such as Quintilian generally only recognize three genres of literary prose: oratory, history, and dialogue. There are, however, a number of other forms that develop literary conventions of their own, including biography as a subdivision of history and variants of oratory or dialogue such as the diatribe and its relative, the homily. In addition, there are many treatises or collections of material, which are basically extended notes.

The ordinary Greek word for such notes or informal treatises is *hypomnēma*, plural *hypomnēmata* (Latin, *commentarii*). Included are notes for a speech made ahead of time, notes on a lecture made at the time or soon after, notes on reading or research, notes on political or historical circumstances, such as Caesar's *Commentaries* on the Gallic and Civil Wars, and the like. These notes are the raw material from which more formal publications can be created (cf., e.g., Cicero, *Brutus* 262). A variant of *hypomnēmata* are *apomnēmoneumata*, which might be translated "memoirs." *Apomnēmoneumata* are notes about the doings or sayings of a person, written either by the person

[17]G. L. Hendrickson, "Literary Sources in Cicero's *Brutus* and the Technique of Citation in Dialogue," *American Journal of Philology*, 27 (1906), 184–199.

or by someone close to him. Although also somewhat informal, *apomnēmoneumata* are usually intended to be published works and not, like most *hypomnēmata*, intended for the private use of the author or friends. *Apomnēmoneumata* (Latin *memorabilia*) is the title traditionally applied to Xenophon's unsystematic memoirs of Socrates. Other *apomnēmoneumata* were Zeno's reminiscences of Crates of Thebes and Philostratus' of the later sophists. The gospels are twice called *apomnēmoneumata* by Justin in the mid-second century (*Apology* 1.66.13; 1.67.8).

Euangelion, of course, is the term coined by the Christians to describe both their message and their written gospels and is the best word for such a published document. Its use is established in Mark 1:1. A term found in some early evidence on the gospels is the neuter plural noun, *logia*. This is regularly used by classical writers to mean "oracles," but literally it only means "that which is proclaimed." There is no reasonable doubt that *logia* in the various fragments quoted by Eusebius means "gospel,"[18] and the connection is doubtless via the concept of proclamation, also seen in *euangelion*, or "good news." *Logia* thus includes both sayings and doings. The problem of whether Eusebius calls the gospels *hypomnēmata* or distinguishes preliminary notes from a formal gospel will be examined below.

Hypomnēmata do not constitute a literary genre, and, from the classical point of view, gospel is not a literary genre. For one thing, a gospel writer's purpose is not literary. The noncanonical gospels illustrate how broadly the term gospel could be used. If one asks how a gospel is formulated, however, the answer would seem to be, by proclaiming it (*keryssein*), and this in turn suggests that the primary formal link between our gospels and the preaching and teaching of Jesus is apt to be found in the preaching and teaching of the Apostles. In this sense, the gospels can be regarded as a nonliterary genre generated, as were the Socratic dialogues, out of the method of the Master. They are rhetorical works in the sense that their intention is to persuade the readers that the Christian message is true or to deepen their understanding of this message.

Historians, Biographers, and Rhetoricians. Perhaps the finest discussion of the source criticism of a particular Greek author

[18]See, e.g., R. Gryson, "A propos du témoignage de Papias sur Matthieu. Le sens du mot logion chez les Pères du second siècle," *Ephemerides Theologicae Lovanienses*, 41 (1965), 530–547.

is that by A. W. Gomme in the introduction to his great commentary on Thucydides.[19] Of course, Thucydides is a special case: he was the most conscientious of the ancient historians; he wrote about contemporary events that he had watched with interest from the start, in some of which he had directly participated, and about which he had doubtless taken notes as they occurred; and he knew the leading actors in these events personally. Gomme enunciates two principles for the historical criticism of Thucydides: first, "if official documents contradict Thucydides, we must believe the former"; second, "if Thucydides states or clearly implies something that contradicts a contemporary pamphleteer or a later historian of the type of Ephoros, Douris, or Diodorus, or Plutarch, Thucydides is to be believed."[20] Gomme subsequently examines two difficult cases: first, in an instance where a natural inference from an official document conflicts with Thucydides, he leans toward trusting Thucydides; second, where Thucydides conflicts with a scholarly writer of the fourth or third century like Aristotle, Gomme is so doubtful as to reach no conclusion.[21] The closest parallel problem in New Testament studies would be that of the relative value of external evidence dating from the times of Papias as opposed to the opinions of later scholarly writers such as Origen or Eusebius.

Within historiography, the study of writings about Alexander the Great and about the history of the Roman republic has a certain pride of place: they both involve the reconstruction of a variety of oral and written sources, documentary and literary, a lengthy history of transmission, and a mingling of supernatural and historical events. Further, a considerable variety of points of view and motivation can be discerned among the writers. Few principles of criticism can be said to emerge from the study of these traditions, save perhaps the conviction that anything can happen and an increasing tendency not to oversimplify the tradition. Nissen's "law" that Livy tends to choose one main written source for a section of his Roman history and then to check it against other sources[22] still seems to hold for some parts of Livy's

[19] A. W. Gomme, *A Historical Commentary on Thucydides*, vol. 1, *Introduction and Commentary on Book I*, rev. ed. (Oxford: The Clarendon Press, 1959), 29–87, esp. 84–87.

[20] Gomme, *A Historical Commentary on Thucydides*, 1:84–85.

[21] Gomme, *A Historical Commentary on Thucydides*, 1:86–87.

[22] Heinrich Nissen, *Kritische Untersuchungen über die Quellen der IV. und V. Dekade des Livius* (Berlin: Weidmann, 1863), 36–52. There are useful surveys of source criticism in *Fifty Years (and Twelve) of Classical Scholarship*,

work, but not for all, and certainly not generally for all historians. It was widely recognized in antiquity that accounts of early history were strongly mythic or poetic and not literal history (see e.g., Quintilian, *Institutio Oratoria* 2.4.18–19), and, though historians referred to sources for such information, they often did so in a vague way. The first ten books of Livy's history contain 133 instances of "they say" or "it is reported that" in various forms.[23]

The best information on the procedures of classical biographers in the use of sources relates to the work of Plutarch and Suetonius. Since their careers are contemporary with or slightly later than the time of the composition of the gospels, it is of interest to summarize what we know about their methods, even though we must recognize significant differences in ambience, objectives, and values between the biographers and the gospel writers.

Plutarch's standards of scholarship were high. In the second chapter of his life of Demosthenes, he speaks as follows:

> But if any man undertake to write a history that has to be collected from materials gathered by observation and the reading of works not easy to be got in all places, nor written always in his own language, but many of them foreign and dispersed in other lands, for him, undoubtedly, it is in the first place and above all things most necessary to reside in some city of good note, addicted to liberal arts, and populous; where he may have plenty of all sorts of books, and upon inquiry may hear and inform himself of such particulars as, having escaped the pens of writers, are more faithfully preserved in the memories of men, lest his work be deficient in many things, even those which it can least dispense with.[24]

Although he refused to abandon his native village lest he further reduce its population, Plutarch traveled in Greece and abroad and read widely everywhere. Recent studies have made clear that, even though he read widely and deeply in both Greek and Latin, he should not be regarded as a systematic researcher. He read works through and took notes on whatever interested him;

---

rev. ed. of *Fifty Years of Classical Scholarship*, ed. Maurice Platnauer (New York: Barnes and Noble, 1968): G. T. Griffith, "The Greek Historians," 182–241, and A. H. McDonald, "The Roman Historians," 465–493.

[23] Henri Bornecque, *Tite-Live*, Bibliothèque de la Revue des cours et conférences (Paris: Boivin & c., 1933), 61.

[24] Quoted from Plutarch, *The Lives of the Noble Grecians and Romans*, trans. John Dryden, rev. A. H. Clough, The Modern Library (New York: Random House, Inc., n. d.), 1022–1023.

he did not ordinarily take a topic and pursue it back through references in a variety of sources. The elder Pliny and other ancient scholars probably worked in a similar way. When they were ready to write systematically, they used their memories and their notes, only occasionally going back to the original. One reason for this was that published works were usually cumbersome scrolls, while notes were often in the more convenient form of a codex.[25] Taking as an example Plutarch's anecdotal work, *On the Virtues of Women*, Philip A. Stadter has shown that it is based not on any published anthology, but on acquaintance with a wide variety of Greek and Roman historians.

It is certain that Plutarch did not read through all these authors simply to gather material for the *Mulierum Virtutes*. On the contrary, this review of the authors used as sources in the *Mulierum Virtutes* leads us to one conclusion: that all Plutarch's historical works, the monumental corpus of biographies together with the several short treatises, share a common foundation formed by Plutarch's extended acquaintance with Greek and Roman history.[26]

Plutarch often quotes from memory, sometimes confessedly (e.g., *Pericles* 24.7), but he also often took notes to which he could later refer. His essay, *On Tranquility of Mind*, he says (464F), was composed hurriedly from *hypomnēmata* in response to the request of a departing friend. He frequently identifies his sources. When he does not, they are usually the standard classics on the subject at hand, which he has read through: Herodotus, Thucydides, Plato, or the like. He makes this procedure clear in the life of Nicias (1.5) where he says that he will summarize important features of Nicias' life as presented by Thucydides and Philistus, but that he will endeavor to bring together "such things as are not commonly known, and lie scattered here and there in other men's writings, or are found amongst the old monuments and archives." This collection of detail is an integral part of his basic purpose, "not collecting mere useless pieces of learning, but ad-

[25] The *locus classicus* is Pliny, *Epistles* 3.5.15, which describes the elder Pliny, accompanied by a *notarius* or stenographer (wearing mittens to keep off the cold!), who has both *libri*, papyrus rolls of books to read aloud to Pliny, and *pugillares* or tablets on which to write at Pliny's dictation. For a general discussion, see Frederic G. Kenyon, *Books and Readers in Ancient Greece and Rome*, 2d ed. (Oxford: The Clarendon Press, 1951). Notebooks are discussed on page 92.

[26] Philip A. Stadter, *Plutarch's Historical Methods: An Analysis of the Mulierum Virtutes* (Cambridge, Mass.: Harvard University Press, 1965), 133.

ducing what may make his [Nicias'] disposition and habit of mind understood."[27] It is this technique of citation that has resulted in the common misconception that ancient historians cite their sources chiefly when they depart from a basic unnamed source. The procedure can also be illustrated from the opening of Plutarch's life of Aristides.

The other great classical biographer of early Christian times, the Roman Suetonius, had less unity of moral purpose and lower critical standards, but he had available to him the resources of Roman libraries and archives from which he read and took notes. When he composed his biographies, he consulted these notes, which, unlike Plutarch's, were arranged topically rather than chronologically. Less conscious than most other writers of the need for harmony of style, Suetonius included in his lives of Julius Caesar and Augustus verbatim quotations from official documents that were available to him as a member of the emperor Hadrian's staff.[28] His goal in writing about the Caesars seems to have been an objective presentation of the evidence regarding various aspects of each emperor's life; he thus sometimes presented divergent accounts of a single event and often seems uncritical. Modern historians, however, have rather welcomed his hesitation to impose his own judgments.

Plutarch and Suetonius are important for the criticism of the gospels primarily as a standard of comparison. They illustrate what constituted learned and literary biography of the times and how the materials were assembled. In the cases of Caesar, Galba, and Otho, we can even compare their differing treatments of the same subjects and of divergent sources, both written and oral. Although the gospels rely on a simpler tradition, in both traditions there occur the stages of collecting the information in notes and regrouping the material into an organized text.

The schools of rhetoric in Hellenistic and Roman times might furnish another analogue to the gospels. The early work of Cicero, *On Invention*, and the approximately contemporary work, entitled *Rhetoric to Herennius*, perhaps to be attributed to an unknown Cornificius, furnish an interesting situation that I have

---

[27]Quoted from Plutarch, *The Lives of the Noble Grecians and Romans*, 627. Cf. A. J. Gossage, "Plutarch," in *Latin Biography*, ed. T. A. Dorey (New York: Basic Books, Inc., 1967), 52; D. A. Russell, *Plutarch* (New York: Charles Scribner's Sons, 1973), 42–62 ("The Scholar and His Books").

[28]See, e.g., G. B. Townend, "Suetonius and His Influence," in *Latin Biography*, ed. Dorey, 87.

elsewhere studied in some detail.[29] I have shown that despite very close similarities in content and even some similarities in wording, neither work is directly dependent on the other. This immediately suggests dependence upon a common source, but certain specific differences between the two cannot well be explained on the basis of derivation from a common source. It appears rather that each is basically derived from the oral teaching of the same unnamed master, to whom indeed Cornificius alludes, but that Cicero studied with this master a few years earlier than did Cornificius. In the interim, the master has made certain changes in the details of his lectures. Now he stresses the novelty of his new views but has preserved verbatim most of his earlier examples and many of his definitions. Clearly, both Cicero and Cornificius had detailed notes of the lectures. In the case of the sayings of Jesus or of material based on the preaching of an Apostle, it should be recognized that slightly different versions of essentially the same pericope may result from varying reports of what was said about the same subject on different occasions. In his ministry, Jesus surely repeated himself far more often than the individual gospels indicate, but not necessarily in exactly the same words. This would hold true also of the preaching of the Apostles, just as of modern preachers and candidates for office.

An unusual example of the possibilities of literal oral transmission of texts is perhaps to be found in the work of the elder Seneca. Seneca was born about the middle of the first century B.C. and educated in the rhetorical schools of Spain and Rome. Though not a professional rhetorician, he remained exceedingly interested in exercises in declamation throughout his life, as did many other Romans of his time. In his old age, about the time of the Crucifixion of Jesus, he wrote an account of declaimers and declamation, of which the greater part is verbatim quotation of extensive pieces of declamation (never a whole speech) delivered many years before (*Oratorum Rhetorum Sententiae Divisiones Colores*). More than one hundred declaimers are represented. In the Preface, Seneca makes a great point of the fact that he is quoting from memory. He claims that he once had a really outstanding memory and could repeat correctly a list of two thousand names after hearing it read only once, though in old age

[29] George Kennedy, *The Art of Rhetoric in the Roman World* (Princeton: Princeton University Press, 1972), 126–138.

his memory is failing.[30] His claim has not always been believed, but there is no good reason to reject it entirely. The art of memory was taught in the schools and cultivated in antiquity. Declamations generally were not published, but Seneca could have heard some of the passages more than once. Adult declamation was *ex tempore* but on a limited number of themes, and declaimers made considerable use of commonplaces repeated in various speeches. Since Seneca was interested in declamation, he collected such passages in his mind and probably reinforced his knowledge of them from time to time by repeating them, as Antiphon did the *Parmenides*, or possibly by asking some of the declaimers what they had said. Eventually, of course, he wrote the passages down, perhaps long before assembling his extant work. Seneca's memory is unusual though not unique. It would have been a much less demanding task for regular hearers of Jesus or of the Apostles to hold in memory a significant part of the teaching they had repeatedly heard and to recite it or write it down at any time there was reason to do so, such as when a congregation was deprived of apostolic teaching. Nevertheless, two individuals with reasonably good memories of this sort would produce two slightly different versions, since it is likely that they would be drawing on different combinations of receptions of the message. Furthermore, studies of oral epic have shown that nonformulaic prose is probably more susceptible to minor variation than is verse. Once a gospel had been composed and published and had achieved wide circulation, it would not be impossible for it to have been virtually memorized by many Christians. Had one of these Christians undertaken to amplify or to abridge this gospel into a new gospel, it would not have been necessary for him to engage in a conscious editorial process based on a written text, because he could have relied on his memory of the original gospel.

Translation and Imitation

Jesus presumably taught in Aramaic, but the gospels are in Greek. Therefore, translation has occurred at some point, whether in the oral tradition, in the composition of the gospels, or in

---

[30] Seneca, *Controversiae* 1. Preface. 2–4. He cites examples of persons with rhetorically trained memories (1. Preface. 18–19). Other famous examples: Simonides of Ceos, Aristotle's contemporary Theodectes, Charmadas of Athens,

the translation of a gospel, such as Matthew's, from Aramaic into Greek. Since I do not know Hebrew or its cognates, my ability to contribute to this subject is limited. I should like, however, to comment briefly on two features of translation from one language to another that were evident in the classical period.

The first is that the concept of translation in classical times was very broad. It included, on the one hand, literal and word for word renderings of texts, such as official inscriptions published in Greek and Latin at the same time (for example, the *Res Gestae Divi Augusti*). On the other hand, it also could include cases that we would think of as closer to imitations. The plays of Plautus and Terence were regularly spoken of as Latin "translations" of Greek originals: "Demophilus scripsit, Maccus vortit barbare," Plautus says of his own *Asinaria* (Prologue.11), while Terence speaks of one of his rivals as having translated well (i.e., literally?) but written badly (*Eunuchus*, Prologue.7). Yet the dramatists felt free to add and subtract characters or scenes and to vary interpretations considerably. Similarly, Cicero's philosophical works are presentations of Hellenistic Greek philosophy in which he sometimes bases much of one book on a single Greek original. It is not surprising, therefore, that he would think of the process as involving "translation," as he says in *De Finibus* (1.7). A flexible concept of translation has been shared in other periods. I am told it can be seen in the Septuagint. Leonardo Bruni's Latin translation of Polybius and of Plutarch's life of Cicero, made in the fifteenth century, include significant amounts of material not in the original Greek.

A second feature of "translation" in New Testament times is a form of the larger phenomenon of *mimēsis*, or literary imitation, which cast a spell over the Greeks and Romans beginning in the late first century B.C. The earliest discussion of *mimēsis* in Greek is by Dionysius of Halicarnassus in a small work, *On Imitation*. The critical assumption behind the theory of imitation is classicism. In each published form there are great models of style (diction, composition, or, to some extent, structure and topics). Success in writing and approval of a public are obtained by successful emulation and/or imitation of these models. In many literary forms, the great models are early or classical Greek:

---

and Metrodorus of Scepsis (see Cicero, *De Oratore* 2.351 and 2.360; and Quintilian, *Institutio Oratoria* 11.51). All four of these may have contributed to the development of the memory system described in *Rhetoric to Herennius* 3.28–40.   144

Homer in epic, Lysias or Demosthenes in oratory. Because Latin literature is derived from Greek, the Romans had always to some extent practiced imitation, which in their case meant both an imitation of some features of a "translated" Greek original and stylistic features of earlier Latin writers in the particular form chosen. A good example is Lucretius, whose philosophical epic *De Rerum Natura* is, loosely speaking, a translation of Epicurus' philosophy into Latin; it shows, however, the influence of the earlier Latin epic poet Ennius as a literary model.

An important figure for the understanding of composition in the apostolic period is Josephus,[31] born in Palestine about A.D. 38, captured by the Romans in 67, and brought to Rome by Titus in 70, where he was given citizenship and a pension. He had kept notes on the Jewish war and, after settling in Rome, revised these notes into a narrative history with the help of collaborators who assisted his Greek (*Against Apion* 1.50). His *Jewish Antiquities* appeared in Greek in the years 93–95, and he later published the so-called autobiography (*Vita*) and the essays, *Against Apion*.

Of Josephus' works the *Jewish War* is both the earliest and the most literary. Critics not unnaturally have assumed that it owes the latter characteristic to the unknown collaborators, who did not hesitate to incorporate literary reminiscences of classical Greek writers such as Thucydides and Sophocles and even some reminiscences of Latin writers.[32]

The case of the *Antiquities* is more complex. There is no explicit testimony that Josephus had help there, and the poorer Greek style is perhaps evidence that he did not. If he did not, he had certainly become more familiar with Greek historical writing during his stay in Rome and had embraced the convention of following literary models. For the general conception of the work, that model was apparently Dionysius of Halicarnassus' *Roman Antiquities*, also in twenty books and with an analogous objective. The literary model, however, was often Thucydides, especially in books 17 to 19, which are replete with Thucydidean

[31] See, e.g., Henry J. Cadbury, in *The Beginnings of Christianity*, pt. 1, *The Acts of the Apostles*, vol. 2, *Prolegomena II. Criticism*, ed. F. J. Foakes Jackson and Kirsopp Lake (London: Macmillan and Company Ltd., 1922), 24–29.

[32] See, e.g., H. St. John Thackeray, *Josephus: The Man and the Historian*, Hilda Stich Stroock Lectures 1928 (New York: Jewish Institute of Religion, 1929); reprinted with a new introduction by Samuel Sandmel (New York: KTAV Publishing House, Inc., 1967), 100–124, esp. 104–106.

grammar, phrases, and techniques of description. The great early-twentieth-century student of Josephus, H. St. John Thackeray, argued that the assistants were still at work and that their contributions could be distinguished in the *Antiquities*: one, the abler, did the greater part of the work for Josephus and was responsible for reminiscences of the poets; the other, the "Thucydidean hack," was responsible for books 17 to 19.[33] More recent scholars have acknowledged signs of Thucydidean, as well as Dionysian and other influences, but have thought the distinction between the two assistants untenable.[34]

If a gospel had been written in Greek at a fairly early date and was reasonably well-known, and if subsequently someone undertook to translate an Aramaic gospel, rather fuller in content, into Greek, it would be in accordance with Greek conventions for the translator to have taken the language of the existing Greek gospel as his model, even to the extent of borrowing some of that familiar language to translate passages of Aramaic that were not literally identical to his text. I understand that when Matthew cites passages of the Old Testament that are also cited by Mark or Luke, these citations are close to the Septuagint and highly consistent in language, whereas when Matthew cites passages of the Old Testament not found in the other gospels, his version is characteristically not that of the Septuagint.[35] To me this suggests that the Greek text of an earlier gospel was a more potent influence on the translator than was the Septuagint itself.

It is interesting to compare what is said about Latin translations of the Scriptures in Augustine's *De Doctrina Christiana* (2.16–19). Augustine indicates that there were many different Latin versions, each lacking any authority and all thus without influence on one another. At times the versions varied greatly or even reflected misunderstanding of the text. Eventually, of course, the Vulgate was created, and, subsequently, its language exercised a strong literary influence. The parallel is not exact, however, for the earliest Greek gospels, with their apostolic

[33] Thackeray, *Josephus*, esp. 106–122.

[34] See, e.g., the review of the reprint of Thackeray by Louis H. Feldman in *Journal of the American Oriental Society*, 90 (1970), 545–546. A recent study of Josephus' literary methods is Zvi Yavetz, "Reflections on Titus and Josephus," *Greek, Roman, and Byzantine Studies*, 16 (1975), 411–432.

[35] Krister Stendahl, *The School of St. Matthew and Its Use of the Old Testament*, 1st American ed. (Philadelphia: Fortress Press, 1968), 45.

authority, would, from the first, have exercised a much greater influence than did any of the later Latin versions.

The External Evidence

In the ordinary methods of classical scholarship, *testimonia* or external evidence regarding authorship, composition, dates, and the like play an important role. The external evidence for the composition of the gospels, chiefly preserved by Eusebius, is often imperfectly cited and sometimes is presented as more inconsistent than it actually is.[36] I should like to comment on two passages in Eusebius' *Church History* that seem to me not to have been correctly understood by modern readers.

The first is the celebrated Papias passage (*Church History* 3.39.15–16). Earlier (2.15), Eusebius had briefly described the circumstances of the composition of Mark, giving as his authority the sixth book of Clement of Alexandria's *Hypotyposes* as confirmed by Papias bishop of Hierapolis. The fuller account from Papias, given in 3.39.15–16, is presumably the confirmation Eusebius had in mind, and we should conclude that he saw nothing basically inconsistent between the two accounts. In the longer account of 3.39.15–16 there are varied problems, but I believe the passage can be translated and explicated as follows:

This is what the elder used to say: Mark, having been the interpreter of Peter, wrote accurately but not in order everything that he [Peter] reported from memory that had been said or done by the Lord. For he [Mark] had not heard the Lord nor followed him, but later, as I have said, followed Peter, who adapted his teaching to the needs of his audience, not making as it were a systematic account of the Lord's gospel (*logia*). Thus Mark was sure of making no mistake in writing some things in this way as he remembered them (*apomnēmoneusen*). For he had a single objective, to omit or falsify nothing that he had heard among these [i.e., the sayings and doings Peter reported]. This is told by Papias on the subject of Mark. On the subject of Matthew this was said [by Papias]: Matthew composed the gospel (*logia*) in the Hebrew dialect, and each one translated it as he was able.

---

[36] See, e.g., William R. Farmer, *The Synoptic Problem: A Critical Analysis* (New York: The Macmillan Company/London: Collier-Macmillan Limited, 1964), 225–227. This book has now been reissued in a very slightly revised edition (Dillsboro, N.C.: Western North Carolina Press, 1976).

   This passage has often been interpreted as a criticism of the order of Mark's Gospel, but that does not seem to me likely, considering what we have seen about the procedures of ancient composition. Mark made notes on Peter's teaching. We have been told in Eusebius' second book (2.15) that the reason for this was the request of Christians to have a record of Peter's teaching when Peter was leaving them. This is likely to have been the usual reason for the first stage of gospel composition, the recording of apostolic sermons. Mark regarded the matter as very important and proceeded with great care. He did not begin by writing a narrative account (i.e., in order) of Jesus' life and teachings. Instead, he first wrote up notes of Peter's preaching exactly as he remembered it, and in Peter's order, which was that of individual sermons. In much the same way, Plutarch would later make running notes on his reading in the order in which it occurred, subsequently drawing on these notes in the composition of systematic works on various subjects. Papias is not describing the actual composition of Mark's Gospel; he is describing the note-taking that was preliminary to composition. Mark's note-taking may have been in Aramaic, and the result was an abstract of Peter's sermons. Subsequently, of course, Mark put the material into narrative order, thus forming a gospel in Greek on the basis of these notes, but Papias is not here telling us about this latter stage. Eusebius does not describe this quotation from Papias as an account of how Mark's Gospel was written, but as "a tradition about Mark who wrote the Gospel" (3.39.14), and the two are not necessarily the same. Considerable time could have elapsed between Mark's note-taking which, in book two (2.14.6), Eusebius dates in the reign of Claudius (A.D. 41–54) and the composition of the Gospel as we have it which on the basis of chapter thirteen of Mark is usually dated in the years between A.D. 65 and 70. According to Eusebius (2.15.1), all that Peter's followers asked of Mark was a *hypomnēma*, notes, though Eusebius remarks there, too, that this is the same Mark whose Gospel is extant and adds that the request to Mark for a *hypomnēma* was the cause of the *euangelion*. There is some evidence (2.15.2) that the *hypomnēma* may have been checked with Peter for accuracy, as the followers of Socrates at times had checked their notes with the teacher; in another account (6.14.7), perhaps more characteristic of Peter, the Apostle refuses to endorse or disown Mark's written version of his preaching.

Acts 10:34–43 indicates what a sermon of Peter might have been like and how such sermons might have formed the basis of a gospel. This passage purportedly gives an abstract of one of Peter's sermons, announcing the good news (*euangelizomenos*) and reporting Jesus' baptism, anointment, ministry of healing in Galilee, arrival in Jerusalem, crucifixion, and resurrection. No doubt, an actual sermon would have been much longer, containing a fuller account, and the details of this account would have varied in different sermons of the same general structure.[37]

What circumstances would lead to the compilation of a systematic gospel out of notes of apostolic preaching? In speaking of the development of apostolic authority, John Howard Schütz has written:

Then comes the second generation, and then the third. The experience of radical conversion disappears. The sensibility of reversal in one's own life is no longer shared by many who are nonetheless Christians. As what was once shared becomes less and less common, the apostle becomes more and more differentiated from others. His status comes to look unique.[38]

The formation of the gospels as we know them may have resulted from this same process. The evidence indicates that the Gospels of Mark and Luke came into existence after the deaths of the Apostles Peter and Paul. It may also be true that the Gospels of Matthew and John came into existence after the deaths of the Apostles of those names, in which case their authors are not the Apostles themselves but members of their "schools." Some extraordinary change was necessary to create the new form. A good possibility is the deaths of the Apostles, since it created the crisis of authority that made gospels necessary.

Although a distinction between the stage of note-taking and that of gospel composition emerges from the Papias passage if analyzed in this way, it is not certain that Eusebius really under-

[37] The speeches in Acts are widely regarded as artificial and literary, but even if they are influenced by literary conventions, they represented to the early church an acceptable picture of apostolic preaching (What else could the Apostles have said?). It is not the content, but the style that is classicizing.

[38] John Howard Schütz, *Paul and the Anatomy of Apostolic Authority*, Society for New Testament Studies Monograph Series 26 (Cambridge: Cambridge University Press, 1975), 280. Schütz also describes the Pauline letters as "an extension of Paul's missionary preaching" (282), which is similar to the view of the gospels taken here.

stood what he was reporting. A similar distinction between note-taking and gospel composition can also perhaps be seen in *Church History* 3.24.5–7, but it is less clear there, since Eusebius has recast his source into his own words and added opinions of his own. He speaks first of *hypomnēmata* by Matthew and John and then of Matthew's *euangelion* in his native language. By the time the latter was published, Mark and Luke had already published their (Greek) gospels. After reading the other gospels, John decided to supplement them by writing his own. Among the problems in unscrambling this passage is the fact that Eusebius has telescoped an elapsed period of time of around fifty years into a few lines.

A final comment needs to be made about the reference to Matthew in 3.39.16, that "each one translated it as he was able." What I see in this statement is first, a reflection of the fact that Matthew's Gospel was known only in Aramaic for a considerable period of time and second, an indication that there was considerable variation in the Greek versions of it that were read out in Christian assemblies. This is exactly the situation in which the well-known Greek text of a gospel such as Mark, which had established itself in the meantime, might be expected to exercise strong literary influence on the translated version of Matthew.

A second passage about which I should like to comment is *Church History* 6.14.5–6, where Eusebius is once again drawing on the *Hypotyposes* of Clement. Eusebius says that Clement reported a tradition of the early elders regarding the composition of the gospels. What modern scholars have usually read in the passage is a report that the gospels with genealogies, that is, Matthew and Luke, were published before the gospels without genealogies. Even if this is unlikely to have been the case, such a tradition could, of course, have existed. But there is at least a possibility that Eusebius has muddied the text of Clement by converting it into indirect discourse. The passage could also be understood as a tradition that the two gospels with genealogies, about which nothing further is said in the passage but which may have been discussed in the context in Clement, and also Mark, the circumstances of whose composition are briefly reported, were *progegraphthai*, "written before." Before what? The Greek particle *de* in 6.14.6 can perfectly well associate Mark with the other two gospels rather than with John, which is specifically said to be the last in order; thus we have a contrast of the Synoptics with John. The account of the composition of Mark in this passage places it in Rome and in the lifetime of Peter. As suggested above, I should prefer to take this as a somewhat confused picture of Mark's notes on Peter's preaching and not the published Greek Gospel of Mark. "Gospel," of course, sometimes means the content or message, sometimes a literary form.

A few chapters later (6.25.4–6) Eusebius reports that Origen, surely the greatest scholar of the early church, says that Matthew in Hebrew (i.e., Aramaic) was the earliest gospel, followed by that of Mark, whom Peter instructed, Luke, and John in this order. Nothing is said about the point in the succession where Matthew's Greek text should be placed. The order, Matthew, Mark, Luke, and John is also supported by St. Augustine (*The Harmony of the Gospels* 1.3), but on the basis of philosophical symmetry rather than of historical evidence. In this interpretation, the canonical order of the gospels is also the chronological order of their composition, the Greek Matthew being substituted for its Aramaic original. Of course, the opening of Matthew formed a very suitable link between Old and New Testaments.

Eusebius' reports regarding the origin of Mark's Gospel are sometimes doubted on the ground that heretics of the second century, among whom Marcion was the most famous, were attacking the authenticity of some gospels and that Papias' assertion of the close connection between Mark and Peter may thus have been based on the desire to affirm the apostolic authority of Mark's Gospel rather than on a reliable tradition.[39] Certainly, there was a great deal of propaganda about the authority of the gospels; we see this, for example, in prologues that were written to accompany the texts.[40] Some evidence may have been invented, but orthodox writers like Irenaeus can also be assumed to have interpreted existing evidence in their favor; it would then not be surprising that they would seize upon evidence (if, indeed, such evidence existed) of a connection between Mark and Peter to give authenticity to Mark's Gospel against the claims of Marcion and perhaps others. On the other hand, there is no reason to associate Papias with anti-Marcionite propaganda. Everything that we know suggests that Papias' activity should be dated around the second or third decade of the second century, twenty

[39] See, e.g., Kurt Niederwimmer, "Johannes Markus und die Frage nach dem Verfasser des zweiten Evangeliums," *Zeitschrift für die neutestamentliche Wissenschaft und die Kunde der älteren Kirche*, 58 (1967), 172–188.

[40] See, e.g., Donatien de Bruyne, "Les plus anciens prologues Latines des Evangiles," *Revue Bénédictine*, 40 (1928), 193–214.

to thirty years before the Marcionite controversy.[41] Papias had his own hobbies to ride, chiefly millennialism, but it remains true that "of all the early Christian books now lost, Papias' *Exegeses* is one we should most like to recover."[42]

Henry J. Cadbury, whom I had the honor of knowing well during my years at Haverford College, commented with great learning on the preface to Luke's Gospel (Luke 1:1-4), showing, among other things, how it combines Greek and Jewish traditions.[43] I have only one point to add. In the passage, there is repeated emphasis on the fact that the order of the incidents has been arranged both by those who have previously written gospels and by Luke himself. This suggests that the raw material of gospel-writing was notes on the preaching of the Apostles, and the major act of composition by a gospel writer was thus the rearrangement of such repetitive material into narrative order.

Conclusion

The experience of classicists seems to suggest that memory of oral teaching, especially if the teaching was heard repeatedly, could be retained with considerable integrity over an extended period of time, even though oral teaching was often converted into running notes by students and these notes were sometimes checked with the original speaker. Of course, both processes might take place: first oral transmission over a period of time, then note-taking. Notes were not usually published, but they were sometimes given limited circulation to interested persons. After oral transmission and note-taking, a third stage would be

[41] See, e.g., E. Gutwenger, "Papias," *Zeitschrift für katholische Theologie*, 69 (1947), 385–416, who dates Papias' work before A.D. 110. Other useful discussions of Papias include H. J. Lawlor, "Eusebius on Papias," *Hermathena*, 43 (1921), 167–222; H. A. Rigg, Jr., "Papias on Mark," *Novum Testamentum*, 1 (1956), 161–183; Bruno de Solages, "Le témoignage de Papias," *Bulletin de létterature ecclesiastique*, 71 (1970), 3–14; and Robert M. Grant, "Papias in Eusebius' *Church History*," in *Mélanges d'histoire des religions offerts à Henri-Charles Puech sous le patronage et avec le concours du Collège de France et de la section des sciences religieuses de l'Ecole pratique des hautes études* (Paris: Presses universitaires de France, 1974), 209–213.

[42] Edgar J. Goodspeed, *A History of Early Christian Literature*, rev. Robert M. Grant (Chicago: The University of Chicago Press, 1966), 92.

[43] Cadbury, in *The Beginnings of Christianity*, ed. Jackson and Lake, 1:2: 489–510.

the publication of a systematic or more literary work. The gospels are not themselves notes on preaching; they are systematic works, with the material appropriately organized. When a work was translated from one language into another, existing traditions in the second language often exercised influence on the form and style of the work, and considerable freedom of rearrangement or restatement was possible even if not inevitable.

The inability of New Testament scholars over a period of two hundred years to agree on the history of the composition of the gospels, despite a general agreement that there are signs of a literary relationship, suggests that the true relationship may be very complex. The original message of Jesus was heard by the disciples on many different occasions, and the disciples' memory of what he did and what he said was influenced by the circumstances and by the reactions of others. Even during his lifetime they surely shared with each other their impressions of him, and after his death, their memories were influenced by what others said. The preaching of the gospel by any one of the disciples differed somewhat from that by any other disciple, and the separate versions were subject to conflation whenever two disciples exchanged memories. At least some of these versions or parts of them, such as the sayings of Jesus, were reduced to written notes, probably at different places and different times, but when given some circulation, these written notes could be modified by material from other sets of notes. What is often called "Q" could represent some stage in this process. The author of a systematic gospel may have drawn primarily on one set of notes, but he may also have consulted other notes, in Aramaic or Greek, or incorporated parts of an oral tradition. Another factor, here as in poetry, is that one must always allow for the possibility of "inspiration": a writer may have felt that it was God's will that he reveal some particular "truth" not contained in any of his sources.

One or more formal gospels were eventually composed in Aramaic and in this form could exercise influence on other writers. Several gospels were eventually circulated in Greek. It is likely that one of these (whether the earliest or the most widely disseminated or the one based on most respected authority) would exercise considerable influence on subsequent gospels in that language. Among these interlocking relationships, it is thus not impossible both that Matthew could have influenced Mark and that Mark could have influenced our text of Matthew: Their authors could have used each other's notes, the second to write a systematic gospel could have had knowledge of the first, and the Greek translation of Matthew, if the Gospel was composed in Aramaic as the external tradition says, could have utilized significant portions of the text of Mark. Luke could have used the notes of Matthew or Mark, the Aramaic text of Matthew, the Greek text of Mark, or the Greek text of Matthew, if a translation was then available, but notes or oral tradition used by Luke could also have been used by Matthew and Mark, and the Greek translation of Matthew, if later than Luke, could have been influenced by Luke, for example, in some of the language of the Sermon on the Mount. John might be the recipient of all possible traditions but presumably could not, in its present form, have influenced the other three Greek gospels. We must also allow for the possibility that the text of the gospels was somewhat fluid into the second century, that the gospels continued to exercise an influence on one another, and that passages were adapted to reflect historical developments and liturgical uses.

In attempting to penetrate this maze, we have a few precious guidelines from the external tradition and whatever signs of the direction of influence we can deduce in comparing specific passages.[44]

Epigraph

It has been a common opinion that the Tower owes its foundation to the Romans, or at least, that its site was once occupied by a fortification, whose origin is attributed to that brave and enterprizing people; and this idea, though unsupported by historical evidence, or by any local discovery of a satisfactory nature, has been confidently adopted by men of rank and of literary reputation. The authority, however, of many of our early writers on subjects of antiquity must not be received without careful examination; for they appear too frequently to have indulged in hypothetical calculations, instead of being guided by plain and unalterable matters of fact: their zeal was not sufficiently tempered by experience, or their ardor was too great to admit of that cool and patient investigation which will allow no favorite notion to implant itself, unless founded on a basis that cannot be overturned by future inquiry.

John Bayley (1830)[45]

[44] I am indebted to my colleague, Professor Philip A. Stadter, for advice on certain matters discussed in this essay.

[45] John Bayley, *The History and Antiquities of the Tower of London, with memoirs of royal and distinguished persons, deduced from records, state-papers,*

Some parts of the complex rest on Roman foundations. The Conqueror built his fortress in the southeast angle of the existing Roman wall around the city; subsequently the Wardrobe Tower was erected on the base of a Roman bastion; and traces of the Roman wall can be seen within. So there are those elements of continuity with Roman power and civilization to satisfy the imagination.

A. L. Rouse (1972)[46]

and manuscripts, and from other original and authentic sources, 2d ed. (London: Jennings and Chaplin, 1830), 1–2.

[46] A. L. Rouse, *The Tower of London in the History of England* (New York: G. P. Putnam's Sons, 1972), 10.

Hypomnēmata from an Untamed Sceptic: A Response to George Kennedy

Wayne A. Meeks

There are times when every discipline becomes too ingrown, when its familiar questions grow stale and its axioms are no longer self-evident. Students of the New Testament, experiencing such a time today, are looking hungrily at both neighboring and distant fields for some methodological refreshment. It is altogether natural that the classics and ancient history should be among the fields being surveyed, for the student of early Christianity who turns to them is, as George Kennedy hints, rather like a prodigal returning home.[1] The allusion should not be pressed; the classicists have no particular reason to kill a

[1] Happily there have been a number of appeals for this homecoming recently: e.g., F. F. Bruce's presidential address at the 1975 annual meeting of *Studiorum Novi Testamenti Societas* ("The New Testament and Classical Studies," *New Testament Studies*, 22 [1976], 229–242); and the several stimulating essays by the Australian classicist, E. A. Judge, especially "St Paul and Classical Society," *Jahrbuch für Antike und Christentum*, 15 (1972), 19–36. Also to be noted are the international *Corpus Hellenisticum Novi Testamenti* project; The Institute for Antiquity and Christianity at Claremont, California; several working groups in the Society of Biblical Literature, including the "Graeco-Roman Religions Group" and the "Social World of Early Christianity Group"; and recent developments, along different lines, in graduate programs in New Testament studies at Harvard and Yale Universities. Of course, one could also name individuals and even institutions, notably the F. J. Dölger-Institut in Bonn, Germany, that have tried through the years to keep Athens and Jerusalem on speaking terms.

fatted calf for us, yet the feast that Kennedy provides is rich enough. To be sure, he warns that he has no magic to impart, no "guild secret discovered since last our disciplines met" (p. 126). He does not pretend that the classicist's perspective will make gospel criticism look simple; on the contrary, the analogies he presents have complex and subtle problems of their own. But it is precisely in thinking through some of these less familiar complexities that the myopia of the New Testament scholar may be relieved, especially since the problems presented emerge from the same cultural milieu, broadly speaking, as that in which the gospels were formed.

The principal lessons that the classicist's experience holds for the source criticism of the gospels are concisely stated in Kennedy's list of "caveats" near the beginning of his essay: (1) "the use of written sources is more complex than it once seemed"; (2) "oral transmission is important and is capable of preserving the integrity of a large text for a considerable period of time"; (3) "there was a great deal of note-taking"; (4) "among published texts there were different conventions in different genres"; (5) "too great an emphasis on abstract principles of criticism is almost certain to distort the evidence"; and (6) "'scientific' scepticism can easily be carried too far" (p. 126). This list would make a rather apt summary of what gospel critics have learned by their own trials and errors in the far country.

Oral Transmission

There would, however, be differences of emphasis. For example, while the recognition of oral transmission's importance is one of the hallmarks of twentieth-century New Testament research, caution is needed in generalizing from the fact that bodies of tradition are sometimes faithfully preserved orally for a long time. Verbatim preservation of such tradition depends upon the existence of some institution, in the broadest sense of the word, for transmission and upon the presence of a social context in which preservation has a higher value than adaptability. The most prominent attempt recently to demonstrate that there were such an institution and such a context for the transmission of sayings of Jesus, the hypotheses of Harald Riesenfeld and Birger Gerhardsson, did not succeed for two principal reasons: first, because the rabbinic model after which the proposed "Jesus-academy" was reconstructed appears to be about a century and a half too late for this purpose; and second, because the forms in which the sayings of Jesus are cast bear hardly any resemblance to the forms produced by the rabbis in question.[2] In this case, at least, scepticism still seems appropriate. Since the question of oral transmission lies outside the area explored by Kennedy, however, this issue need not be carried further here.

Note-Taking

An item that might not be on the New Testament critic's list is note-taking. Since Schleiermacher's *"diēgēsis* hypothesis" early in the nineteenth century,[3] New Testament scholars have almost totally ignored the possible function of notes in the preservation of early tradition and the formation of early Christian literature. Nevertheless, many of the intermediate forms that have been suggested by various critics over the past few decades, such as catenae of miracle stories, collections of sayings, and "testimony" lists of scriptural texts interpreted as prophecies, could more readily be understood as private or limited-circulation *aides-mémoire* than as "published" compositions. We might even con-

---

[2] Harald Riesenfeld, "The Gospel Tradition and Its Beginnings," in *The Gospel Tradition*, trans. E. Margaret Rowley and Robert A. Kraft (Philadelphia: Fortress Press, 1970), 1–29, originally published in monograph form (London: A. R. Mowbray & Co. Limited, 1961); Birger Gerhardsson, *Memory and Manuscript: Oral Tradition and Written Transmission in Rabbinic Judaism and Early Christianity*, trans. E. J. Sharpe, Acta Seminarii Neotestamentici Upsaliensis 22 (Lund: C. W. K. Gleerup/Copenhagen: Ejnar Munksgaard, 1961). Riesenfeld and Gerhardsson argued that the disciples memorized the teaching of Jesus, much as students of the Jewish rabbis memorized the interpretations of their masters, that this practice was continued in the early church, where Christians memorized the teaching of the Apostles, and that, as a result, what eventually passed into the written gospels was the actual life story and teaching of Jesus with very little alteration. For criticisms of this argument, see, e.g., W. D. Davies, "Reflections on A Scandinavian Approach to 'The Gospel Tradition,' " in *Neotestamentica et Patristica. Eine Freundesgabe Herrn Professor Dr. Oscar Cullmann zu seinem 60. Geburtstag überreicht*, Supplements to Novum Testamentum 6 (Leiden: E. J. Brill, 1962), 14–34; Morton Smith, "A Comparison of Early Christian and Early Rabbinic Tradition," *Journal of Biblical Literature*, 82 (1963), 169–176. For Gerhardsson's reply, see his *Tradition and Transmission in Early Christianity*, trans. E. J. Sharpe, Coniectanea Neotestamentica 20 (Lund: C. W. K. Gleerup/Copenhagen: Ejnar Munksgaard, 1964). For further criticism, see Jacob Neusner, *The Rabbinic Traditions about the Pharisees before 70*, pt. 3, *Conclusions* (Leiden: E. J. Brill, 1971), 143–179.

[3] On this, see, e.g., Werner Georg Kümmel, *Introduction to the New Testament*, rev. ed., trans. Howard Clark Kee (Nashville and New York: Abingdon Press, 1975), 45–46.

jecture that the advantage of "notebooks" may be one reason why Christians abandoned the scroll, which was used both for Jewish Scriptures and for pagan literary texts, and adopted the codex form, which was so much easier to use for reference, even for their scriptural texts.[4] In any case, the *hypomnēma* stands on the fluid border between tradition and "literature," and thus Kennedy correctly emphasizes its potential importance for the process of composition of the several gospels. In his proposal about the Papias testimony, he has given one fairly detailed example of how recognition of the importance of notes can affect our reading of texts. This will be discussed more carefully below.

Genre

The question, to what genre, if any, of Greco-Roman literature the gospels can be assigned, is one that has exercised scholars for a long time and has enjoyed some revival of late. Kennedy accepts the widespread view that the gospels constitute a distinct genre, developed in response to the teaching of Jesus (and, I should want to add, in response to the situation of the early Christian groups) somewhat as the dialogue was developed by the followers of Socrates (p. 135). He shifts our attention away from the quest for a comparable genre and inquires instead about the process by which writers did their work.

There is good reason to follow Kennedy's lead, for the question, whether "gospel" names a genre, is not a simple one. How many examples must exist before one can speak of a genre, and how widely recognized must a genre be before anyone who wrote in that mode would find his composition consciously or unconsciously shaped by conventions that "belonged" to the genre? Does it make any sense at all to speak of Mark's having invented the genre (assuming for a moment that the Two-Source Hypoth-

---

[4]I owe this suggestion to my colleague, Nils Alstrup Dahl, who called my attention to P. Yale 1 (Inv. no. 419, Beinecke Rare Book and Manuscript Library). If C. B. Welles' dating is correct, this leaf from a codex of Genesis is the earliest Christian manuscript known and attests the use of the codex format for Scripture as early as A.D. 80–100; see his "The Yale Genesis Fragment," *Yale University Library Gazette*, 39 (1964), 1–8 + 2 plates. Most early biblical manuscripts that are identifiably Christian are from codices. Of the few nonbiblical codices known from second-century Egypt, most are handbooks of one kind or another. See also C. H. Roberts, "P. Yale 1 and the Early Christian Book," in *Essays in Honor of C. Bradford Welles*, ed. A. E. Samuel, American Studies in Papyrology 1 (New Haven: American Society of Papyrologists, 1966), 25–28.

esis is roughly correct) and the others having adapted it, except in retrospect, and would such a retrospective abstraction tell us anything at all about the process of each gospel's composition? The problem is complicated further by the fact that the title "gospel" was used in antiquity for documents that to the modern critic seem to belong to widely diverse types of literature, so that the Gospel of Truth, for example, has less in common with the Gospel according to Mark than either has with other documents that are not called gospels.[5] Kennedy prudently avoids this thicket of questions and admits that "there is no perfect classical analogue" to the problem of the origin of the New Testament gospels (p. 129). Instead, he offers two sets of instructive partial analogies: the formation of the Socratic literature and the common procedures in historiography, biography, and rhetoric.

Classical Analogues to Source Criticism of the Gospels

The principal lesson to be learned from the four "gospels" of Socrates is that even though both notes and good memories must have been involved in the production of all four, the major formative factor was the freedom of Aristophanes, Xenophon, Plato, and Aristotle each to shape the tradition to say what he wanted to say, within the bounds of the developing conventions of the genre he was using. This lesson is certainly in harmony with the viewpoint of recent "redaction (or composition) criticism," which has corrected a tendency of the analytic stage of form criticism to minimize the role of the Evangelists as "authors." On the other hand, the four "gospels" of Socrates may in some respects more fruitfully be compared with the four primitive types of gospel literature reconstructed by Helmut Koester—collections of sayings (*logoi*), collections of miracle stories (aretalogies), revelation discourses, and canonical type gospels[6]—than with the four canonical gospels. For one thing, the interesting chronological "rhythm" pointed out by Kennedy (pp. 134–35) would better fit Koester's hypothetical model.

---

[5] The most valuable discussion of this range of issues that I know is by Norman R. Petersen, Jr., in an unpublished paper, "So-Called Gnostic Type Gospels and the Question of the Genre 'Gospel,' " presented at the 1970 annual meeting of the Society of Biblical Literature.

[6] Helmut Koester, "One Jesus and Four Primitive Gospels," in James M. Robinson and Helmut Koester, *Trajectories through Early Christianity* (Philadelphia: Fortress Press, 1971), 158–204.

One comparison that Kennedy makes with the Socratic tradition seems somewhat wide of the mark. He suggests that Antisthenes has played a role in Socratic source criticism comparable to that of "Q" in Synoptic studies (p. 132). Not quite. In Antisthenes we have a real person mentioned in ancient sources, on whom modern source theories have been hung; on the other hand, "Q" is a modern hypothesis, not to be identified with anything mentioned in ancient sources, but suggested by data in extant texts. The precise parallel to Antisthenes is thus not "Q" but the "*logia* in Hebrew dialect" that Papias said Matthew wrote and that some modern scholars have too hastily identified with "Q." Kennedy himself gives Papias' report rather more credence, "Q" rather less, than I, but more about that later.

Kennedy's discussion of the way historians, biographers, and rhetors worked in antiquity is filled with suggestive details that cannot be more neatly summarized than he has done. These details can be of most help to New Testament scholars by being absorbed into their general *Gestalt* of the cultural ambience of early Christianity. If any general rules emerge, they are those that Kennedy derives from considering the Alexander literature and the histories of the Roman republic: "anything can happen" in ancient writers' use of sources and "not to oversimplify the tradition" (p. 138). If there are still New Testament students who decide casually about, say, Luke's composition of speeches on grounds that "that's the way ancient historians always worked," they can learn here to expunge this "always" from their vocabulary. Oversimplification, on the other hand, does not seem to be an overwhelming danger at this particular moment in the history of our discipline.

Kennedy describes classical writers' uses of sources in ways that are essentially positive; that is, an author draws information from documents, normally depending upon notes that he has made as he read the documents. In such cases the crucial question is how accurately and reliably the author has reported this information. Kennedy does not discuss another kind of use of sources, one that has been very prominent in some New Testament hypotheses, namely, the quotation from a source in order to refute its main content. It is not hard, of course, to find ancient examples of *explicit* polemic like that in Origen's *Contra Celsum* or Irenaeus' refutations of various heretics. It is an altogether different matter, however, if, as is now frequently suggested, the author of Mark incorporated the collection of Jesus' miracles

162

into his book not because he regarded it as containing valuable information, but because he disliked the Christology implicit in the miracle stories and wanted to correct it by putting it into a new context;[7] or, to give another example, if the author of the Letter to Colossians quoted a Wisdom-hymn to Christ not because he approved of it, but because it epitomized the beliefs of the heretics whom he wrote to accuse.[8] In each case, the hypothesized polemic is so implicit and so subtle that it escaped detection until the last decade. If Kennedy knows of any comparable use of sources by pagan writers in antiquity, it would be most illuminating.

Translation

The context in which Kennedy sets the question of translation is helpful, emphasizing the breadth of the concept and the importance of literary models in the receptor language. The former point is relevant to the interest of many New Testament scholars in the Targums (Aramaic interpretive translations or paraphrases of Scripture lections) as an analogy to early Christian interpretation both of Scripture texts and of Jesus' sayings.[9] The primary illustration of the second point, of course, is the fact that the Septuagint served as the primary literary model of New Testament writers, in various ways and to various degrees. This fact itself has obscured the whole question of translation, since it is often impossible to distinguish "Semitisms" from "Septuagintisms."

The question of translation of early Christian traditions and documents is even more complicated than Kennedy allows. Kennedy's opening sentence in the section on "Translation and Imitation" (p. 143) is accurate, but not complete: In all likelihood,

[7] See, e.g., Theodore J. Weeden, *Mark—Traditions in Conflict* (Philadelphia: Fortress Press, 1971).

[8] See, e.g., Ernst Käsemann, "A Primitive Christian Baptismal Liturgy," in *Essays on New Testament Themes*, trans. W. J. Montague, Studies in Biblical Theology 41 (Naperville, Ill.: Alec R. Allenson, Inc., 1964), 149–168, esp. 164–165.

[9] From the large and growing literature, suffice it to mention Roger le Déaut, *Introduction à la littérature targumique* (Rome: Pontifical Biblical Institute Press, 1966); Martin McNamara, *Targum and Testament: Aramaic Paraphrases of the Hebrew Bible: A Light on the New Testament* (Grand Rapids: William B. Eerdmans Publishing Company, 1972); the fine survey by M. P. Miller, "Targum, Midrash and the Use of the Old Testament in the New Testament," *Journal for the Study of Judaism*, 2 (1971), 29–82.

Jesus did speak Aramaic, but he may well have also spoken Hebrew and Greek. Christianity was born in a trilingual culture,
and the archaeological discoveries and epigraphic collections of
recent years have made it difficult to be quite so certain as Gustav
Dalman and all his followers have been that the earliest traditions of and about Jesus *must* have been formulated in Aramaic.[10]
We are not yet in a position to speak with certainty about the
linguistic shift that may have occurred when the cities of the
eastern empire superseded Palestine as the center of gravity of
the Christian movement. Furthermore, we know next to nothing
about any possible continuity between different rural and presumably Semitic-speaking areas (Palestine and the eastern and
rural western parts of Syria). Was there any direct contact between Aramaic-speaking Jewish Christians in Palestine and
Syriac-speaking Christians, or did Syriac Christianity receive
its traditions by (re-?) translation from Greek, urban missions?
What little evidence there is suggests the latter. In any case,
the standard rule of thumb about the Jesus traditions, "Semitic
early; Greek late," looks more and more dubious.

The question, whether the Gospel of Matthew was originally
written in Aramaic, which Kennedy takes for granted, is far from
settled. The recent tendency among New Testament scholars
has been to doubt that it was, despite the tradition to the contrary. This tradition is likely based solely on Papias,[11] and it
remains uncertain precisely what Papias meant. Did "Hebrew
dialect" (*hebrais dialektos*) mean "Aramaic"? This seemed a
reasonable assumption so long as the opinion of Dalman prevailed
that Hebrew was a dead language in first-century Palestine.

[10] See, e.g., H. Ott, "Um die Muttersprache Jesu. Forschungen seit Gustaf
Dalman," *Novum Testamentum*, 9 (1967), 1–25; J. N. Sevenster, *Do You Know
Greek? How Much Greek Could the First Jewish Christians Have Known?* Supplements to Novum Testamentum 19 (Leiden: E. J. Brill, 1968); James Barr,
"Which Language Did Jesus Speak?—Some Remarks of A Semitist," *Bulletin
of the John Rylands Library*, 53 (1970), 9–28; Joseph A. Fitzmyer, "The Languages of Palestine in the First Century A.D.," *The Catholic Biblical Quarterly*,
32 (1970), 501–531; and Ch. Rabin, "Hebrew and Aramaic in the First Century,"
and G. Mussies, "Greek in Palestine and the Diaspora," in *The Jewish People in
the First Century: Historical Geography, Political History, Social, Cultural
and Religious Life and Institutions*, ed. S. Safrai and M. Stern, 2 vols., Com-
pendia Rerum Iudaicarum ad Novum Testamentum 1 (Philadelphia: Fortress
Press, 1974–1976), 2:1007–1039, 1040–1064.

[11] J. Kürzinger, "Irenäus und sein Zeugnis zur Sprache des Matthäusevangeliums," *New Testament Studies*, 10 (1963), 108–115; on this point, 110–111. It
is not so certain that Clement knew Papias, but it seems likely.

With the discovery of the Dead Sea Scrolls, however, most of which were written in Hebrew, it appears that Hebrew was very much alive in the first century, at least as a literary language, and other evidence suggests that it was also used as a spoken language in some circles.[12] There is thus no reason why "Hebrew" in Eusebius cannot mean precisely that.[13] Of course, this is not to say that it *must* mean "Hebrew." In John 19:13, for example, *hebraisti* introduces *Gabbatha*, which is the Grecized form of an Aramaic word.[14] Greek-speaking residents of Hierapolis or Alexandria may not have had a very precise knowledge of the different Semitic dialects. When they spoke of the *hebrais dialektos* they meant the language spoken by "the Hebrews," i.e., the Jews.

Thus, Josef Kürzinger goes so far as to say that *hebrais dialektos* in the Papias report (Eusebius, *Church History* 3.39.16) does not mean "Hebrew language" at all, but "a Jewish style."[15] This is not convincing, but Kürzinger does make some very important observations about the way the sentence from Papias is to be understood. First, Eusebius has interrupted the continuity by inserting his own comment: "This is reported by Papias about Mark, and about Matthew this was said . . ." Read without the interruption, the Papias quotation does not present an independent statement about Matthew, but rather contrasts Mark, who did not make a literary composition, with Matthew, who did. Thus the emphasis is not on *hebraidi dialektō*, whatever it may mean, but on *synetaxato* ("composed"). Moreover, the contrastive clause that follows, which has so baffled modern interpreters, is not talking about translation at all. "Each" still refers to Matthew and Mark,[16] *hērmēneusen* means "presented, expounded, reported," and the meaning is that Matthew and Mark each expounded the gospel as best he could.[17] Thus, if

---

[12] See the works cited above in n. 10.

[13] See, e.g., Ott, "Um die Muttersprache Jesu," 22.

[14] Fitzmyer, "The Languages of Palestine in the First Century A.D.," 528.

[15] J. Kürzinger, "Das Papiaszeugnis und die Erstgestalt des Matthäusevangeliums," *Biblische Zeitschrift*, n. F. 4 (1960), 19–38, esp. 30–34. He finds this supported in Irenaeus' use of Papias ("Irenäus und sein Zeugnis zur Sprache des Matthäusevangeliums"), but his argument in this latter article is not so rigorous as in the earlier one.

[16] Kürzinger is certainly right that the distinction between plural and dual is frequently disregarded in Hellenistic Greek.

[17] Kürzinger, "Das Papiaszeugnis und die Erstgestalt des Matthäusevangeliums," 26–27; cf. H. J. Lawlor's review of the usage of *hermēneia, exēgēsis,*

Papias did know about a Semitic Gospel of Matthew, he does *not* describe its translation into Greek, *nor is a translation of Matthew ever described by the writers who repeat Papias' testimony.*

If the external evidence is obscure, the internal evidence is no clearer. Matthew's language abounds with Semitisms, perhaps more than any other New Testament document,[18] but redactional analysis suggests that its basic structure was composed in Greek. Kennedy's own tentative hypothesis is that the Aramaic Matthew mentioned by Papias was later translated into Greek by someone who, in accord with normal Greek practice, would have used an available Greek gospel, i.e., Mark, as a "pony" (p. 146). Kennedy supports this hypothesis by paraphrasing a sentence from Krister Stendahl regarding the non-Septuagint character of Matthew's formula-quotations.[19] Stendahl, however, at this point is only summarizing old observations by John C. Hawkins, and Kennedy ignores the next sentence: "A closer study of the material, however, yields a more complicated picture." The more complicated picture includes the facts that the formula-quotations of Matthew, while deviating from the Septuagint, do not ally themselves simply with the Masoretic or any other single, familiar text type and that other quotations and allusions peculiar to Matthew do depend on the Septuagint. Thus, Stendahl concludes, and this conclusion is reiterated in the preface of his second edition, that Matthew "was produced as a Greek original, dependent on the Greek Mark and a Greek Q."[20]

---

and the cognate verbs in "Eusebius on Papias," *Hermathena*, 43 (1921), 173–188. Lucian, describing the historian's craft, uses *hermēneuein* in precisely the sense Kürzinger proposes (*How to Write History* 6, where K. Kilburn [*Lucian.* With an English translation by A. M. Harmon, K. Kilburn, and M. D. Macleod, 8 vols., The Loeb Classical Library (Cambridge, Mass.: Harvard University Press/ London: William Heinemann Ltd., 1959), 6:9] appropriately translates, "to put the facts into words"). What both Matthew and Mark were "putting into words" was the *logia* of the Lord. It is now generally conceded, as Kennedy observes, that this cannot mean only "sayings," but *ta hypo tou kyriou ē lechthenta ē prachthenta*, i.e., "the gospel."

[18] See Klaus Beyer, *Semitische Syntax im Neuen Testament*, vol. 1, *Satzlehre*, pt. 1, 2d ed. (Göttingen: Vandenhoeck & Ruprecht, 1968), 296–299 *et passim.* H. Ott ("Um die Muttersprache Jesu," esp. 21–22) claims that Matthew's Semitisms clearly betray a Hebrew rather than an Aramaic orientation, but he thinks the language of composition was Greek.

[19] Krister Stendahl, *The School of St. Matthew and Its Use of the Old Testament*, 1st American ed. (Philadelphia: Fortress Press, 1968), 45.

[20] Stendahl, *The School of St. Matthew and Its Use of the Old Testament*, x.

External Evidence

The issue of translation leads us to the question of the external evidence, especially the report of Papias. It is here that Kennedy has made his most original and interesting suggestions. He contends that, in the excerpt from Papias' *Logiōn kyriakōn exēgēs(e)is* reproduced by Eusebius (*Church History* 3.39.15–16), "Papias is not describing the actual composition of Mark's Gospel; he is describing the note-taking that was preliminary to composition" (p. 148). Kennedy supports this suggestion by observing that earlier (2.15) Eusebius, depending on Clement's *Hypotyposes*, reports that Peter's followers asked from Mark only a *hypomnēma*, a set of notes. There is even stronger support, however, from another writing attributed to Clement, the fragmentary Letter to Theodore discovered by Morton Smith in 1958 and recently published. After summarizing the *Hypotyposes* report ("during Peter's stay in Rome he wrote an account of the Lord's doings [*praxeis*] . . ."), this document goes on to tell of Mark's coming to Alexandria, "bringing both his own notes (*hypomnēmata*) and those of Peter, from which he transferred to his former book the things suitable to whatever makes for progress toward knowledge. Thus he composed a more spiritual Gospel . . ."[21] If this letter is authentic, and Smith has made a powerful case that it is, then we have here Clement's own authoritative expansion of his *Hypotyposes* report, and it agrees precisely with Kennedy's reconstruction of the two stages of note-gathering and gospel composition, while adding yet a third stage, revision into a second, esoteric gospel.[22]

---

[21] Fol. 1 recto, 16–22. Translation in Morton Smith, *Clement of Alexandria and a Secret Gospel of Mark* (Cambridge, Mass.: Harvard University Press, 1973), 446.

[22] One puzzle introduced by the Letter to Theodore is the question, what relationship Clement may have seen between the "Secret Gospel of Mark" and the Gospel of John, for there is striking similarity between the language of this passage, which calls the esoteric Mark a *pneumatikōteron euangelion*, and the *Hypotyposes* passage quoted by Eusebius in *Church History* 6.14.5–7, where Clement contrasts all the Synoptics with John, a *pneumatikon euangelion*. Did both serve somewhat esoteric functions in the Alexandrian church? The picture is further complicated by the fact that the added passages quoted by Clement from the Secret Mark have several Johannine elements, including a parallel to the Lazarus story. Some have tried to show that these elements are drawn from the canonical John (e.g., Helmut Merkel, "Auf den Spuren des Urmarkus? Ein neuer Fund und seine Beurteilung," *Zeitschrift für Theologie und Kirche*, 71 [1974], 123–144; Raymond E. Brown, "The Relation of 'the Secret Gospel of Mark' to

It is interesting to compare both the Papias and the Clement reports with the way Lucian said history ought to be written:

He [sc. the *syggrapheus*] should for preference be an eyewitness, but, if not, listen to those who tell the more impartial story. . . . When he has collected all or most of the facts let him first make them into a series of notes (*hypomnēma ti*), a body of material as yet with no beauty or continuity. Then, after arranging them into order (*taxin*), let him give it beauty and enhance it with the charms of expression, figure, and rhythm.[23]

This clearly is the kind of procedure that Papias and Clement imagine the gospel writers to have followed. Papias (or the Elder) and Clement in the *Hypotyposes* describe only the first stage of writing, the *hypomnēma*; in the Letter to Theodore, Clement mentions also the finished composition and its later revision, not to add beauty for the public eye, but to add further content for those initiated "into the great mysteries."

The problem with this reconstruction is that Eusebius himself appears to have identified the *hypomnēma* produced by Mark with the canonical gospel itself. Granting with Kennedy that the statement in *Church History* 2.15 need not identify the two, it is nevertheless difficult to read the second version of the same report (6.14.6) in any other way. There, too, the crowds persuade Mark to "write up what was spoken," and Clement says, "When he had done this, he distributed the Gospel among those that asked him."[24] Of course it may be, as Kennedy suggests, that Eusebius has "a somewhat confused picture" (p. 151) while Clement himself had another stage of composition in mind. The Letter to Theodore would support this. On the other hand, Kür-

---

the Fourth Gospel," *The Catholic Biblical Quarterly*, 36 [1974], 466–485), but, on the whole, Smith's argument that both depend on a common source is more convincing, even if one does not accept his entire reconstruction (see his *Clement of Alexandria and a Secret Gospel of Mark*, 146–163; "Merkel on the Longer Text of Mark," *Zeitschrift für Theologie und Kirche*, 72 [1975], 133–150).

[23] Lucian, *How to Write History* 47–48, translation by K. Kilburn in *Lucian*, Loeb 6:61.

[24] The early sixth century Latin translation and adaptation of parts of the *Hypotyposes* apparently also understands the Gospel of Mark as the immediate product of Mark's note-taking: "Marcus . . . praedicante Petro evangelium . . . coram quibusdam Caesareanis equitibus . . ., petitus ab eis, ut possent quae dicebantur memoriae commendare, scripsit ex his, quae a Petro dicta sunt, evangelium quod secundum Marcum vocitatur . . ." (*Adumbrationes Clementis Alexandrini in Epistolas Canonicas* 3.206.17ff, as quoted by Smith in *Clement of Alexandria and a Secret Gospel of Mark*, 20).

zinger has argued persuasively that Papias intended to portray precisely the canonical Gospel of Mark as a *hypomnēma*. The Gospel should not therefore be disparaged, Papias was saying, for lacking the elegance expected of a literary composition (*taxis*), because such elegance had not been Mark's purpose. Though Matthew had indeed made such a literary composition (*synetaxato*), in "Hebrew" dialect, the point is that each was presenting the facts (*hērmēneusen*) as he was able.[25]

Kennedy's suggestion about *Church History* 6.14.5–6 also merits careful consideration. He interprets the passage to mean not that Clement regarded the two gospels with genealogies (Matthew and Luke) as having been written prior to Mark, but rather that Clement contrasted all three with John, which was written last. Kennedy concedes that Origen, in a passage quoted later by Eusebius (*Church History* 6.25.4), does put (Hebrew) Matthew first (*prōton men . . .*), but this latter passage may not count heavily in the question of order, for Origen is not discussing this question. Rather, he is insisting that *only four* gospels are to be taken as authoritative and is defending such a claim for each of the four, following the order that had already become most common. Origen may also assume that this order was the chronological order of composition, but he does not explicitly claim to have information about this latter point.

There is another question, however, that must be raised about all these testimonies. Is everything reported by these authors as "learned by tradition" really based on early reports, or does "tradition" also incorporate learned deductions that the fathers have made from internal evidence in the New Testament writings? The question sounds like just the kind of scepticism about which Kennedy is sceptical, but, at least in the case of Clement's *Hypotyposes*, it can be shown in one instance to be well-grounded. Just before the passage about the gospels, Eusebius has quoted another excerpt from the *Hypotyposes*:

---

[25] Kürzinger, "Das Papiaszeugnis und die Erstgestalt des Matthäusevangeliums." I have paraphrased in accordance with Kürzinger's translation (35). Similarly, Lucian is willing to excuse a historian who has compiled a *hypomnēma tōn gegonotōn gymnon*, for, though it is apparent that the writer is an amateur (*idiōtēs*), he has performed a valuable labor, which a trained writer might use later (*How to Write History* 16). Strabo called his forty-seven-book history only *hypomnēmata*, and his chief claim for it was that it was "useful." In contrast, the *Geography*, composed with similar aims, but perhaps more ambitiously, was a *syntaxis* (1.1.23).

And as for the Epistle to the Hebrews, he [sc. Clement] says indeed that it is Paul's, but that it was written for Hebrews in the Hebrew tongue (*hebraikę phonę*), and that Luke, having carefully translated it, published it for the Greeks; hence, as a result of this translation, the same complexion of style is found in this Epistle and the Acts.[26]

Clement goes on to explain (6.14.3) why Paul's name is not mentioned in the superscript of Hebrews and supports this by what "the blessed Elder used to say" (6.14.4). I think no one who has read Hebrews carefully will give this report an ounce of credence. According to Eusebius, Origen records it briefly, together with an alternative tradition, and rejects both. "But who wrote the epistle," he says, "in truth God knows" (*Church History* 6.25. 13–14). How did the "tradition" arise? Evidently by Clement, or someone before him, making a deduction from (1) the growing acceptance among Catholics of Hebrews as "Pauline," (2) its actual anonymity, (3) some superficial observations about style (Luke-Acts and Hebrews are fairly similar, Paul quite different), and (4) the fact that Luke was known as Paul's disciple.

Origen's own speculation, which he candidly expresses as such (*Church History* 6.25.13), is also illuminating for our problem. Hebrews was written, he suggests, by someone who "called to mind (*apomnēmoneusantos*) the Apostle's teachings and, as it were, made short notes (*scholiographēsantos*) of what his master said."[27] This is precisely the way Papias described the relation between Peter and Mark, as clarified by Kennedy! Moreover, both Clement and Origen base the relationship between Peter and Mark, as well as Mark's presence in Rome, on the statement in 1 Peter 5:13 (*Church History* 2.15; 6.25.5), and in Eusebius' summary of Papias' work, the only epistles mentioned are 1 John and 1 Peter (3.39.17). Is it then hypersceptical to conjecture that Papias' tradition from the Elder of Ephesus originated as a learned deduction from 1 Peter 5:13 and the unrhetorical style of Mark's Gospel?

In any case, there are grave limits to the probative power of all these reports. (1) Most surprisingly, in view of the use to which they have often been put, they are completely uninter-

---

[26] Eusebius, *Church History* 6.14.2; translation from Eusebius, *The Ecclesiastical History*. With an English translation by Kirsopp Lake and J. E. L. Oulton, 2 vols., The Loeb Classical Library (Cambridge, Mass.: Harvard University Press/London: William Heinemann Ltd., 1926–1932), 2:47.

[27] Translation from Eusebius, *The Ecclesiastical History*, Loeb 2: 77–79.

ested in the "Synoptic Problem." Both Papias and Clement write as if there were *no literary connection* between any of the gospels. The insistence that Mark was the *hermēneutēs* of Peter precludes, in Papias' picture of things, Mark's having depended on Matthew. Papias mentions Matthew after he mentions Mark, and he contrasts the two, but he does not suggest that Matthew depended on Mark. Clement and Origen, on the other hand, mention the gospels in the orders, respectively, Matthew, Luke, Mark, John and Matthew, Mark, Luke, John, but neither has a word to say about dependence. (2) Even when these authors speak of the order of the gospels, it is not certain that it is the *chronological* order with which they are concerned. (3) The Hebrew (Aramaic?) *logia* composed by Matthew remains a will-o'-the-wisp. (4) There is great difficulty in connecting these reports with what we actually see in the extant gospels. What parts of Mark would one identify as summary notes on Peter's preaching?

Other Issues

Though there are many other parts of Kennedy's essay that deserve careful discussion, the response ought not to become longer than the primary statement. Thus I shall mention only two general issues that he raises. First, he does not directly address the question of the social setting in which traditions are transmitted and documents composed. If I read him correctly, the implication of his comparisons is that the early Christian transmitters and authors belonged to a relatively learned circle, analogous to the rhetorical schools. This kind of analogy is certainly not to be dismissed out-of-hand, as has so frequently happened under the influence of the Deissmannesque presumption that all early Christians belonged to the "non-literary classes."[28] Yet, even if the social status of all the Christians was not too low to expect contemporary rhetorical and literary models to be effective, one must question the extent to which the examples Kennedy puts forward are really analogous to the internal lit-

---

[28] For an important discussion of recent evidence that tends to redress the balance, see the work by my colleague, Abraham J. Malherbe, *Social Aspects of Early Christianity*, Rockwell Lectures, Rice University (Baton Rouge and London: Louisiana State University Press, 1977), esp. 29–59 ("Social Level and Literary Culture").

erature of a *sect*. Perhaps if we knew more about the (Neo-)Pythagoreans or the Epicureans, we might have a better vantage point from which to answer this question.

Second, Kennedy's emphasis on the *preaching* of the Apostles as the core of the material organized by the Evangelists is reminiscent of Martin Dibelius' assumption that missionary preaching was the primary *Sitz im Leben* of the Synoptic traditions.[29] Has Papias exerted undue influence here? This limitation to missionary preaching does not suit either what we should expect, a priori, to be happening as a new sect constituted itself or the hints in the epistolary literature about the ways in which traditions were in fact used. Neither does it fit what we can deduce from the forms of the individual pericopes in the gospels. The process by which the early Christians "remembered" the sayings and doings of Jesus was virtually coextensive with the shape of the Christian groups and their activities: their rituals, their catechesis, their hymns and chants, their ecstatic speech and prophecy, their *paraenesis*.[30] It is useful to focus, as Kennedy does, on one aspect of this process, an aspect that can be illuminated from common practices in the Greco-Roman world, but it is also probable that just as there is no "perfect classical analogue" to the source criticism of the gospels, so there is no precise sociological analogue to the Christian sect among the other movements in the Greco-Roman world.

Conclusion

George Kennedy has not pretended to offer a solution to our problems, but he has done something far more useful. He has allowed us to overhear him thinking out loud, as it were, about a number of problems that parallel and overlap our own. To watch a learned, supple, and disciplined mind at work is always an exciting experience, and in this case the experience is precisely tuned to set our own imaginations humming.

[29] See, e.g., Martin Dibelius, *From Tradition to Gospel*, trans. Bertram Lee Woolf (New York: Charles Scribner's Sons, 1934), 13, originally published in German in 1919.
[30] See Nils Alstrup Dahl, "Anamnesis: Memory and Commemoration in Early Christianity," in *Jesus in the Memory of the Early Church* (Minneapolis: Augsburg Publishing House, 1976), 11–29, and also the afterword, "The Early Church and Jesus," in the same volume, 167–175.

Classics and the Gospels: The Seminar

Reginald H. Fuller

Complexity of the Synoptic Problem

In the final section of his essay, George Kennedy concludes that the relationships among the Synoptic Gospels are anything but simple:

> The inability of New Testament scholars over a period of two hundred years to agree on the history of the composition of the gospels, despite a general agreement that there are signs of a literary relationship, suggests that the true relationship may be very complex. (p. 153)

Kennedy then suggests that the reason for this complexity is the probable fact that the Evangelists did not simply copy their predecessors. Rather, and more importantly, there may well have been a good deal of cross-fertilization from the use of each other's notes and from ongoing oral tradition:

> . . . it is . . . not impossible both that Matthew could have influenced Mark and that Mark could have influenced our text of Matthew: Their authors could have used each other's notes, the second to write a systematic gospel could have had knowledge of the first, and the Greek translation of Matthew, if the Gospel was composed in Aramaic . . . could have utilized significant portions of the text of Mark. Luke could have used the notes of Matthew or Mark, the Aramaic text of Matthew, the Greek text of Mark, or the Greek text of Matthew, if a translation

was then available, but notes or oral tradition used by Luke could also have been used by Matthew and Mark, and the Greek translation of Matthew, if later than Luke, could have been influenced by Luke. . . . (pp. 153–54)

Most New Testament scholars, even those who advocate an alternative to the Two-Document Hypothesis, still assume a simple solution to the Synoptic Problem. One of the unintended consequences of attempts by William R. Farmer and others to revive the Griesbach Hypothesis, however, has been that a few have come to recognize the complexity of the problem. For instance, Frederick Houk Borsch wrote a decade ago:

We also have many reservations about this hypothesis [sc., that Matthew and Luke used Mark] and welcome, without accepting his conclusion, the overdue challenges of W. R. Farmer. . . . It is our view that, despite all their attractions, the simpler solutions to the source problem are manifestly insufficient. The complexity of the evidence suggests a need to reconsider theories which respect the capacities of oral tradition or, at the least, possibilities concerning different recensions of Mark or a source common to the three Gospels.[1]

Somewhat later, E. P. Sanders expressed himself in a similar vein:

I rather suspect that when and if a new view of the Synoptic problem becomes accepted, it will be more flexible and complicated than the tidy two-document hypothesis. With all due respect for scientific preference for the simpler view, the evidence seems to require a more complicated one.[2]

We might add that such a new view will likely "be more flexible and complicated" than any other tidy hypothesis such as the Augustinian or neo-Griesbachian.

Two other New Testament scholars have gone further, seeking an explanation of this complexity in the cross-fertilization of oral traditions. In 1975, reviewing the discussion of the Synoptic Problem during the ten years after the publication of Farmer's book, I suggested that:

Farmer has compelled those who accept the two-document hypothesis to demonstrate its tenability pericope by pericope. . . . Henceforth,

[1] Frederick Houk Borsch, *The Son of Man in Myth and History*, The New Testament Library (London: SCM Press Ltd, 1967), 17, n. 3.

[2] E. P. Sanders, *The Tendencies of the Synoptic Tradition*, Society for New Testament Studies Monograph Series 9 (Cambridge: Cambridge University Press, 1969), 279.

when we work on the synoptic tradition, all the available direction indicators must be applied afresh to every pericope. We must even be prepared to find them working in opposite directions, without committing ourselves in advance to one synoptic theory. Normally, for instance, I have found that the redaction goes from Mark to Matthew/Luke, but in working recently on the double commandment of love I found that it seemingly went from Matthew to Mark. This . . . may mean . . . the continued circulation of oral tradition after it had assumed written form in the gospels.[3]

More recently, John A. T. Robinson has noted the probable complexity of the relationships among the Synoptic Gospels and offered an explanation similar both to my own of a year before and to part of what Kennedy suggested in his essay:

We have been accustomed for so long to what might be called linear solutions to the synoptic problem, where one gospel simply 'used' another and must therefore be set later, that it is difficult to urge a more fluid and complex interrelation between them and their traditions without being accused of introducing unnecessary hypotheses and modifications. But if we have learnt anything over the past fifty years it is surely that whereas epistles were written for specific occasions (though they might be added to or adapted later), gospels were essentially for continuous use in the preaching, teaching, apologetic and liturgical life of the Christian communities. They grew out of *and with* the needs. One can only put approximate dates to certain states or stages and set a certain *terminus ad quem* for them, according to what they do or do not reflect. At any stage in this development one must be prepared to allow for cross-fertilization between the on-going traditions. This does not mean that all interrelationships are equally probable or that rigorous sifting of various hypotheses to explain them is not required.[4]

Although Robinson was concerned with the dating of the gospels rather than with the relationships among them, his words correspond remarkably with Kennedy's conclusions, which, in turn, are supported by Borsch, Sanders, and my own earlier suggestion. Kennedy has added the further complicating factor, however, of the Evangelists' use of each other's notes, of which more anon.

The most significant point made by Kennedy's essay may well

[3] Reginald H. Fuller, "The Synoptic Problem: After Ten Years," *The Perkins School of Theology Journal*, 28 (1975), 67.

[4] John A. T. Robinson, *Redating the New Testament* (Philadelphia: The Westminster Press, 1976), 94. The entire passage (93–95) is well worth reading, even if most of us would not accept Robinson's attempt to prove that all of the New Testament writings were produced before the fall of Jerusalem in A.D. 70.

be that regarding the complex relationships and cross-fertilization of oral tradition and notes at different stages through the final composition of the Synoptic Gospels. This means that future study of the redaction of the gospels must be conducted without presuming a simplistic solution to the Synoptic Problem. We can no longer assume in any given pericope that the relationship goes in one particular direction; it may go either way. Indeed, during the seminar discussion, Kennedy maintained that, given the "fluidity" of the situation in first-century Christianity, any given passage of any of the Synoptic Gospels could have been influenced by any passage of any of the other Synoptics.[5] In this connection, the sharpening of what Farmer has called the "canons of criticism" and others have called "criteria" or "direction indicators"[6] is an urgent necessity, not with the hope of "solving the Synoptic Problem," which, at the present juncture, seems both impossible and unnecessary, but in order to distinguish in any given instance between tradition and redaction.

External Evidence Regarding Origin of the Gospels

The Value of External Evidence. Perhaps the greatest surprise occasioned by Kennedy's essay was the weight that he attached to the external evidence regarding the composition of the gospels and particularly to the quotations from Papias in Eusebius. In the seminar discussion, Kennedy went even further than he had done in his essay, accepting as "hard evidence" derived from Papias not only the material from Eusebius, *Church History* 3.39.15–16, but also the information in 3.24.5–7. Putting this material together, he argued, in the absence of compelling evidence to the contrary, for the following order in the composition of the gospels: Aramaic Matthew, Mark's *hypomnēmata*, Mark's Gospel, Luke, Matthew in Greek, and John.

New Testament scholars have had increasing reservations about the value of external evidence regarding the composition

---

[5] Subsequent references to the seminar discussion will not be documented. In the preparation of this paper I used audio tapes of the discussion, and these tapes will be retained by the editor of this volume.

[6] William R. Farmer, *The Synoptic Problem: A Critical Analysis* (New York: The Macmillan Company/London: Collier-Macmillan Limited, 1964), 227–229. Farmer's book is now available in a very slightly revised edition (Dillsboro, N.C.: Western North Carolina Press, 1976), but unless otherwise indicated, all references will be to the first edition.

of the gospels and particularly of the testimony of Papias. To begin with, the meaning of many words and phrases in the citations from Papias and others is highly uncertain and subject to various conflicting interpretations. Then, the successive movements of source, form, and redaction criticism have all contributed to the erosion of confidence. First, source criticism deduced that there was a direct literary relationship among the Synoptics, about which Papias (and the rest of the external evidence prior to Augustine) said nothing, and that Matthew's apparent use of Mark as a source invalidated Papias' statement that Matthew was originally written in Aramaic.[7] Second, form criticism concluded that the gospels were the end product of oral transmission, that they constituted collections of originally isolated units (pericopes), and that they thus could not be regarded as direct, or even second-hand, records of apostolic preaching.[8] Finally, redaction criticism suggested that the motives for composing the gospels were much more complex and theological in character than the simple desire to preserve the teaching of the Apostles after their deaths. In addition, the negative attitude toward Papias arising from source, form, and redaction criticism seemed to have the support of Eusebius himself, who did not think very highly of Papias' intelligence.[9] The common critical attitude toward Papias is well summed up by Werner Georg Kümmel:

Admittedly the meaning of the words used by Papias to characterize Mt and Mk, and accordingly the translation of the passage as a whole, are highly disputed, so that it is methodologically inappropriate to try to clarify the literary relationships between the Synoptics, and the origin of Mt and Mk, by appeal to the information from Papias, as is widely done even today.[10]

Kennedy, on the other hand, insisted in the seminar discussion that the appropriate method, as used by classical scholars when dealing with any piece of ancient literature, was to go to the external evidence *first* before resorting to modern methods of ana-

[7] Supporters of the Two-Document Hypothesis have occasionally invoked Papias in support of Marcan priority on the ground that he mentions Matthew after Mark.

[8] Form critics have occasionally appealed for support to Papias' characterization of Mark as written *ou taxei*, taking *taxis* to mean chronological order.

[9] Eusebius describes Papias as *sphodra . . .smikros ton noun* (*Church History* 3.39.13).

[10] Werner Georg Kümmel, *Introduction to the New Testament*, rev. ed., trans. Howard Clark Kee (Nashville and New York: Abingdon Press, 1975), 53.

lyzing the text. The external evidence must be taken very seriously and only abandoned if this is made necessary by internal considerations that are irreconcilable with the external data. Moreover, Kennedy pointed out, Papias is very early, antedating Marcion and the particular ecclesiastical motivations that developed after the middle of the second century for claiming apostolic authorship for Christian writings; thus Papias should not be suspected at this point of fabrication for polemical reasons. In response, it was conceded that New Testament scholars generally have not taken the external evidence (especially that of Papias) seriously enough, that they have accepted Eusebius' verdict on Papias too easily, and that they have tended to concentrate on isolated snippets from his writing without adequate attention to the form and function of the quotations.

Note-taking as Intermediate Stage in Gospel Composition: The Papias Testimony. Kennedy later agreed that he would not press for the acceptance of the details of Papias' statements. He would not attach too much importance, for instance, to the names of Peter and Mark. He would plead, however, for acceptance of the central core, which is that the gospels, or at least Mark, came into being in three stages: first, the apostolic preaching; second, the compiling of notes (*hypomnēmata*); third, the composition of gospels. It was agreed on all sides that Kennedy had rendered an important contribution by introducing the intermediate stage of note-taking in the process of gospel composition, but the question was raised, whether there is a congruity between the internal and external evidence on this point. Does Mark, in fact, look as if it was based on the *hypomnēmata* of preaching? Kennedy replied that it did, pointing out that Mark's Gospel follows the three stages of ancient rhetorical composition: (1)*logos*: initial assertion of the divinity of Jesus; (2)*ēthos*: selection of events in the life of Jesus proving the truth of the assertion; and (3)*pathos*: the rhetorical tension of the passion. In response to an expression of scepticism about using rhetorical patterns as a key to the structure of Mark on the grounds that such patterns could be found in almost any composition, Kennedy acknowledged that it was, in large part, his personal interest in ancient rhetoric (he is currently planning to write a book on early Christian rhetoric) that led him to approach the gospels as records specifically of early Christian *preaching*.

It was pointed out that, when Mark is broken down into pericopes, these smaller units of material seem to have served func- 178 tions other than just preaching. Martin Dibelius perhaps over-emphasized preaching, and now one recognizes a whole variety of activities in the early communities that led to the shaping of the material: catechetical, liturgical, apologetic, controversial, etc. Later in the discussion, this observation was fleshed out, and a plausible suggestion was offered for the role of *hypomnē-mata* behind Mark. Wayne A. Meeks called attention to the view that various collections of sayings, miracle stories, scriptural texts interpreted as prophecies, and the like were produced in the early church, suggesting that such pre-gospel collections were the sort of thing that might initially have been recorded in the form of *hypomnēmata*.

If scholars are prepared to grant this, I believe that some of the conclusions of form criticism can and probably should be modified in a significant way. The form critics started out by emphasizing the kerygmatic nature of the gospel tradition, viz., the shaping of the Jesus-tradition as a means of proclaiming the eschatological salvation event, but they developed their work along lines that emphasized rather the importation of alien forms and alien ideas into the tradition (especially in the miracle stories, where Jesus was portrayed in Hellenistic terms as a *theios anēr* or "divine man"). If, however, we give more weight again to the Papias tradition; if, in agreement with Kennedy, we view the first stage of gospel writing as the reduction into notes of the oral proclamation (in its widest sense, of course, including catechesis, apologetic, controversy, aetiological cult narratives, etc.) of the apostolic witnesses (symbolized for Papias by the figure of Peter); and if we see these notes, in turn, as the basis for the Evangelists' composition; then it becomes possible to overcome the excessive scepticism of which Kennedy not unjustly complains. The whole process of the development of the gospel tradition, under the assumption of a direct link (via the *hypomnēmata*) between the gospels and the original apostolic witnesses, becomes much more controllable and less subject to outside accretion. Of course, one must still allow for the constant reinterpretation of the Jesus-tradition by his followers. The first major development is the reassessment of this tradition in the light of the Easter faith. It is precisely this reassessment that makes the Jesus tradition apostolic. At this point it becomes no longer the memories of the words and deeds of a dead prophet, but the vehicle for the proclaiming of the risen Lord and his continued Lordship in the post-Easter community. Papias, then, allows us to infer that it was the same apostolic witnesses, at least at first, who continued to adapt this tradition to the needs[11] of their successive hearers, that the *hypomnēmata* which the Evangelists used recorded these adaptations, and that the Evangelists finally redacted these *hypomnēmata* to meet the further needs of their own times (though Papias does not talk of the final stage of gospel composition here). In short, if we take Papias seriously, it will mean not that we shall revive his precise theory regarding the connection of Mark with Peter, but that we shall become less sceptical about the development of the gospel traditions. They were continually *adapted* to meet new needs, not created anew either from extraneous sources, as the form critics too often supposed, or by the Evangelists themselves, as the redaction critics so often suggest. If extraneous importations were occasionally made (e.g., the Gadarene Swine or the Cana Miracle), this was done in the service of the kerygma. To sum up: Kennedy's introduction of the *hypomnēmata* as an intermediate stage in the process of gospel composition demands a reassessment and a revision of the more sceptical historical assumptions of form and redaction criticism.

Other Points in the Papias Testimony. Certain other details of the Papias testimony in Eusebius, *Church History* 3.39.15–16, received attention in the seminar discussion. Kennedy's interpretation of *ou . . . taxei* ("not in order") as implying a contrast between the *hypomnēmata* and the finished gospel (cf. *syntaxin*, "a systematic account," and, with reference to Matthew, *synetaxato*, "composed") was generally regarded as suggestive and helpful, and most were apparently convinced that the term, *logia*, referred not just to "sayings" but rather to "[what] had been said or done by the Lord," i.e., to a gospel as such. In response to a question about the precise meaning of *ouden hēmarten*, which he had translated "Mark was sure of making no mistake" (p. 147), Kennedy replied that *hamartanein* means, literally, "to miss the mark" and that *ouden hēmarten*, therefore, is neither a complaint about Mark's poor style or lack of

---

[11] Greek: *pros tas chreias*. Bernard Orchard noted the interpretation of *chreiai* as "chriai" or short biographical *apophthegms*, a view first advanced by R. O. P. Taylor in his *The Groundwork of the Gospels* (Oxford: Oxford University Press, 1946), 75–90. Cf. also J. Kürzinger, "Das Papiaszeugnis und die Erstgestalt des Matthäusevangeliums," *Biblische Zeitschrift*, n. F. 4 (1960), 23, n. 7. Such an interpretation has the advantage of not requiring some additional phrase like "of his hearers."

rhetorical training, as had been suggested by Josef Kürzinger,[12] nor a reference to his absence of chronological order, as is often held.[13] Rather, it must simply mean that someone has questioned the accuracy of Mark's notes as a record of Peter's preaching, and Papias is insisting that Mark made every effort to be accurate.

It was suggested that the phrase, *hērmēneusen d'auta hōs ēn dynatos hekastos*, be translated to mean that "each expounded Matthew" and to equate "each" with Luke and Mark, successively, which, of course, would support the Griesbach Hypothesis. Attention was also called to Kürzinger's suggestion that Eusebius has split the Papias citation into two by inserting his own comments ("This is told by Papias on the subject of Mark. On the subject of Matthew this was said [by Papias]."), that the citation regarding Mark and Matthew was continuous, and that the implied subject of the last verb, *hērmēneusen*, was "Matthew and Mark" (each of them).[14] Kennedy thought this latter suggestion worth considering but insisted that *hērmēneusen* could only refer to translation, not to exposition.

There was a general scepticism in the seminar regarding Kennedy's inference from Papias that canonical Matthew was a translation from Aramaic. Kennedy appreciated the difficulties but was sure that they could adequately be accounted for by the classical concept of translation, which could include anything from literal translation through paraphrase to the use of already existing literature as a "pony." At the moment of translation, there would have been great pressure to conform the translation to similar documents in the recipient language; in this instance to conform Greek Matthew to Mark. At other times, the pressure might operate in the other direction, that of variation.

Following the external evidence, Kennedy attributed the literary crystallization of the gospel tradition to the crisis occasioned by the deaths of the Apostles and the disappearance of the original eyewitnesses. In response to the suggestion that composition of the gospels was motivated primarily by the concerns of emerging catholicism (*Frühkatholizismus*), such as the delay of the parousia and the emergence of false teaching, Ken-

[12] Kürzinger, "Das Papiaszeugnis und die Erstgestalt des Matthäusevangeliums," 23–25.

[13] See n. 8 above.

[14] Kürzinger, "Das Papiaszeugnis und die Erstgestalt des Matthäusevangeliums," 21–23.

nedy acknowledged that the delay in the parousia was a possible factor in the situation, but he argued that the reason given by Eusebius, the deaths of the Apostles, was a plausible one, even though there may also have been others. Indeed, the deaths of the Apostles and the consequent need to preserve the apostolic witness in the next generation is itself one of the features of *Frühkatholizismus*, and since the other features were of a more temporary and changing character, the need to preserve the apostolic witness would be the one feature that continued to be emphasized in the second century. Eusebius' explanation of the cause of gospel writing is thus not necessarily inconsistent with the explanations of modern scholarship.

Other "Hard Evidence." The Papias testimony was not the only piece of "hard evidence" regarding the origin of the gospels brought forward by Kennedy. He also introduced into the discussion two passages from the New Testament. One was Mark 14:9, "wherever the gospel is preached in the whole world, what she [*sc.* the woman who anointed Jesus] has done will be told in memory of her" (cf. Matthew 26:13). To Kennedy, this showed that Mark's Gospel was the deposit of Christian *preaching*. To the modern redaction critic, however, it is doubtful whether this passage can be used in this way, since most would regard it as part of the Marcan redaction[15] and see it as referring not to the pre-literary stage of the tradition, but to Mark's Gospel itself. Mark understood his work as gospel. It had kerygmatic character. This does not mean, however, that Mark understood his work to be the deposit of preaching in the narrower sense of the word.

Kennedy's third bit of "hard evidence" was the Lucan prologue (Luke 1:1-4). Kennedy was fully aware of the stylized character of the prologue, but he maintained that since Greek had distinct forms for the singular, the dual, and the plural numbers, the presence of the plural form, *polloi* ("many"), clearly refers to a plurality, thus implying at least three gospels before Luke. To the suggestion that the singular, *diēgēsin* ("a narrative"), meant that "many" (the Matthean "school"?)[16] had joined together to produce a single *diēgēsis* or gospel, Kennedy

---

[15] See, e.g., Willi Marxsen, *Mark the Evangelist: Studies on the Redaction History of the Gospel*, trans. James Boyce, Donald Juel, William Poehlmann with Roy A. Harrisville (Nashville and New York: Abingdon Press, 1969), 122–125.

[16] See Krister Stendahl, *The School of St. Matthew and Its Use of the Old Testament*, 1st American ed. (Philadelphia: Fortress Press, 1968).

replied that since the natural interpretation of the Greek was that each had produced his own *diēgēsis*, he would not find the alternative suggestion persuasive in the absence of other evidence to support it.

Bernard Orchard called attention to the remarkable verbal parallels between the statement about Mark in the Papias testimony (Eusebius, *Church History* 3.39.15), *akribōs egrapsen, ou mentoi taxei* ("he wrote accurately, not, indeed, in order"), and the words in the Lucan prologue (1:3), *akribōs kathexēs . . . grapsai* ("to write accurately in order").[17] Noting the surprising fact that the Papias testimony, as quoted by Eusebius, makes no reference to Luke, which surely had been written by Papias' time, Orchard suggested that Papias had, in fact, been discussing Luke just prior to the point where Eusebius' quotation begins. This suggestion was not pursued, however, in the seminar discussion.

Summary. As a result of Kennedy's essay and the subsequent discussion, New Testament scholars have been challenged to take more seriously the external evidence regarding the origin of the gospels than they have been wont to do in the recent past. They likely will not agree with Kennedy that it must be given priority over the internal evidence, but they must henceforth exercise great caution when they spin off theories about the internal evidence that flatly contradict the external evidence. Clearly, another necessity is that experts in the field make a more careful study of the actual contents of the external evidence, particularly that deriving from Papias, within the context of its own *Sitz im Leben*, insofar as this can be determined. This should be one item for the agenda of future studies of the relationships among the gospels.

Sociological Questions Regarding the Origin of the Gospels

Much of the seminar discussion centered around three topics of a more or less "sociological" nature, which were posed by Meeks, and most of this discussion is relevant, either directly or indirectly, to the question of the relationships among the gospels.

The Sociology of Early Christian Rhetoric. Meeks noted that in the early part of this century, Adolf Deissmann, approaching the gospels from a study of the recently discovered papyri, had

[17] Cf. also *anataxasthai* in Luke 1:1 [editor's note].

concluded that the Evangelists belonged to a social class similar to that of the people who wrote the papyri, that is, an essentially nonliterary class.[18] Meeks then observed that this theory has recently been called into serious question by, among others, his colleague, Abraham J. Malherbe.[19] The question that Meeks posed to Kennedy was twofold: To what social class did the Christians who produced the gospels belong? What were the levels of penetration in the late first century, in terms of social strata, of the different kinds of rhetoric practiced by classical authors?

Here, Kennedy felt that the question of what he called "provenience" and what New Testament scholars usually call "provenance" was important. Where the gospels were written would have made a great deal of difference in the rhetorical standards of the writers and in the rhetorical expectations of their communities. If Mark, for example, was written in Rome, as the external evidence claims, its rhetorical level might be expected to be relatively sophisticated. Expectations would likely be much lower, however, in Palestine, Syria (the provenance of Matthew?), or Ephesus (the provenance of John?). It must be remembered that by the time the gospels were being produced, Hellenization had been in process for more than three hundred years, and Greek was the official language in the towns, though perhaps not in the countryside, even in Palestine. The origins of formal rhetoric in Greece and Rome were closely tied to the law courts and the functions of the bureaucracy. One had to know how to present a case in public and argue for it. At a lower level, people would come into contact with tax review boards, for example, or be involved in such matters as disputes over real estate boundaries and would have to make public presentations of their cases. Thus, some knowledge of rhetorical techniques and conventions inevitably would have filtered down to the lower levels of society and would have colored the expectations, perhaps unconsciously, of those who listened to early Christian preachers or read early Christian literature. On the other hand, according to

---

[18] Adolf Deissmann, *Light from the Ancient East: The New Testament Illustrated by Recently Discovered Texts of the Graeco-Roman World*, rev. ed., trans. Lionel R. M. Strachan (New York: George H. Doran Company, 1927; reprinted, Grand Rapids: Baker Book House, 1965).

[19] Abraham J. Malherbe, *Social Aspects of Early Christianity* Rockwell Lectures, Rice University (Baton Rouge and London: Louisiana State University Press, 1977), esp. 29–59 ("Social Level and Literary Culture").

Kennedy, the gospels do not exhibit a conscious artifice of style designed for rhetorical effect. The Johannine prologue, for example, has a very crude and primitive rhythm and shows little sense of the conventions of rhythm found in formal Greek writing.

Kennedy suggested that there likely was considerable variety, so far as the level of education among early Christians was concerned, but that the evidence seemed to point generally to a primarily urban, lower middle class, where formal education would be rare but common rhetorical conventions and techniques would be familiar and appreciated. Meeks tended to agree, suggesting that the communities out of which the gospels emerged were something above the proletarian groups about which Deissmann had romanticized half a century ago. The early Christian converts in the Hellenistic cities may well have come largely from the "God-Fearers," including such people as merchants, artisans, and other members of society whose upward mobility tended to be blocked by higher classes. Meeks also called attention to some Scandinavian scholarship comparing the Greek of the New Testament authors with that of certain specialized groups, such as physicians, artisans, and other technical writers,[20] suggesting that the closest analogy to New Testament Greek might be found in such literature. Kennedy thought such comparisons well worth exploring but wondered what "controls" would be applicable.

The Functions of Early Christian Literature. Meeks posed the question: What are the differences in function between the kinds of literature written specifically for the use of a "sect" and those kinds of literature intended for a more public clientele? Kennedy found it difficult to answer this question in terms of the rhetorical intention of the Evangelists, but he suggested that the gospels belong generally to that class of rhetoric which aims at the strengthening and deepening of opinions or convictions already held, namely, epideictic, rather than, as was the case of the missionary sermons in Acts, the persuasion of people to accept new beliefs.

Attention was called to the sudden shift of style from the

[20] Albert Wifstrand, "Stylistic Problems in the Epistles of James and Peter," *Studia Theologica*, 1 (1947), 170–182; and Lars Rydbeck, *Fachprosa, vermeintliche Volkssprache und Neues Testament. Zur Beurteilung der sprachlichen Niveauunterschiede im nachklassischen Griechisch*, Acta Universitatis Upsaliensis, Studia Graeca Upsaliensia 5 (Stockholm: Almquist & Wiksell, 1967).

Lucan prologue (Luke 1:1–4) to the ensuing infancy narrative (Luke 1:5–2:52), and it was suggested that, in the prologue, if anywhere, there was a self-conscious desire on the part of the author to conform to recognized literary and rhetorical standards. Kennedy proposed that Luke intended this conformity to make the Gospel more palatable to his clientele from the outset, but that he likely changed to the highly Semitized style at the beginning of the actual narrative, not because of the introduction of new subject matter, but rather because at this point he began following a source exhibiting Semitic features.

This, of course, touches upon a very sensitive point in current Lucan scholarship. Many, including the present writer, would say that Luke deliberately modeled his style from Luke 1:5 on that of the Septuagint. The reason for this would be that Luke's public expected to hear or read salvation history, for which the Septuagint provided the recognizable model in Greek. Thus, Luke 1:5 would mark a change of style determined both by the subject matter and by the recipients. Moreover, this Semitized change of style is not completely dropped after the infancy narrative, for, as Tim Schramm pointed out in his analysis of Luke's use of Mark, the Semitized style is continued in the introduction to the Marcan pericopes.[21] While Schramm explained this phenomenon from Luke's use of a non-Marcan source alongside of Mark, it is perhaps better attributed to Luke's deliberate attempt to cast a Septuagintal aura over his narrative by the use of a limited number of stock turns of expression. Thus, the third Evangelist conveys the impression that he is writing salvation history, which would fulfill the expectations of previous adherents of the Hellenistic synagogues.

One interesting point that emerged was Kennedy's observation that a distinct difference of style between a writer's *prooemium* and the ensuing treatise was not at all unusual. In fact, it was possible for an author to buy a *prooemium* ready-made. Cicero once used the same *prooemium* for two different works, a circumstance that caused him not a little embarrassment!

From the entire discussion, Luke emerged as the most consciously rhetorical of the Evangelists, a point not altogether irrelevant to the question of the relationships among the gospels.

The Institutionalization of Transmission. Meeks' concern

[21] Tim Schramm, *Der Markus-Stoff bei Lukas*, Society for New Testament Studies Monograph Series 14 (Cambridge: Cambridge University Press, 1971).

here had to do with the question, how and by whom the traditions were transmitted in the early Christian communities. Specifically, he wanted to know why the codex became the standard format for the books of these communities and whether the Christians were different from other contemporary groups in using the codex form for their writings.

Kennedy pointed out that notes (*hypomnēmata*) were almost always written on codices, since the codex was originally employed for all informal kinds of writing, but that the codex was just beginning to be used for literary works at the time when the New Testament documents were being written. Literary works in codex form would be written on parchment, however, rather than on wood covered with wax, as was the case with informal works. Kennedy suggested that the Christian adoption of the codex form may have had something to do with expense and observed that it was fortunate that the development of the codex for literary use coincided with the beginnings of Christian literature.

Meeks and other members of the seminar seemed more impressed by the early Christian need to look up references as a factor encouraging the adoption of the codex. It was much harder to find one's place in a scroll! Kennedy agreed that this would have been an added bonus but thought that it was not the initial reason for the choice of the codex format, because ancient authors were not much given to checking their references and usually quoted either from memory or from notes.

The implications of this for the relationships among the gospels are important. Perhaps we should think of an Evangelist not as closely copying his sources, but rather as reproducing them from memory. Indeed, Kennedy reported that he had remarked earlier during the Colloquy to Farmer that *if* the view were accepted that Mark was a conflation of Matthew and Luke (a view, of course, which Kennedy himself did not accept), then he could imagine Mark not as copying Matthew and Luke alternately, but rather as recollecting and combining his sources from memory. New Testament scholars who have worked on the Synoptic Problem, however, have always advanced the matter of order, rather than verbal agreement, as decisive proof for literary dependence. Kennedy did not suggest it at the time, but, in retrospect, one may perhaps suggest that a writer using his sources by memory might first list the order of the pericopes he wished to use in his preparatory *hypomnēmata*. If this were the case, the phenomenon of order would cease to be so conclusive a proof of direct literary dependence.

Other Topics

Publication. Kennedy noted that publication was a vague concept in ancient times. It took two main forms: public utterance and dissemination of copies by the author. In the first instance a poet, for example, might read his newly written poem aloud to an assembled audience. In the second case, the author might distribute copies of the work. In addition, there could be unauthorized publication, such as when students published the lectures of Quintilian from their class notes without the latter's approval! Authors in those days had very limited control over their "published" works.

Kennedy suggested that, as far as the gospels were concerned, publication took the form of liturgical use. Certainly this was true of at least some of the epistles, as we know from Colossians 4:16, where *anagnōsthei* and *anagnōte* mean public reading in the Christian assembly, but it is not clear just how soon the gospels were used liturgically. Orchard insisted that the use of the Old Testament Scriptures in the synagogue liturgy provided the precedent for the Christian use of the gospels. M. D. Goulder has attempted to demonstrate, from his study of Matthew's midrashic technique, that Matthew's Gospel was prepared for liturgical use.[22] The problem with such attempts, like the earlier attempt of Philip Carrington,[23] is that there are no external "controls" on the proposals. Carrington tried to show, from the liturgical marks in the margin of Codex Vaticanus, that Mark was composed as a lectionary. This only proves, however, that at some point Mark was used for lectionary purposes, not that such lectionary divisions go back to the author of Mark himself or account for his arrangement of the pericopes. Lectionary use has also been proposed as the origin of John[24] but has not been

[22] M. D. Goulder, *Midrash and Lection in Matthew*, The Speaker's Lectures in Biblical Studies 1969–71 (London: SPCK, 1974).

[23] Philip Carrington, *The Primitive Christian Calendar: A Study in the Making of the Marcan Gospel*, vol. 1, *Introduction and Text* (Cambridge: Cambridge University Press, 1952); cf. also his article, "The Calendrical Hypothesis of the Origin of Mark," *The Expository Times*, 67 (1955), 100–103.

[24] Aileen Guilding, *The Fourth Gospel and Jewish Worship: A Study of the*

worked out for Luke.[25] The whole question of the liturgical use of early Christian literature is an important one calling for further investigation, but such investigation is fraught with difficulties because of the insufficiency of hard evidence. To begin with, we know very little even about the synagogue use of Scripture in New Testament times. In fact, our earliest evidence of the use of Scripture in the synagogue service comes from the New Testament itself, from Luke 4:16–19. Further, the earliest evidence for the use of the gospels in Christian liturgy comes from Justin Martyr (c. A.D. 150). In response to a question, Kennedy said that he knew of no analogies in the cultic sects of antiquity to the Christian liturgical use of written documents.

Genre. There was no real consensus within the seminar regarding the particular genre to which the gospels should be assigned. Indeed, Kennedy was not at all happy with the term itself; to him, as a classicist, it suggested a self-conscious attempt on the part of the Evangelists to conform their work to an already established and recognized literary model. He pointed out that the concept of genre was evolved at Alexandria for the purpose of library classification: one looked for a book in the library according to its genre. What is important for the gospels is not the question of genre *per se*, but the purpose the Evangelists had in writing and the expectations of their readers. It has often been maintained in recent years that Mark "created the gospel genre." In the light of Kennedy's observations, this claim sounds questionable. Of the four gospels, Luke seems most nearly to reflect a conscious and deliberate attempt at conformity to an already existing literary genre. Certainly, the Lucan prologue, as has already been noted, suggests that Luke was deliberately modeling his Gospel on contemporary historiography. The difference between Luke and the other gospels in this regard supports Kennedy's questioning whether, indeed, the gospels can be brought under a single genre at all and Meeks' observation that each of the four gospels really represents a different genre. Kennedy noted that there are many examples of classical literature that conform to no established genre (e.g., the *Agricola* by Tacitus). The four gospels are thus in good company.

Relation of St. John's Gospel to the Ancient Jewish Lectionary System (Oxford: The Clarendon Press, 1960).

[25] On the entire subject, see John Reumann, "A History of Lectionaries: From the Synagogue at Nazareth to Post-Vatican II," *Interpretation*, 31 (1977), 116–130, esp. 120–122.

In connection with the subject of genre, the question of the meaning of the term "literary" was raised. What does it mean to call a writing a "literary work"? Kennedy denied that the gospels had a literary intent, despite the fact that in his essay he had compared the gospels to works that did have such an intent. He had understood that this was a part of his assignment, but he had been at pains to emphasize that classical literature offered no perfect analogue to the gospels, and this absence of analogues must involve, among other things, the lack of literary intent in the gospels. The gospel writers were not producing art for art's sake.

Two further elements of confusion in the use of the term "literary" were mentioned. First, there is the long-standing tradition of speaking of the source analysis and other introductory studies of the gospels as "literary criticism," which, strictly speaking, is a misnomer. Quite recently, too, there have been attempts by Dan Otto Via, Jr., and others to apply the methods of modern literary criticism to the study of the gospels, particularly the parables.[26] Meeks argued that despite the gospels' lack of conscious literary intention, something could be gained by the use of such techniques. He himself had profitably applied the methods of character analysis and thematic analysis, derived from contemporary literary criticism, to the study of the Fourth Gospel.[27] He fully realized, however, that the gospels were not novels, and, on the whole, he remained sceptical about the recent attempts to apply literary critical methods wholesale to the gospels.

Memorization. Kennedy had maintained that early Christian writers may, at times, have reproduced previously written sources from memory, rather than by direct copying, and that memorization may thus have played a significant role in the de-

---

[26] See, e.g., Dan Otto Via, Jr., *The Parables: Their Literary and Existential Dimension* (Philadelphia: Fortress Press, 1967); Norman Perrin, *Jesus and the Language of the Kingdom: Symbol and Metaphor in New Testament Interpretation* (Philadelphia: Fortress Press, 1976).

[27] Wayne A. Meeks, *The Prophet-King: Moses Traditions and the Johannine Christology*, Supplements to Novum Testamentum 14 (Leiden: E. J. Brill, 1967); "The Man from Heaven in Johannine Sectarianism," *Journal of Biblical Literature*, 91 (1972), 44–72; "The Divine Agent and His Counterfeit in Philo and the Fourth Gospel," in *Aspects of Religious Propaganda in Judaism and Early Christianity*, ed. Elisabeth Schüssler Fiorenza, University of Notre Dame Center for the Study of Judaism and Christianity in Antiquity 2 (Notre Dame and London: University of Notre Dame Press, 1976), 73–67.

190

velopment of the gospel tradition. In response to the suggestion that there was also memorization at the pre-literary or oral stage, however, he insisted that there was no classical precedent for the memorizing of oral tradition. Similarly, Meeks observed that despite the theory of Harald Riesenfeld and Birger Gerhardsson that the followers of Jesus memorized the sayings of Jesus and recited them by heart after the later fashion of the rabbinic schools,[28] no such precedent in Judaism could be found as early as the first century.

Nevertheless, the role of memory at the oral stage of the gospel tradition should not be ruled out altogether. In his remarks on the place of memory in oral traditional literature, Albert B. Lord had made the point that it is not the exact wording but the outline or structure of a narrative that is retained in folk memory. At any given recitation, the outline or structure would be reproduced exactly, but the precise wording would vary compared with other occasions, even when the same person was reciting (pp. 37–38). Bernard Orchard noted that the gospel pericopes with Synoptic parallels tend to have a fixed outline or structure. One or more of the elements can be omitted by any given Evangelist, but the general structure remains constant from one gospel to another. Into this structure, the Evangelist fits his own wording, which can vary considerably among or between the parallels. This seems to tie in neatly with Lord's observations regarding oral traditional literature. Orchard also insisted, however, that there was memorization at the oral stage and promised to set out the evidence for this in a forthcoming publication. A study of this evidence will, in my view, contribute significantly to an understanding of the relationships among the gospels. It should tend to diminish (and, as I believe, this is the trend today) the emphasis upon direct literary dependence among written documents and to enhance the possibility of cross-fertilization of oral traditions as a major clue to these relationships.

Conclusions

Kennedy rounded off his contribution by stating what he had hoped to achieve by his total participation in the Colloquy. First, he had hoped to encourage New Testament scholars to re-examine and to take more seriously the external evidence regarding

[28] See n. 2 in Meeks' response to Kennedy, p. 159.

the origin of the gospels. Second, he had intended to indicate just how literary composition was done in the first century, including the use of source materials, and, particularly, to call attention to the importance of note-taking (*hypomnēmata*) as an intermediate stage between oral proclamation and gospel writing. Third, he had sought to emphasize the importance of translation (conceived in the broadest possible sense and including everything from literal rendition to extensive paraphrase, together with the employment of earlier versions) as a factor in the literary evolution of the gospels and as a clue to their relationships.

It was agreed that Kennedy had amply fulfilled his intention and that New Testament scholarship must henceforth take very seriously the three areas of concern that he had raised. Meeks, for his part, had insisted upon the importance of the sociological background for understanding the compositional intent of the gospel writers and the expectations of their hearers/readers.

Kennedy has impressed upon us once again the fact that scholarly theories of one generation so often become unquestioned assumptions of the next and, in this regard, has had the effect of reinforcing some of the results (not always intended) of the work of Farmer and, more recently, of Robinson. To use a term that acquired a good deal of popularity in the classics seminar, we are entering into a period of great "fluidity" so far as acceptable views regarding the relationships among the gospels and other introductory matters are concerned. Perhaps Kennedy, Meeks, the classics seminar, and the Colloquy as a whole have demonstrated that a universally acceptable solution of the Synoptic Problem will not be found and that a pluralism of viewpoints is perfectly respectable in this as in many other matters and indeed is the only viable possibility for today.

3
JUDAIC STUDIES
and the GOSPELS

"Habent Sua Fata Libelli": The Role of Wandering Themes in Some Hellenistic Jewish and Rabbinic Literature

Lou H. Silberman

Introduction

Proposal. The proposal being made here is, frankly, quite simple. It suggests merely that attention to the way in which certain items, yet to be defined, make their appearance and function in various works stemming from the Jewish communities of the Hellenistic cultural area may illuminate some problems arising from an examination of other works, the gospels, that stem from the same general milieu. Although the proposal is simple, the hypothesis lying behind it is less so. What will be argued is that there existed a large body of thematic materials within the thought of the Jewish communities; that these materials came into expression for particular occasions at various times, in various ways, with various emphases; and that the various uses of particular themes may be entirely inconsistent one with the other. This essay is not intended to be an exercise in "parallelomania," to use Samuel Sandmel's splendid terminology.[1] I would

[1] Samuel Sandmel, "Parallelomania," *Journal of Biblical Literature*, 81 (1962), 1–13, reprinted in his *Two Living Traditions: Essays on Religion and the Bible* (Detroit: Wayne State University Press, 1972), 291–304. Sandmel did not coin the term but resurrected it from an earlier work, *circa* 1830, whose author and title he had forgotten; see his note 1, page 1.

argue that a parallel requires total congruence of form, content, and setting and is, hence, to borrow a term from mathematicians, uninteresting. Indeed, the claim will be made that, in significant instances, the same is not the same and that our task is to recognize and to recover the un-sameness.

Point of Departure. The point of departure is the opening chapter, or a part thereof, of *Pirqê 'Abot*, "The Chapters of the Fathers":[2] "Moses received Torah from Sinai and delivered it to Joshua, and Joshua to the Elders, and the Elders to the Prophets, and the Prophets delivered it to the Men of the Great Synagogue." This statement is taken to be correct, not necessarily in a literal sense, but as a cultural fact: the possession by a community of a body of ideas, practices, precepts, formulae, activities that form and inform its existence. Louis Finkelstein has argued cogently that this chapter is the charter of rabbinic Judaism as it found its self-identity; hence Torah, in this context (a rabbinic one), does not mean Scripture or Pentateuch but points, as has been stated, to something of a wider scope, the whole cultural heritage of the community.[3] The content of this heritage, in its variety although not in its subsequent quantity, was present at various levels of consciousness from the time of the community's emergent self-identity. Over the years, decades, and centuries, this content, as it grew, evoked a variety of organizing structures that made possible its preservation and its being brought to effective consciousness in the existence of the community. Some of this structured content found its ever more sharply defined expression in an ever less variable mode, writing (i.e., Scripture). But whatever its level of organization, much of it remained oral and thus more liable to motion, combination, disintegration, and recombination.

An analogy, with all of its dangers and distortions, is that of a chemical solution out of which, in the presence of a catalytic agent, some elements crystalize and precipitate while others

[2] A convenient and helpful edition is R. Travers Herford, *Pirke Aboth: The Tractate "Fathers," from the Mishnah, Commonly Called "Sayings of the Fathers,"* 3d ed. (New York: Jewish Institute of Religion, 1945), reissued as *The Ethics of the Talmud: Sayings of the Fathers*, 1st Schocken Paperback ed., Schocken Books 23 (New York: Schocken Books, 1962). There are many more editions, however. The quotation is from 1.1 (page 19 in the 1962 edition).

[3] Louis Finkelstein, *Mbw' lmsktwt 'bwt w'bwt drby Ntn (Introduction to the Treatises Abot and Abot of Rabbi Nathan)*, Texts and Studies of the Jewish

remain in suspension for a longer period of time, and when in turn these are induced to precipitate, they do so otherwise than did the first batch. This is, I am sure, a highly unscientific analogy, and it is suggested merely as a partial indication of how the dynamics of the situation are perceived. It is really the latter half of the analogy that is the source of difficulty, for in the chemical solution once an element is precipitated out, it is out, while in the situation I am discussing the material comes to expression without inhibiting yet another use of it in a quite different situation.

Preview. To return to the theme and to move from abstraction to concreteness, I would argue for the correctness of the rabbinic understanding of Torah as *šebikětab* and *šebě'al peh*, written and oral. I would further argue that the latter, the oral tradition, while it was not disorganized, nonetheless had a loose enough structure that items within it (themes and thematic episodes in the instances I shall be examining) could break away and enter into new, unexpected, and even contradictory alliances with other such items. (These then are the "wandering themes" in the title of this essay.) Such themes and thematic episodes were thus available not as fixed forms but as free content to be expressed, disposed, arranged, or modified as the occasion of their use may have required. These items may have been used well or poorly; they may have served the purposes for which they were chosen or obscured that which, for whatever reason, they were expected to illuminate. It is just this use of themes and thematic episodes that I wish to illustrate, with the intimation that observation of this procedure within the thought of Jewish communities in the Hellenistic culture area may afford another vantage point from which to view the way in which themes and thematic episodes within the gospels may have been variously used and arranged in response to a variety of occasions and occurences (or, to return momentarily to the analogy, in response to different catalytic agents).[4]

Theological Seminary of America 16 (New York: The Jewish Theological Seminary of America, 1950), 5–18 (Hebrew), x–xi (English summary).

[4] I have been wary of providing examples of this from the gospels, for it was my understanding that my task was to offer a methodology, not to impose it upon the gospel material without much more careful consideration. However, I have indicated the presence in the gospels of some of the themes that form the axis of this essay. I shall return to this subject briefly in n. 58.

Creation and Torah

I have chosen to examine themes and thematic episodes relating to Moses and most particularly to his early life, for in doing so attention can be focused on the way in which the story of a person is related—a program not distant from the central concern of this volume. The themes and thematic episodes are taken from Philo, Josephus, and some rabbinic sources.

Moses as Rhetor: Philo and Josephus. I begin with Philo and his first mention of Moses (I do not mean to suggest by this anything about the order of composition of the Philonic corpus but refer merely to the first mention in order of reading). It occurs at the beginning of *De Opificio Mundi*:

> While among other lawgivers some have nakedly and without embellishment drawn up a code of the things held to be right among their people, and others, dressing up their ideas in much irrelevant and cumbersome matter, have befogged the masses and hidden the truth under their fictions, Moses, disdaining either course, the one as devoid of the philosopher's painstaking effort to explore his subject thoroughly, the other as full of falsehood and imposture, introduced his laws with an admirable and most impressive exordium. He refrained, on the one hand, from stating abruptly what should be practised or avoided, and on the other hand, in face of the necessity of preparing the minds of those who were to live under the laws for their reception, he refrained from inventing myths himself or acquiescing in those composed by others. His exordium, as I have said, is one that excites our admiration in the highest degree. It consists of an account of the creation of the world, implying that the world is in harmony with the Law, and the Law with the world, and that the man who observes the Law is constituted thereby a loyal citizen of the world, regulating his doings by the purpose and will of Nature, in accordance with which the entire world itself also is administered.[5]

Josephus, too, introduces Moses at the beginning of the *Jewish Antiquities*:

> Such, then, being the lesson which Moses desired to instil into his fellow-citizens, he did not, when framing his laws, begin with contracts and the mutual rights of man, as others have done; no, he led their thoughts up to God and the construction of the world; he convinced them that of all God's works upon earth we men are the fairest; and when once he

[5] Philo, *De Opificio Mundi* 1–3. Translation from *Philo*. With an English Translation by F. H. Colson, G. H. Whitaker, and Ralph Marcus, 10 vols. and 2 supplementary vols., The Loeb Classical Library (Cambridge, Mass.: Harvard University Press/London: William Heinemann Ltd, 1929–1953), 1:7.

had won their obedience to the dictates of piety, he had no further difficulty in persuading them of all the rest.[6]

Notice how Josephus turns the meaning of Philo's ideas. The
latter suggests not that the exordium is intended to lead man's
"thoughts up to God and the construction of the world," to win
"their obedience," but rather to demonstrate the harmony of
nomos (Law) and *kosmos* (world). The notes to the German
translation suggest that Philo "sieht in dem Umstande, dass die
Thora mit der Weltschöpfung beginnt, eine Übereinstimmung
mit der Lehre der Stoiker, nach der die wahre Sittlichkeit darin
besteht, dass man der Natur folgt und nach der Natur lebt . . ."[7]

Josephus shifts the emphasis to the point noted above and adds
to Philo the idea that "our legislator . . . having shown that God
possesses the very perfection of virtue, thought that men should
strive to participate in it, and inexorably punished those who did
not hold with or believe in these doctrines." He does, however,
seem to follow, off-handedly, Philo's observation concerning the
harmony of Law and nature: "everything, indeed, is here set
forth in keeping with the nature of the universe."[8]

We see at once that both Philo and Josephus found it necessary to explain why the creation story precedes *nomos* (assuming that this latter term meant "what should be practiced or
avoided"). While it has been suggested that Josephus took something over from Philo, it is also clear that, if so, the borrowing
was not slavish, for the direction of Josephus' explanation is
quite different from that of Philo's. If Philo wishes to point to
agreement with Stoic ideas, Josephus' thought has a more "political" quality: obedience or punishment.[9]

Rhetoric without Rhetor: Mekilta and Tanḥuma. But is the
question itself (why the creation story before the statement of

[6] Josephus, *Jewish Antiquities* 1.Preface.4 (1.21). Translation from *Josephus*.
With an English translation by H. St. J. Thackeray, Ralph Marcus, Allen
Wikgren, and L. H. Feldman, 9 vols., The Loeb Classical Library (Cambridge,
Mass.: Harvard University Press/London: William Heinemann Ltd, 1926–1965),
4:11–13.

[7] L. Cohn, I. Heinemann, M. Adler, and W. Theiler, eds. *Die Werke Philos von
Alexandria in deutscher Übersetzung*, 6 vols., Schriften der jüdisch-hellenistischen Literatur in deutscher Übersetzung (Breslau: M. & H. Marcus 1900–
1937), 1:28, n. 1.

[8] Josephus, *Jewish Antiquities* 1.Preface.4 (1.23) and 1.Preface.4 (1.24).
Translation from *Josephus*, Loeb 4:13.

[9] See Thackeray's n. b in *Josephus*, Loeb 4:11; and Colson's n. c in *Philo*, Loeb
6:xvii–xviii.

the Law?) originally Philonic, or may it belong to the philosophical-theological (if such words are in order) discussions at a variety of levels that took place and continued to take place within the cultural field of the Eastern Mediterranean world? I say "took place and continued to take place" because the query emerges again in a quite different literary milieu from that of Philo or Josephus. The *Mekilta*, commenting on the first words of the Ten Commandments (*nomos* in the most specific sense), reads:

> Why were the Ten Commandments not said at the beginning of the Torah? A parable is in order. To what may this be compared? To the following: A king who entered a province said to the people: May I be your king? They replied: You have done nothing good for us that you should rule over us. What did he do then? He built for them the walls, brought in the water supply, fought their battles. Then said he to them: Let me rule over you! They replied—Yea! Yea! So God: He brought forth Israel from Egypt; divided the sea for them; brought down manna for them; caused the well to spring up for them; brought the quail for them; battled with Amalek for them. Said he to them: Let me rule over you and they responded—Yea! Yea![10]

When one compares the *nmšl* or explanation of the parable with the *mšl* or parable itself, it seems evident that the explanation is truncated, for all it refers to, in a strict sense, is the third item, "fought their battles." The first two items of the parable, building the city walls and bringing in the water supply (which at least suggest the creation narrative), are not reflected in the explanation. All that is present are references to the earlier chapters of Exodus, that is, the "battles." This is not the end of the matter, however. In *Tanḥuma*, in the midst of an extended discussion of creation, it is reported that R. Isaac said:

> It was necessary only to commence writing the Torah with the words: *hḥdš hzh lkm* "this month shall be to you" (Ex. 12.2); why then did it begin with *brʼšyt* "in the beginning"? In order to make known the extent of his power, as it is said: *kḥ mʻśyw hgyd lʻmw ltt lhm nḥlt gwym* "His power by his works, he manifested to his people, by giving them the patrimony of nations" (Ps. 111.6).[11]

[10] Tractate "Bahodesh" V (Exodus 20:2). Translation in part from Jacob Z. Lauterbach, ed., *Mekilta de-Rabbi Ishmael: A Critical Edition on the Basis of the Manuscripts and Early Editions with an English Translation, Introduction and Notes*, 3 vols., The Schiff Library of Jewish Classics (Philadelphia: The Jewish Publication Society of America, 1933–1935), 2:229–230.

[11] *Bereshit* 11. S. Buber, ed., *Midrash Tanchuma. Ein agadischer Commentar zum Pentateuch von Rabbi Tanchuma ben Rabbi Abba*. Zum ersten male nach Handschriften aus den Bibliotheken zu Oxford, Rom, Parma und München

The meaning of this laconic and truncated statement is made clear by R. Solomon b. Isaac (Rashi, the famous commentator), who quotes it at the very beginning of his commentary on Scriptures. I shall not burden you with a detailed discussion of the discrepancy between the full text in Rashi and the truncated text in *Tanḥuma*. Abr. Berliner deals with the matter in the commentary to his edition of Rashi and concludes that Rashi had an earlier text of *Tanḥuma* before him, one we no longer possess.[12] Only the first part is now found in *Tanḥuma*; the remainder, however, is quoted by Rashi in his comment on Genesis 1:1:

Said R. Isaac: It was not required that Torah begin otherwise than with "this month shall be unto you", for this is the first commandment with which Israel was commanded. Why then did it begin with "in the beginning"?—because of the phrase, "his power by his works, he manifested to his people, by giving them the patrimony of the nations," for should the nations of the world say to Israel, "you are robbers, for you have conquered the lands of the seven [Canaanite] nations!" they can reply to them: "the entire earth belongs to The Holy One Blessed be He, He created it and gave it to whomsoever He wished. In accord with His will He gave it to them and in accord with His will He took it from them and gave it to us."[13]

What is of interest to us is that Rashi's version of the *Tanḥuma* passage, like the material in Josephus and Philo, occurs in connection with a discussion of the creation story, yet each of the three, while dealing with the same theme, offers his own particular response to the common question. Philo understands the precedence of the creation story to indicate the harmony of *nomos* and *kosmos*; Josephus, to inculcate the piety necessary for obedience; and R. Isaac, in *Tanḥuma*, to affirm the right of the *kosmokratōr* to dispose of his creation "in accordance with his will."

Now it is evident from both Philo and Josephus that existential questions guide their responses. Both are concerned with the wisdom of Moses, indeed with his very special qualities as lawgiver, and this suggests the possibility of a polemic-apologetic situation, in which mythologies (for so the creation story may be

---

herausgegeben. Kritisch bearbeitet commentiert und mit einer ausführlichen Einleitung [auf Hebräisch] versehen (Vilna: Romm, 1885), 2:7. Translation mine.

[12] Abr. Berliner, ed., *Raschi. Der Kommentar des Salomo b. Isak über den Pentateuch* (Frankfurt a. M.: J. Kauffman, 1905), 424 (Hebrew).

[13] Berliner, ed., *Raschi*, 1 (Hebrew).

depicted) are under attack, so that the particular cogency of the
account as exordium to the laws has to be defended. On the other
hand, no such conflict seems to lie behind R. Isaac's comment,
or does it? Wilhelm Bacher, dealing with the mention by Procopius of a Phoenician inscription referring to *Iēsou tou lęstou*
("Joshua the robber"), cites this passage in the several versions
in which it occurs, both in the name of R. Isaac and in that of
R. Levi. Bacher writes:

> In conclusion, attention must be called to a passage in Josephus,
> "Against Apion," where among the reasons that he gives why the Jews
> for so long a time remained unknown to the Greeks, he brings forward
> this, that the forefathers of the Jews did not, as the Greeks did, become
> sea-robbers, nor did they engage in wars for the sole purpose of gaining
> more wealth (Contra Apionem, I.xii.4). For piracy he employs the term
> that indicates robbery in general, *lęsteia*, in the use of which he could
> hardly have had in mind any charges that had been hitherto levelled
> against the Jews that they were a "nation of robbers." The remark of
> Josephus just quoted is not so much apologetic as aggressive, upbraid-
> ing the Greeks, whose ancient history was sullied by piracy. It was only
> after the time of Josephus that it was sought to prove from their own
> historical sources that the Jews were a "nation of robbers . . ."

At the end of his article, Bacher points to the fact that Procopius
came from Caesarea, "where hostility to the Jews was an old
tradition among the inhabitants";[14] this suggests the background of the debate reflected in the *Tanḥuma* passage, for
R. Isaac also lived in Galilee, in Caesarea.

It will be recognized at once that far from being caught up
in "parallelomania" and thus being under bondage to demonstrate source and precedence, I am concerned here with the function of similar materials in their own respective situations. What
relates all of the passages—Philo, Josephus, *Mekilta*, and *Tanḥuma*—is not the answer but the question *mh ṭ'm, mpny mh*
(why?), which is, by the very nature of the situation, earlier than
any answer. Saul Lieberman comments on this point:

> One of the fundamentals of research is to ask "why", to inquire into the
> reasons of a given matter. *Mpny mh* "why," is the common term used
> by the Rabbis in their interpretation of Scripture. Similarly, Didymus
> the grammarian likes to introduce his disquisitions with *zētoitai, dia ti,*

---

[14]W. Bacher, "The Supposed Inscription upon 'Joshua the Robber' (Illustrated from Jewish Sources)," *The Jewish Quarterly Review*, o.s. 3 (1891), 357.

etc., and the *zētēmata* constituted a notable part of the philologic, the philosophic and the juridical literature.[15]

But the question need not always be expressed, of course. Even when the answer does not formally appear to be an answer, it presupposes the question, the question that ultimately relates the variety of responses.

With regard to the material being examined here, one cannot know with any certainty what was floating about back there, behind the earliest answer available, Philo's. Bacher, in the passage quoted above, precludes an early date for the contents of R. Isaac's reply, holding that the accusation it seeks to refute did not arise before the time of Josephus. Yet it is altogether possible that the reply represents an early level of the traditional material, albeit in a new statement, for it can be argued that the very structure of the Hexateuch, the narrative from creation to the settlement in the Land, is (among the many other things it is) a response to any challenge made to Israel's right to possess the Land. This is not a point I would push too strenuously (indeed, I prefer not to push it at all), but it is possible to see this coalescence of the tradition as a defense of the claim of those returning from Babylon to their ancestral land. *Mpny mh* may provoke all sorts of answers—good, bad, indifferent, but it is in and of itself a potent question that cannot be sidestepped. The question is the theme.

Traditions and Sources

It is beyond dispute that, as noted at the beginning, rabbinic Judaism saw itself as the heir of a deep and wide tradition, into which it dipped or plunged to garner the materials required to build a structure of life both communal and private and to recommend this structure as necessary for convenantal existence. But rabbinic Judaism alone did not make the claim to be privy to such a heritage. Philo, too, in undertaking to recount the story of Moses, claims that his knowledge of this story is closer than that of others, for he has learned it *kak biblōn tōn hierōn . . . kai*

---

[15] Saul Lieberman, *Hellenism in Jewish Palestine: Studies in the Literary Transmission, Beliefs and Manners of Palestine in the I Century B.C.E.–IV Century C.E.*, Texts and Studies of the Jewish Theological Seminary of America 18, 2d ed. (New York: Jewish Theological Seminary of America, 1962), 48.

para tinōn apo tou ethnous presbyterōn ("both from the sacred books . . . and from some of the elders of the nation"). (There is no intention at this point or at any other to resurrect the argument concerning the meaning of *agraphos nomos* or "the unwritten law" in Philo. It is irrelevant. What cannot be gainsaid is Philo's own explicit claim that what he knew about Moses came to him not only from "the sacred books" but "from some of the elders of the nation.") More than this, Philo tells us of his procedure: *ta gar legomena tois anaginōskomenois aei synyphainon* ("for I have always interwoven what I was told with what I read").[16]

This stands in contrast, or so it seems, to what Josephus says of his undertaking at the beginning of *The Antiquities*:

The precise details (*ta . . . akribē*) of our Scripture records will, then, be set forth, each in its place, as my narrative proceeds, that being the procedure that I have promised to follow throughout this work, neither adding nor omitting anything (*ouden prostheis oud' au paralipōn*).

This provoked the modern translator, H. St. John Thackeray, to comment: "In fact he 'adds' some curious legends, on Moses in particular, and there are some few pardonable omissions." But, indeed, one does not have to read far into *The Antiquities* to discover that what this statement meant to Josephus and what Thackeray understood it to mean are worlds apart.[17]

The key to Josephus' understanding of his task is found somewhat earlier, in the paragraph to which Thackeray refers in support of his wry note, where Josephus states that his work "will embrace our entire ancient history and political constitution, translated from the Hebrew records." To this Thackeray appends a note: "Josephus bases the first part of his narrative on the Biblical story; but his rôle as 'translator' is limited."[18] If this is the case, then Josephus may, indeed, have had something other than "translation" in mind when he wrote *methērmēneumenēn*. Without attempting a full-dress examination of the philological material, it can be argued with considerable plausibility that the counterpart of the Greek *methērmēneumenēn* is *mytrgm*, which means both "translate" and "interpret," thus

[16]Philo, *De Vita Mosis* 1.4. Translation from *Philo*, Loeb 6:279.

[17]Josephus, *Jewish Antiquities* 1.Preface.3 (1.17). Translation from *Josephus*, Loeb 4:9; see Thackeray's n. b.

[18]Josephus, *Jewish Antiquities* 1.Preface.2 (1.5). Translation from *Josephus*, Loeb 4:5; see Thackeray's n. a on p. 4.

paying attention to Lieberman's statement: "But the first rudiment of the interpretation of a text is the *hermēneia*, the literal and exact equivalent of the Hebrew *trgwm*, which means both translation and interpretation."[19] If this suggestion has merit, then it is evident that Josephus had not promised a translation but an interpretation, and *ta . . . akribē* are the precise details from a wider tradition than Scripture by itself. So, too, Philo in his introduction to *De Vita Mosis*, to which I shall soon turn, wrote that he "believed [him]self to have a closer knowledge than others of his [Moses'] life's history" (*edoxa mallon heterōn ta peri ton bion akribōsai*).[20] In the same way, Luke wrote in the introduction to his Gospel of his "having followed all things closely for some time past" (*parēkolouthēkoti anōthen pasin akribōs*).[21]

The Life of Moses

Introduction: Apologetics and Polemics. Turning back then to Philo's *De Vita Mosis* (for in attending to the gospels we have in sight a Life, and it may be helpful to observe how some contemporaries, broadly understood, of the Evangelists recounted a Life), we are faced with an apology, which is, as all apologies are, a polemic as well. Philo wrote:

I hope to bring the story of this greatest and most perfect of men to the knowledge of such as deserve not to remain in ignorance of it; for, while the fame of the laws which he left behind him has travelled throughout the civilized world and reached the ends of the earth, the man himself as he really was is known to few.

The continuation at this point is a rebuke to the Greek men of letters who had refused to pay him any attention and had indulged in the composition of "comedies and pieces of voluptuous licence," rather than using "their natural gifts to the full on the lessons taught by good men and their lives." But, Philo concluded, "I will disregard their malice, and tell the story of Moses (*ta peri ton andra*) as I learned it, both from the sacred books . . . and from some of the elders of the nation."[22]

Josephus, too, in connection with the explanation of what the

---

[19] Lieberman, *Hellenism in Jewish Palestine*, 48.
[20] Philo, *De Vita Mosis* 1.4. Translation from *Philo*, Loeb 6:279.
[21] Luke 1.3.
[22] Philo, *De Vita Mosis* 1.1–4. Translation from *Philo*, Loeb 6:277–279.

creation story is doing at the beginning of Scripture, noted that he "must first speak briefly of him [Moses]" and, following Philo (but far more briefly) or a common tradition, contrasted Moses and his work with what "others have done."[23] It is not until later in *The Antiquities* that his encomium of Moses is to be found.[24]

The Land of Egypt. Before examining the life of Moses (or rather some episodes of his life as found in Philo, Josephus, and certain rabbinic texts), it is interesting to note a subtle variance between Philo's and Josephus' setting of the background. Philo begins with words of praise for the land of Egypt. This breaks into the narrative almost at its beginning, for, having mentioned Moses' ancestry and the famine that brought his forefathers to Egypt, Philo continues: "Egypt is a land rich in plains, with deep soil, and very productive of all that human nature needs . . ." This "interruption" ends with the statement that it is only a visitation of the anger of God because of "the prevailing impiety of the inhabitants" that prevents a plentiful crop.[25] This concluding statement is almost thrown away and could indeed be thought of as a mere reference to the past, yet when one turns to Josephus one sees that it is hardly innocuous. Josephus refers to the Egyptians as "a voluptuous people and slack to labour, slaves to pleasure in general and to a love of lucre in particular."[26] These statements may express no more than personal prejudices, but given the frequent reference to the sensuality of the Egyptians in Jewish literature as noted by Louis Ginzberg, it would seem plausible to discern a common tradition lurking in the background.[27] Such references do not appear in this same connection in rabbinic texts but rather in other contexts. For example, in *Tanḥuma*, in the account of Abraham's and Sarah's journey down to Egypt, the vulgate text reads: "My daughter, Egypt, is a whorish land, as it is written, 'The flesh of asses is their flesh.'" In S. Buber's text, Abraham is reported as saying: "The

[23] Josephus, *Jewish Antiquities* 1.Preface.4 (1.18, 21). Translation from *Josephus*, Loeb 4:11.

[24] Josephus, *Jewish Antiquities* 2.9.5–6 (2.225–231).

[25] Philo, *De Vita Mosis* 1.5–6. Translation from *Philo*, Loeb 6:279.

[26] Josephus, *Jewish Antiquities* 2.9.1 (2.201). Translation from *Josephus*, Loeb 4:251.

[27] Louis Ginzberg, *The Legends of the Jews*, trans. Henrietta Szold and Paul Radin, 6 vols. and Index vol. by Boaz Cohen (Philadelphia: The Jewish Publication Society of America, 1909–1938), 5:220–221, n. 68.

Egyptians are steeped in whoredom."[28]

To return, for a moment, to Philo. He wrote in *De Josepho*, by the way, of Jacob's concern for Joseph: "For he knew how natural it is for youth to lose its footing and what licence to sin belongs to the stranger's life, *particularly in Egypt* where things created and mortal are deified, and in consequence the land is blind to the true God."[29]

What these several items suggest is a common attitude that is carried along in the stream of the community's stock of themes and that, in an appropriate situation, comes to expression in a fashion relevant to the occasion. This by no means implies, however, a slavish reproduction of some necessarily supposed literary source or even fixed oral tradition.

The Perfect Man. But to return more directly to the life of Moses. Philo called him "this greatest and most perfect of men" (*andros ta panta megistou kai teleiotatou*).[30] Josephus wrote of him as "having surpassed in understanding all men that ever lived" and spoke of "the superlative quality of his virtue."[31] Such praise is commonplace, of course, and is reflected in rabbinic texts as well. In *Sifre Bamidbar, Bahalotekha* (§101) to the second half of the verse, Numbers 12:3 ("Now the man Moses was very meek, above all the men that were upon the face of the earth"), R. Yose responds to the comment, "more than any man upon the face of the earth [i.e., alive in his time] but not than the patriarchs," with the emphatic statement, "even than the patriarchs!"[32] In *Midrash Tannaim*, in the midst of a discussion of Moses' hesitation to mention the divine name in the poem *h*ᵓ*zynw* (Deuteronomy 32) until the twenty-first word, we read: "so that if Moses, master of the prophets, than whom there has not been one greater in the world . . ."[33] Thus, too, *Abot d'Rabbi Nathan* in both recensions: "Moses our master, the

[28]*Midrash Tanḥuma* (Piotrkov: J. Cedarbaum, 1930), *lekh lekha* 5 (34); editio Buber (see n. 11 above), *lekh lekha* 9, 2:65–66. Translation mine.

[29]Philo, *De Josepho* 254. Translation from *Philo*, Loeb 6:263; emphasis mine.

[30]Philo, *De Vita Mosis* 1.1. Translation from *Philo*, Loeb 6:277.

[31]Josephus, *Jewish Antiquities* 4.8.49 (4.328, 331). Translation from *Josephus*, Loeb 4:633, 635.

[32]H. S. Horovitz, ed., *Siphre de'be Rab*, Fasciculus primus, *Siphre ad Numeros adjecto Siphre zutta*, Schriften, herausgegeben von der Gesellschaft zur Förderung der Wissenschaft des Judentums: Corpus Tannaiticum 3:3:1 (Leipzig: G. Fock, 1917), 99–100. Translation mine.

[33]D. Hoffmann, ed. *Midrash Tannaim zum Deuteronomium*, 2 vols. (Berlin: M. Poppelauer, 1908–1909), 2:186 (to Deuteronomy 32:3).

wisest of the wise, father of the prophets" and "lord of the prophets."[34]

Again, while it is possible that each of these statements, and others besides, is a natural response to the person of Moses described in Scripture, yet the variety of places in which they occur suggests that such encomia belong to an ongoing tradition that finds its moments of expression in diverse ways.

The Counter-Tradition. Equally important in this connection is a counter-tradition: one that either plays down the superior role of Moses or, in what is the most extreme and therefore the most telling instance, that does not merely disregard such praise but totally ignores the presence of Moses. Sir Walter Scott, in the Introduction to *The Talisman*, comments on the "playbill, which is said to have announced the tragedy of Hamlet, the character of the Prince of Denmark being left out." But in the Jewish tradition it is, *mirabile dictu*, possible to tell the entire story of the Egyptian bondage, the plagues, and the going forth from Egypt including the crossing of the sea without a single mention of Moses. Whoever has recited the *Haggadah* of Passover at the Seder table knows that in this central liturgical act which enacts the passion of the people of Israel, not only is Moses not mentioned but his absence is not even noticed, for the commanding presence (to use Emil Fackenheim's potent phrase)[35] is "I and not an angel . . . I and not a seraph . . . I and not a messenger . . ."

Less drastic, yet of similar significance, is a passage at the beginning of *Abot d'Rabbi Nathan*. On the surface, it is an argument between R. Yose the Galilean and R. Akiba over the interpretation of Exodus 24:16. Does *wykshw h'nn* mean "and the cloud covered him" (i.e., Moses) or "and the cloud covered it" (i.e., the mount)? Yet as Judah Goldin points out in the Appendix to his translation of the first chapter of *Abot d'Rabbi Nathan*: "What *is* at the root of the controversy is the rabbinic attitude toward Moses." Here, he educes the evidence that there was a

[34] S. Schechter, ed., *Aboth de Rabbi Nathan* (London; D. Nutt/Vienna: Ch.D. Lippe/ Frankfurt a.M.: J. Kaufmann, 1887), 3. See the English translation of version A: Judah Goldin, trans. *The Fathers According to Rabbi Nathan*, Yale Judaica Series 10 (New Haven: Yale University Press, 1955), 7; and the translation of version B: Anthony Saldarini, *The Fathers According to Rabbi Nathan* (Abot De-Rabbi Nathan) *Version B: A Translation and Commentary* (Leiden: E. J. Brill, 1975), 21.

[35] Emil Fackenheim, *God's Presence in History* (New York: New York University Press, 1970), 14–16.

distinctive tendency "to qualify his [Moses'] greatness"—a tendency expressed by R. Akiba but (this is my enlargement of Goldin's discussion) perhaps stemming from earlier times and reflecting a response to the adoring attitude toward Moses found among the Essenes. According to Goldin:

> One may say that the so-called ambivalence toward Moses is typical of many sages. All of them accept that there hath not risen a prophet like Moses; on the other hand, all of them took great precautions in their interpretations, lest the figure of Moses be magnified beyond human proportions.[36]

The Theme of the "Seventh." To continue: Philo wrote of the outstanding qualities of Moses' parents and of the fact that "he was the seventh in descent from the first settler [Abraham], who became the founder of the whole Jewish nation."[37] Josephus, too (in a passage questioned by some authorities), wrote: "He was the seventh from Abraham, being the son of Amaram, who was the son of Caath, whose father was Levi, the son of Jacob, who was the son of Isaac, the son of Abraham."[38] Once again the same tradition is reported in rabbinic texts, but in such diverse contexts as to make it evident that we are not dealing with a literary or even a fixed oral source but with free-floating thematic material.

There are fascinating examples of how this theme—Moses, seventh from Abraham—became part of discussions totally unconcerned with the genealogical interests of both Philo and Josephus. The material occurs in three different contexts. In *Bereshit rabba* (19, 7) the verse commented upon is *wyšm'w 't-qwl yhwh 'lhym mthlk bgn lrwḥ hywm* "they in the garden at eventide heard the voice of the Lord God departing."

Said R. Abba bar Kahana: it is not written here *mhlk*—"he was walking"—but *mthlk*—"it was leaping upward". Originally the presence was among the terrestrials; when the first man sinned it arose to the first firmament. When Kain sinned, it went up to the second firmament. When the generation of Enosh sinned it went up to the third. When the generation of the Flood sinned, to the fourth; the generation of the

---

[36] Schechter, ed., *Aboth de Rabbi Nathan*, 1. The translation and the Appendix thereto are found in the *Mordecai M. Kaplan Jubilee Volume on the Occasion of his Seventieth Birthday* (New York: Jewish Theological Seminary of America, 1953), English Section, 263–280.

[37] Philo, *De Vita Mosis* 1.7. Translation from *Philo*, Loeb 6:279.

[38] Josephus, *Jewish Antiquities* 2.9.6 (2.229). Translation from Josephus, Loeb, 4: 263–265; see Thackeray's n. a on p. 264.

Dispersal, to the fifth; the Sodomites, to the sixth; the Egyptians in the days of Abraham, to the seventh. Counter to this there arose seven righteous ones, Abraham, Isaac, Jacob, Levi, Kohath, Amram, Moses and they brought it down to earth. Abraham from seventh to sixth. Isaac brought down from sixth to fifth. Jacob brought down from fifth to fourth. Levi brought down from fourth to third. Kohath brought down from third to second. Amram brought down from second to first. Moses brought it down below.[39]

The same material occurs in *Shir ha-Shirim rabba* with some unimportant textual variations, but in a different context to provide it with a different import. The biblical text is *b'ty lgny*—"I have entered into my garden" (Song of Songs 5:1).

Said R. Menahem the son-in-law of R. Eleazar bar Abuna in the name of R. Simeon b. R. Yosna: It is not written "to the garden" but "to my garden"—i.e., *lgnwny*: to my bridal chamber, to the place where I was originally;—and was not the presence originally among the terrestrials?[40]

The question is answered by citing the entire previous passage as proof that, indeed, God's presence was originally on earth. There is yet another occurrence of the material with a serious dislocation in the first section (the movement of the presence from earth to the seventh heaven), but this in no way affects the outcome: the righteousness of Moses, the seventh righteous man, bringing the presence back to earth. This is found in *Pesiqta d'Rab Kahana* in a *petiḥah*, an introduction to the reading of the Scriptural lesson, in this case Numbers 7:1, the lesson for the festival of Hannukah. In this occurrence, the way in which the material is fitted in is instructive.

As just noted, a *petiḥah* is an introduction to the reading of the scriptural lesson. It begins with what has been called an "extraneous" verse and concludes with the first verse of the lesson. The reason for the choice of the so-called "extraneous" verse has been a matter of debate among modern scholars, but it can be shown that in a great many, perhaps in all cases the verse contains a word that assonates with a significant word in the opening verse of the lesson. In the instance at hand the "extraneous" verse is Psalm 37:29: *ṣdyqym yyršw 'rṣ wyšknw l'd 'lyh* ("The

---

[39] J. Theodor and Ch. Albeck, eds., *Midrash Bereshit Rabba: Critical Edition with Notes and Commentary*, 2d printing with additional corrections by Ch. Albeck (Jerusalem: Wahrmann Books, 1965), 1:176–177. Translation mine.

[40] *Shir ha-Shirim rabba* to Song of Songs 5:1. Translation mine.

righteous shall possess the land and shall dwell upon it forever"). R. Isaac quotes this verse and follows it with a little humorous by-play: "And what will the wicked inherit? Are they to fly around in the air?" Then he gets down to cases: "What does *wyšknw l'd 'lyh* signify?" This introduces the tally word, *wyšknw*, which assonates with *'t-hmškn* in the first verse of the lesson. R. Isaac then proposes to read the "extraneous" verse other than with the traditional pointing: *wyškynw škynh b'rṣ* ("they [the righteous] cause the presence to dwell on earth"). The material quoted above from *Bereshit rabba* is now cited (with a serious dislocation in the first series, as has already been indicated), leading to the mention of Moses, who as the seventh in the series brought the presence back to earth, and concluding with the quotation of Numbers 7:1 (*wyhy bywm klwt mšh lhqym 't-hmškn*), which must be understood to mean that Moses completed (*klwt*) the series of acts that resulted in the return of the presence (*mškn* = *škynh*) to the earth.[41] Here we have, with some textual variations, a thematic episode that serves no genealogical interest as in Philo and Josephus and yet is clearly related to the notices in these authors, for again it is Moses, in seventh place, who is a significant person.

This theme comes to its paradigmatic expression in another place in *Pesiqta d'Rab Kahana*:

All sevenths are beloved. In the celestial sphere, the seventh is beloved: heaven, heaven of heavens, expanse, vault, habitation, dwelling, *arabot—swlw lrwkb b'rbwt* "Praise the rider in Arabot (= clouds)" (Psalm 68:5). In the terrestrial realm— *'rṣ 'dmh 'rq' gyh ṣyh nṣyh tpl— whw' yspwṭ tbl bṣdq* "He will judge Tebel with righteousness" (Psalm 9:9). In the sequence of the generations: Adam, Seth, Enosh, Kenan, Mehalalel, Jared, Enoch—(I Chron. 1:2–3—*wythlk hnwk 't-h'lhym*, "And Enoch walked with God." (Gen. 5:24). So too with the Patriarchs, the seventh was beloved: Abraham, Isaac, Jacob, Levi, Kohath, Amram, Moses—*wmsh 'lh 'l h'lhym* "And Moses ascended to God" (Ex. 19:3).

---

[41] This translation is based upon the text given in B. Mandelbaum, ed., *Pesikta de Rav Kahana*. According to an Oxford manuscript with variants from all known manuscripts and genizoth fragments and parallel passages with commentary and introduction, in Hebrew and English, 2 vols. (New York: The Jewish Theological Seminary of America, 1962), 1:2–3. The translation in *Pĕsikta dĕ Rab Kahăna: R. Kahana's Compilation of Discourses for Sabbaths and Festal Days*, trans. William G. (Gershon Zev) Braude and Israel J. Kapstein (Philadelphia: Jewish Publication Society of America, 1975), 5–6, is acceptable but for its interpretation of the concluding verse. It does not recognize the assonance of the tally word with the text word.

Of the sons [of Jesse] the seventh was beloved: Eliab, Abinadab, She-mael, Nethanel, Raddai, Ozem the sixth, and the seventh, David. Of the kings, the seventh was beloved: Saul, Ish bosheth, David, Solomon, Rehaboam, Abijah, Asa—*wyqr⁾ ⁾s⁾ ⁾l-yhwh* "And Asa cried unto the Lord, *etc.*" (II Chr. 14:10).

The passage then continues with several more lists of seven and concludes with the words from Leviticus 23:24: "In the seventh month on the first day." This is a *petihah*, an introduction to the reading of Scripture on Rosh ha-Shanah, the New Year, that occurs on the first day of the seventh month.[42]

One can conclude from this evidence that the theme of the be-loved "seventh" was widespread and could be used in many situations to underscore a particular "seventh." It is, of course, well known that the genealogy at the beginning of Matthew places Jesus in just such a "beloved" situation, at the end of a sixth seven-member chain, and that the genealogy in Luke places him at the end of the eleventh seven-member chain. Another expres-sion, it would seem, of the theme *hšby ⁽ym hbybyn* "The sevenths are beloved."[43]

The "Annunciation" Theme. There is, in connection with the birth of Moses, a theme that may be designated the "annuncia-tion." It occurs in two versions. In Josephus' *Antiquities* it is reported that Amram, in response to the decree condemning all of the male children of the Hebrews to death (a biblical theme interestingly developed in the gospels; see Matthew 2), entreated God to prevent the destruction of the race. God appeared to him in his sleep, "exhorted him not to despair of the future" and told him that the child his wife was carrying (who was, indeed, the child, the prediction of whose birth was the threat that had caused the wicked decree) would be delivered and would in turn be the deliverer of his people.[44] A similar theme occurs in *Mekilta* but, as noted above, with a different nuance. The text commented upon is Exodus 15:20: "Miriam the prophetess took." The com-ment expresses surprise: "But where do we find of Miriam that she uttered prophecies? She had said to her father, 'You will yet beget a son who will arise and save Israel from the power of the

[42] Mandelbaum, ed., *Pesikta de Rav Kahana*, 2:343–344. See, too, the Braude-Kapstein translation (pp. 359–360) cited in the previous note. Again, I interpret some of the material in a different fashion.

[43] Matthew 1:2–16; Luke 3:23–28.

[44] Josephus, *Jewish Antiquities* 2.9.3 (2.210–216). Translation from Josephus, Loeb 4:255–259.

Egyptians'." The comment continues by quoting Exodus 2:1–3, which is taken as Amram's response to the prophecy: "And there went a man of the house of Levi and took . . . And the woman conceived and bore a son . . . And when she could no longer hide him," continuing:

> . . . then her father rebuked her, saying "Miriam, what about your prophecies!" But she held fast to her prophetic statement, as it is said, "And his sister stationed herself at a distance, to learn what would befall him" (Ex. 2:4). Now, "taking up a station" is nothing other than a reference to the Holy Spirit, as it is said, "I saw the Lord station himself beside the altar" (Amos 9:1), and it says, "And the Lord came and stationed Himself" (I Sam. 3:10), and it says, "Call Joshua, and station yourselves *etc*." (Deut. 31:14).

Likewise it is demonstrated that "at a distance," "to learn," and "what would befall him," all phrases in the verse, refer to the Holy Spirit (i.e., to Miriam's prophetic gift).[45] The same material in a truncated form appears in the Babylonian Talmud, tractate *Megillah* (14a), in an extended discussion of prophets and prophetesses.[46] In both these latter instances, unlike the passage in Josephus, the center of interest is not in Moses but in Miriam as a prophetess. The appearance of this theme in Pseudo-Philo is of interest, for it reflects both versions: Miriam has the dream, rather than Amram, and reports it to her parents.[47] Again we see how thematic material is used freely to serve the needs of the narrator or interpreter.

It seems to me that the theme also appears, elaborated and

[45] *Mekilta*, tractate *Shirata* X (Exodus 15:20). Lauterbach, ed., *Mekilta de-Rabbi Ishmael*, 2:81. See also Judah Goldin, *The Song at the Sea* (New Haven: Yale University Press, 1974), 242–246.

[46] Tractate *Megillah* 14a, *The Babylonian Talmud*; for English translation, see Maurice Simon, "Megillah: Translated into English with Notes, Glossary and Indices," in *The Babylonian Talmud: Seder Mo'ed: Translated into English with Notes, Glossary and Indices*, ed. I. Epstein, 4 vols. (London: The Soncino Press, 1938), 4:Megillah":82. Cf. also Tractate *Soṭah* 12a and 12b–13a; for English translation, see A. Cohen, "Soṭah: Translated into English with Notes, Glossary and Indices," in *The Babylonian Talmud: Seder Nashim: Translated into English with Notes, Glossary and Indices*, ed. I. Epstein, 4 vols. (London: The Soncino Press, 1936), 3:"Soṭah":60 and 65.

[47] M. R. James, ed., *The Biblical Antiquities of Philo* (New York: KTAV Publishing House, Inc., 1971 reprint), ix, 10 (p. 102). See, too, Daniel J. Harrington, ed., *The Hebrew Fragments of Pseudo-Philo's Liber Antiquitatum Biblicarum Preserved in the Chronicles of Jerahmeel*, Society of Biblical Literature Texts and Translations, Pseudepigrapha Series 3 (Missoula, Mont.: Scholars Press for The Society of Biblical Literature, 1974), 38, 39.

embellished but unmistakably the same, in the annunciations in chapter one of both Luke and Matthew.[48]

Moses' Precocity. This leads to a further and on this occasion final theme (but in terms of the material it is hardly final), that of the precocity of Moses. Philo reports:

> As he grew and thrived without a break, and was weaned at an earlier date than they had reckoned, his mother and nurse in one brought him to her from whom she had received him. . . . He was noble and goodly to look upon . . . so advanced beyond his age . . . he did not bear himself like the mere infant that he was . . . [etc., etc.]"[49]

Josephus, too, notes:

> . . . she [the princess], at sight of the little child, was enchanted at its size and beauty. . . . His growth in understanding . . . far outran the measure of his years. . . . When he was three years old, God gave wondrous increase to his stature; and none was so indifferent to beauty as not, on seeing Moses, to be amazed at his comeliness.[50]

The theme of Moses' maturity appears in rabbinic texts in a slightly less direct fashion but clearly visible. To the verse (Exodus 2:6), "When she opened it she saw the *yld* (= infant); and lo, the *n'r (=* lad) was crying," the commentator in *Tanḥuma* noted: "it does not say 'the infant was crying' but 'the lad.' This teaches that though he was an infant he had a lad's voice." Further on in the same text, to the verse (11), "It happened, when Moses was grown up *(wygdl mśh),*" the commentator queries: "do not all things grow?, man, cattle, beasts, birds, all grow. This teaches that his growth was out of the ordinary."[51] In yet another text we are told that when Moses was but five years old he appeared as though he were eleven years of age.[52] As to Moses' comeliness, the continuation of the first comment declares: "Pharaoh's daughter kissed him and hugged him and loved him and would not permit him to leave the king's palace,

---

[48] Luke 1:8–23, 26–38; Matthew 1:20–23.

[49] Philo, *De Vita Mosis* 1:18–20. Translation from *Philo*, Loeb 6:285–287.

[50] Josephus, *Jewish Antiquities* 2.9.5–6 (2.224–231). Translation from *Josephus*, Loeb 4:261–265.

[51] *Midrash Tanḥuma*, Shemot 8, 9; (cf. n. 28 above), 125. Translation mine.

[52] *Tanḥuma*, Va'era 17, editio Buber, 2:33. See, too, V. Aptowitzer, *Kain und Abel in der Agada, den Apokryphen, der hellenistischen, christlichen und muhammedanischen Literatur*, Veröffentlichung der Alexander Kohut Memorial Foundation 1 (Wein and Leipzig: R. Löwit, 1922), 110–111, n. 32.

for he was so very beautiful that all desired to behold him, nor would anyone who saw him pass him by."

And is this not the same theme that sounds thrice in the Gospel of Luke: *to de paidion ēuxanen kai ekrataiouto pneumati* ("And the child grew and became strong in spirit"); *to de paidion ēuxanen kai ekrataiouto plēroumenon sophią* ("And the child grew and became strong, filled with wisdom"); and *kai Iēsous proekopten en tę sophią kai hēlikią kai chariti para theǫ kai anthrōpois* ("And Jesus increased in wisdom and in stature [or years] and in favor with God and man")?[53]

Conclusion: How to Hear a Text

It is important to indicate that all of the material dealt with in this essay is easily available, so that no claim can be made that anything new has been discovered. What is crucial, however, is the insistence that this material must be viewed anew. It is less than helpful, no matter how valuable, to bring such material together as was done almost one hundred years ago by Heinrich Bloch in his painstaking work, *Die Quellen des Flavius Josephus*, if one is misled by Bloch's title or, for that matter, by the attempt (then regnant in scholarship and perhaps related to problems that inspired the Colloquy on the Relationships among the Gospels and this volume) to establish the literary source of each item in Josephus.[54] A century ago, scholars assumed unquestioningly that a literary work had its sources in literary works (for, after all, were not these scholars themselves ransacking literary works to fabricate new literary works?). And even now, when we have come to affirm that behind some or many of the literary works we deal with there is an oral tradition, we still manipulate such traditions as though they too were "literary" works. We have not come to terms with a fecund world of ideas, to leap beyond my original metaphor long since inundated by the rain of quotations. We still march along the straight black line of the Gutenberg galaxy.

[53] Luke 1:80; 2:40; 2:52.

[54] Heinrich Bloch, *Die Quellen des Flavius Josephus in seiner Archäologie* (Wiesbaden: Dr. Martin Sandig OHG, 1968 reprint of 1879 ed.); also Salomo Rappaport, *Agada und Exegese bei Flavius Josephus* (Wien: Alexander Kohut Memorial Foundation, 1930); and Ginzberg, *The Legends of the Jews*, 7(Cohen): 547–550.

More than fifty years ago, Victor Aptowitzer wrote in the introduction to his work, *Kain und Abel in der Agada, den Apokryphen, der hellenistischen, christlichen und muhammedanischen Literatur*:

1. The legends of the agada are part folk, part literary legends. Folk legend is the mother of exegesis, whilst literary legend is the last born daughter.
2. Many literary legends owe their formation to particular tendencies or polemics and many folk stories, their rearrangement to the same.
3. Tendentiousness and polemic have caused ancient Jewish legends to vanish for centuries from Jewish writings, only to reappear in late agadic works—when the tendentiousness is devoid of application and the polemic has become unnecessary. This is the emigration and return home of the legend. But there are as well legends that are really "wild shoots in the vineyard of Israel." This is the immigration of legends.
4. Similar situations encourage the formation of similar stories, or parallels. Such parallels also arise in connection with different persons and situations because of a particular tendency. For example, the similarities between Cain-Abel, Esau-Jacob and Abel-Enoch stories.
5. There are agadas that have nothing in common as far as external form is concerned but internally are closely related, for they are rooted in one and the same point of view, from which alone they can be understood. Similarly, there are agadas that can be understood only by reference to halakhah [legal materials] and halakhahs that are understood only in connection with agadas. This is the coherence between agada and halakhah.
6. The contiguities between Philo and rabbinic agada are far wider and deeper than has previously been recognized. The same is true for Jewish agada and the churchly authors.[55]

I quote this at length not to indicate agreement with all that Aptowitzer wrote, but to point out that one must be particularly sensitive to dynamic inner relationships.

As has been indicated throughout this essay, simply by juxtaposing materials *in their contexts*, storytelling (for this is what we have been looking at) is something other than redaction. In a recent review, David L. Tiede, summarizing a point made by Gerd Theissen, wrote: "The 'redactor' is much more dependent

---

[55] Aptowitzer, *Kain und Abel in der Agada, den Apokryphen, der hellenistischen, christlichen und muhammedanischen Literatur*, V–VII; translation mine. I assume that when Aptowitzer wrote of folk legend he was thinking of oral tradition and that by literary legend he had text, i.e., something written, in mind. The distinction between folk song and art song may help to clarify the distinction.

upon the possibilities that are latent in the structure of the tradition than generally has been observed."[56] "Redactor" thus understood is one who senses the *latent* possibilities within a tradition and, by his placing of the tradition in a particular context, manifests *a* possibility that may obscure but not efface others. To hearers at home in a tradition, it is the tension between manifestation and latency that enriches and enlarges the meaning of the story. An example from a different, yet related field may illuminate this point. In the synagogue, the Book of Esther is read traditionally at a rather rapid rate with its own distinctive cantillation. Five verses, however, are chanted more slowly and with the chant reserved for the Book of Lamentations. The verses are: 1:7: "And they gave them to drink in vessels of gold . . ."; 2:6: "who had been carried away from Jerusalem with the captives that had been carried away with Jeconiah king of Judah, whom Nebuchadnezzar the king of Babylon had carried away"; 3:15: "but the city of Shushan was thrown into confusion"; 4:16, which concludes with the words "and if I perish, I perish"; and finally 8:6, whose opening words *ky ʾykkh* "how can I" echo the opening word of Lamentations, chapters 1, 2, and 4, *ʾykh*. The reason for this anomaly is evident for several of the verses, but to understand its presence in the first, one must know that, according to a *haggadah*, the vessels used by the king and his courtiers were none other than the sacred vessels of the Temple of Jerusalem. The words in 3:15 are *h ʿyr šwšn nbwkh*, in which the last word, it seems to me, assonates with the root *bkh* "to weep." Indeed, attention to "the structural force of wandering motifs," to use Eric Werner's insightful phrase in connection with the music of the Synagogue, can provide a texture of understanding that goes far beyond concern with the "theological" idiosyncrasies of mere redactors, for it is the story as a whole that is the center of the storyteller's thought and to which he devotes, consciously and unconsciously, his art.[57]

[56] David L. Tiede, review of *Urchristliche Wundergeschichten. Ein Beitrag zur formgeschichtlichen Erforschung der synoptischen Evangelien*, by Gerd Theissen, in *Journal of Biblical Literature*, 95 (1976), 483.

[57] Eric Werner, *A Voice Still Heard: The Songs of the Ashkenazic Synagogue* (University Park: Pennsylvania State University Press, 1976), 83–84 ("Cantillation of Esther") and 38; see also "General Index," s.v., "Motifs, wandering." I have used "wandering themes" throughout this essay in much the same sense as Werner uses "wandering motifs." The two terms are interchangeable in the present setting.

What this suggests to me, as I contemplate the present state of the study of the gospels, is the need to withdraw, at least temporarily, from our preoccupation with questions of chronology and literary relationships and to focus rather on the gospels as manifestations of the storyteller's art. It is the storyteller who has at his disposal the forms and modes of expression that give texture to the tales. The themes and thematic episodes belonging to the environment provide the means of illuminating or shadowing events, of transforming them in such ways as shall capture the attention, compel the acquiescence, and, ultimately, command the allegiance (if this is what is sought) of the hearers.[58] Neither Philo nor Josephus nor the midrashic expositors were mere retailers of raw folk traditions. Rather were these traditions the stuff, the constituent elements, that, when imaginatively seized upon, were given shape that disclosed, were set in tension with context that enchanted, were provided form that grasped, so that at last (to use the late Ian Ramsey's beguiling phrase)[59] they broke the ice, and the sought-after or even unexpected new was now revealed. To be a teller of tales is no mean feat. To be a hearer of tales, too, is a high accomplishment, a noble art.

[58] As indicated in n. 4 above, I have made occasional references to passages in the gospels that pick up some of the themes I have been concerned with (see notes 21, 43, 48, 53, and their references in the text). I have done this not to play the game of parallels or of Jewish sources but to illustrate what I understand to be the role of wandering themes. Indeed, were one to go to H. L. Strack and Paul Billerbeck, *Kommentar zum Neuen Testament aus Talmud und Midrasch*, 5 vols. in 6 (München: Beck, 1922–1956), and, after careful and suitable winnowing, examine the congruent thematic materials that remain from this perspective, one would, perhaps, come away from the reading and hearing of the gospels with a livelier sense of what they were as stories before they became texts. To discover this, it seems to me, is far more important than to answer the questionable question of who used whom, but it is just this discovery that has been lost sight of in modern and contemporary scholarship. With this in mind, then, I chose the Latin tag, "habent sua fata libelli," understanding it to mean "stories have their luck," as the title of my essay.

[59] Ian T. Ramsey, *Religious Language: An Empirical Placing of Theological Phrases* (London: SCM Press Ltd, 1957), 49.

The Gospels and the Canonical Process: A Response to Lou H. Silberman

James A. Sanders

Lou H. Silberman's essay attacks some of the basic assumptions underlying source criticism as inherited from the nineteenth century and criticizes the whole exercise of this discipline as it might apply to various bodies of Jewish literature in the Hellenistic cultural area, including the gospels. Here, Silberman joins a growing company of students of the Bible, Old Testament and New, who are scrutinizing not only the results of source criticism but also its assumptions and methods. He puts his case sharply: "A century ago, scholars assumed unquestioningly that a literary work had its sources in literary works (for, after all, were not these scholars themselves ransacking literary works to fabricate new literary works?)" (p. 215). Silberman notes that even when we now speak of oral traditions "we still manipulate such traditions as though they too were 'literary' works," suggesting that we need to "come to terms with a fecund world of ideas" (p. 215) and "to focus . . . on the gospels as manifestations of the storyteller's art" (p. 218).

Silberman speaks of "a large body of thematic materials" that "at various times, in various ways, with various emphases," "came into expression for particular occasions" (p. 195). He stresses themes, or using Eric Werner's phrase, "wandering motifs" (p. 217) on the one hand, and, on the other hand, the many and varied particular contexts to which these themes and motifs were applied. In the different applications "the various uses of particular themes may be entirely inconsistent one with the other" (p. 195). The same theme in two different contexts or literary deposits may be very different, even contradictory.

Earlier this century, at a time when source criticism of the Old Testament had become almost a caricature in the hands of its most devoted adherents, Hermann Gunkel made some of the same observations about it. Source critics had begun to split infinitives and slice off conjunctions in pursuit of the kind of consistency that Silberman denies to his ancient themes.[1] Gunkel brought to bear another kind of criticism on the book of Genesis, however, which but substituted the method of form criticism for that of source criticism. At about the same time, source criticism was being attacked by archaeologists and philologists, and in Germany form criticism soon developed into tradition criticism.[2] There were parallel developments in work on the four gospels.[3] The result of such critical dialogue within biblical criticism has been the continued use of the sigla devised by source criticism, such as "J," "E," "D," "P," "Q," "logia," and the like, but only as indicating possibilities of traditions rather than discreet palpable documents. Certainly in the case of the Pentateuch one cannot now find a serious scholar anywhere arguing for the date and provenance of "J" or of any putative stratum within it. Attention is now focused elsewhere.

---

[1] For an example of how far source criticism went, see Cuthbert A. Simpson, "The Growth of the Hexateuch" and "The Book of Genesis: Introduction and Exegesis," in *The Interpreter's Bible: The Holy Scriptures in the King James and Revised Standard Versions with General Articles and Introduction, Exegesis, Exposition for Each Book of the Bible*, ed. George Arthur Buttrick *et al.*, 12 vols. (New York and Nashville: Abingdon Press, 1951–1957), 1:185–200 and 1:437–829. Hermann Gunkel wrote voluminously, but for an easily accessible statement of his approach, see his *The Legends of Genesis: The Biblical Saga and History*, trans. W. H. Carruth, 1st Schocken Paperback ed. (New York: Schocken Books, Inc., 1964 reprint of 1901 edition); see also "Fundamental Problems of Hebrew Literary History," in *What Remains of the Old Testament and Other Essays*, trans. A. K. Dallas (New York: The Macmillan Company, 1928), 57–68.

[2] See, e.g., John Bright, *Early Israel in Recent History Writing: A Study in Method*, Studies in Biblical Theology 19 (London: SCM Press Ltd, 1956), esp. 34–55.

[3] See, e.g., Werner Georg Kümmel, *Introduction to the New Testament*, rev. ed., trans. Howard Clark Kee (Nashville and New York: Abingdon Press, 1975), 35–247.

A Response to Lou H. Silberman

Old Testament Textual Fluidity and Canonical Open-endedness

The observations that Silberman makes are congruous with some basic developments today in Old Testament text criticism and canonical criticism.

The recovery of the Dead Sea Scrolls has revolutionized Old Testament text criticism. Until their impact was absorbed by the field, text criticism was understood to be the exercise of biblical criticism that engaged in establishing the biblical text. By nearly universal agreement, this meant recovering the original text. One was free to mix philological observations with archaeological discoveries, literary critical analysis with scrutiny of ancient texts and versions, in order to come up with more and more brilliant and ingenious scholarly conjectures as to what the original of a difficult text was. One has but to look at the apparatus in the various editions of Rudolf Kittel's *Biblia Hebraica*[4] and now also in that of the *Biblia Hebraica Stuttgartensia*[5] to see the purpose of text criticism as it has been understood until recently. Examples of the end result of this view of text criticism can be found in *The Jerusalem Bible* (English version based on the first French edition)[6] and *The New English Bible*.[7]

The older view was part of a general "primitivist" tendency within biblical studies. *Biblische Wissenschaft*, whether source criticism or text criticism, was dedicated to recovering points originally scored. The first of anything was the best. The closer one could tune into the *ipsissima vox* of Jeremiah or Jesus, for example, the closer one approached truth. How could it be otherwise?

The assumption was that an *ipsissima vox* would in utter clarity convey the speaker's intention. The full impact of the meaning of "context" for understanding "text" seems to have struck us fully only in recent times. While we may be a bit overwhelmed now with the scepticism forced upon us by the

---

[4] Rud. Kittel, ed., *Biblia Hebraica*, 3d ed., completed by A. Alt and O. Eissfeldt (Stuttgart: Privilegierte Württembergische Bibelanstalt, 1937); the 15th ed. (1968) is a revised and augmented reprinting of the 3d ed.

[5] K. Elliger, ed., *Biblia Hebraica Stuttgartensia* (Stuttgart: Privilegierte Bibelanstalt, 1968–1976), in fascicles.

[6] Alexander Jones, ed., *The Jerusalem Bible* (Garden City, N.Y.: Doubleday & Company, Inc., 1966).

[7] *The New English Bible with The Apocrypha* (London: Oxford University Press/Cambridge: Cambridge University Press, 1970).

sociology of knowledge, it is nonetheless wise to be aware of assumptions. Even some earlier critics, who insisted most strongly that the Bible was a product of history, did not always take into account that whatever we might have from Jeremiah or Jesus had of necessity come through the understanding and formation of early believing communities.

Form criticism made such observations with a sort of vengeance, but text criticism continued to include conjecture about original readings until the realization dawned that in the period up to ca. 100 C.E., an important characteristic of biblical texts was not only their relative stability but also their relative fluidity. The degree of fluidity varied between Torah, Prophets, and Hagiographa, with Torah considerably more stable than the others, but it has become increasingly clear that a marked change took place in the course of the first century C.E. Moshe Greenberg was the first to call attention to this change in 1956, and he was followed soon thereafter by Dominique Barthélemy, Shemaryahu Talmon, Frank Moore Cross, and Moshe H. Goshen-Gottstein.[8] In the so-called "Accepted Texts Period,"[9] that is up to about 100 C.E., there were different families of texts (Cross) or autonomous local texts (Talmon). Even handsome, official copies of biblical books had been adapted by textual alteration to the major theological beliefs of those who copied and read the books. As Talmon has shown, even proto-Masoretic or Pharisaic scribes in the Persian-Hellenistic period contributed to the Scriptures they copied.[10] But they did so within their understanding of piety and faith. Whatever *tiqqunê sopherim* (corrections by the scribes)

[8] Moshe Greenberg, "The Stabilization of the Text of the Hebrew Bible, Reviewed in the Light of the Biblical Materials from the Judean Desert," *Journal of the American Oriental Society*, 76 (1956), 157–167; and see the several articles by Dominique Barthélemy, Shemaryahu Talmon, Frank Moore Cross, Moshe H. Goshen-Gottstein, and others, all to the point, in *Qumran and the History of the Biblical Text*, ed. Frank Moore Cross and Shemaryahu Talmon (Cambridge, Mass., and London: Harvard University Press, 1975).

[9] For sketches of the history of transmission of the Hebrew text see M. H. Goshen-Gottstein, "Hebrew Biblical Manuscripts, Their History and Their Place in the HUBP Edition," *Biblica*, 48 (1967), 243–290; James A. Sanders, "Text Criticism and the NJV Torah," *Journal of the American Academy of Religion*, 39 (1971), 193–197; the brilliant reconstruction by D. Barthelemy, "Text, Hebrew, History of," in *The Interpreter's Dictionary of the Bible: An Illustrated Encyclopedia*, supplementary vol., ed. Keith Crim *et al.* (Nashville: Abingdon Press, 1976), 878–884.

[10] See the incisive and pivotal new paper by Shemaryahu Talmon, "The Tex-

there were would have taken place in this period: Scribes could alter the text in the light of a major theological belief.[11] Especially at Qumran the fluidity of biblical texts was exploited. As Talmon has so brilliantly shown:

> In contradistinction [to the later rabbis], the Qumran Covenanters did not subscribe to the idea that the biblical era had been terminated, nor did they accept the concomitant notion that 'biblical' literature and literary standards had been superseded or replaced by new conceptions. It appears that the very concept of a 'canon of biblical writings' never took root in their world of ideas, whatever way the term 'canon' is defined. Ergo, the very notion of a closing of the canon was not relevant. This applies to the completion of the canon of Scriptures as a whole, and also to the closure of its major components. It would seem that not only did the complex of the Hagiographa remain an open issue, but also the collection of prophetic books was not considered sealed.[12]

Talmon goes on to recognize my own arguments about the openendedness of the Psalter at Qumran.[13]

In other words, the gospels were shaped and then written precisely at the end of the period when in Judaism both the text and the canon of Scripture were to an extent fluid and openended. S. Vernon McCasland was wrong; Matthew did not twist the Scriptures when he so often reshaped his citations of the Old Testament to suit his overriding theological convictions concerning Christ and the Church.[14] Neither did the other New Testament writers. This was the thing to do. It was the greater piety. Here Qumran and the early church shared the same eschatological belief that God was doing another righteousness in their day like the ones recounted in Scripture, but even more important in

---

tual Study of the Bible—A New Outlook," in *Qumran and the History of the Biblical Text*, ed. Cross and Talmon, 321–400.

[11] See D. Barthélemy, "Les Tipqunê Sopherim et la critique textuelle de l'Ancien Testament," in *Congress Volume, Bonn 1962*, Supplements to Vetus Testamentum 9 (Leiden: E. J. Brill, 1963), 285–304; see now Bruce Nielsen, *Tqwny Sprym* (M.Div. thesis, Union Theological Seminary in the City of New York, 1977), the most complete study of the topic to date.

[12] Talmon, "The Textual Study of the Bible—A New Outlook," 379.

[13] Talmon, "The Textual Study of the Bible—A New Outlook," 379 and n. 254; cf. James A. Sanders, "Cave 11 Surprises and the Question of Canon," in *New Directions in Biblical Archaeology*, ed. David Noel Freedman and J. C. Greenfield (Garden City, N.Y.: Doubleday & Company, Inc., 1969), 113–130.

[14] S. Vernon McCasland, "Matthew Twists the Scriptures," *Journal of Biblical Literature*, 80 (1961), 143–148.

that he was now eschatologically bringing all the earlier episodes of his holy history to completion, to climax and fulfillment.[15]

At Qumran the Psalter was open-ended because of the belief that David wrote 4,050 psalms, and the greater piety was to be sure not to deny to him some psalm he might indeed have written. The idea of cutting the Psalter back to a "paltry psaltry" of 150 psalms would have been blasphemy for the Qumran community, whether other branches of Judaism had done so or not. It would have been as much a betrayal of their essential identity as God's True Israel (the right denomination) as using a different calendar.[16] In study of the Psalter we can see well what Eric Werner meant by "wandering motifs" in religious music,[17] for in the non-Masoretic psalms at Qumran, as well as in some of the 150 Masoretic psalms, we find refrains, incipits, and many phrases deposited in more than one psalm. It would appear sheer folly to try to bring the methods of source criticism to bear on such phenomena, for what often happened was that many psalmists used common liturgical phrases and words. These wandering motifs and liturgical phrases belonged to everybody.

Fifteen years after Albert C. Sundberg, Jr., wrote his dissertation at Harvard University on the Old Testament in the early churches, his main point has been amply confirmed: whereas Judaism was able at the Council of Jamnia to stabilize its canon (with lively discussion continuing about a few literary units: Esther, Song of Songs, Qohelet, and even Proverbs and Ezekiel) at the end of the first century, Christianity, whose break with

---

[15] See the basic statement by Karl Elliger on the hermeneutics of the author of the *pseher* on Habakkuk in his *Studien zum Habakuk-Kommentar vom Toten Meer*, Beiträge zur historischen Theologie 15 (Tübingen: J. C. B. Mohr [Paul Siebeck], 1953), 275–287; see also James A. Sanders, "From Isaiah 61 to Luke 4," in *Christianity, Judaism and Other Greco-Roman Cults: Studies for Morton Smith at Sixty*, ed. Jacob Neusner, 4 parts, Studies in Judaism in Late Antiquity 12 (Leiden: E. J. Brill, 1975), 1:75–106; Daniel Patte, *Early Jewish Hermeneutic in Palestine*, Society of Biblical Literature Monograph Series 22 (Missoula, Mont.: Scholars Press for The Society of Biblical Literature, 1975), 209–314.

[16] See col. 27 of 11QPs[a] in James A. Sanders, *The Psalms Scroll of Qumran Cave 11 (11QPs^a)*, Discoveries in the Judean Desert (of Jordan) 4 (Oxford: The Clarendon Press, 1965), 91–93; also, James A. Sanders, *The Dead Sea Psalms Scroll* (Ithaca, N.Y.: Cornell University Press, 1967), 15–21, 134–135, and esp. 155–159.

[17] Eric Werner, *A Voice Still Heard: The Songs of the Ashkenazic Synagogue* (University Park: Pennsylvania State University Press, 1976), 83–84 ("Cantillation of Esther") and 38; see also "General Index," s.v., "Motifs, wandering."

Judaism was definitive by the year 70, did not benefit from such standardization, so that the churches continued to have many of the books that some Jewish denominations before 70 had held sacred. The churches in the east retained the so-called Apocrypha and Pseudepigrapha and those in the west the so-called Apocrypha.[18] Published in the same year as Sundberg's dissertation was a paper by Jack P. Lewis, which showed that the occurrence of the so-called Council of Jamnia in 90 C.E. cannot be supported by hard literary evidence.[19] Sundberg's principal thesis remains valid, however: the stabilization that took place in Judaism by the end of the first century and that is amazingly attested to in the biblical manuscripts now available from between the First and Second Jewish Revolts simply did not take place in Christianity. On the other hand, the standardization and stabilization of text and canon that took place in Judaism between 70 and 135 cannot be read back, as was done until recently, into the pre-70 period. For Judaism the pre-70 period was one of comparative textual fluidity and canonical open-endedness. Whatever antecedents to standardization there were before 70 cannot be viewed as official, normative, or the like.[20]

Old Testament Stabilization and Standardization

The New Testament, then, came into being precisely at the end of the period of Old Testament textual fluidity and canonical open-endedness, that is, at the end of what Talmon calls "the biblical period." For Christianity the process of stabilization and standardization was less intense and was to continue for some time. Not until the reformation would Christianity attempt to limit the Old Testament to the radically curtailed canon of Judaism. To the degree that Christianity remained eschatologically oriented into the second century C.E., it remained open to whatever God might momentarily do, through the parousia or perhaps through some other re-creative or apocalyptic act. All of the New Testament literature, with only the possible exceptions of a few of the latest epistles, would have come from such an

[18] Albert C. Sundberg, Jr., *The Old Testament of the Early Church*, Harvard Theological Studies 20 (Cambridge, Mass.: Harvard University Press, 1964).

[19] Jack P. Lewis, "What Do We Mean By Jabneh?," *The Journal of Bible and Religion*, 32 (1964), 125–132.

[20] See Barthelemy, "Text, Hebrew, History of."

eschatological ethos in the churches. Judaism had for the most part turned the corner of stabilization after the catastrophe of 70, but Christianity continued largely in the same eschatological vein of thinking with which we are familiar from the vast resources of non-Masoretic Jewish literature either preserved by the churches in the Apocrypha and Pseudepigrapha or discovered by archaeology at Qumran and elsewhere. If I read Hans von Campenhausen, Werner Georg Kümmel, Kurt Aland, and others correctly, Christianity did not even attempt to turn its corner of stabilization until the middle of the second century when Marcion shocked it into doing so. Until that time the churches in their christological and ecclesiological arguments not only engaged in midrash on Scripture (the "Old Testament") but firmly believed in listening to the voice of the living Lord and of the Spirit in determining what could be used in worship and instruction.[21] The dangers that Jeremiah was apparently willing to live with in his time, when, as a part of his polemic against Deuteronomy, he insisted on continually listening to the voice of Yahweh (Jeremiah 7:23 *et passim*) became too great for the churches in the face of the disintegrating forces of multiplying heresies.

But we should also note that as the New Testament thinkers and authors made use of the Old Testament they retained well past the year 70 the type of freedom that characterized the era of textual fluidity which we know from the Qumran literature. The kind of narrow sense of midrash that was introduced after 70 in Judaism, in which the midrashist cited the biblical text accurately but then could use all sorts of rules to break it up and make it relevant and adaptable, did not take hold in Christianity until after Marcion and probably not until the time of Origen.[22] This observation is parallel to that by Sundberg concerning the canon of the Old Testament in the early churches. Christian thinkers still had the earlier conviction of the ontology of canon: it was both relatively adaptable and relatively stable tradition. They cited it and adapted it and wove it into their new literature just

---

[21] See esp. Hans von Campenhausen, *The Formation of the Christian Bible*, trans. J. A. Baker (Philadelphia: Fortress Press, 1972), esp. 103–163; Kümmel, *Introduction to the New Testament*, 475–484; Kurt Aland, *The Problem of the New Testament Canon*, Contemporary Studies in Theology 2 (London: A. R. Mowbray & Co. Limited, 1962), esp. 8–18.

[22] Roger Le Déaut, "Apropos a Definition of Midrash," *Interpretation*, 25 (1971), 259–282.

as most Jews had been doing since the beginnings, way back into biblical times.[23]

The shift in ontology of Scripture, from being primarily adaptable to being primarily stable, which culminated by the end of the first century C.E. with an almost stable text and canon for Judaism, had antecedents in the first century B.C.E. Beginning in the reign of Salome Alexandra, with the activity of the Pharisees when they had some power, and culminating in the Pharisaic survival of the First Jewish Revolt when they alone remained after the destruction of Jerusalem, the ontology of the Bible made the shift it would retain for 1800 years thereafter, until the rise of biblical criticism. The idea of verbal inspiration of the Torah was introduced by the proto-Masoretic Pharisees beginning in the first century B.C.E. and then not long thereafter the concept of literal inspiration.[24] There had long been shamanistic ideas of inspiration, especially of Torah. But the concepts of verbal and literal inspiration were new and helped to solve some of the problems of relevance. The concepts were applied first, and primarily, to laws within Torah.

The problem of relevance of the old Bronze and Iron Age laws was met in two basic ways. The first, as Silberman has noted (p. 197), was *Torah šebĕ ʿal peh* ("oral Torah"). To attribute laws to Moses was the basic means of legitimizing them. To do so the tradition arose, as noted in *Pirqè ʾAbot*, that Moses, after his consultation with God on Sinai, passed much more on to Joshua in oral form than in written form. The concept of *Torah šebĕ ʿal peh* thus guaranteed the continuing adaptability and relevance of the Law. But along with this concept also rose that of verbal inspiration. If the *peshat* (plain meaning) of a passage did not make sense in a new situation, or if no *peshat* of any passage met a new problem arising out of new situations, then the *peshat* had to be by-passed in some way.[25] In its inception verbal inspiration must have been one of the most "radic-lib" ideas ever to arise; if

[23]James A. Sanders, "Adaptable for Life: The Nature and Function of Canon," in *Magnalia Dei: The Mighty Acts of God: Essays on the Bible and Archaeology in Memory of G. Ernest Wright*, ed. Frank Moore Cross, Werner E. Lemke, and Patrick D. Miller, Jr. (Garden City, N.J.: Doubleday & Company, Inc., 1976), 531–560.

[24]See notes 9 and 20 above.

[25]See R. Loewe, "The 'Plain' Meaning of Scripture in Early Jewish Exegesis," in *Papers of the Institute of Jewish Studies* (Jerusalem: Hebrew University Press, 1964), 140–185.

the plain meaning of a verse was not relevant then one could break up the syntax of the verse, focus on one word in it, and find a vehicle to a solution by locating the same word in another passage and bringing the two passages together. Once the *peshat* was thus by-passed to focus on isolated words, one could then create a new literary context by taking separate verses out of their original contexts and combining them. Actually the literary aspect of the practice had been going on a long time. Many larger literary units in the Old Testament were formed because two smaller units both had the same word in them. This was the old redactional technique we call *Stichwörter*, and we should not be surprised to find the practice continued in this new and different way. What was new was the gradual shift in ontology of the Bible to its verbal inspiration, which eventually triumphed in both synagogue and church. But in our period, which Silberman calls the "Hellenistic cultural area," the shift had but begun and at first only among Pharisees or, generally speaking, the proto-Masoretic thinkers of Early Judaism. To accompany the new view of Scripture there soon developed the seven hermeneutic rules of Hillel, the thirteen of Ishmael, and the final traditional thirty-two rules, each set accommodating itself more and more to the view of verbal inspiration as over against *peshat* exegesis. But even so, these rules never entered Christianity because they apparently did not become a part of the thinking of any of those eschatological denominations of Early Judaism that fed into Christianity and because it all happened too late. Early Christians, like many other Jews of the time, fully believed that they lived still in the period of textual fluidity and canonical open-endedness or what Talmon calls "the biblical period."

Torah as Halakah *and Torah as* Haggadah

Some of the hermeneutic techniques that were developed to render new *halakot* (legal interpretations) from old laws came to be applied also to biblical narrative to render haggadic midrashim.[26] Silberman correctly notes that Torah was not limited in reference to the Pentateuch. As I tried to say in a recent article, Torah also meant all divine revelation, including the targumim,

[26]See M. Gertner, "Terms of Scriptural Interpretation: A Study in Hebrew Semantics," *Bulletin of the School of Oriental (and African) Studies*, 25 (1962), 1–4; and M. P. Miller, "Midrash," in *The Interpreter's Dictionary of the Bible*, supplementary vol., 593–597.

developing commentaries, the Talmud, and midrashim.[27] Indeed, in some biblical passages Torah meant oracle or instruction and not law at all. It can even be affirmed that Torah has always included both narrative and stipulation, gospel and law, *haggadah* and *halakah*. Abraham Heschel, in one of the last articles he wrote before his untimely death in 1972, makes the point so beautifully in his inimitable way.

What we know about Abraham and of Rabbi Akiba is not only law. In fact, most of what is contained in the Chumash or Tenach is non-legal ideas or tales. Similarly rabbinic literature contains both halacha and agada, and the thinking of Judaism can only be adequately understood as striving for a synthesis between receptivity and spontaneity, a harmony of halacha and agada. . . . Halacha gives us norms for action; agada vision of the ends of living. Halacha prescribes, agada suggests; halacha decrees, agada inspires; halacha is definite; agada is allusive. The terminology of halacha is exact, the spirit of agada is poetic, indefinable. Halacha is immersed in tradition, agada is the creation of the heart. . . . To maintain that the essence of Judaism consists exclusively of halacha is as erroneous as to maintain that the essence of Judaism consists exclusively of agada. The interrelationship of halacha and agada is the very heart of Judaism. Halacha without agada is dead, agada without halacha is wild.[28]

To observe with Philo, therefore, "dass die Thora mit der Weltschöpfung beginnt,"[29] is to make but an elementary statement about the basic nature of Torah. Not only does Torah begin with creation, it goes on to deal with many important biblical topics including human sin, the relations among the nations, the election of Israel's ancestors, God's dealing with a family that sells its brother into slavery, God's work as liberator, redeemer and desert guide—all before anything at all is said about the will of this God as to how his people should shape their society and conduct their lives. And if Gerhard von Rad's form critical analysis of many traditions in the Bible is correct, the stop at Sinai (where, according to tradition, the Law was given) was not considered important enough to be mentioned anywhere in the

[27] J. A. Sanders, "Torah," in *The Interpreter's Dictionary of the Bible*, supplementary vol., 909–911.

[28] Abraham Heschel, "A Time for Renewal," *Midstream* (1972), 46–51, esp. 47–48.

[29] The words are from the notes to the German translation of Philo: L. Cohn, I. Heinemann, M. Adler, and W. Theiler, eds., *Die Werke Philos von Alexandria in deutscher Übersetzung*, 6 vols., Schriften der jüdisch-hellenistischen Literatur in deutscher Übersetzung (Breslau: M. & H. Marcus, 1900–1937), 1:28, n. 1.

extra-pentateuchal recitals of the whole Torah story.[30] The question is not whether creation begins the Torah, but rather how and when certain denominations in Judaism came to focus so much on Sinai that the narrative portions, the whole setting into which Sinai was placed, were devalued. I have tried to answer this question elsewhere.[31]

In Early Judaism, almost from its inception in the Exile, there seem to have been two major groupings of the scattered and multiplying Jewish denominations: those that focused on Torah as *halakah* and those that stressed its nature as *haggadah*. None stressed one to the exclusion of the other, but the one group searched the old pre-exilic traditions for light on what Jews scattered about the Persian Empire should do to retain their identity; the other searched these traditions for indications of what God would do to alleviate their burdens and liberate them once again from oppression. The latter developed into the heavily eschatological denominations, whose works we know in the Apocrypha, the Pseudepigrapha, and the newly recovered literature from Qumran. The former developed into those denominations, particularly the Hasidim and Pharisees, whose works we know as preserved by later rabbinic Judaism. We have far more of the literature of the eschatological denominations datable to the pre-70 period than of the Pharaisaic literature precisely because Christianity is heir to the former and, as noted, did not benefit from the intense stabilization and standardization process that culminated for Judaism around 100 C.E. (the discoveries of archaeology have also added to the store of this eschatological literature). Furthermore, the proto-rabbinic traditions are notoriously difficult to date: very little can be dated surely before 70. Jacob Neusner's form critical work on these traditions but underscores the point.[32]

Jewish denominations that were extant before 70 can be placed at the two ends of the spectrum just described: those that em-

[30] Gerhard von Rad, "The Form-Critical Problem of the Hexateuch," in *The Problem of the Hexateuch and Other Essays*, trans. E. W. Trueman Dicken (New York: McGraw-Hill Book Company, 1966), 1–78; cf. James A. Sanders, *Torah and Canon* (Philadelphia: Fortress Press, 1972), ix–xx.

[31] See n. 27 above and my "Torah and Paul" in *God's Christ and His People: Essays honoring Nils Alstrup Dahl on the occasion of his Sixty-Fifth Birthday*, ed. Wayne A. Meeks and Jacob Jervell (Oslo: Universitetsforlaget, 1977), 132–140.

[32] Jacob Neusner, *The Rabbinic Traditions about the Pharisees before 70*, 3 pts. (Leiden: E. J. Brill, 1971).

phasized Torah and hence Judaism as a story of what God has done and will do and those that emphasized Torah as stipulations for what Jews have done and should do. There were many shades between, with some perhaps preferring to stress the role of Wisdom in Jewish heritage, but the great preponderance of the literature datable to the period indicates the two major groupings.

After Marcion the central question of canon for Christians may well have been whether the Old Testament was to be retained as Scripture. But the central question about the New Testament, precisely in the period of which Silberman writes, was whether, so to speak, the New Testament was biblical.[33] Paul and the Evangelists had the *ḥuspāh* to claim that the God who created the world, redeemed the slaves from Egyptian bondage, gave them the law at Sinai, guided them through the desert, brought them into the Promised Land, and occupied Jerusalem with David, has just now brought this *haggadah* to its fulfillment and climax: the Torah story is now complete. Paul puts it succinctly: Christ is the *telos* of the Torah righteousness-wise for all who believe (Romans 10:4), i.e., for all who read the Torah as a record of what God has done, as *haggadah*. As Silberman very movingly stresses, the specific *haggadah* for the Passover Seder insists that God was the principal actor in the story of Israel's redemption (p. 208). So also, if the New Testament is read theocentrically, rather than anthropocentrically or christocentrically, in continuity with the Old Testament, one can see its central argument: God has done it again, this time a mighty act of redemption and creation in one, in Christ.

Conclusion: Reading the Gospels Midrashically

I am constrained to agree with the overall thrust of Silberman's essay: source critical work on the formation of the gospels does not now seem to be the most fruitful avenue of approach to them (p. 218). All the earliest Christians knew and applied the Old Testament (Law, Prophets, Psalms, and other writings) to their christological and ecclesiological claims. In addition they had traditions about Jesus' words and parables, as well as some form of the basic kergyma of the early church about the work of God

[33] James A. Sanders, "Torah and Christ," *Interpretation*, 29 (1975), 372–390, esp. 372–375; also see "Torah and Paul."

in Christ. These latter grew in authority through the middle third of the first century to have weight equal eventually to that of the Old Testament Scriptures.[34] Knowing what we do about the period (considering the observations brought by Silberman and those that I have tried to bring about comparative scriptural fluidity and open-endedness), it is simply very difficult to imagine Mark or Matthew, Luke or John, at their desks copying great reams of a gospel *Vorlage* or to imagine that these literary works had their sources in previous literary works, at least not quite in the way source critics have supposed.

On the other hand, it cannot be ignored that there is an amazing amount of verbatim agreement in detailed phrasing among the Synoptics. We cannot agree with Birger Gerhardsson that memory work among early Christians would account for this phenomenon: he simply did not convince very many of us.[35] Silberman's suggestion about free-floating themes will not suffice by itself to account for the Synoptic phenomenon, nor will my observations alone halt the perennial debate regarding the priority of Mark or Matthew, or even Luke.

But I do have a suggestion to make, and it evolves out of the hint that the central christological and ecclesiological arguments of the New Testament become clear if the New Testament is read theocentrically rather than christocentrically. My suggestion is that the New Testament be studied midrashically, through the disciplines of comparative midrash and canonical criticism, before the methods of source and form criticism are applied. I am convinced that we need all the subdisciplines of biblical study so far developed but that they are complementary to each other. I am equally convinced that New Testament students need to see the New Testament as the product of a denomination of Judaism in the first century and to approach it in the light of the history of all the Jewish literature from the fourth century B.C.E. to the end of the first century C.E. Of course, the New Testament has a lot of Hellenism in it, but as Martin Hengel has brilliantly shown, so did much of the rest of the Judaism of the period have a great deal of Hellenism in it.[36] For that matter, the Old Testa-

---

[34] See n. 21 above.

[35] Birger Gerhardsson, *Memory and Manuscript: Oral Tradition and Written Transmission in Rabbinic Judaism and Early Christianity*, trans. E. J. Sharpe, Acta Seminarii Neotestamentici Upsaliensis 22 (Lund: C. W. K. Gleerup/Copenhagen: Ejnar Munksgaard, 1961).

[36] See Martin Hengel, *Judaism and Hellenism: Studies in their Encounter*

ment has a lot of Bronze, Iron, and Persian Age cultural idiom in
it. But none of these should be absolutized. If one studies the
Bible holistically, or canonically, in the stream of history, and if
one approaches the New Testament "from its top side," one gets
a perspective that the great bulk of New Testament source and
form criticism has hardly considered.

My students, among themselves, call the work of comparative
midrash on the New Testament "coming up through the floor-
boards of the New Testament." New Testament scholars agree
that Scripture, or the Old Testament, was the first reference of
authority for all New Testament writers, and especially for Jesus
himself. The Old Testament cuts across the whole question of
gospel sources, whether the source was Jesus, his sayings, "Q,"
logia, Mark, Matthew, or whatever. One need but ask of the Old
Testament citation or allusion (and sometimes it is only an Old
Testament theme woven into the fabric of a gospel passage or, as
Silberman notes, floating themes of the Jewish times, which
nonetheless nearly all have roots in Old Testament tradition)
what its function is in the passage. And one does this first by
drawing up a history of the function of this same Old Testament
passage or theme since its inception in Old Testament times right
through Early Judaism, until it shows up in the New Testament.
The job would not be complete, of course, until the work of the
other subdisciplines had also been brought to bear on the New
Testament passage in question.

One of the poignant observations that one makes, when he or
she has completed an exercise in comparative midrash, is one of
Silberman's first points in his paper: when an old tradition or
theme comes into expression for a particular occasion it may be
quite inconsistent with the way it functioned on another particular occasion. Often, as he rightly says, "the same is not the same"
(p. 196).

We can observe this far back in biblical times. The reference to
the theme of Abraham being one person and inheriting the land
is utterly rejected by Ezekiel (33:24–29) but is advanced as divine truth by Deutero-Isaiah fifty years later (51:1–3). And
many other such examples in the Bible can be given. Such a pluralistic observation can be expanded to the general insight brilliantly stated by James Barr: "It is the shape of the tradition

---

in Palestine during the Early Hellenistic Period, trans. John Bowden, 2 vols.
(Philadelphia: Fortress Press, 1974).

that leads Jesus to the finding of his obedience; but it is also the shape of the tradition that leads his enemies to see him as a blasphemer and to demand that he should be put to death."[37] The student of the Qumran scrolls often gets excited when he or she observes the entirely different functions of the same Old Testament passage or theme in a Qumran commentary over against its appearance in the New Testament. They sometimes serve in the two different contexts to say precisely opposing things.[38] Can we be surprised to observe that some of the very traditions of the Old Testament that the New Testament calls upon to support its christological claims were called upon by other Jews of the period to reject these claims? There are two observations here: (1) The Bible is highly pluralistic; and (2) its traditions are by their very nature as canon adaptable to differing contexts and needs. Whatever was not ambiguous enough to have meaning or value in at least two generations and in more than one context simply was not picked up, read again, and passed on. I hope that this point about canon is abundantly clear by now.[39]

But the Bible is also pluralistic. In the Neo-Orthodox period, when I was a student, we were on constant quest for the unity of the Bible. Today my students know that when they think they have found a point clearly scored in biblical literature, they must then begin a search for its contrapositive. Isaiah 2:4 and Micah 4:3 say that at some future point Judah will beat her swords into plowshares and her spears into pruning hooks, but Joel 3:10 (4:10 in Hebrew) says that she will beat her plowshares into swords and her pruning hooks into spears. Little wonder that the Fourth Gospel says Jesus gave peace (John 14:27), whereas Luke says he came to bring not peace but dissension (Luke 12:51–53).

Study of true and false prophecy in the Old Testament has taken a new turn in the past few years and is one of the more exciting areas of biblical study at the moment, especially the disputation passages, where two ancient theologians or colleagues

[37] James Barr, *Old and New in Interpretation: A Study of the Two Testaments*, The Currie Lectures delivered at Austin Presbyterian Theological Seminary, Texas, February 1964 (New York: Harper & Brothers, Publishers, Inc., 1966), 27.

[38] See James A. Sanders, "Habakkuk in Qumran, Paul and the Old Testament," *The Journal of Religion*, 39 (1959), 232–244, and "The Ethic of Election in Luke's Great Banquet Parable," in *Essays in Old Testament Ethics: J. Philip Hyatt In Memoriam*, ed. James L. Crenshaw and J. T. Willis (New York: KTAV Publishing House, Inc., 1974), esp. 248–253.

[39] See n. 23 above.

can call on the same ancient tradition and apply it to the same historical and political context in ancient Israel or Judah but do so in opposing ways.[40] Isaiah's colleagues could say that even though the Assyrian forces were gathering outside the city gates and setting up their siege works to attack Jerusalem, God would at the right moment rise up as on Mt. Perazim and be angry as in the valley of Gibeon back there when he helped David defeat the Philistines (2 Samuel 5:17–25) and help Judah repel the Assyrians in 701 B.C.E. Isaiah responded that God would rise up right enough as on Mt. Perazim and be wroth as in the valley of Gibeon to do his deed, but strange would be his deed and alien his work, for this time he would as Holy Warrior be at the head of the enemy troops attacking his own people (Isaiah 28:21). Incidentally, Isaiah's colleagues, the so-called false prophets, were right and Isaiah wrong in terms mechanically of what happened in 701. Their hermeneutics were different. But it is Isaiah that is in the canon and not the others.

So in New Testament study I am much more interested in determining the function of Old Testament themes in a given New Testament passage than in determining which Evangelist was copied by the others. There are always three variables in the study of the function of an authoritative tradition: the old text or tradition called upon, the historical context into which it is cited, and the hermeneutics used in doing so. The Bible is full of unrecorded hermeneutics from earliest Old Testament times to the last New Testament book, and we have only begun to ferret them out and look at them. The believing communities, synagogues and churches, have for so long imported hermeneutics to the Bible to render it relevant to ongoing generations that we have failed to see that the Bible is one long record of adaptation of authoritative traditions or themes in many shapes, forms, and styles to ever-changing situations and contexts. Could it not be that recovery of these hermeneutics might give us a clue as to the hermeneutics we might use today to hear afresh what some of

[40] See James L. Crenshaw, *Prophetic Conflict: Its Effect Upon Israelite Religion*, Beihefte zur Zeitschrift für die alttestamentliche Wissenschaft 124 (Berlin and New York: Walter de Gruyter, Inc., 1971); Frank Lothar Hossfeld and Ivo Meyer, *Prophet gegen Prophet. Eine Analyse der alttestamentlichen Texte zum Thema: Wahre und falsche Propheten*, Biblische Beiträge 9 (Fribourg: Verlag Schweizerisches Katholisches Bibelwerk, 1973); James A. Sanders, "The Hermeneutics of True and False Prophecy," in *Canon and Authority: Essays in Old Testament Religion and Theology*, ed. George W. Coats and Burke O. Long (Philadelphia: Fortress Press, 1977), 21–41.

these themes might say to the believing communities that find their identity in them?[41] My suspicion is that if we do just this, we may recover the power for life that the canon has had for these believing communities for nearly three thousand years, including the power to liberate ourselves from ancient and modern cultural forms and mores that sponsor repression of the weak and corrupt the consciousness of the powerful. To focus on the gospels as manifestations of the storyteller's art could begin with a consideration of how the various stories update and contemporize the Old Testament traditions and themes they held to be authoritative. To read the New Testament theocentrically, rather than christocentrically, might indicate how biblical it really is despite the odd, sometimes puzzling Hellenistic idiom in which its stories are recited. To do so might also help us become liberated from absolutizing the equally odd Bronze, Iron, and Persian Age idioms of the Old Testament.

The early churches in their astounding wisdom provided themselves four quite different gospels so that we might not get hung up on any one of them. Nor should we permit ourselves to get hung up on any of the Ancient Near Eastern idioms in which the Bible recites its story of the way God does what he does and says what he says in any age. To experience this liberation might indicate how we can also be liberated from the recent, Modern Near Western idioms that serve us so well in this and other scholarly gatherings, whether the idiom be literary criticism, or source criticism, or form criticism, or rhetorical criticism, or redactional criticism, or canonical criticism . . . .

[41] See J. A. Sanders, "Hermeneutics," in *The Interpreter's Dictionary of the Bible*, supplementary vol., 402–407.

Judaic Studies and the Gospels: The Seminar

Joseph A. Fitzmyer, S.J.

Both the Christian gospels and the post-canonical literature of the Jews grew out of the relationship of certain bodies of tradition to a common Palestinian matrix, namely, the Hebrew Scriptures. Even though one admits at the outset a broad and fundamental difference between these two bodies of tradition, indeed a *chasma mega*, yet because they are developments of a common scriptural matrix, one does at times detect items of affinity and kinship. Moreover, since some of the traditions in post-biblical Jewish literature have persisted in multiple forms, the query surfaces whether the study of this multiplicity of form might reveal some analogues to the problems posed by the multiplicity of the Christian gospels. Certainly this area of comparative study deserves as much attention as that devoted to the insights derived from oral traditional literature, classical literature, or refined literary criticism. Is there something in the field of Judaic studies that will shed light—by way of approach, perspective, methodology, or parallelism—on the vexed question of the relationships among the gospels?

Silberman's Essay and Sanders' Response

Since the full texts are available earlier in this volume, I shall make no attempt in the following paragraphs to summarize the

237

overall contents of the essay by Lou H. Silberman and the response by James A. Sanders. Rather, I shall isolate only those elements in the essay and the response that bear directly upon the issue of the relationships among the gospels and that seem most pertinent to the discussion that took place in the Judaic Studies Seminar during the Colloquy on the Relationships among the Gospels.

Silberman. Silberman treats certain motifs in Jewish literature stemming from communities in the Hellenistic cultural world and dealing with the person of Moses and suggests that such motifs might serve as an analogue for the varying traditions in the gospels surrounding the person of the Palestinian Jew, Jesus of Nazareth.

He compares and analyzes various ways in which the theme of Moses the lawgiver, who prefaced his legislation with the account of creation, wandered and played its role in Philo's *De Opificio Mundi*, in Josephus' *Jewish Antiquities*, and in some rabbinic materials. In each document the question has been posed at least implicitly, "Why does the creation story precede the Law?" The similarity in the passages is obvious. But the answer given by each writer to the question varies. One cannot be sure of the form of the answer that would have floated around in a tradition prior to its earliest written attestation (in Philo), but one can be sure that the question is pre-Philonic and can see that the answer was at times shaped by a challenge made to a developing situation in Israel's history.

Silberman further cites the theme of the superior quality of Moses' character, which is found in varying forms of an encomium in Philo, Josephus, and some rabbinic materials, as well as subordinate themes about a knowledge of Moses from "sacred books" and from "elders of the nation" (Philo and Josephus), about Egypt as a land of luxury, which led to its license, sloth, and debauchery (Philo, Josephus, and rabbinic writings), and even a countertheme of the omission of Moses from stories of the Exodus, with which he was intimately related (rabbinic materials).

Similarly, Silberman appeals to the theme of Moses as "the seventh" from Abraham (Philo, Josephus, and rabbinic writings) or, more generally, to the theme of "the beloved seventh" (rabbinic material), to the theme of the "annunciation" of the birth of Moses (Josephus and rabbinic writing), and to that of Moses' precocity (Philo, Josephus, and rabbinic materials). In these themes one notes some elements that have even crept into the gospel tradition.

Thus Silberman shows how a number of themes have wandered about in Jewish writings and yet have played different roles in the redactional composition of different writers. He stresses the unsameness as well as the sameness of these themes, their "dynamic inner relationship," their dependence on oral tradition (despite their eventual written, literary distillation), and their "manifestations of a storyteller's art." Silberman writes: "Neither Philo nor Josephus nor the midrashic expositors were mere retailers of raw folk traditions. Rather were these traditions the stuff, the constituent elements, that, when imaginatively seized upon, were given shape that disclosed, were set in tension with context that enchanted, were provided form that grasped, so that at last . . . they broke the ice, and the sought-after or even unexpected new was now revealed" (p. 218).

Sanders. Sanders' response to Silberman agrees with and supports the latter's contention that what is needed in "the present state of the study of the gospels" is a withdrawal, "at least temporarily, from our preoccupation with questions of chronology and literary relationships . . ." (pp. 231, 218). Sanders lauds Silberman's attack on "some of the basic assumptions underlying source criticism as inherited from the nineteenth century" (p. 219) and recounts the advance in biblical studies from source criticism to form and tradition criticism, and even to canonical criticism. Sanders criticizes as "primitivist" a tendency in biblical scholarship to regard "the first of anything" as the best and regards the quest for the *ipsissima vox* of a Jeremiah or Jesus as a neglect of the context of the believing community in which the traditions were preserved. He stresses the fluidity of the text-traditions of the Old Testament prior to A.D. 100, the openness of the canon at this time, and the composition of the Christian gospels precisely at a time when such fluidity and openness reigned in contemporary Judaism. The use of the Old Testament in the New was not a "twisting of the Scriptures" but an interpretative process with an overriding theological and eschatological concern that manifests fluidity and openness.

Sanders further supports Silberman's idea of wandering themes or motifs by citing the use of "refrains, incipits, and many phrases" of the "Masoretic psalms" in the non-Masoretic psalms of the literature of the Jews of Qumran. He thus introduces a dimension of "Judaic studies" that was not touched on in Silberman's paper. But he adds that it "would be sheer folly to try to bring the methods of source criticism to bear on such phenomena, for . . . many psalmists used common liturgical phrases and words" (p. 224).

Sanders also stresses the wider sense of Torah and the grouping of two sets of traditions that focused on it respectively as *halakah* and as *haggadah*—a grouping that characterized Jews of differing denominations: one Pharisaic/rabbinic, which emphasized what Jews had done and should do; the other apocalyptic/eschatological, which emphasized what God had done and would do. In the new Christian tradition it was stressed rather that God had done it again: by "a mighty act of redemption and creation in one, in Christ" (p. 231).

Maintaining that "source critical work on the formation of the gospels does not now seem to be the most fruitful avenue of approach to them" (p. 231), Sanders finds it "very difficult to imagine Mark or Matthew, Luke or John, at their desks copying great reams of a gospel *Vorlage* or to imagine that these literary works had their sources in previous literary works, at least not quite in the way source critics have supposed" (p. 232). Yet he does not think that "Silberman's suggestion about free-floating themes" will "suffice by itself to account for the Synoptic phenomenon" (p. 232). He suggests rather that the New Testament be "read theocentrically" and that it be "studied midrashically, through the disciplines of comparative midrash and canonical criticism, before the methods of source and form criticism are applied" (p. 232). "One need but ask of the Old Testament citation or allusion . . . what its function is in the passage" (p. 233). Thus Sanders stresses the difference in function of the Old Testament quotation or allusion in the *new* context, whether this context be that of Qumran literature or of the New Testament. Hence the student of the New Testament should be "more interested in determining the function of Old Testament themes in a given New Testament passage than in determining which Evangelist was copied by the others" (p. 235).

Further Comments by Silberman and Sanders

Silberman's essay and Sanders' response had been distributed and read prior to the Colloquy; thus the first session of the Judaic Studies Seminar began with brief oral presentations by both

Silberman and Sanders, followed by Silberman's response to Sanders' comments.[1]

Silberman. Silberman summarized his understanding of the movement of traditional materials in the world of Judaism at about the time of the emergence of Christianity by commenting on three elements of this movement: (a) the nature and dynamic role of tradition; (b) the cultural area or setting in which the tradition moved; and (c) the individual sensibilities that adapted and mediated the tradition in situations of cultural change.

Regarding the nature and dynamic role of tradition, Silberman stressed that although *Pirqê ᵓAbot* in a rather traditional way sought the origin of Mosaic tradition (both written and oral) in the Sinai experience, its authors really knew that the matrix of this tradition was much more the experience of Torah in the structured, ongoing life of the Jewish community. Torah is the tradition of the community. Its written distillation at any given point was the result of particular catalytic agents in the community's life. At first, there was an interdiction against setting the oral tradition in writing, but this eventually yielded to particular needs. Even so, the oral tradition continued to function in the life of the community as a companion to the written Torah; it filled in the interstices of the latter by enlarging, complementing, supplementing, and specifying. In a way, it resembled "Common Law" in the Anglo-Saxon world, and its dynamism derived from the life of the community.

The cultural setting in which the tradition moved affected the speed of this tradition's growth. For example, the slow cultural development during the period after the return from the Babylonian Captivity is reflected in the large span of tradition of "the men of the great synagogue" (*ᵓanšê hakkĕneset haggĕdôlāh*); this tradition is characterized by anonymity, lack of "schools," and lack of individual names. On the other hand, the cultural changes of the Ptolemaic-Seleucid periods, with the influx of Hellenistic modes of life and thought, produced more rapid development, which is reflected in the traditions of this period. Challenges from various cultural settings resulted in new problems, new social requirements, new legal demands, and an intellectual ferment that grafted new forms and structures onto the tradition.

---

[1] Subsequent references to the seminar discussion will not be documented. In the preparation of this paper I used audio tapes of the discussion, and these tapes will be retained by the editor of this volume.

When the tradition encountered new cultural worlds, the interplay between tradition and the changed situation produced individual sensibilities (sensibilities not merely of single persons but much more of groups, "schools," and even communities), and these sensibilities in turn adapted and mediated the tradition. Here one thinks of the individual reactions of the Qumran community (mentioned by Sanders in his response), of the Sadducees, and of the Pharisaic-rabbinic form of Judaism. Major crises, some caused by the First and Second Revolts, played a part in producing these individual sensibilities; those parts of the community that were capable of adjusting to the new situations survived, but others did not.

The Christian gospels seem to represent literary deposits emerging from a tradition, a community, and a cultural matrix that were in many respects similar to those of Palestinian Judaism; thus, much of what has been said about the movement of traditional materials in the world of Judaism would also apply to early Christianity.

Silberman concluded with a note of caution: One should be wary of drawing too sharp a line between Hellenism and Hebraism, between Greek thought and Judaic thought, for Palestinian Jewish communities were not isolated from the larger eastern Mediterranean world with its deposits of late classical culture, Greek thought, Roman legal structures, oriental cults, and the like. In such a world, foreign ideas and practices did affect Palestinian Judaism, as is reflected even in the codification of oral legal traditions about the time of R. Judah the Patriarch (ca. A.D. 200).

Sanders. Sanders' comments focused on the following points: (a) the highly pluralistic situation in Judaism from very early times; (b) the genre or shape of New Testament books; and (c) the relations among the various New Testament books (i.e., the shape of the canon).

Rather than to speak of a basic tradition that may have been either enriched or contaminated as various cultural changes took place, Sanders preferred to emphasize the fact of Jewish pluralism in different historical situations. Recent discoveries have shown that George Foot Moore's picture of "normative Judaism" in pre-Christian times has to be modified, since it does not reflect the pluralism that existed.[2] Figurines found in Palestinian ar-

---

[2] George Foot Moore, *Judaism in the First Centuries of the Christian Era: The Age of the Tannaim*, 3 vols. (Cambridge, Mass.: Harvard University Press,

chaeological excavations were not all Canaanite, for example; some were Jewish. Jeremiah inveighed against polytheism because it was rampant; and so on. What is interesting is the "canonical process," that is, the process of selection, and the factors (socio-political and other) that went into this process in the midst of such pluralism. S. Z. Leiman of Yale University has recently published a list of Jewish writings mentioned in the Old Testament but now lost.[3] What happened to those documents? Many other writings that are still extant (or recently discovered) were ultimately rejected as not authoritative. Did the *Tenak* (i.e., the Hebrew Bible as finally "canonized"), then, represent the best in this filtering process or only that which was favored by the "Yahweh-only party" (to use Morton Smith's term)?[4] Is one certain that what is in the Mishnah represents not just a minority opinion, at least in terms of the wide scope of Jewish history? How does the Qumran literature fit into this picture? Is it not strange, for example, that this literature is not much more heavily influenced by Hellenistic ideas than it is? At any rate, it must be clear that there was no "great wall of China" around Palestine in the first century.

As for the shape of the New Testament writings and of the gospels in particular, it may be a form of *ḥuspāh* to insist on their uniqueness. Morton Smith, for example, regards the gospels as aretalogies and nothing more.[5] But are they not much more like such documents as *Enoch, Jubilees*, and the *Testaments of the Twelve Patriarchs* and thus only further expressions of Judaic

---

1927–1930); "The Rise of Normative Judaism," *Harvard Theological Review*, 17 (1924), 307–375; 18 (1925), 1–39.

[3] S. Z. Leiman, *The Canonization of Hebrew Scripture: The Talmudic and Midrashic Evidence*, Transactions of the Connecticut Academy of Arts and Sciences 47 (Hamden, Conn.: Archon Books, The Shoe String Press, 1976), 16–26.

[4] Morton Smith, *Palestinian Parties and Politics that Shaped the Old Testament*, Lectures on the History of Religions sponsored by the American Council of Learned Societies, new series 9 (New York and London: Columbia University Press, 1971), 29 *et passim*. Smith actually uses the term, "Yahweh-alone party."

[5] See, e.g., Moses Hadas and Morton Smith, *Heroes and Gods: Spiritual Biographies in Antiquity*, Religious Perspectives 13 (New York: Harper & Row, Publishers, Inc., 1965); Morton Smith, "Prolegomena to A Discussion of Aretalogies, Divine Men, the Gospels and Jesus," *Journal of Biblical Literature*, 90 (1971), 174–199; Morton Smith, *The Aretalogy Used by Mark*, Protocol of the Sixth Colloquy of the Center for Hermeneutical Studies in Hellenistic and Modern Culture (Berkeley, Calif.: The Center for Hermeneutical Studies in Hellenistic and Modern Culture, 1975). Cf. Howard C. Kee, "Aretalogy and Gospel," *Journal of Biblical Literature*, 92 (1973), 402–422.

pluralism? To be sure, none of these pre-Christian Jewish writings is exactly like the gospels, but there are striking similarities at certain points. These include a common interest in: (1) a message for the times and a messenger; (2) a congruity between the message and the messenger (and at times an incongruity as well); 3) the effect that the message has on the messenger's life and fate; (4) the effect that the message and messenger have on the people and on the various symbols and institutions of society; and (5) the words and works of the messenger. These features can be found in the book of Jeremiah; they can be found in the books of Moses; they are also found in the gospels (with the addition of the Crucifixion and the Resurrection). This suggests that the gospels wish to be understood as "biblical books," that is, as standing in the line of the earlier tradition about what God has done. Their basic theocentrism (see Sanders' response to Silberman, p. 236) reveals that they *are* biblical books and expressions of a Jewish pluralism. In addition, there is their widespread use of the Old Testament: quotations (with and without introductory formulas), phrases, allusions, and themes; indeed, there is even the same shape of individual units.

Lastly, the relationships among the gospels should be looked at not only in terms of the intentions of the original authors but also in terms of the particular needs of the believing communities that shaped the canon. What needs were being met, for example, when Luke and Acts were separated and John was placed between them? Would not a better order in the canon have been: Matthew, Mark, John, Luke, Acts, Romans, Corinthians . . . ? In his book, *Torah and Canon*, Sanders had suggested a reason for the placing of Deuteronomy between Numbers and Joshua;[6] would it be possible to suggest something similar about the placing of John?

Silberman. In his response to Sanders' comments, Silberman made two points:

(a) Sanders' emphasis on the pluralism within first-century Judaism is correct. An interesting passage in the Babylonian Talmud even ascribes the destruction of Jerusalem to the sectarian quarrels that were taking place in the community there; this is an indication that the rabbinic tradition itself knows of the variety. It is inaccurate to speak of the emergence of "normative" or rabbinic Judaism as a "system" before A.D. 135 or even

[6]James A. Sanders, *Torah and Canon* (Philadelphia: Fortress Press, 1972), 36–45, esp. 44–45.

A.D. 140, and even then it was not a "closed system." Certainly, there was no real uniformity before this time. The monolithic view of orthodox Judaism that one often finds in New Testament introductions is really only the product of nineteenth-century scholarship (in Germany). Of all the varieties of Judaism that existed, the only two that managed to survive to modern times, according to Samuel Sandmel, were rabbinic Judaism and Christianity.[7] The emergence of the Christian gospels and the relationships among them must be seen against the background of such diversity within Judaism.

(b) The emergence of a canon of Scripture has to be understood as the result of a problem that arises when a particular group emerges as more or less dominant. The problem is: how to instruct the whole community and thus insure its unity. "Canonization" of Torah means nothing more than "authorized to be read in the synagogues" (to paraphrase the title page of the King James Version of the Bible). Hence "canon" became something about which the community could rally, the centerpiece of its teaching. The same would have been true of the gospels. Out of a variety of gospels, four came to be regarded as authorized to be read publicly. The others could be read for edification, but not with any guarantee that they would insure entry into the Kingdom of Heaven.

The Seminar Discussions

In the discussions, members of the seminar sought to relate the data laid before them by Silberman and Sanders more specifically to the source criticism of the gospels and the question of their literary interrelationships.

Parallels. The first issue to emerge was that of parallels. It was pointed out that "there are parallels and then there are parallels." *Thematic parallels*, of the sort treated by Silberman, are to be found in the gospels and indeed in the whole corpus of Christian literature, and much of the background of such thematic parallels in the New Testament lies in Jewish discussions of the same topics. There are also specific *verbal parallels*, however, which, along with other parallels of details, cry out for an explanation and which actually gave birth to the source criticism

---

[7] Samuel Sandmel, *Philo's Place in Judaism: A Study of Conceptions of Abraham in Jewish Literature*, augmented ed. (New York: KTAV Publishing House, Inc., 1971), 211.

of the gospels. Another aspect of the question of parallels is the time-spans involved in the traditions being compared: more than a thousand years in the Jewish biblical tradition, at least three hundred in the rabbinic tradition, but fewer than seventy years for the gospel tradition. In this short time, gospels emerged from a tradition in diverse forms, but with verbal parallels. The question, then, is not so much why gospels emerged, but, having emerged, how they are related. Is there literary dependence among them, and if so, of what sort? It was suggested that the real danger here is not that of "parallelomania" but of "backgroundomania," stressing the Old Testament tradition in the gospels to the obscuring of the parallels among the gospels. The specific, word-for-word parallels in the gospels also raise the question, how this phenomenon should be viewed in the context of a growing tradition in the living community of the church, a tradition analogous to that in the living community of Judaism to which Silberman's essay appealed. How was the redaction of the various gospels affected by the ongoing tradition, whether one prefers the priority of Mark or that of Matthew?

Appeal was made to numerous instances in Jewish literature where a high degree of verbal agreement can be found in parallel texts. For instance, Numbers 5:11–31 gives legislation about a wife suspected of adultery. In the halakic commentary of *Sifre*, this legislation is commented on in the biblical order, but in the tractate *Soṭah* of the Mishnah and Tosephtah, a thematic presentation of the same legislation is given. Yet all this material can be put in parallel columns and studied in the same way as the Synoptic parallels; judgments can be made about the growth of the tradition. A similar study could be devoted to the parallel accounts of the four modes of atonement ascribed to R. Ishmael. Such material (and many more examples could be cited) shows that Jews did memorize things word-for-word, did copy things verbatim, and did revise or modify the material thus memorized or copied on the basis of other texts or traditions.[8] The writings here referred to date roughly from A.D. 135–235, but one can also appeal in Qumran literature to variant forms of the War Scroll (1QM, 4QM^{a-f}) and of the Manual of Discipline (1QS, 4QS^{a-j}) for

[8] At this point, E. P. Sanders made reference to the work of E. Z. Melamed, *Hyhs Šbyn Mdršy-hlkh Imšnh wltwspt⟩: ⟩· Šmwšm šl Mdršy Hlkh bmšnh wbtwspt⟩, The Relationship between the Halakhic Midrashim and the Mishna and Tosefta: The Use of Mishna and Tosefta in the Halakhic Midrashim* (Jerusalem: Research Foundation of the University of Tel Aviv, 1967).

earlier parallels.[9] It was proposed that this sort of material should have been used and exploited along with the "wandering themes" to shed light on the relationships among the Synoptic Gospels, since the Synoptic Problem would appear to be primarily a literary problem.

Silberman expressed surprise, however, that one would use Jewish *halakic* material (with its complicated process of growth) as an analogue for the *narrative* materials of the gospels. In Jewish halakic material there is the phenomenon of "back-editing" or "back-revision," i.e., the modification of an earlier text in the light of a decision given by an authoritative rabbi of a later date. This complicates the comparison of halakic parallel texts with the narrative material of the gospels. In such back-editing, the concern was to get two laws governing conduct to agree, but this was scarcely a concern in the case of *haggada*, where it matters little if two related anecdotes do not agree. Silberman also suggested that a real problem in appealing to rabbinic parables as analogues to gospel parallels would be that of explaining how a community originally composed of Galilean peasants under the leadership of a charismatic teacher could in such a short time have accomplished the rather technical and sophisticated process of developing an oral tradition, putting this into written form, back-editing it, and the like. This was countered, however, by a reference to the surprising speed with which the highly sophisticated theology of Paul emerged in an even shorter span of time.

Silberman raised the question, What constitutes a "parallel"? Noting a tendency to regard verbal agreement as the primary mark of parallelism, he argued that a true parallel does not exist unless two passages have similar *functions*; in the absence of such congruity of function, mere verbal agreement is not significant. It appeared, however, that members of the seminar did not completely agree at this point.

A somewhat different tack was taken in the discussion when reference was made to Silberman's essay, where he had compared four passages and concluded that the prior question underlying the similar material, "Why?" (*mpnh mh*), was really the theme uniting the answers given in the four passages (p. 202).

[9] For details of these Qumran texts, see Joseph A. Fitzmyer, *The Dead Sea Scrolls: Major Publications and Tools for Study (With an Addendum, January 1977)*, Society of Biblical Literature Sources for Biblical Study 8 (Missoula, Mont.: Scholars Press, 1977), 14, 29–30, and 32.

The query was raised, whether this was also true for the gospels, where it appears that the answer is often earlier and, in fact, forces the question. Are not those who converse with Jesus (as in John 3-4), for example, really only "straw figures," who supply artificial questions for him to answer? Do not Rudolf Bultmann's "apophthegms," in which the narrative framework is secondary to the pronouncement, reveal the same priority of answer to question?[10] Is there perhaps a difference here between the Christian traditions and the traditions of other contemporary Jewish denominations, a difference that has affected the growth of the material as it was handed on? Some members of the seminar, however, felt that the query could really be put the other way around. Are there not some areas in the gospel tradition where the question is actually prior to the answer? For instance, did not a prior question give rise to the two different Infancy Narratives in Matthew and Luke? And yet, one does not detect this priority of question to answer in the parallel sayings materials, where the similarities are great.

Sanders interjected two observations at this point. The first concerned how an old tradition is picked up and used in a new setting. The story of the Great Supper (*deipnon*) in Luke 14:16-24, for example, has a parallel in Matthew 22:1-10 (as *gamos* or marriage feast), and there is considerable verbal agreement between the two. But what should be of real concern here is not the parallelism as such, but the use of Deuteronomy 20 in Luke and of Zephaniah 1 (as preserved in the Targum) in Matthew. In this instance, source criticism, if focused on by itself, distracts from another important dimension of the parallel stories, namely, the hermeneutical dimension implied in their use of Old Testament materials. When this latter is recognized, the verbal parallels take on a new aspect. Apropos of the difficulty of using the parallels of halakic material for comparison with the gospel parallels, Sanders observed that one apparently has to go down as late as *Tanḥuma* 20 (which begins and ends with Psalm 121) to find haggadic materials with parallels, and this text is dated anywhere from the sixth to the eleventh century A.D.! Here Silberman objected that parallels in haggadic materials are found earlier than *Tanḥuma* and that these parallels exhibit overlapping influence. In his essay he had limited himself to materials from

[10]Rudolf Bultmann, *The History of the Synoptic Tradition*, trans. John Marsh, rev. ed. (New York and Evanston: Harper & Row, Publishers, Inc., 1968), 11-69.

the first two Christian centuries (Philo, Josephus, and the halakic midrashim) and steered clear of the midrashim of a later date, particularly the Galilean materials of the fourth and fifth centuries. In these latter midrashim there is much parallel material, indeed, sometimes verbatim, but again the function that the parallels play is important. For example, there is one small block of material in the Palestinian Talmud, where the text reads *šbh*, "repentance," but which is identical with a passage in the Babylonian Talmud, which reads *glt*, "exile," instead. It is usually considered that the latter has been substituted to adapt the text to the Babylonian situation of Jews dwelling far from the Holy Land. It was pointed out, however, that consideration of the substitution verges on the question of redaction criticism in texts that are otherwise parallel.

It was suggested that since verbatim agreements do appear in the different bodies of literature, one should ask about the institutional forms of the process that produced the literature. Does the agreement result from books being copied, memorization by students in a "school," midrashic interpretation of the Old Testament, or what? What was the institution or process in the Christian community that resulted in the formation of the gospel tradition? In the Greco-Roman world there was widespread "note-taking," as George Kennedy pointed out (p. 126). Would this have a bearing on the formation of the gospel tradition, even though its counterpart in their Jewish background has yet to be discovered? Something of a relevant analogue might be seen in the Qumran *pesharim*, where the use of the Old Testament and its relation to the contemporary beliefs and practices of the Essenes can be analyzed.

It was pointed out that although an explanation of how the gospels came into such a sophisticated state of being in the first generation of Christians might be difficult, one should remember that these gospels were the products of the second or even third generation of Christians, which might be expected to be a reflective, collecting, and literary community. To the question, whether an analogous situation could be found in Judaism with a multiplicity of documents from the second or third generation of a new religious development exhibiting extensive parallels among themselves, Silberman acknowledged that he could not produce anything specific. He did note, however, that at one point of his preparation for the Colloquy he had considered analyzing the various traditions about the *Pĕtîrat Mōšeh* (death of Moses) but had abandoned it in favor of earlier material.

The discussion of parallels took on a new dimension when it was shifted from the usual Matthew/Mark/Luke comparison to a comparison of parallels in one or another of the Synoptic Gospels and in John (and even at times in Acts). From another standpoint, it was asked whether in a Colloquy on the Relationships among the Gospels (not restricted to the canonical gospels) one should not also consider the form that some of the parallel materials take in the apocryphal gospels. For example, the parable of the Great Supper has another form in the Coptic *Gospel According to Thomas* (64). The affinity of such noncanonical parallels to one or more of the Synoptic forms raises the question, whether the material was simply copied from one of the Synoptic Gospels or whether it depends on a different source. In still another respect, it was suggested that some of the gospel parallels might fruitfully be compared with parallels in pseudepigraphical writings, such as *The Testament of Abraham*, the *Apocalypse of Moses*, or the *Life of Adam and Eve*, which come from a Jewish background.

The Institution or Process That Preserved and Transmitted the Gospel Tradition. Several aspects of this topic emerged in the discussion. The first centered on the views of Birger Gerhardsson.[11] In general the reaction was negative to Gerhardsson's thesis that the early Christians had the same sort of institutional process for transmitting the words and deeds of Jesus as did the rabbis for transmitting their traditions, a process involving the memorization of material and its transmission from teacher to pupil. There seems to have been nothing in the Christian communities that was similar to this well-known institution in Judaism, and, in fact, it appears that Gerhardsson has read back into the first-century situation a process that did not exist even in Judaism until the second century, after the Hadrianic persecution, when the Hillelite family achieved its dominance and authority and the *nśy'* ("prince") emerged as a figure recognized in the Roman world. Moreover, Jesus' sayings did not function within the Christian communities in the same way as did the Torah or the sayings of the rabbis within Judaism. The process

[11] Birger Gerhardsson, *Memory and Manuscript: Oral Tradition and Written Transmission in Rabbinic Judaism and Early Christianity*, trans. E. J. Sharpe, Acta Seminarii Neotestamentici Upsaliensis 22 (Lund: C. W. K. Gleerup/Copenhagen: Ejnar Munksgaard, 1961).

of which Gerhardsson speaks was largely identified with the halakic (legal) materials, whereas most of the tradition about Jesus would have to be regarded as haggadic (narrative). In the Jewish haggadic materials, the same saying is at times attributed to different rabbis, but in such cases what is important is not the multiple attribution but the saying itself (even with possible variants).

These reactions to Gerhardsson's thesis are important, but some members of the seminar felt that they did not wholly minimize his claim that memory and a process of transmission played some role in early Christianity. It was pointed out, for example, that Paul is aware of such a process when he uses the Greek words *paradidonai* and *paralambanein*, the equivalents of Hebrew *msr* ("hand on") and *qbl* ("receive"), which are the words that characterize the transmission in the Pharisaic-rabbinic tradition. And Paul uses these words not only of the kerygma (1 Corinthians 15:3) but also of the words of Jesus (1 Corinthians 11:23; cf. 1 Corinthians 11:2; 7:10 [cf. Luke 16:18]). This Pauline evidence cannot be understood in terms of Christian "schools" or of Christian rote memorization, but it has to be related to an oral tradition that functioned somehow in the pre-written stage of the formation of the gospels. Two possible parallels were cited: a body of orally transmitted materials in the Mithraic cults of the same period and the collection of sayings of Jesus that has come to light in the Coptic *Gospel According to Thomas*, known to have existed in an earlier Greek form as well.

Implicit in the discussion of the institution or process behind the gospel tradition is some view of the person about whom the tradition was passed on. It was suggested that regarding him as a rabbi (even though he is given this title in the New Testament) in the sense of the rabbinic schools of the post-Hadrianic era is perhaps an appeal to the wrong model. Does he not better fit the picture of Old Testament prophet: the "prophet like Moses," as the New Testament itself suggests (Acts 3:22–23 citing Deuteronomy 18:15–18), or a prophet like Jeremiah, whose oracles were later collected by disciple(s). Sanders observed that if "prophet" was one of the earliest titles applied to Jesus, then his disciples may have been concerned to remember and preserve what the "prophet" said, even before the appearance of any developed Christology.

Various members of the seminar emphasized that the tradition about Jesus' words and deeds was as fluid in the early period of

251

Christianity as was the Old Testament text itself during the same period. Silberman suggested that some powerful institutional center in early Christianity was responsible for the very rapid establishment of the gospels as authoritative crystallizations of the Christian tradition, a center somewhat akin to what the Jewish tradition itself seems to suggest apropos of the academy at Jamnia,[12] which stabilized the text-tradition and acted as a canonizer of the Hebrew Scriptures in the face of the socio-political challenges offered to the survival of Palestinian Judaism. In response to this suggestion, it was argued that there is no evidence that such a center existed in early Christianity and that the conformity desired in the stabilization of the text of the Hebrew Scriptures has its counterpart later in the Christian period, when scribes, copying the New Testament documents, sought to harmonize sayings of Jesus in the various gospels.[13] It was pointed out, however, that not even these scribes eliminated the nonconformity in a large number of sayings, such as Mark 6:9 and Matthew 10:10 (usually regarded as parallel) with their conflicting instructions about whether Christian disciples on their evangelical missions were to wear sandals. The effort at conformity, produced by "back-editing" in the Jewish halakic tradition, was found by most members of the seminar to be of little value in explaining parallels in the gospels. These parallels do not seem to be the product of such a process, and the evidence for the back-editing of Jesus' sayings in the written stage is minimal at best. A form of back-editing may have been operative in a given community in the pre-written stage of the gospel tradition, but it does not appear that Jesus' words about divorce (see Mark 10:11), for example, were back-edited in the light of Matthew's exceptive phrases (Matthew 5:32; 19:9), save in the later scribal harmonization of the particular text tradition mentioned above, which is a different matter.

It was pointed out that, in time, Jesus' words began to be regarded almost as "Scripture" (see Acts 20:35). When records

---

[12] On this matter, see Sanders' comments (p. 224–25 above).

[13] See, e.g., Matthew 6:33 (and what happens to Jesus' saying in the *Koine* text-tradition and in Codex Koridethi); Matthew 5:11 (harmonization with Luke 21:12 in some manuscripts). Better still, one should consult the *apparatus criticus* on Luke 11:2–4 (the "Our Father") for the attempts to harmonize its text with that of Matthew 6:9–13. See further Bruce M. Metzger, *The Text of the New Testament: Its Transmission, Corruption, and Restoration* (New York and London: Oxford University Press, 1964), 197–198.

of his words and deeds were written, these records appear to have been modeled in various ways on the biblical documents, and, in the words of Sanders, they "intended" to *be* "biblical." Luke-Acts has been regarded as a prime example of an effort to cast the memory of Jesus ("the events that have come to fulfillment among us") in the mold of a biblical book,[14] although some members of the seminar thought that Matthew (with *hē genesis* in the first verse) or even John (with *en archē*) would be a better example. Such an effort is not without relation to the question about the institution or process behind the formation of the gospel tradition (nor is it irrelevant to the question of the "genre" of the gospels, as was pointed out). It was agreed, however, that the gospels are not examples of "parabiblical literature" (to use a phrase of H. L. Ginsberg)[15] among the Jews, such as the *Genesis Apocryphon*, *Jubilees*, or *Enoch*. The latter are more of a paraphrase or midrashic treatment of Old Testament books, whereas the gospels intend rather to be imitative.

The view was expressed that, though one has to allow for oral tradition at some point in the process, one can scarcely think of a body of free-floating oral Jesus-tradition in the Greek world in which the Christian communities of the early period took shape; the problem of the relationships among the gospels is, at least in part, a documentary problem. It was pointed out, however, that Galatians 1:18 speaks of Paul going up to "get information from Cephas" (*historēsai Kēphan*), which, for a number of New Testament interpreters, has meant that Paul used Cephas as a source of information about Jesus.[16]

If the intent to write a "biblical" book was part of the process of the formation of the gospels and was in any way responsible for the shape of the gospels, then one might further ask what the canonical order of the gospels says about the relationship among them. To what need of the community was a response being given, for example, when John was inserted between Luke and

[14] See Nils Alstrup Dahl, "The Purpose of Luke-Acts," in *Jesus in the Memory of the Early Church* (Minneapolis: Augsburg Publishing House, 1976), 87–98, esp. 88.

[15] H. L. Ginsberg, review of Joseph A. Fitzmyer, *The Genesis Apocryphon of Qumran Cave I: A Commentary*, in *Theological Studies*, 28 (1967), 574.

[16] The interpretation of this phrase is controverted; for the view expressed here, see Raymond E. Brown, Karl P. Donfried, and John Reumann, eds., *Peter in the New Testament: A Collaborative Assessment by Protestant and Roman Catholic Scholars* (Minneapolis: Augsburg Publishing House/New York, etc.: Paulist Press, 1973), 23–24.

Acts? Does this position reflect any particular theological view of John or of the gospels as a group? Most of the answers to this question from members of the seminar were on the negative side. It was observed that there are prior questions that would have to be raised, such as: Given the canonicity of John, is the order stable within the canon? Are there not manuscripts that have the order Matthew, John, Luke, and Mark?[17] Does one not have to look at the varying positions of Acts in different manuscripts? What about the order of the Pauline corpus? Within this corpus, the familiar canonical order is usually explained by appeal to such "mechanical" considerations as the order of the longest to the shortest, the letters to the churches before those to individuals, and the like. Finally, does not one detect a desire in the canonical order to keep John with the Synoptics simply because all four are "gospels," narratives of what Jesus said and did? Thus, it was generally felt that some arcane theological reason behind the canonical order was highly unlikely.

Whether the canonical order has anything to say about the parallels to be found at times between John and Luke or between John and some other Synoptic Gospel, or even between John and Acts, is an area that needs further investigation. Judgment can be made only when these alleged parallels are published and studied in detail.

Reflections of the Seminar Leader

From the Seminar on Judaic Studies and the study of Silberman's essay and Sanders' response, as well as of the tapes that recorded the discussion, I came away with a heightened interest in the bearing of Jewish tradition on the background of the gospel tradition. The post-canonical tradition among the Jews had its matrix in Palestine prior to and contemporary with the growth and development of the Christian gospel tradition. The sense of

---

[17]See, e.g., Werner Georg Kümmel, *Introduction to the New Testament*, rev. ed., trans. Howard Clark Kee (Nashville and New York: Abingdon Press, 1975), 516: "The sequence of the various parts of the NT is the same in almost all the Greek manuscripts: Gospels, Acts, Catholic letters, Pauline letters, Rev. A few of the newer editions of the NT have followed this order [e.g., von Soden, Tischendorf, Westcott-Hort], but other sequences are represented as well, e.g., in א and A (Gospels, Pauline letters, Acts, Catholic letters, Rev) or the Muratorian Canon (Gospels, Acts, Pauline letters, Catholic letters, Rev)." Cf. A. Wikenhauser and J. Schmid, *Einleitung in das Neue Testament*, 6th ed. (Freiburg im B./Vienna: Verlag Herder KG, 1973), 79–80.

a tradition, which also had its origins in Palestine and which terminated in gospel-deposits about Jesus, is something that is perhaps not stressed enough today in New Testament study. There is, indeed, a willingness to acknowledge the Palestinian origin of the primitive kerygma, but there is also a strong inclination to seek the roots of the multiform gospels themselves in extra-Palestinian, eastern-Mediterranean Christian experience. The seminar discussion about wandering themes, their adequacy to explain the gospel relationships, and aspects of the institutionalization of the Jewish traditions, even though these are never identical with the gospel traditions, made one aware of a refined sense of tradition with which one has ultimately to reckon.

Beyond this, I should like to make the following points:

(1) Any solution of the Synoptic Problem has to reckon, first of all, with a pre-literary oral tradition about what Jesus did and said; this was built on memories and recollections of his deeds and his words. The specific form of this tradition that Gerhardsson has proposed, as memorization within a school of transmission, may not be convincing.[18] The tradition was carried on in a social environment that cannot be assimilated to the "schools" or the halakic tradition of post-Hadrianic rabbinism. Jesus and his followers were not related simply as rabbi and disciples. Yet some sort of oral tradition (involving catechesis, liturgy, and preaching) has to be considered at this stage.

(2) The literary interdependence of the written gospels is not ruled out by anything discussed in this seminar based on data from the rabbinical tradition. The specific verbatim parallels in the gospels cannot simply be explained either as coincidences in early Christian oral tradition or as deriving from free-floating

[18]See my review of Gerhardsson's *Memory and Manuscript*: Joseph A. Fitzmyer, "Memory and Manuscript: The Origins and Transmission of the Gospel Tradition," *Theological Studies*, 23 (1962), 442–457. Cf. also the following reviews: B. Brinkmann in *Scholastik*, 37 (1962), 426–430; P. Benoit in *Revue biblique*, 70 (1963), 269–273; E. Lohse in *Theologische Zeitschrift*, 18 (1962), 60–62; and Morton Smith, "A Comparison of Early Christian and Early Rabbinic Tradition," *Journal of Biblical Literature*, 82 (1963), 169–176 (but see the reply: Birger Gerhardsson, *Tradition and Transmission in Early Christianity*, trans. E. J. Sharpe, Coniectanea Neotestamentica 20 [Lund: C. W. K. Gleerup/Copenhagen: Ejnar Munksgaard, 1964]). See further W. D. Davies, *The Setting of the Sermon on the Mount* (Cambridge: Cambridge University Press, 1964), 424; Jacob Neusner, "The Rabbinic Traditions about the Pharisees before A.D. 70: The Problem of Oral Transmission," *Journal of Jewish Studies*, 22 (1971), 1–18; Birger Gerhardsson, *Die Anfänge der Evangelientradition* (Wuppertal: R. Brockhaus, 1977).

themes or wandering motifs. When sixty out of sixty-four Greek words in the Baptist's eschatological preaching agree (Matthew 3:7–10; Luke 3:7–9), to cite but one example, something more is obviously involved. Moreover, the literary interdependence that these specific parallels imply may be *superficially* compared with verbal parallels in the Jewish halakic tradition, but in the long run one has to deal with an entirely different institution or process that brought these halakic parallels into being (i.e., the concern for conformity in legal decisions, resulting in the "back-editing" of materials that would cause "parallels" of a sort not really present in the gospels). One also has to reckon with the distinction between the redaction and the use of sources that were at work in this process. More study of the Jewish tradition has to be undertaken, especially the study of parallels in early haggadic midrashim. But even if this be pursued, will it do more than bring to light an analogous process of literary composition? Will it reveal some new methodology as yet untried in Synoptic research?

(3) If one admits that the Christian gospels came into being roughly between A.D. 65–100 and that the rabbinic texts used for comparison, for all their dependence on the "men of the great synagogue," only assumed literary form in the post-Hadrianic period, as Silberman insisted, we are at least confronted with a caution against the extrapolation of would-be analogies. Members of the seminar alluded at times to parallels in different forms of the *War Scroll* and of the *Manual of Discipline*, i.e., in Essene Jewish literature of an earlier date. Yet even here the parallel may not walk on all fours, for these are ostensibly revisions of the same texts, and whether the different recensions should be regarded as having the same literarily autonomous purpose, conception, or composition as do the four gospels is a major question. In this regard, a possibly better analogue from the same period might be found in the interesting and provocative comparisons suggested by Jeffrey H. Tigay, who dealt with the Documentary Hypothesis of the Pentateuch and examined Old Testament passages in the Masoretic Text, Qumran Proto-Samaritan texts, and the Samaritan Torah.[19]

(4) When we come to the "sixty-four-dollar question," whether anything emerged from the Seminar on Judaic Studies that would speak to the prevailing modes of explaining the Synoptic Prob-

[19] Jeffrey H. Tigay, "An Empirical Basis for the Documentary Hypothesis," *Journal of Biblical Literature*, 94 (1975), 329–342.

lem, I should have to say no. Nothing was said that could not easily be fitted into the modified form of the Two-Source Theory that is used by what was called at the Colloquy "the establishment" among modern New Testament scholars. By the same token, I should have to admit that nothing was said either that could not be fitted into the efforts of those who are seeking to resurrect the Griesbach Hypothesis.[20]

(5) Indeed, one must insist that the Colloquy in no way contributed to any alleged "eroding" of the dominance of the Two-Source Theory.[21] The renewed emphasis on the function of oral tradition and other forms of traditional material can easily be assimilated into the modified form of the Two-Source Theory with which many New Testament scholars work today. Beyond the oral stage of the tradition about Jesus, one can easily reckon with its influence in the following way. If the two main literary sources of the Synoptics are still to be regarded as Mark (or *Ur-Markus*) and "Q," and if one allows in addition for the individual sources "M" and "L" (without, however, understanding the latter so rigidly as solely written sources), then there is ample room for the influence of oral tradition even in the literary stage of gospel formation. Here, of course, it is difficult to draw the line between, say, "L" and Lucan composition. But, to cite an example, I should ascribe the "traditional" elements in the Matthean and Lucan infancy narratives to oral "M" or oral "L," accounting for the rest by Matthean or Lucan composition. Further, I have

---

[20]See William R. Farmer, "Modern Developments of Griesbach's Hypothesis," *New Testament Studies*, 23 (1977), 275–295. Pages 283–293 are devoted to answering nine objections that I had formulated against the Griesbach Hypothesis in my article, "The Priority of Mark and the 'Q' Source in Luke," in *Jesus and Man's Hope*, vol. 1, ed. David G. Buttrick, A Perspective Book (Pittsburgh: Pittsburgh Theological Seminary, 1970), 131–170. This is not the place to comment on Farmer's answers; suffice it to say that, on the basis of his response to my criticism, I do not see the attempt to resurrect the Griesbach Hypothesis as posing any serious threat to the "establishment's" position.

[21]I prefer to use this terminology rather than to speak of the Two-Document Hypothesis, because it may alert some unsuspecting student of gospel relationships to the fact that most of us who hold for the priority of Mark and "Q" use a considerably modified form of the so-called Two-Document Hypothesis. To admit "M" (special Matthean source-material) and "L" (special Lucan source-material) is already to admit that there were *four* sources; moreover, to admit that either "M" or "L" could have been in part oral is yet another modification. Remarks about the Two-Document Hypothesis sometimes verge on caricature and reveal how little acquaintance some have with the form in which the hypothesis is often used today.

always worked with the possibility that "Q" might be a well-translated Greek form[22] of Aramaic *logia*, thus relating to the Two-Source Theory some of the data of the Papias testimony.

(6) Finally, a comment about "canon criticism." It obviously has something to do with "the interrelationships among the gospels." That it really has much to do with Judaic studies and their bearing on the Christian gospels or more specifically on the interdependence of the Synoptic Gospels, the concern which really called the Colloquy into being, is, however, another matter. Aside from the "prior questions" that surfaced in the seminar discussion, there is a more fundamental question about "canon criticism." This has to do with the use of the term itself and with the designation of it as a "discipline." The question, What does it mean that John was put between Luke and Acts?, is in reality a pseudo-question. While it is legitimate to speak of "source criticism," "form criticism," "redaction criticism," and "composition criticism" as disciplines, because each has its own methodology or demarcated lines of procedure and each copes with realities in the literary text being analyzed, none of these things is true of so-called canon criticism. To take the term "criticism" from the former procedures and apply it to a question about the position that a book may have in the canon is to make an equivoque of it. As stated above, the question in itself is legitimate, but the question or its possible answer says nothing about the formation of the gospel tradition. It might say something about the formation or the development of the canon and the forces at work here, but it is hardly a "criticism" of the gospels. And hence "canon criticism" has to be regarded as a non-discipline in studies of the gospels as such.[23]

[22]See further Robert M. Grant, *A Historical Introduction to the New Testament* (New York and Evanston: Harper & Row, Publishers, Inc., 1963), 41.

[23]This comment on "canon criticism" should not be understood to include the question that was at times related to it in the seminar discussions, viz., that of parallels between John and Luke or some other of the Synoptics, or even Acts. This is a tantalizing question, but more has to be done with it before any judgment can be made. Moreover, it is indeed a question that concerns the relationships among the gospels, but what pertinence it has to the topic of the gospels and Judaic studies is another matter.

4
LITERARY CRITICISM and the GOSPELS

The Synoptic Problems and Analogies in Other Literatures

Roland Mushat Frye

For the New Testament scholar, the gospels pose many problems that are similar to problems faced by scholars of other types of literature. Of course, the gospels differ in subject matter from secular writings, and for very good reasons they are more important to more people than are even the greatest secular masterpieces. This importance is not because of style or belle lettristic finesse but rather because of the significance of the gospels' central character and of their message. Once these and other differences are acknowledged, however, it is generally agreed that valid methods used in studying other literature also apply to the study of the gospels. When scholars from other literary fields were invited to participate in the Colloquy on the Relationships among the Gospels and to contribute to this volume, it was with the expectation that the ways in which we have dealt with our own areas of study would be relevant to the gospels. In my case, this means the analysis of critical work on the gospels in the light of comparable work on English literary history. This is a welcome opportunity for me, because I have been interested in New Testament scholarship for a quarter of a century, since my own seminary days.

The prospectus for the Colloquy begins with the following proposition: "Crucial to any attempt to understand the origins and early development of Christianity is the question of the chronological and literary relationships among the gospels."[1] Explicit here is a concern for the chronological order of the gospels, and the first part of my essay is devoted specifically to this subject. But more is involved, and this is expressed in the reference to literary as well as chronological relationships and in the emphasis upon the origins and early development of Christianity. It is often assumed that certain types of form critical and redaction critical techniques make it possible to move behind the literary texts of the gospels through earlier stages in the development of the gospel tradition and thus to approach closer to the origins of Christianity. To deal only with the chronological relationships among the gospels and to ignore these widely employed methodologies would be to address only part of the problem. It would also imply acquiescence in approaches to the gospels that are of dubious literary-historical value, as I shall indicate in the second part of this essay by analyzing some close analogies between the gospels and other literature. As a result of this analysis, it should be clear why a literary historian accustomed to the disciplines of secular literary study cannot honestly accept certain form critical and redaction critical techniques as reliable guides to the tradition behind the gospels, but must regard them as intricate and learned illusions.

I. On Sequence and Dependence: The Griesbach Hypothesis

Approaching the Problem of Linear Sequence. The hypothesis of Marcan priority was so firmly established during my days as a student that it hardly seemed open to challenge, and I recall very few who did challenge it in a rational and scholarly way. One of the most notable events in modern New Testament scholarship occurred when William R. Farmer cogently attacked the arguments for the priority of Mark and advocated instead the succession of Matthew, Luke, and Mark according to the Griesbach Hypothesis. Subsequent work by Farmer, David L. Dungan, Thomas R. W. Longstaff, and others has further undermined the arguments for the priority of Mark and reinforced those for the priority of Matthew, and the debate continues.[2]

[1] Brochure prepared and distributed prior to the Colloquy on the Relationships among the Gospels (1976).

[2] William R. Farmer, *The Synoptic Problem: A Critical Analysis* (New York: The Macmillan Company/London: Collier-Macmillan Limited, 1964); this book has

262

Fortunately, no one expects a critic of English literature to be able to solve the Synoptic Problem. Surely, if the problem is to be solved at all, the solution must come from within the New Testament field. What an outsider can do is to appraise hypotheses by reference to analogies in literature. For example, the credibility of the Griesbach Hypothesis could be severely damaged if it were possible to show that conflation of the kind it postulates simply never took place elsewhere in literature; conversely, the hypothesis could be supported by evidence that similar developments did take place in other fields. Thus, although it will not be possible in this way to determine whether the Griesbach Hypothesis is correct, it should be possible at least to evaluate certain major objections that have been raised to it.

In analyzing the Griesbach Hypothesis from this point of view, I shall first make some tentative suggestions about the argument that Mark is the most Aramaic of the gospels and therefore should be presumed to be the earliest. On the basis of linguistic developments with which I happen to be acquainted, I shall maintain that this argument appears doubtful. Turning, then, from linguistic to literary analogies, I shall consider two major arguments. In the first place, it is sometimes assumed that increased length evidences a later stage of development, so that Matthew and Luke are regarded as later embellishments upon the briefer Mark. But the equation between greater length and later date applies primarily to the development of a single work by a single author and not to the recension of an earlier text by a later writer, where the result may at least equally well be a shortening of the text. In the second place, critics have argued against the

---

now appeared in a very slightly revised edition (Dillsboro, N.C.: Western North Carolina Press, Inc., 1976), but, unless otherwise indicated, all references will be to the first edition; cf. also Farmer's *Synopticon: The verbal agreement between the Greek Texts of Matthew, Mark and Luke contextually exhibited* (Cambridge: Cambridge University Press, 1969). See, e.g., David Laird Dungan, "Mark—the Abridgement of Matthew and Luke," in *Jesus and Man's Hope,* vol. 1, ed. David G. Buttrick, A Perspective Book (Pittsburgh: Pittsburgh Theological Seminary, 1970), 51–97; and "Reactionary Trends in the Gospel-Producing Activity of the Early Church? Marcion, Tatian, Mark," in *L'Évangile selon Marc. Tradition et Rédaction*, ed. M. Sabbe, Bibliotheca Ephemeridum Theologicarum Lovaniensium 34 (Gembloux: Editions J. Duculot/Louvain: Louvain University Press, 1974), 188–194; Thomas R. W. Longstaff, *Evidence of Conflation in Mark? A Study in the Synoptic Problem*, Society of Biblical Literature Dissertation Series 28 (Missoula, Mont.: Scholars Press for The Society of Biblical Literature, 1977).

Griesbach Hypothesis on the grounds that Mark's postulated shortening of Matthew and Luke, joined with his lengthening of individual pericopes, is inherently unlikely. Perhaps this is so logically, but it is not necessarily so historically, where every example of literary conflation that I have been able to find operates in much the same way as the Griesbach advocates propose.

One basic qualification must be made explicit at the outset: I approached the alternatives of Marcan and Matthean priority entirely within the perimeters of the kind of linear, developmental, or source relationship that has been accepted as a basic postulate by most New Testament scholars. Since completing my reflections on the Griesbach Hypothesis (the first part of this essay) within this ground rule, I have read John A. T. Robinson's recent *Redating the New Testament*, and I suspect that Robinson's bombshell will reverberate as widely as has Farmer's. Robinson recognizes that the old acceptance of Burnett Hillman Streeter's "fundamental solution" to the Synoptic Problem has been disrupted and holds that "it is far too early yet to say what new patterns or modifications of older patterns will establish themselves." More directly pertinent to our concerns is his contention that the gospels are "parallel, though by no means isolated, developments of common material for different spheres of the Christian mission, rather than a series of documents standing in simple chronological sequence." Thus, he finds among the gospels "a more fluid and complex interrelation" than the linear possibilities that have been generally accepted.[3] Significant comments by George Kennedy and Albert B. Lord would also support the possibility of such "synchronic" relationships among the Synoptic Gospels.[4] Without denying this possibility, I have pursued my analysis within the prevalent assumption that two of the Synoptics are sequentially derived from an original.

The Criterion of Language. It is sometimes argued that the linguistic style and construction are much more heavily Aramaic in Mark than in Matthew and Luke and that such heavy Aramaism is evidence of an earlier date for Mark because it is closer to the spoken versions of *koiné* Greek in the time of Jesus.[5] For the purposes of this analysis, let us assume that the language

[3] John A. T. Robinson, *Redating the New Testament* (Philadelphia: The Westminster Press, 1976), 92–94, see also 15.

[4] See the essays by Albert B. Lord and George Kennedy in this volume.

[5] See, e.g., H. Maynell, "Some Unorthodox Solutions of the Synoptic Problem," *Theology*, 70 (1970), 391–396.

patterns in Mark are closer to what many native speakers of Aramaic would have used when speaking in the *lingua franca* than are those in Matthew and Luke. It does not necessarily follow, however, that such a style is earlier than the more standard Greek of Matthew and Luke. There is some evidence, in fact, to suggest that writing (as opposed to speaking) in a stylistic form like Mark's would be expected to come later. The extent to which such evidence is typical must be left to linguistic specialists to decide.

First, however, I wish to present the case of Lucian (c. A.D. 120–180) as a cautionary example of the importance of the atypical. Born into a poor Syrian family at Samosata on the Euphrates and apprenticed as a boy to a stonecutter, Lucian presumably spoke Aramaic as his native tongue, but he became one of the acknowledged masters of Attic Greek, writing a pure, polished, and sparkling prose. Modelling his style on Plato, he used Greek with an unaffected ease and fluency that betray nothing of his Aramaic background. To be sure, his works occasionally contain forms and compounds that are post-Platonic and show evidence of Latin influence, yet on stylistic grounds it would be impossible to identify his Syrian origins—and this at a time when many of his contemporaries and compatriots were writing in various degrees of creolized forms. The point is not that Matthew or even Luke were on the plane of Lucian as Greek stylists but that style alone is not a dispositive guide to points of origin and of time. Issues of the individual's education, ability, and taste are more informative than the simple question of provenance. In the final analysis, the individual writer is the decisive factor in literary analysis.

We should also go beyond the individual to consider linguistic groups. The facts of conquest and/or colonization are well known in past history and in our own time, and of remarkable interest are the interactions of language as between the language of colonization, the contact vernacular, and creolized language. The language of colonization has been defined as "the language of a politically, economically or culturally superior or strong nation which is imposed upon a conquered or dependent nation, or adopted by the latter, as a language of official dealings, business, and as a cultural medium, parallel with or replacing the native language." Even where the native language continues in use, there is also a contact vernacular developed for dealings between colonizers and natives of a particular part of the world. An example would be Pidgin English. The contact vernacular may develop as a creole language, characterized by simplifications and adaptation of the language of colonization from which it is derived.[6]

In all of this, an important distinction needs to be preserved, the distinction between the spoken vernacular of the colonized people in their daily contacts with the colonizers and the written language adopted by the same colonized people when expressing themselves in a somewhat more formal context and preserving their words on paper or parchment. Although it may be presumed that a *spoken* form of a creolized language that is closer to the language of colonization would indicate greater and presumably longer contact with the latter,[7] it does not follow that the same would be true of the language as *written* by spokesmen for colonized people. Written and spoken language always represent different efforts, and the same rules do not apply to both.

But the question of typicality remains: When a conquered or colonized people begin to *write* in the language of colonization, do they *typically* show care to observe the standard forms of this language, as Matthew and Luke do with Greek, or do they *typically* introduce into their writings the type of creolized forms that have been noted in Mark? Apposite parallels can be found in the creolization of classical Latin in Gaul, as it developed into the Old French vernacular, and then in the similar process by which Norman French was heavily creolized in England after the Norman Conquest as a result of the Anglicizing influence. I suspect that the patterns emerging in these instances are fairly typical of what would be found elsewhere under similar circumstances, but I defer to professional linguistic scholars for judgment on this issue. In addition to such macro-linguistic changes, there is the micro-linguistic problem of uses of the rhetoric of persuasion by a minority group seeking to change attitudes within the broader culture by writing in the language of colonization. Here, the focus will be upon black English, which may offer even closer and more apposite parallels to the linguistic problems of the Synoptic Gospels.

I turn first to the history of classical Latin and its creolization in the direction of Old French after the Roman conquest of Gaul.

---

[6] The definitions of terms are from Mario A. Pei and Frank Gaynor, *A Dictionary of Linguistics* (New York: Philosophical Library, 1954), 119, 47, 219, and 50.

[7] See Leonard Bloomfield, *Language* (New York: Henry Holt and Company, 1933), 473–474.

According to M. K. Pope, "Officially the language introduced in the wake of the conquest was the written language of Rome, the language of law, literature and education." Some of the major sources of our knowledge here are the inscriptions, which in Gaul "from the time of Augustus and Tiberius on, are for the most part couched in a Latin as correct as Italian ones of the same period." Even though there were, of course, marked differences between the spoken language and the written language, in this earlier period these differences rarely appeared in the Latin documents. Standard written Latin was thus typical even among those whose daily speech was in the *lingua vulgaris*.[8] The intrusion of this *lingua quotidiana* into written forms came later. The most authoritative recent student of these developments, Gerhard Rohlfs, notes the beginnings of this change in the third century. As the central power of Rome declines, "the *sermo urbanus* of the capital is no longer considered the model to be followed . . . even by the writers. Henceforth, colloquial expressions crept into the language of the educated class (Commodian, Marcellus Empiricus, Palladius, Anthimus)."[9]

One of the later languages into which vulgar Latin developed was Norman French, which for a time was the "established" language of England. For a decade or more before the Norman Conquest, English as a language was in process of being supplanted in courtly circles by Norman French, and after 1066 this process was rapidly expanded. Though English continued to be spoken by the conquered majority and also appeared in written form, it did not re-emerge as the standard written language of the country for two or three centuries.[10] In the meanwhile, most of the documents (whether literary, religious, legal, or commercial) that were not written in Latin were written in French. The

[8]M. K. Pope, *From Latin to Modern French with Especial Consideration of Anglo-Norman: Phonology and Morphology* (Manchester: Manchester University Press, 1966), 2, 4.

[9]Gerhard Rohlfs, *From Vulgar Latin to Old French: An Introduction to the Study of the Old French Language*, trans. Vincent Almazan and Lillian McCarthy (Detroit: Wayne State University Press, 1970), 21.

[10]The re-establishment of English as the written as well as the spoken language of all classes in England is in one sense irrelevant to our concern, because there was no parallel re-establishment of Aramaic as the language of all Christians. It may in another sense be relevant to note, however, that the English that emerged to replace French was heavily creolized with French elements, so that some analogies might also be drawn between this development and the Aramaicized Greek of Mark.

precise extent and proportion of French dominance, both geographical and social, cannot be determined in every instance, but it is quite clear that among the educated and among those whom the twelfth-century Robert Wace called "the rich men who have the rents and the money," French was the essential language until well after the loss of Normandy by the English kings early in the thirteenth century.[11] Even in the middle of the fourteenth century, the English monk Ranulf Higden commented that Englishmen who could not understand each other because of differences in dialect could still communicate through "the language of Normandy."[12] For a long time, therefore, even English natives of Anglo-Saxon heritage continued to use written (as well as spoken) French or employed a scribe to do so for them.

After a time, however, the French that was used in this way began to show signs of English influence. By the end of the twelfth century, French natives in France were ridiculing the Anglo-Norman spoken in England, but it was in the following century that evidence accumulates for the creolization of the written language under influences from English.[13] By the late thirteenth century and early fourteenth century, written French forms appear that are so noticeably corrupted or "magnetized" by English that we can observe a kind of "franglais" in operation, to adopt a derogatory term from twentieth-century French criticism. This process of creolizing the written language can be observed between 1292 and 1333 in the bills or petitions to justices in eyre, where professional scribes or parish priests write up the appeals of individuals seeking redress of grievances, documents of a kind that would earlier have been written in standard French. By this time, however, French "declension and conjugation are often in-

---

[11] Wace is quoted by Rolf Berndt, "The Linguistic Situation in England from the Norman Conquest to the Loss of Normandy (1066–1204)," *Philologica Pragensia*, 8 (1965), 161; see the entire article, 145–163. For other analyses of the French influence in England after the Conquest, see M. Dominica Legge, "The Rise and Fall of Anglo-Norman Literature," *Mosaic*, 8 (1975), 1–6; "L'Anglo-Normand: Langue Coloniale?" in *Congrès International de Linguistique et Philologie Romane 1971* (Quebec: Les Presses de l'Université Laval, 1976), 85–91; William Rothwell, "The Role of French in Thirteenth-Century England," *Bulletin of the John Rylands University Library of Manchester*, 58 (1976), 445–466; R. M. Wilson, "English and French in England 1100–1300," *History*, n.s. 28 (1943), 37–60.

[12] Legge, "L'Anglo-Normand," 89–90.

[13] Rothwell, "The Role of French in Thirteenth-Century England," 454 *et passim*.

correct or peculiar, and the writers make the most obvious mistakes in gender, such as using *la* before a man's name and *le* before a woman's."[14] In the late fourteenth century, Chaucer made gentle fun of the French used by his Prioress:

> And French she spake full fair and fetishly,
> After the school of Stratford-at-Bow,
> For French of Paris was to her unknowe.[15]

Pope, a leading authority on these developments, writes that "the acquirement of French by people with a different organic base induced gradually many modifications," and it is important to note that this creolization was gradual rather than immediate.[16] Such evidence suggests that closer to the time of the Norman Conquest, written French in England was likely to have been more nearly standard (analogous to the Greek of Matthew and Luke), whereas a French that was heavily creolized by the influence of the native language (rather like Mark's Greek) came later.

The developments of black English are even closer to our concerns than are the changes in Latin and French just discussed. When black writers sought to convert their readers from one set of attitudes to another, to induce in their readers a change of heart and mind, their purpose was not radically dissimilar, at least in rhetorical terms, from the purpose of the Evangelists. It is therefore especially pertinent to note the use of standard English and of creolized English by such black writers as they employed the rhetoric of persuasion.

Typically, the early published writings by blacks in the United States and in the British West Indies seem to have been characterized for the most part by a careful adherence to standard English usage and an equally careful attempt to eliminate any signs of patois, while the appearance of creolized or ghetto English in written form typically came later, indeed only in recent decades. (Of course, there were exceptions to this general pattern, but the point in question here is typicality.) When the West

---

[14] Albert C. Baugh, *A History of the English Language*, 2d ed. (New York: Appleton-Century-Crofts, Inc., 1957), 162. See also W. C. Bolland, *Select Bills in Eyre, A.D. 1292–1333* (London: Selden Society, 1914).

[15] Chaucer, *The Canterbury Tales*, "General Prologue," lines 124–126, where I have slightly modernized the spelling.

[16] Pope, *From Latin to Modern French with Especial Consideration of Anglo-Norman*, 431.

Indian J. J. Thomas stated the case for his fellow blacks against the racial aspersions of James Anthony Froude in 1889, he modestly disclaimed any ability to match Froude in style, but this disclaimer was merely tactical, for Thomas wrote standard English as impeccable (though perhaps not with the same "old school tie" tone) as that of the Regius Professor of History who was his antagonist. It is only in the twentieth century that typical West Indian black spokesmen have written and published their racial claims in creolized forms of English.[17]

The same observations about style can be made regarding blacks writing for publication on the continental mainland of North America. The work of Phyllis Wheatley (c. 1753–1784) is a good example. Brought from Africa and sold when about eight years old to a Boston merchant named John Wheatley, she was educated in the Wheatley family and showed early signs of a precocious ability to write. Her *Poems on Various Subjects,* published in 1773, were written in an eighteenth-century style heavily influenced by Alexander Pope and were on a plane with much of the better colonial versifying of the time. When she visited London at the age of eighteen, she created quite a stir. Some Englishmen questioned her authorship of works thought to be beyond the stylistic capacity of a slave girl, but there is no doubt about the authenticity of her writings. Although Thomas Jefferson did not regard her verse highly, Voltaire described her as "une Négresse qui a fait de très bons vers anglais." It is clear that Wheatley did not write in the typical spoken patois of American blacks in 1773, and it is equally clear that she did write in the standard forms of the language of colonization at that time.[18]

Much the same observation applies to the prose writings of the escaped slave and Methodist minister Josiah Henson (1789–1883), whose autobiography dates from 1849, and to the abolitionist works of Frederick Douglass (1817–1895). It was by using the standard literary language that these and other black writers caught the attention of the general reading public, and this lan-

---

[17]Selections from Froude and Thomas can be found and compared in Lambros Comitas and David Lowenthal, eds., *Slaves, Free Men, Citizens: West Indian Perspectives* (Garden City, N.Y.: Doubleday & Co., Inc., 1973), 150–170.

[18]Merle A. Richmond, *Bid the Vassal Soar: Interpretive Essays on the Life and Poetry of Phyllis Wheatley and George Moses Horton* (Washington: Howard University Press, 1974), 53–54. See also William H. Robinson, *Phyllis Wheatley in the Black American Beginnings* (Detroit: Broadside Press, 1975).

guage differed greatly from the daily patois of the folk whom they represented. B. A. Botkin's comments are pertinent here:

> In contrast to the more consciously produced narratives of racial leaders, many of which, like those of Josiah Henson (the original Uncle Tom) and Frederick Douglass, have become classics, the oral statements of ex-slaves may seem crude and casual. But as folk-say—what the people have to say about themselves—and oral literature on an illiterate or semiliterate level, they will be found to possess literary qualities of their own, close to folk literature.[19]

Only later did the patois of slaves, ex-slaves, sharecroppers, and more recently ghetto blacks begin to appear in the published works of black writers. In the 1930s, the Federal Writers Administration began collecting comments by ex-slaves upon the slave times. At about the same time as this collection of folk-say and increasingly thereafter, black writers began to show a tendency to utilize creolized English in their published works. With a greater sense of self-confidence and the expectation of a more open or even favorable response from their readers, speakers of the black dialects introduced these dialects into their published writings. This development parallels what the Griesbach advocates see as the movement from the more standard Greek of Matthew and Luke to what some would regard as the more heavily creolized style of Mark.

These developments in Latin, in Anglo-Norman French, and in black English represent linguistic phenomena that are analogous to phenomena found in the Synoptic Gospels. At least on the basis of my own observations, therefore, I cannot accept the claim that Mark's Aramaicized Greek represents the most typical early form in which a colonized or conquered people would *write* the language of colonization. What emerges here is the need to consult with linguistic scholars who are familiar with interactions in writing between standard and creolized forms of many languages, in order to discover more broadly typical sequences in development.

The Criterion of Comparative Length. In Synoptic studies,

---

[19] B. A. Botkin, ed., *Lay My Burden Down: A Folk History of Slavery* (Chicago: University of Chicago Press, 1945), xiii. This quotation should not be read as implying that Mark's language is illiterate or semiliterate. I refer merely to the generally accepted view that Mark wrote a style closer to that of ordinary folk speech than did Matthew and Luke.

those who advocate the priority of Mark assume that the shorter work is likely to be earlier, the longer one later.[20] In my observation, this use of greater length as a sign of posteriority is valid when all the documents under scrutiny are by a single author or at least reflect the development of a single text. A simple example can be found in the two-stage development of a rather wooden narrative poem published in the early decades of our republic. Widely hailed upon its appearance as a great American epic, Joel Barlow's *The Vision of Columbus* was first published in 1787. In 1807, it appeared in a second, much expanded form under the title *The Columbiad*. Even if we did not have the dates of publication of these ponderous and turgid works, we could readily establish the chronology in terms of a single author's expansion of his own original plan. Here we see the recognized phenomenon of a relatively simple original growing through the addition of material at the hands of a single author into a more complex work.

A similar progression can be noted in the medieval allegorical poem *Piers Plowman*, which is attributed to William Langland. This poem exists in three quite different versions known as the A, B and C Texts, with insertions, additions, and alterations from one to another of these three texts, which move the initial length of 2,579 lines through an intermediate text of 7,241 lines to a final length of 7,353 lines.[21] What is undeniable is that a single "core" text is being altered and developed throughout, and on this basis the sequence of texts, A to B to C, is unmistakable.[22]

Apparently insoluble problems of chronology can arise in cases where changes have been made in relatively short internal passages within a single text by a single author, when the changes represent something akin to tinkering or fine tuning but do not go so far as the kind of total overhaul or reworking that we find in Barlow and Langland. Thus in *Hamlet*, the 1604 quarto text is about two hundred lines longer than that of the 1623 folio, but

[20] See, e.g., William Barclay, *Introduction to the First Three Gospels: A Revised Edition of* The First Three Gospels (Philadelphia: The Westminster Press, 1976), 87.

[21] Questions have been raised as to whether a single author, William Langland, was responsible for all three versions, but most students of the subject are now comfortable with the traditional postulate of a single author who has carried the work through three recensions.

[22] For guidance to the scholarly literature on *Piers Plowman*, see Albert C. Baugh, "The Middle English Period (1100–1500)," in *A Literary History of Eng-*

the folio, with a total of 3,904 lines, contains about eighty-five lines that are missing from the quarto. We cannot be certain how to distribute all of these almost three hundred lines among early composition, late addition, and various stages of deletion, and chronological problems of this kind probably cannot be definitively resolved unless extratextual evidence happens to be available. In the cases of Barlow's epic works and the successive versions of *Piers Plowman*, the problems are more manageable than they are with *Hamlet*.

The medieval allegory and the early American epic, then, provide handy paradigms for the assumption that greater length is likely to constitute evidence of later composition. At any rate, this would be a workable starting point if we were considering two or more versions of a single developing text, and unless contradictory evidence intervened, it would presumably also be our conclusion. Thus, for example, if we had two or more texts available for Matthew, we should do well at least to begin with the assumption that the longest text was the latest. But this is not the situation we face with the Synoptic Gospels, and for this reason the Synoptic Problem cannot be resolved simply by an appeal to length as evidence of lateness.

Because we do not have in the Synoptics a single basic text in the same sense as with Barlow and *Piers Plowman* and because we have three different author-editors, the problem is considerably more complicated. Nevertheless, when the Griesbach progression places the two longer Synoptics first and sees Mark as a kind of independent abridgment of the fuller and earlier treatments, this accords with a progression that we can identify elsewhere. To cite a rather commonplace example, *Reader's Digest* synopses appear after popularity has been established for works in their uncut versions. On a more academic level, long scholarly biographies of important historical figures are frequently followed by the appearance of shorter and derivative lives. In a specifically theological field, John Calvin systematically expanded and refined his *Institutes of the Christian Religion* through successively longer editions until his death in 1564, but once this work was widely recognized as a kind of Reformed *Summa*, the process of abridgment set in, and in 1579 there ap-

---

land, ed. Albert C. Baugh, 2d ed. (New York: Appleton-Century-Crofts, Inc., 1967), 241–247 and S 241–247.

peared the first of a long series of compends.[23] Other examples
of a similar process might be cited.

Epitomators flourished in the classical period. The writings of
Aristotle and Strabo, as well as the Greek epic cycles, were all
subject to abbreviation, as were the works of numerous Roman
writers and historians. For the techniques and patterns to be
found in these works, I can say nothing of professional value
but refer to the 1922 study by Marco Galdi, *L'epitome nella
letteratura latina*.[24]

One thing seems certain: writers in the field of biography and
history (broadly conceived) often make what appear to us to be
strange omissions in the use of their sources. It has sometimes
been objected against the Griesbach Hypothesis that Mark would
not likely have omitted, for example, the birth narratives, which
are so conspicuous a part of Matthew and Luke. Equal curiosity
has been aroused, however, by the absence of information about
the birth, childhood, and youth of Charlemagne in the *Vita
Karoli*, even though Einhard completed this biography within
twenty years of his subject's death and had immediate access to
the living tradition of the time. Neither, for that matter, does
Einhard ever quote directly from Charlemagne, even though he
declares that he himself directly witnessed many of the events
that he recounts. Perhaps we can do no better at this point than
to cite the explanation of Plutarch regarding his comparison of
the lives of Alexander and Julius Caesar:

. . . because of the number of their deeds to be treated, I shall make no
other preliminary statement than to beg my readers not to criticize me
if I do not describe everything or narrate fully any of their celebrated
exploits in each case, and if instead I curtail most of these. For I am writing biography, not history. . .[25]

Because Plutarch based his *Lives* on multiple sources, his comment provides an apt transition from the subject of simple abbreviation to that of conflation.

The Criterion of Conflation: Old English Examples. The processes of conflation are central to the Synoptic Problem. Long-

[23] Cf. Hugh Thomson Kerr, Jr., ed., *A Compend of the Institutes of the Christian Religion by John Calvin* (Philadelphia: Presbyterian Board of Christian
Education, 1939), iv–v.

[24] Marco Galdi, *L'epitome nella letteratura latina* (Napoli: P. Federico &
G. Ardia, 1922).

[25] Plutarch, *Alexander* 1.1–2, as quoted by E. I. McQueen, "Quintus Curtius
Rufus," in *Latin Biography*, ed. T. A. Dorey (New York: Basic Books, 1967), 18.

staff's study, which appeared too late for use in this essay, will be an important contribution,[26] but perhaps post-classical examples that are different from those with which he worked may also be relevant. It is possible to identify certain literary works from the Anglo-Saxon period and the English Renaissance that were produced by conflation of identifiable influences from known and extant *Vorlagen*. In such cases, the chronology and the direction of influence are entirely beyond dispute. It is then possible to compare the results with Mark in terms of the Griesbach Hypothesis. After the enactment of the first authors' copyright law in England in 1709, literary borrowing was not the same, and more recent examples of conflation would be harder to find.

The *Advent*, sometimes also known as *Christ I*, was composed by an Anglo-Saxon poet of the ninth century on the theme of the Advent season of the Christian year.[27] The text as we have it contains 439 lines, and while it contains admonition, exposition, and some dialogue (between Mary and Joseph and between Mary and the dwellers in Jerusalem), it consists primarily and pervasively of invocation and petition, hymn-like in style and tone. Early in the twentieth century, Albert S. Cook and Johannes Bourauel discovered independently that these Old English lyrics were structured on the basis of certain antiphons of the early medieval church. Subsequent study has confirmed and extended their conclusions, and the following pattern emerges: *Advent* begins with two *Antiphonae Majores* as the source for the first two lyrics, shifts then to the "Monastic" or "Additional" Antiphons for the next two, returns to the *Antiphonae Majores*, moves to a text compiled by Alcuin, incorporates a motif from the traditional "Doubting of Mary" (cf. Matthew 1:18–20), and returns to two "Monastic" Antiphons. Thus far, the lyrics cited derive primarily from the greater and lesser antiphons that, between December 17th and 23rd, are chanted at Vespers before and after the *Magnificat*, but another lyric derives from two antiphons of the Trinity Sunday service of Lauds and still another (the eleventh) from the *Sanctus* and *Benedictus* of the Mass.[28]

[26] Longstaff, *Evidence of Conflation in Mark?*

[27] See Kemp Malone, "The Old English Period (to 1100)," in *A Literary History of England*, ed. Baugh, 79–80.

[28] See Michael J. B. Allen and Daniel G. Calder, *Sources and Analogues of Old English Poetry: The Major Latin Texts in Translation* (Cambridge, England, and Towota, N.J.: Rowman & Littlefield, Inc., 1976), 70–77, for commentary, bibliography, and translations of the sources; and Charles W. Kennedy, *Early*

Here we see an instance of a writer who has based his composition on ancient liturgical texts and who has chosen to be guided now by this antiphon, now by that, usually in the services for Advent but at times in the Lauds for Trinity Sunday, in the Mass, or in the "Doubting of Mary" tradition. His principal sources, however, are the Major Antiphons and the Monastic or Additional Antiphons, between which he alternates. If we total the combined length of the available services for the Advent season, that for Trinity Sunday, the Mass, and the relevant "Doubting of Mary" accounts and compare this total with the shorter length of the *Advent*, the difference in length between the *Advent* and the sources upon which its author depended is roughly comparable to the difference in length between Mark and a combination of Matthew and Luke. At the same time, the particular antiphons that the Old English writer has chosen to treat are considerably expanded in the sections or "fits" of his poem, again in a manner comparable to Mark's expansion of pericopes as over against the parallel treatments in the other two Synoptics. Although not precise, the parallel is instructive and can be illustrated by comparing Monastic Antiphon *O Hierusalem* ("O Jerusalem, city of the Great God: lift up thine eyes round about and see thy Lord, for he comes to loose thee from thy chains") with the following translation of the verses derived from it, which is italicized to provide a ready comparison with the source:

> *O Holy Jerusalem*, Vision of peace,
> Fairest of royal seats, *City of Christ*,
> Homeland of angels, in thee for ever
> Rest the souls of the righteous alone
> In glory exulting. No sign of sin
> In that city-dwelling shall ever be seen,
> But from thee all evil shall flee afar,
> All trouble and toil. Thou art wondrously filled
> With holy hope, as thy name is named.
>
> *Lift up thine eyes* on the wide creation,
> The dome of heaven, on every hand;
> *Behold His coming*; the King of glory
> *Himself approaches* to seek thee out,
> To abide in thee, as the blessed prophets
> In their books foretold the birth of the Christ,

English Christian Poetry Translated into Alliterative Verse; with Critical Commentary (London: Hollis & Carter, 1952), 75–92, for critical commentary and translations of the Old English verse.

> To thy comfort spoke, thou fairest of cities!
> Now is the Babe come born to transform
> The works of the Hebrews. He brings thee bliss,
> *Looses thy bondage*, draws nigh unto men,
> For He only knows their harrowing need,
> How man in his wretchedness waits upon mercy.[29]

As illustrated here, the *Advent* provides a clear instance of the abbreviation of various *Vorlagen* (i.e., the numerous antiphons, the Trinity Sunday Lauds, the Mass, and the "Doubting of Mary") coupled with the expansion of chosen parts. There may appear to be a logical contradiction in such abbreviation joined with expansion, but history is not governed by logical considerations, and neither is literary history.

Another example of "a mosaic of borrowings" can be found in the Old English *Last Judgment*, also known as *Christ III*.[30] For the most part, the patterns of derivation here are quite clear, though they are more complex than for the *Advent*. As Michael J. B. Allen and Daniel G. Calder write, "parts of the poem come from specific sources, parts seem to reflect patristic writings generally, and parts seem to stand alone."[31] The poet takes his basic structure or succession of parts from a single source (here differing from the Griesbach understanding of Mark's alternation between Matthew and Luke), this source being the hymn *Apparebit repentina dies magna Domini*, which is quoted by the Venerable Bede in his *De Arte Metrica*. The hymn consists of about fifty Latin lines, and these are expanded in the *Last Judgment* into 798 lines of Old English verse. In the expansion, the poet was influenced by far more extensive sources, including *De judicio et compunctione* by Ephraem Syrus, the *Liber Cathemerinon* by Prudentius, the *Moralia* and *Homilies* of Gregory, two sermons by Caesarius of Arles, *De Trinitate* by Augustine, and various works of the Pseudo-Augustine and the Pseudo-Bede, as well as numerous Old and New Testament texts. The combined length of these is considerably greater than that of the Anglo-Saxon writer's resulting text. All of this material the writer uses macaronically, shifting from one source to another as suits his dramatic needs, and in this regard his practice is even more intricate than that postulated for Mark in

[29] Kennedy, *Early English Christian Poetry*, 86–87, emphasis added.
[30] See Kennedy, *Early English Christian Poetry*, 254–258, 268–289; Allen and Calder, *Sources and Analogues of Old English Poetry*, 84–107.
[31] Allen and Calder, *Sources and Analogues of Old English Poetry*, 84.

the Griesbach Hypothesis. Yet, as with the Griesbach suggestion, the result is a considerable reduction of the combined length
of the sources, often linked with an expansion of certain details
and episodes.

Even more interesting and more suggestive for the Synoptic
Problem is the way in which a later writer can be seen to alter his
sources to provide a larger measure of vivid, concrete details, a
fresher and more circumstantial character, indeed a sense more
nearly approaching that of eyewitness involvement, than did the
earlier treatments of the same subject. It is sometimes said that
in Mark we have a more "straightway" story and that the details
and action of the narrative argue for an earlier date than that of
the other gospels. But in literary history we often find that it is a
later, not an earlier, writer who gives us this sense of eyewitness
vividness. This important point can be illustrated by comparing a
single passage from Caesarius of Arles (c. 500) with the unmistakably derivative passage from the ninth century English *Last
Judgment*. A striking feature of both accounts of the Last Judgment is the picture of Christ actively interrogating sinners about
their ingratitude for his redemption. Both passages are moving
and even powerful but that by Caesarius somewhat less so than
that of the man he obviously influenced. Caesarius imagines
Christ in Judgment demanding of sinners, "Why have you
afflicted me on the cross of your crimes, which is heavier than the
one on which I once hanged?"[32] This dramatic question is taken
up directly by the Anglo-Saxon writer, is somewhat expanded,
and is given an even more direct immediacy and sense of personal
involvement:

> Why did you hang me on a Cross of your own hands
> Where I hung more heavily than on that once of old?
> Lo! this seems the harder. More bitter to Me,
> The Cross of your sins. . .[33]

[32] Allen and Calder, *Sources and Analogues of Old English Poetry*, 106.

[33] Kennedy, *Early English Christian Poetry*, 284. Because few can read Old
English, I have provided modern renditions, but in order that the points I make
may not be thought to reside only in Kennedy's translation, I cite also the following version by Robert K. Gordon, *Anglo-Saxon Poetry* (London: J. M. Dent,
1950), 177: "Why dost thou hang me on the cross of thy hands more painfully
than long ago I hung? Lo! this seems harder to me. Now the rood of thy sins. . ."
Gordon's ending of the sentence after "me" is debatable, and Kennedy's reading
seems more convincing. Aside from this minor problem, the comparison between
the poet and his source stands in either translation as representing the original
Old English passage.

The Anglo-Saxon has caught the precise gist of the earlier writer, but whereas the original had "Why have you afflicted me," the later rendition is more graphic as "Why did you hang me"; similarly, "the cross of your crimes" is given greater impact by "a cross of your own hands"; and instead of the simple comparison by which the cross people have made for Christ from their sins is merely "heavier," we now have the far more intimate and striking words of Christ, "where I hung more heavily." One could go through the Old English *Last Judgment* at great length, finding examples of the way in which the later writer has provided a greater sense of immediate involvement than did the earlier sources from which he derived his inspiration. In phrase after phrase, we find a heightening of dramatic impact by the addition of minor details and the substitution of more graphic words.

This is quite similar to what we find in comparing Mark with the other Synoptics, where greater immediacy is often cited as evidence for an earlier date for Mark. Immediacy, impact, and vivid detail do not necessarily indicate priority of authorship in accounts within a single tradition, but depend instead upon the abilities and interests of the different narrators. The most notable example of this general phenomenon is of course Shakespeare, whose accounts of the English Civil Wars are so characterized by picturesque details and evocative elements that they make us feel closer to the original events than do the extant accounts of people who were involved in the events or the intermediary histories upon which Shakespeare relied. Another instance, among many, is the most realistic of the narratives devoted to the American Civil War, *The Red Badge of Courage*. This is often cited as the most convincing evocation of battle by any American writer, but the author, Stephen Crane, was not born until several years after the Civil War, and his treatment of it was based upon his reading of history.

On the basis of the evidence just surveyed and of more that could be cited, I can only conclude that the presence of corroborative details within a fast-moving and convincing narrative does not necessarily indicate the early date of a particular account within the historical tradition of which it is a part. What is decisive here is not chronology, but narrative proclivity and technique.

The Criterion of Conflation: Shakespearian Examples. I turn now to a famous example of conflation in Shakespeare, in *Julius Caesar*. Shakespeare's respect for what he regarded as authori-

279

tative works on English and Roman history is well known and often remarked upon; thus it is appropriate in a discussion of the Synoptic Problem to cite parallels to one of his Roman plays. (He was far more cavalier in his use of fictitious sources for non-historical plays.) When the most informative recent editor of *Julius Caesar* comments upon Shakespeare's adaptation of Plutarch's three separate biographies of Caesar, Brutus, and Antony into a single play, he does so in words similar in conception to those used in describing Mark's conflation of Matthew and Luke according to the Griesbach Hypothesis: According to T. S. Dorsch, Shakespeare has transmuted "Plutarch's three comparatively leisurely narratives into a single closely knit and swiftly moving drama."[34]

Distinctions must be kept clear, however. Plutarch wrote three separate biographies, and his accounts overlap even as the events reported in them overlapped historically; Shakespeare then combined these three sources into a single dramatic history. Obviously this is a different situation from that envisioned by the Griesbach Hypothesis, where three different authors treated a single life with the first work forming the basis for the second and these two together forming the basis for the third. In Shakespeare, we have an author developing a single account from three overlapping but distinct narratives about three individuals and doing so by a process of moving back and forth among the three. With Mark, according to the Griesbach Hypothesis, we have a single author preparing a single account on the basis of two narrative sources about the same individual and doing so by moving back and forth between the two. Technically, Mark's task would appear to have been simpler to perform than Shakespeare's and to have demanded less art, but despite the obvious differences between the two, there are structural parallels that make a comparison appropriate.

Against the Griesbach Hypothesis, it has been argued that a writer would not or could not have alternated between his sources as Mark is said to have done. We have already seen something quite similar to such alternation in Old English literature, however, and we see it again in Shakespeare's *Julius Caesar*. The drama opens on Caesar's Roman triumph when, as one character in the play describes it, the plebs "strew flowers

[34] T. S. Dorsch, ed., *Julius Caesar*, The Arden Edition of the Works of William Shakespeare (Cambridge, Mass.: Harvard University Press, 1955), xvii.

in his way,/That comes in triumph over Pompey's blood" (1.1. 50–51). This episode was found in Plutarch's *Life of Julius Caesar*. Shakespeare's next scene opens with the Feast of Lupercal, at which time Mark Antony thrice offers Caesar the diadem. This too came from the same work by Plutarch. Both before and after the presentation of the diadem, however, Shakespeare introduces Cassius' attempt to persuade Brutus to join the conspiracy against Caesar; for this he relied upon Plutarch's *Life of Marcus Brutus*. Next, for the fearful prodigies that precede Caesar's death, Shakespeare returns to the *Life of Caesar*, after which he recurs to the *Life of Brutus* for the troubled thoughts of Brutus as he weighs his responsibilities, for the whole treatment of Brutus' wife Portia, and for other details about developments within the conspiracy. But Shakespeare returns to the *Life of Caesar* for the account of Calpurnia's fearful and ominous dream that almost prevents Caesar from venturing forth on the Ides of March and of the actual persuasion of Caesar to go out on that fatal day. Then the playwright returns to the *Life of Brutus* for the dramatic detail of Portia's anxiety, to the *Life of Caesar* for Artemidorus' final warning to Caesar, and back to the *Life of Brutus* for a suspenseful detail when the conspirators fear that their plans have been betrayed. The principal details of the assassination itself come from the *Life of Caesar*. The major patterns consist of alternating material drawn from the two *Lives* of Caesar and Brutus, but this pattern is somewhat complicated by the inclusion of details of characterization and description taken from the *Life of Antony* as well as from the other two *Lives*. After the assassination, there is an occasional backwards glance to the *Life of Caesar*, but the primary reliance henceforth alternates between the *Lives* of Antony and Brutus, with principal reliance upon the latter.

Here, as in the other conflationary works we have observed, we see a "wiggling back and forth" between *Vorlagen*, to cite a pejorative description of the Griesbach postulate.[35] Some of Shakespeare's lines are taken almost verbatim from one or another of his three sources, often they are extensively paraphrased, sometimes abbreviated and sometimes expanded, but always they are endowed with immediacy and circumstantial

---

[35] F. W. Beare, Review of *The Synoptic Problem: A Critical Analysis*, by William R. Farmer, in *Journal of Biblical Literature*, 84 (1965), 296. See also "wiggled back and forth" in Reginald H. Fuller, "The Synoptic Problem: After Ten Years," *The Perkins School of Theology Journal*, 28 (1975), 65.

detail. Without positing any slavish parallels, we can nonetheless say that Shakespeare's process of adaptation here is essentially similar to that which has been postulated for Mark's use of Matthew and Luke.[36] Although Mark has not executed his conflation on the same aesthetic level as has Shakespeare, there is no reason to doubt that he could readily have done the same kind of thing in a technical sense. Nothing in the process is beyond the capacity of a narrator such as Mark.[37]

Neither Shakespeare nor Mark thought it effective to report everything available to him. Thus, Shakespeare's *Julius Caesar* is only about 37 percent as long as the three basic *Lives* by Plutarch, and Mark's length is approximately 30 percent that of Matthew and Luke combined.[38] Although Mark did not include

[36] Those who wish to follow Shakespeare's procedure in detail will find all they need in the New Arden text: Dorsch, ed., *Julius Caesar*.

[37] Also relevant to our concern is the conflation of separate episodes in a source into a single episode in the derivative work. As with the larger patterns of conflation, here, too, we find a parallel in the conflation of particular events, which can be illustrated in Shakespeare and in the Gospel of Luke. Whereas Shakespeare telescopes the decisive Battle of Philippi into two encounters on a single day, Plutarch's *Life of Brutus* recounts two major battles, separated from each other by almost three weeks' time. A comparable conflation in the Synoptic Gospels can be seen when Matthew 14:13–21 and 15:32–39 recount two separate miracles of multiplying loaves and fishes, the first to feed 5,000 and the second 4,000, but Luke (9:12–17) has only a single account. Whether the two accounts in fact derived from a single episode in the ministry of Jesus, which Matthew reported in two ways, is irrelevant to our present concern, for, according to the Griesbach Hypothesis, Luke would have found in Matthew two feedings, just as Shakespeare found two battles in Plutarch's *Brutus*, but both Luke and Shakespeare intensified the drama by reporting only a single occasion. See Shakespeare, *Julius Caesar*, act five, scenes two through five, and the reprint of Plutarch's *Life of Brutus* in Dorsch, ed., *Julius Caesar*, 163–165 (cf. also xvi).

[38] For Plutarch, statistics are reached by calculating average numbers of words to the page of the original text in The Loeb Classical Library edition and multiplying by the total number of pages in the three *Lives*; see *Plutarch's Lives*. With an English translation by Bernadotte Perrin, 11 vols., The Loeb Classical Library (Cambridge, Mass.: Harvard University Press/London: William Heinemann Ltd., 1914–1926), 6:125–247; 7:137–333; 9:441–609. For Shakespeare, the word count is taken from Marvin Spevack, *A Complete and Systematic Concordance to the Works of Shakespeare*, vol. 3, *Drama and Character Concordances to the Folio Tragedies and Pericles, The Two Noble Kinsmen, Sir Thomas More* (Hildesheim: Georg Olms Verlagsbuchhandlung, 1968), 568. The resulting ratio of former to latter is approximately 51,730 to 19,110 words. For the Synoptic Gospels, the figures are from Barclay, *Introduction to the First Three Gospels*, 86, as follows: 661 verses in Mark, 1,068 in Matthew, and 1,149 in Luke. The resulting comparisons, though only approximate, are close enough.

all that was available in Matthew and Luke, he did expand upon what he chose to use. Thus, "606 verses from Mark occupy only about 500 verses in Matthew," [39] so that Mark expanded upon his chosen passages in Matthew by 21.2 percent for those passages that appear in both. Dorsch has excerpted from Plutarch's three *Lives* the passages upon which Shakespeare primarily relied for *Julius Caesar* and has reprinted the results in approximately 15,700 words. [40] The play itself runs to 19,110 words. Thus we see that Shakespeare has expanded upon his chosen passages in Plutarch by 21.7 percent, whereas, according to the Griesbach Hypothesis, Mark expanded upon his chosen passages in Matthew by 21.2 percent. The close convergence between these two sets of comparative figures certainly does not prove that Mark was using the other Synoptics as Shakespeare was using Plutarch's three separate *Lives*, but it does show that if he was indeed following the conflation procedure proposed by Griesbach, he was doing so in a way similar to that of one of the recognized masters of the technique. Thus the Griesbach Hypothesis accords with what we know about practices of conflation from these other examples in literary history.

Appraisals and Probabilities. Before summarizing my own appraisal of the Griesbach Hypothesis, it is necessary to consider one issue in the scholarly debate that seems to me to have been a "red herring." This concerns the "canons of criticism" that Farmer proposed for recognizing a secondary or derivative form of a tradition. [41] Whereas Reginald H. Fuller regarded the formulation of these canons as "a notable contribution," [42] I have always seen them as an unnecessary weakness that could divert attention from Farmer's major argument and achievement. They are a weak link, but as a link they are not really a part of the chain of his argument but rather an attachment to it. To show what happened in history or in literary history as between particular literary works (which is Farmer's main purpose) is one thing, and a very desirable thing indeed, but to postulate laws of history is a very different and more dubious enterprise, and Farmer's canons are too much like laws of history in my reading.

History, including literary history, is too idiosyncratic, too unpredictable even in hindsight, too vagarious in its develop-

[39] Barclay, *Introduction to the First Three Gospels*, 86.
[40] See Dorsch, ed., *Julius Caesar*, 131–166.
[41] For the canons, see Farmer, *The Synoptic Problem*, 227–229.
[42] Fuller, "The Synoptic Problem," 64, cf. 67–68.

ments to make the formulation of such generalized laws and canons practicable. Such generalizations may be useful as brief summaries of a particular argument or as mnemonic devices, but they are too far abstracted from the raw stuff of literary history to be decisive instruments for interpreting this history on an *a priori* or deductive basis. Furthermore, such canons and laws can be cited to support conflicting answers to too many questions, and it is therefore not surprising that Charles H. Talbert and Edgar V. McKnight were able to turn these canons against Farmer's position and use them at certain points to support Marcan priority.[43] The result, I would suggest, is not a falsification of the basic hypothesis that Farmer advocates, but rather a falsification of certain laws or canons of history that are not essential to the hypothesis.

As for the basic issue, Farmer and his associates have forced us to re-examine the Synoptic Problem and to do so with a new rigor. One result has been the exposure of the accumulated prejudgments in favor of Marcan priority as being made up, like most prejudgments, of about nine parts of conditioned habit to one part of hard evidence. So much to the good. But has the Griesbach Hypothesis been proven? "Proof" is and should be a hard word, a most demanding word. As I understand literary-historical proof, there is simply not enough objective, externally supported evidence to allow us to say that either Marcan or Matthean priority has been proved. As for demonstrable proof in the present state of the evidence, then, I should have to choose a Scottish verdict of *non liquet* for all of the sequential arguments regarding the relationships among the Synoptic Gospels.

If the Griesbach Hypothesis has thus far neither been proven nor disproven, what then of the probabilities? These probabilities, at least in the present state of our understanding, cannot be established like actuarial tables, for we do not have such a statistical base for comparison and analysis. Rather, we must rely on how such literary relationships as those among the Synoptics can be explained internally within the gospels and correlated externally with similar relationships elsewhere in literary history. It is on such grounds that I would accept the Griesbach explanation as, overall, the most credible of the linear hypotheses. I recapitulate and summarize as follows:

1. In terms of language, arguments from the "creolized"

[43] Charles H. Talbert and Edgar V. McKnight, "Can the Griesbach Hypothesis Be Falsified?," *Journal of Biblical Literature*, 91 (1972), 338–368.

Greek of Mark are surely not decisive for establishing priority in a written and published work. On the contrary, creolization accords with what in certain other circumstances would seem to be a typically later appearance. Here the issue of typicality should be submitted to linguistic scholars who can take the analysis beyond the rather fragmentary impressions that I have recorded.

2. In terms of length, the argument that the greater length of an account evidences a later development holds true for stages in the work of a single author but not for redactions by different authors. Digests typically and even by definition follow the prior establishment of the importance of longer works.

3. In terms of conflation, the procedure postulated for Mark in the Griesbach Hypothesis conforms closely to what can be seen wherever I have found a literary work in which conflation is demonstrable beyond a shadow of doubt. There are probably exceptions of which I am unaware, but the following characteristics are widespread enough to be regarded as highly typical: alternation between or among *Vorlagen*, condensation of overall or total length of the *Vorlagen*, frequent expansion within pericopes, and addition of lively details to provide a fresher and more circumstantial narrative. Here the conformity to general literary patterns that we find in the Griesbach explanation of Synoptic order is not only very impressive, but telling evidence in its favor.

On the other hand, arguments for Marcan priority in a linear development are more cumbersome, requiring the postulation not only of that omnium gatherum "Q," but of other entities as well, which are introduced "to save the appearances." It is more economical to explain source relationships among the three Synoptics by viewing Mark as a conflater of Matthew and Luke than it is to start with Mark and construct the devious ways of its expansion into the two longer gospels.

4. For this reason among others, the postulate of Matthew leading to Luke and then to Mark leaves less work for "Ockham's razor," with fewer excrescences to require pruning and cutting. When the fourteenth-century philosopher William of Ockham formulated the principle known as the law of parsimony, he made a major contribution to all scholarly and scientific analysis: "Entia non sunt multiplicanda praeter necessitatem." If we operate within an assumption of sequential source relationships, Matthean priority and the Griesbach Hypothesis cover the data we

have in the three Synoptics at least as adequately as does Marcan priority, but with greater simplicity and elegance. If the Griesbach Hypothesis covered the data less effectively, even though more simply, it should be rejected, of course, but since it includes and explains appearances with at least equal appositeness and with fewer complexities, it is preferable.

I do not come away from my analysis with a feeling of certainty regarding the source relationships. We do not have preserved from the first century the kinds and extent of evidence that render certainty possible in other literary historical contexts. Perhaps such evidence may yet come to light, or perhaps new methods of approaching the present evidence may make demonstration possible. Perhaps too the arguments for synchronic and overlapping developments as advanced by Robinson and independently supported in this volume by Kennedy and Lord will ultimately prove to be convincing. We shall see: *Veritas filia temporis*. In the meantime, I have more confidence in the Griesbach explanation than I have in the alternatives among the hypotheses of linear development.

II. On Disintegrating the Gospels

Disintegrating Criticisms of Shakespeare: A Parallel. Secular literary history can contribute more confidently and more helpfully to other areas in the critical study of the gospels than to attempts at solving the problem of chronological relationships, where the nature of the evidence is so problematical. In recent years, uncertainty about the sequence of the gospels has combined with other equally important concerns to produce an increasing desire for a wide reassessment of gospel studies. Calls for a re-evaluation have come from several quarters and notably from younger biblical scholars. E. P. Sanders has posed one aspect of the problem with force and clarity:

If both form and redaction criticism rest on the two-source hypothesis (and they do), and if our understanding of the gospels and of Jesus depends on our ability to apply these and other methods of criticism to the gospels (and it does), and if there is widespread disenchantment in the English and French speaking worlds with the traditional source hypothesis (which there is), *why is synoptic research not being redone from top to bottom?*[44]

[44] E. P. Sanders, "The Synoptic Problem: After Ten Years," *The Perkins School of Theology Journal*, 28 (1975), 70–71.

If reappraisals are in order, it will be helpful for New Testament scholars to consider the experience and perspective of other literary-historical disciplines.

No literary historian could fail to be impressed by the intellectual energy that has characterized much New Testament scholarship and by the many brilliant critical arguments and interpretations that have resulted. It is a fact, however, that New Testament scholars have been accustomed to accepting certain approaches and techniques as adequate and productive, and the accepted methodology seems "natural." At this point, coming from outside the "system," as a representative of literary history in the secular fields, I must observe that few if any of the leading literary historians in secular fields would be comfortable with the widespread assumption among New Testament critics that it is possible, in the present state of the evidence, to move backwards in time from passages in the extant gospel texts in such a way as to identify previous stages or forms through which the tradition has supposedly developed and, ultimately, to arrive at or near the original life and teachings of Jesus; or that it is possible, through a similar procedure, to explain the Synoptic redactions as we now have them. No one would deny the desirability of the objective, but the methods of pursuing it should be questioned, even though these methods are currently acceptable to many who work within the biblical and theological fields.

Here, some New Testament critics may object that I have admired many results of their work and ask how I can do this and yet remain unshaken in my scepticism as to the methodology that I question. An astronomical analogy may help to clarify the point here. Although many observations made by astronomers who accepted the Ptolemaic system are still valid, it remains true that the Ptolemaic astronomers were operating around the wrong methodological center (metaphorically) and that their efforts were circumscribed by the wrong questions and by a "disorbited" view of the reality they approached. This analogy is useful, but a more instructive parallel to gospel studies can be found in English literary studies.

During the nineteenth century and the first decades of the twentieth, it was fashionable among literary critics to engage in what is known as "disintegration." Looking at the available Shakespearian texts, for example, critics would suggest, for any of a number of plausible reasons, that certain passages did not represent what Shakespeare himself had written. Of course, in some cases the *textus receptus* may itself indicate garbling, or we may have external evidence of tampering with the text, but these types of cruces were not the concerns that characterized the disintegrators. Their aim was to rediscover the real Shakespeare by eliminating from the corpus "those lines, speeches, scenes, or whole plays which [were] aesthetically or morally unacceptable" to their best understanding of Shakespeare.[45] Among the leading disintegrators were F. G. Fleay (1831–1909) and J. M. Robertson (1856–1933), both intelligent and learned men, whose views were reflected by a considerable number of enthusiastic students. No one can justly accuse these people of frivolity or willful chicanery, but it is now universally recognized that their detailed and impressive analyses moved from equivocal uses of evidence to subjective conclusions. They moved within what we might call a "Ptolemaic system," which is now thoroughly discredited.

Whenever some passage in the plays impressed Robertson and others as un-Shakespearian, they argued that it represented the detritus from an earlier writer, whom Shakespeare had only partially revised, or that it resulted from a later revision of Shakespeare by someone else. Of course, if and when we know objectively an earlier work that Shakespeare rewrote, this method can be put to impeccable uses, but alas the disintegrators were for the most part not objectively comparing known texts but rather hypothesizing lost earlier texts (of whose mere existence there is often no evidence) in order to account for elements in Shakespeare's canon that they found objectionable. An admirer of Robertson's method summarized it as follows: because certain "passages leave on his aesthetic sense an unsatisfactory impression, he recalls his experience of previous or contemporary dramatists and assigns them to one or the other. . . . The result is that Shakespeare is exalted, not belittled."[46] When a passage is thought to be "undignified or unworthy," then we are assured that we "are probably reading either alien work rewritten by Shakespeare or Shakespeare curtailed and interpolated by an-

---

[45] S. Schoenbaum, *Internal Evidence and Elizabethan Dramatic Authorship: An Essay in Literary History and Method* (Evanston, Ill.: Northwestern University Press, 1966), 111.

[46] Augustus Ralli, *A History of Shakespearean Criticism*, 2 vols. (Oxford: Oxford University Press, 1932), 2:371.

other." [47]

All of this was presented with elaborate learning, with extensive critical apparatus and sophisticated arguments, often with statistical tables and charts, and with repeated appeals to "science." Adherents of this methodology thought that something had been proved when an intellectually impressive exercise led them to eliminate from the text what they found distasteful or bothersome and reassured them with results that they found more pleasing. Robertson's aim here was as noble as that of certain New Testament scholars, whose methodology is so like his own: as a follower summarized, he aimed "to trace the Master by his style, and reach a final vision of him, if at all, only when his real work [was] made fairly sure." [48]

Following this purpose, Robertson looked at the problems and mysteries of *Hamlet* (e.g., indecision, delay, violence, Machiavellian scheming) and postulated that Shakespeare was not responsible for such troublesome and puzzling elements, but that he had merely taken them over from an earlier play on the same story, the so-called *Ur-Hamlet*. In this case such an earlier play is known to have existed, but it is not preserved for us; thus, by an elaborate scissors-and-paste job, Robertson could ascribe to the earlier play everything that he wished to remove from Shakespeare. His long series of ingenious conjectures, salted with occasional pieces of objective evidence, was a fascinating and in many ways a brilliant exercise, but in the consensus of modern Shakespearian scholars, the result was "the almost total divorce of character from plot, of Hamlet from *Hamlet*, and, indeed, of Hamlet at one moment from Hamlet at another." [49]

New Testament scholars who wish to explore the relevance of such "disintegrating" criticism for the study of the Synoptic Gospels will enjoy a close reading of *The Disintegration of Shakespeare* by Sir Edmund K. Chambers. [50] This compact essay, one of the landmarks in the development of literary history, originated as the Annual Shakespeare Lecture delivered in 1924

[47] Ralli, *A History of Shakespearean Criticism*, 2:416. For Ralli's praise of Robertson, see, e.g., 123, 232, 371, 420–421.

[48] Ralli, *A History of Shakespearean Criticism*, 2:553.

[49] Paul Gottschalk, *The Meanings of Hamlet: Modes of Literary Interpretation Since Bradley* (Albuquerque, N.M.: University of New Mexico Press, 1972), 17.

[50] E. K. Chambers, *The Disintegration of Shakespeare*, The British Academy: The Annual Shakespeare Lecture 1924 (Oxford: H. Milford, Oxford University Press, 1924). Although Chambers does not mention New Testament criticism, scholars in this field will have no difficulty in identifying similarities in approach.

before the British Academy. In it, Chambers summarized many features of the disintegrating approach that can be seen as strikingly similar to much New Testament analysis, and he judged the approach inadequate for rigorous literary-historical scholarship. There was nothing simplistic in Chambers' approach. He freely admitted that "there are inconsistencies of narrative and time-sequence" in Shakespeare, that "analysis often reveals the co-existence in one and the same play of features belonging to different stages of development, and sometimes of features which it is difficult to place in the line of development at all," and that "an examination of the texts shows such eccentricities and dislocations as to raise a doubt whether they can have come to us just as Shakespeare left them." Chambers further recognized that the disintegrating critics were often men of "fertile and ingenious mind." After an unbiased analysis of their attempts to sort out within the texts "strata belonging to different dates" and to ascribe these variously according to systems that they claimed were scientific and inexorable, he concluded that disintegrating criticism approaches "the point where scholarship merges itself in romance."[51]

Attempts to separate "strata belonging to different dates" within the gospels, so as to disclose the process of redaction or to identify the authentic earliest stratum, involve essentially the same modus operandi as that employed by the disintegrators, who led us *from* what we have in the best established texts of Shakespeare but instead of leading us closer *to* the authorial originals, substituted intricate new understandings, which, however subjectively satisfying for a time, have eventually been recognized as learned illusions. The same recognition is already overtaking comparable exercises in biblical studies. As a contribution to this ongoing process, I shall now, in the light of comparable situations in secular literature, appraise certain representative examples of "disintegrating" the gospels. Many other examples could have been chosen from the corpus of twentieth-century gospel criticism, but these should suffice at least to show the nature of the problem and the weakness of such methodology.

Parables Followed by Aphorisms. In Luke 14:11, Jesus concludes the parable of the guest at a marriage feast with the *chreia* or *aitia*, "For everyone who exalts himself will be humbled, and he who humbles himself will be exalted," an expression that also

---

[51] Chambers, *The Disintegration of Shakespeare*, 10, 3, 6, 7, 10.

occurs with only slight variation in the Greek of Matthew 23:12. Luke 18:14b records the same aphorism after the parable of the Pharisee and the tax collector who went up to the Temple to pray. Some New Testament critics regard such concluding aphorisms as "secondary and expanded interpretations," evidences of "a strong tendency to add conclusions to the parables in the form of generalizing logia," as Joachim Jeremias put it.[52] But why, we may ask, should such expressions be regarded as additions? Two rationales operate here, the first having to do with repetition as such and the second with the parable as a form.

The first rationale apparently presupposes that Jesus said only once that "everyone who exalts himself will be humbled, and he who humbles himself will be exalted," and that one or the other use of these words therefore derives from Luke the editor rather than from Jesus the teacher, as though a teacher would not repeat himself. But I wonder how many teachers really teach this way; I doubt that many do. Every "good line" (which Luke 14:11 and 18:14b certainly are) that also makes an important point tends to be repeated. I have known a goodly number of great teachers, and they have all had certain favorite expressions that recur in their teaching, with or without variations. But my response thus far is only part of the answer, though an important part. Literarily, what we have here is an example of incremental repetition, which usually signals that an important thematic development is at work. So, at least, it works with repetitions of this kind elsewhere in literature, and such repetitions are not unusual. Readily accessible examples can be found in Shakespeare, where two pairs occur in the same play. In *Richard II*, the Duke of York says of the impetuous young king that "all in vain comes counsel to his ear," and two dozen lines later he repeats the image as "all too late comes counsel to be heard."[53] In another instance, the Duchess of York declares that her lord "sets the word itself against the word," while two scenes later Richard says that his thoughts "do set the word itself/Against the word."[54] As the famous critic Kenneth Burke has written,

---

[52] Joachim Jeremias, *The Parables of Jesus*, rev. ed., trans. S. H. Hooke (New York: Charles Scribner's Sons, 1963), 110; cf. also 107–108.

[53] Shakespeare, *Richard II*, act two, scene one, line four, and act two, scene one, line twenty-seven.

[54] Shakespeare, *Richard II*, act five, scene three, line one hundred twenty-two and act five, scene five, lines thirteen and fourteen.

"repetition itself is not a fault," and it may indeed be a sign that the narrator knows exactly what he wishes to emphasize.[55]

Another rationale for regarding the aphoristic conclusion to the parable as a secondary addition concerns the parable as a form, and this poses perhaps an even more basic problem. It is sometimes assumed that the parables told by Jesus were originally independent units and that such summarizing epigrams as follow the parable of the Pharisee and tax collector at prayer are "accumulated redactional additions" to the simple story, which Jesus told without comment of his own.[56] But why make such an assumption? Was there only one form of the parable that Jesus always used, and did he never add aphoristic comments at the end of the story told in the parable? On literary-historical grounds, there is no hard evidence that Jesus, as a first-century Palestinian rabbi, would not or could not or did not append to the parable of the seating arrangements at the wedding feast or to the parable of the two men praying in the Temple the admonition that "everyone who exalts himself will be humbled."

Here the rabbinic parables are relevant, but surely these do not include all possible variations of the parable as a literary form. Every literary form that I know has been subject to alteration and development by its various practitioners, especially if these practitioners happen to have possessed originality (and at the very least Jesus would appear to have been original). The variations and embellishments or adaptations of the parable form that we find in the gospels are entirely within the range of a single individual, even of an individual considerably less gifted than Jesus seems to have been. This should be clear from what is known, in literary history at large, of established literary forms and of the variations that are played upon them.

As a case in point, consider the sonnet form. It is the most rigorously systematized literary form I know, with its tightly structured fourteen lines and careful interlinear rhyming. Yet it has been adapted and shaped into a number of quite distinct types. Fortunately, these different types have been preserved in sufficient numbers so that we can trace the developments of

[55] Kenneth Burke, *Counter-Statement* (New York: Harcourt, Brace and Company, 1931), 125.

[56] Robert A. Spivey and D. Moody Smith, Jr., *Anatomy of the New Testament: A Guide to Its Structure and Meaning*, 2d ed. (New York: Macmillan Publishing Co., Inc./London: Collier Macmillan Publishers, 1974), 205.

the form without encountering those lacunas and gaps of evidence that can make New Testament criticism puzzling and allow it to become speculative.

But assume for our purposes of analysis that only a fraction of these sonnets have in fact been preserved and passed on to us, comparable in number to the preserved parables of Jesus and others. Assume further that we have sizeable collections of the so-called Italian form of the sonnet, which originated with Petrarch and then spread all over Europe. In this type, the fourteen lines were divided into an initial eight lines called the octave (containing two quatrains) and a concluding six lines called the sestet. The structure of this Italian type precluded or at least restricted the opportunity to provide an aphoristic conclusion to the sonnet, because it is difficult to turn six intricately inter-rhymed lines into an aphorism. But then let us assume that we also have preserved a few instances of a very different type of sonnet, a type that progresses through three successive quatrains of four lines each and is climaxed by a brilliantly aphoristic couplet that summarizes or comments in two lines upon all that has gone before. What I have described, of course, is first the Italian sonnet (for example, Milton's "How Soon Hath Time" or Keats' "On First Looking into Chapman's Homer") and the later variation upon it known as the English sonnet, which was epitomized but not originated by William Shakespeare. To someone who did not have such prolific evidence of the sonnet's total development as is actually available to us, it might seem that Shakespeare's final couplet that passes judgment on the preceding twelve lines was as extraneous to the sonnet form as, in the judgment of some New Testament critics, are the concluding aphorisms to the parables upon which they comment.

Suppose, however, that we encountered a perfect Italian sonnet, for which an aphoristic comment had been supplied after the fourteenth line. Should we regard the aphorism as a redactional addition? No, because here we have the *sonetto caudato* or tailed sonnet, in which the basic form is that of the Italian sonnet with octave and sestet, to which couplets or tercets or quatrains are added at will so that the author can provide whatever moral or other commentary he chooses. An example is Milton's "On the New Forcers of Conscience." These various subtypes of the sonnet could and did exist at the same time in the same country and even in the works of a single writer.

293 A literary form is highly flexible, and even in that most rigor-

ously structured of literary forms, the sonnet, it is subject to far greater variation than New Testament form criticism sometimes allows in its treatment of an apparently more flexible form such as the parable. From this brief account of the sonnet, it should be obvious that there are grave dangers in establishing a single prototype for a literary form and then assuming that variations from this norm are due to editorial manipulations or other intrusions upon the original words or the early tradition. To assume that an aphorism following a parable is inauthentic because it does not conform to an abstract literary form is to grant less flexibility to such forms than secular literary historians are accustomed to recognize.

Aphorisms. No scholar could object to the hypothesis that the aphorism, "For everyone who exalts himself . . . ," was not originally attached to the parable as told by Jesus or that it was not included in the earlier tradition preserving this parable, if the hypothesis were supported by solid evidence. Surely the Synoptic writers could and did on occasion ascribe words to Jesus that he did not speak in their present form. Every example of dramatic history that I know includes such ascriptions, for reasons that I have suggested elsewhere.[57] Acknowledging that there is growth and change within a tradition, we should recognize, however, that claims to reconstruct the stages of such growth and change will usually be speculative guesses, however much they may be overlayed with learned apparatus, *unless* one or more of the following types of evidence are available:

1. There may be clear instances of changes within a text, of movement from an unaltered to an altered state. Such changes occur between the first edition of *Paradise Lost* in 1667 and the second edition of 1674, for example, and when two different names are assigned to a single character at various points within the single text of a Shakespeare play.

2. There may be objective internal evidence within a text that correlates with objective external evidence in such a way that we know changes have taken place. Ben Jonson, for example, asserted that Shakespeare wrote of Julius Caesar, "Caesar did

[57] See Roland Mushat Frye, "A Literary Perspective for the Criticism of the Gospels," in *Jesus and Man's Hope*, vol. 2, ed. Donald G. Miller and Dikran Y. Hadidian, A Perspective Book (Pittsburgh: Pittsburgh Theological Seminary, 1971), 193–221 and esp. 206–214; and "On the Historical-Critical Method in New Testament Studies: A Reply to Professor Achtemeier," *Perspective*, 14 (1973), 28–33.

never wrong, but with just cause," and Jonson castigated this statement as ridiculous. In the preserved text of Shakespeare, however, we now read, "Caesar doth not wrong, nor without cause/Will he be satisfied."[58] Granting the well-attested accuracy of Jonson's verbal memory, we are justified in assuming that, under his stern critique, Shakespeare altered his own words from what Jonson says they were to what we find in the present text.

3. There may be objective evidence entirely external to a text that points to developments and alterations within the text. For example, Milton's notebooks record his earlier plan to write *Paradise Lost* not in its present epic form, but as a drama. We do not know how far he progressed with this dramatic composition, but we do know that the famous soliloquy of Satan, which now occurs early in Book Four of the epic, had originally been composed to serve as the first speech in the play, and we know this because Milton's nephew tells us so in his life of his uncle.[59]

Of these three types of evidence for alteration of a tradition, we find famous examples of the first type in the gospels, such as the obvious "early" ending of Mark (16:8), to which concluding material has been added, as attested by different manuscript editions. Still falling within this type is the case of the end of John, where the next to the last chapter concludes with verses appropriate to concluding the whole Gospel, and yet another chapter follows this "false conclusion." But for the other two types of evidence, we find little or nothing that can help us in an objective way in moving backwards through earlier stages of the tradition.

To focus upon a representative problem, let us consider the question of short, tersely worded statements that memorably summarize some truth or opinion. Akin to the proverb and adage, into which category such statements sometimes move as a result of popular acceptance and repetition, the literary form itself can variously be called epigram, aphorism, maxim, *chreia*, or mot. Under whatever name, expressions of this kind abound in the gospels. Here, as elsewhere, certain readers may wish to speculate that some of these are redactional additions to the tradition

---

[58] Shakespeare, *Julius Caesar*, act three, scene one, lines forty-seven and forty-eight; cf. the notes in Dorsch, ed., *Julius Caesar*, 65.

[59] Milton, *Paradise Lost*, book four, lines thirty-two to forty-one; see Edward Phillips, "The Life of Mr. John Milton," in *The Early Lives of John Milton*, ed. Helen Darbishire (London: Constable & Co Ltd, 1932), 72–73.

or to Jesus' own words, but however couched in learned apparatus such speculations may be, it is hard to see how, in the present state of the evidence, these aphorisms in the gospels can be discredited on anything approaching sound literary-historical grounds.

Given sufficient evidence, of course, the ascription of aphorisms can be discredited. Everyone has heard the Duke of Wellington quoted to the effect that "The Battle of Waterloo was won on the playing fields of Eton," and few people have doubted that he actually said it. It certainly sounds like Wellington, who was so famous for coining such phrases that the phrases were known among his contemporaries and among later history buffs as "Wellington's laconics," and there is nothing on stylistic grounds to throw doubt on the "playing fields of Eton" saying. In all probability, however, Wellington did not originate this most famous of his laconics, and we know this because of the careful tracing of extant evidence of a growing tradition that we find in the authoritative two-volume biography of Wellington by Elizabeth Longford. Nothing approximating the epigram was associated with Wellington until three years after his death, and then it was introduced by a Frenchman, the Count de Montalembert, in 1855. According to his account, the Iron Duke returned to Eton late in his life, noted the vigor shown by the students in the organized games, recalled his own days there, and commented: "C'est ici qu' a été gagnée la bataille de Waterloo." As Longford shows, however, there were no organized sports at Eton when Wellington attended it, and he shunned such impromptu games as were available. The specific detail about the playing fields was explicitly added some twenty years later when Sir Edward Creasey, in his *Eminent Etonians*, described the aged Duke who, as he passed the "playing fields" of Eton, paid tribute to the "manly character" they nurtured: "There grows the stuff that won Waterloo." This version was the first to appear in English and it came from an unauthoritative source. From it there shortly developed the famous saying as we know it.[60]

Legends and legendary statements do indeed grow, and here we have a fine instance, readily traceable and documented over a period of a third of a century. But all of this involves masses of evidence, preserved and available to the scholar. For Wellington, this kind of "form-critical" study will work. As for the Syn-

[60] Elizabeth Longford, *Wellington: The Years of the Sword* (New York: Harper & Row, Publishers, 1969), 15–17.

optics, alas, efforts to postulate similar developments will rest for the most part on sheer speculation. Such speculation may be fun for those who do it and interesting for those who read it, but it is not literary history as this discipline is widely known and practised in secular fields.

The Great Supper and the Wedding Feast. Returning now to the parable form as such, let us consider the representative case of a single story situation cast into two different narrative formats: the parable of the great supper in Luke 14:16–24 and that of the wedding feast in Matthew 22:1–14. Assuming as some do that these two passages are not two forms of the story as varied by Jesus on different occasions, but that they vary according to the redactional intent of the two Evangelists, it is possible (depending, of course, upon the chronology one accepts for the two gospels) to chart a progressive adaptation of Jesus' original story in the course of influences playing upon each editor. Jeremias, for example, thus sees Matthew's account as a reflection of historical circumstances after A.D. 70, including the Jewish rejection of Christian claims and the destruction of Jerusalem by Roman armies (Matthew 22:7: "The king was angry, and he sent his troops and destroyed those murderers and burned their city"), as Matthew "transformed our parable into an outline of the plan of redemption from the appearance of the prophets, embracing the fall of Jerusalem, up to the Last Judgment."[61] But is all this necessary? Are we justified in assuming that the original teller of a story told it only once or told it invariably in only one form or that it was preserved in only one form? Surely this is not what we find with great storytellers other than Jesus or in other literary traditions.

Two examples from secular literature illustrate the point, the first from the dramatic histories of William Shakespeare and the second from the purer invention of William Faulkner. In his sequence of four plays called the Great Tetralogy, Shakespeare traces English history from the feeble reign of King Richard II through the tumultuous times of usurping King Henry IV to a climax in the victorious exploits of King Henry V, the erstwhile Prince Hal. In these plays, the following situation occurs successively on three different occasions: on the eve of a military confrontation a leader considers his prospects, his followers report that his forces are outnumbered by the enemy, and the leader reacts. In Shakespeare, the basic situations in the three accounts

297   [61]Jeremias, *The Parables of Jesus*, 69; see also 63–66, 67–69, 176–180.

are no more dissimilar than are the basic situations in the great supper in Luke and the marriage feast in Matthew, where a host invites guests to a feast, finds that they do not come, and proceeds to provide himself with other guests. The difference is that Shakespeare tells the story not twice but three times: first with Richard II as the outnumbered leader, second with Hotspur in this role, and third with Henry V,[62] and the basic situation is skillfully varied in each instance to convey a conception of each leader. Are we to assume that Shakespeare was responsible for only one of these accounts and that the other two represent "redactional additions"? Certainly not, and there is no more reason to make such an assumption about the two versions of the parable ascribed to Jesus in Matthew and Luke. The range of variation upon a single theme found in the two versions is easily within the scope of a skilled narrator, who adjusts a basic story to different situations. In other words, there are no convincing literary-historical reasons for denying to Jesus, as narrator, the two divergent recountings of this story or for assuming that the differences are to be ascribed to Matthew or Luke as redactors rather than to Jesus as original narrator.

Or take the case of the late William Faulkner, who would write different accounts of the same fictional situation, with discrepancies between the accounts fully as marked as those between the two parables discussed above, but with the basic situation clearly the same. Faulkner's editor, Malcolm Cowley, once called certain of these variations to Faulkner's attention, and Faulkner replied that the story itself "was still alive and growing" in his mind and that the two versions should be allowed to stand as evidence of this fact. In Faulkner's mind, such changes in a basic story pattern were inevitable if his work was to have life.[63]

Why should it be different with Jesus and with the traditions preserved about him? Why must changes within two tellings of what is essentially the same story necessarily indicate editorial intervention? If Jesus was at all comparable to other storytellers and to other teachers, as he surely must have been, then the similar practices of Shakespeare and Faulkner are clearly rele-

---

[62] Shakespeare, *Richard II*, act three, scene two; *I Henry IV*, act four, scene one; and *Henry V*, act four, scene three.

[63] See James B. Meriwether, "Notes on the Textual History of 'The Sound and the Fury,' " *Papers of the Bibliographical Society of America*, 56 (1962), 311, where the references are not only to the work cited in the title but also to *The Mansion*.

vant to him. In terms of secular literary history, there is no reason to deny that Jesus cast the same story into two shapes, as preserved by Matthew and Luke. To assume otherwise, without strong external evidence, is gratuitous. And the same is true for other examples of similar parallels in the gospels.

In none of the foregoing do I mean to assert that these gospel passages provide the *ipsissima verba* of Jesus. Indeed, it seems natural to assume that some remarks attributed to Jesus in the gospels originated after his death. Such attributions would not only be natural but insofar as they faithfully exemplified or summarized the principal emphases or the *ipsissima vox* of his teachings, they would be useful additions. What is questioned here is the practicability of separating what Jesus actually said from redactional additions ascribed to him, because, in the present state of the evidence, there is unfortunately no literary-historical methodology that can perform this separation with any assurance.

Historical Developments or Stages in Stories. For examples of literary traditions in which stages of development can be traced, I turn again to Shakespeare, not because there are not other examples, but because his works are most readily accessible. In or about the year 1599, Shakespeare wrote *Julius Caesar*, and for his basic historical information, as we have seen, he consulted Plutarch's *Parallel Lives*, where we can identify the precise source of his knowledge and often of the very words he used. His Plutarch was the English version of 1579, which Sir Thomas North had translated not from the original but from the 1559 French version of Jacques Amyot, who in turn had translated from the original, both translators introducing changes along the way. Plutarch (b. A.D. 50, d. + A.D. 120) in turn had himself mined various sources for his materials.

Here, we have a veritable gold mine for tracing stages and forms in the development of a literary-historical tradition. It can be both interesting and instructive to trace particular characterizations, speeches, and events through these stratified layers, moving from earliest to latest or reversing the direction and moving backward in time. But let us suppose that Shakespeare's *Julius Caesar* was all that we had, that all earlier versions were lost. Could we then move backwards to restore the tradition and identify stages of its development? This in essence is what is often attempted for the gospels. Let us test a hypothesis: If it is possible, with any degree of assurance, to take the Synoptics as we have them and to move backwards in time so as to identify earlier forms of the traditions they record, then it should also be possible to apply the same procedure to Shakespeare. On these grounds, in other words, it should be possible to analyze Shakespeare's text taken by itself, just as though its sources were lost to us, and from it to deduce what he had found in North's Plutarch. If we wish to extend the range of this operation *ad absurdum*, we might even seek to postulate, not only how Shakespeare diverged from North's version, but also how North had changed Amyot, and how Amyot had altered the original Plutarch.

Or we might take a somewhat less complex problem, associated with Shakespeare's great cycle of English historical drama ranging from *Richard II* through *Henry V*. For these four plays, written between 1595 or 1597 and 1599, the magisterial source was Raphael Holinshed's *The Chronicles of England, Scotland and Ireland* in its second edition of 1587, which enlarged the first edition of 1577. Shakespeare was even more careful to be essentially (though never literally or slavishly) faithful to the English history he knew than he was in comparable uses of Roman history. He made changes, of course, such as when he represented Hotspur as a contemporary of Prince Hal even though Hotspur had been old enough to be Hal's father, but the essential fidelity was there. Here we find three stages of a developing tradition, all of them preserved for our examination, all in English, and all fitting within a span of no more than twenty-two years, with the major transmission restricted to only twelve years. Surely, if it is possible to move backwards from Synoptic texts to one or more earlier stages in the development of some speech or episode, it ought to be possible to do so in the comparable circumstances of Shakespeare's great histories. It should, in other words, be possible to employ the methodologies of form criticism or of the new hermeneutic in such a way as to concentrate only on Shakespeare and, in ignorance of his sources, deduce from his text the tradition lying only a dozen years earlier in Holinshed's revised second edition and perhaps also to go back ten more years and recover Holinshed's first edition. The results could then be compared with the preserved writings in order to see how well or how poorly the methodology operates.

Granted that there might be a number of accurate deductions as to what Holinshed or North's Plutarch had provided, is it not apparent that there surely would also be at least an equally large (and probably far larger) number of postulates far wide of the mark? How then could we distinguish the one set of deductions from the other? Without preserved records of the earlier tradition (which we have for the dramatic histories of Shakespeare but not for the gospels), we should be at sea in a tempest of speculations and conjectures.

And this is what the methodologies in question yield: not sound literary history, but a mass of speculations and conjectures, a labyrinth of pseudo-historical constructs. Efforts to move backwards from the written records of the gospels through various stages of postulated developments so as to arrive at earlier phases of the traditions about Jesus, and to analyze these, may and often do constitute very impressive intellectual exercises, but they are not recognizable as literary history to one who represents this field in secular scholarship.

The Open Door. I do not wish to close on a negative note, for I do not see the problem as hopeless but only a particular methodology as deluding. What I see as immensely hopeful is the prospect that the gospels should be analyzed with the standard techniques (both historical and critical) employed in the study of other literature. How do the symbols work? What patterns of symbols are present? How do various rhetorical devices operate, and what do these contribute to meaning? What themes are introduced, how, and how are they interrelated? What patterns of imagery are there, and how are these used and to what effect? How do incidents relate to each other? What is the meaning evident in patterns of succession and juxtaposition? Where are we being *led* by all these devices, and what do they "add up to"? What happens when we analyze the characterization of Jesus by the same techniques used in approaching Mark Antony or King Richard II or Prince Hal? These are only hints of the rich possibilities that are available for making the gospels come fully alive to modern readers. When such possibilities are explored in sufficient depth, Jesus will become recognizably alive to people who have previously found him remote.

What I am advocating is not a closed door but an open door or rather a turning away from one door, which has only led us into a maze of mirrors, to another door, which offers good promises of leading us to Jesus. After my paper, "A Literary Perspective for the Criticism of the Gospels," was read at the Pittsburgh Festival on the Gospels in 1970, the African scholar E. Bolaji Idowu commented that most New Testament criticism could be summed up in the words of Mary Magdalene at the empty tomb: "They have taken my Lord away, and I know not where they have laid him."[64] My proposal is that *first* we use the readily available techniques of secular literary-historical criticism for bringing the character of Jesus to life literarily, *then* we compare the figure (or figures) of Jesus emerging from the four gospels (each with its distinctive presentations and emphases), and *finally* we may be able better to assess the historical figure who lies behind the four characterizations and his relevance to us: we can only get back to the Jesus of history through the Jesus of literature.

[64] Note, again, as an apposite parallel that the disintegrating criticism of *Hamlet* resulted in "the almost total divorce . . . of Hamlet from *Hamlet*, and, indeed, of Hamlet at one moment from Hamlet at another" (Gottschalk, *The Meanings of Hamlet*, 17).

Basic Affirmation with Some Demurrals: A Response to Roland Mushat Frye

William R. Farmer

The title of Roland Mushat Frye's essay is nicely phrased. The use of the plural, "Synoptic Problems," rather than the singular, "Synoptic Problem," is deliberate. Frye intends to address attention not only to the problem of the sequential relationships among the gospels, i.e., the order in which they were written (the "Synoptic Problem" as it is usually understood), but also to the problem involved in attempting to work back from the extant gospel texts through earlier stages of the tradition to the original life and teachings of Jesus. To this end, Frye appropriately divides his essay into two parts. The first part addresses the problem of the sequence in which the gospels were written and in particular assesses the merits of the Griesbach Hypothesis, according to which Matthew was written first, Luke second, and Mark third. The second part addresses the question, how to bring the character of Jesus to life literarily, and concludes with the proposal that after the Jesus of each gospel has thus been brought to life, the characters can be compared and an attempt made to assess both the historical figure of Jesus and his contemporary relevance.

In both parts of the essay, Frye critically evaluates current methods of literary study of the gospels, and in both parts he makes his own original critical contributions.

303

On Sequence and Dependence: The Griesbach Hypothesis

In the first part of his essay, Frye makes no attempt at the kind of comprehensive discussion of the Synoptic Problem that would give equal attention to all of the major hypotheses. Rather, as an informed onlooker since the days of the Pittsburgh Festival on the Gospels in 1970,[1] he confines his attention to what he perceives as the nexus of the actual debate now underway among gospel critics. The central question, as Frye sees it, is whether the Griesbach Hypothesis, which is now receiving support from an increasing number of New Testament scholars, or the Two-Document Hypothesis, which has long been accepted by an overwhelming majority of critics, more adequately accounts for the various literary phenomena that constitute the Synoptic Problem. Neither solution has been or can be proven, but the literary analogies that Frye has examined lead him to prefer the Griesbach Hypothesis. He presents his evidence for this preference under three headings. The first two relate to arguments that have been used to support Marcan priority: the criterion of language and the criterion of comparative length. The third deals with a matter that is of paramount importance for the Griesbach Hypothesis, i.e., the phenomenon of conflation.

The Criterion of Language. Frye suggests that the alleged Aramaic or Semitic character of Mark's text, far from pointing to Marcan priority as advocates of the Two-Document Hypothesis sometimes argue, is actually an indication of a later, more "creolized" style than that of Matthew and Luke. Before such a suggestion can carry substantive weight, however, it will be necessary to establish criteria for determining exactly what constitutes "Aramaic" or "Semitic" influence in a Greek text, and the attempt to establish such criteria is at best "still in its infancy." It has never been established to my satisfaction that Mark's text is any more "Aramaic" or "Semitic" than are the texts of either Matthew or Luke.

This does not mean that Frye's *tour de force*, whereby he

---

[1] For his own contribution to the Festival, see Roland Mushat Frye, "A Literary Perspective for the Criticism of the Gospels," in *Jesus and Man's Hope*, vol. 2, ed. Donald G. Miller and Dikran Y. Hadidian, A Perspective Book (Pittsburgh: Pittsburgh Theological Seminary, 1971), 193–221. For a response, see Paul J. Achtemeier, "On the Historical-Critical Method in New Testament Studies: Apologia pro Vita sua," *Perspective*, 11 (1970), 289–304; for Frye's reply, see his "On the Historical-Critical Method in New Testament Studies: A Reply to Professor Achtemeier," *Perspective*, 14 (1973), 28–33.

argues *against* Marcan priority on the basis of the alleged "Aramaic" or "Semitic" character of Mark's text, is of no value. It only means that, as an argument, its value is mainly rhetorical rather than scientific. Properly stated, the rhetoric would run as follows: It is often claimed or widely believed that the "Aramaic" or "Semitic" character of Mark's text constitutes evidence in favor of the hypothesis of Marcan priority; it would be useful, therefore, for opponents of Marcan priority to demonstrate that if Mark's text were in fact more "Aramaic" or "Semitic" than the text of Matthew and/or Luke, this fact could indicate that Mark was written after and not before Matthew and/or Luke. What Frye has produced is a useful counterargument. It can, and I trust will, be used to raise questions in critics' minds about a particular plank in the platform on which the consensus for Marcan priority has rested. In my opinion, however, it would be unfortunate if this very interesting, and I think important, argument were accepted as having more value than that of a substantial literary counter-move. Frye's observations about the criterion of language may have undermined a particular argument for Marcan priority, but was this argument ever more than pure fantasy in the first place?

If Frye's argument on this count has long-term value, I should expect it to lie in the direction of stimulating competent critics to develop: (1) an inclusive and discriminating set of criteria for identifying "Aramaic" or "Semitic" influence in Greek texts and (2) an appropriate method for comparing texts of Matthew, Mark, and Luke, with a view to determining which if any is more or less "Aramaic" or "Semitic" than the others. This having been successfully accomplished, the "creolizing" phenomena noted by Frye, as well as other relevant considerations, could then receive careful consideration. Until then, we shall not be in a position to say what if any probative value this particular type of literary data has for resolving the Synoptic Problem.

In any case, what I have said about this part of Frye's work is only a relatively minor caveat and is not meant to blunt the force of Frye's achievement along this line of investigation. He has literally turned the tables and added another instance where it has been possible not only to nullify an argument for Marcan priority, but, granting its assumptions, to reverse it.

One further point is perhaps relevant here. It might be possible to develop an argument regarding the sequence of the gospels by detaching the "creolizing" phenomenon as such from any

question of specifically Aramaic or Semitic influence and interpreting it more generally as a tendency in the early church to
use less standardized Greek (standardized Greek meaning the
Greek employed by authors who aspired to an Attic style). Thus,
it might be argued that Mark's text, which is further from standardized Greek than are Matthew's and Luke's, is indicative of
a later date for Mark.

The Criterion of Comparative Length. Here, as was the case
with the criterion of language, Frye has succeeded in taking a
type of argument that has been held by advocates of Marcan
priority to favor their view and reversing the outcome. According to the nineteenth-century analogy of biological growth, it
became popular to think of the shortest gospel as the earliest
and the longer gospels as forms that developed later. Twentieth-
century literary experts, however, acknowledge that there is no
canon of criticism according to which one can correlate length
with chronology. There are both too many instances where a secondary work is shorter and too many where it is longer than the
more original for the criterion of comparative length to be of
significant value in determining which of the two is earlier. Thus,
on first reading, there appears to be nothing new in Frye's conclusions under this heading. On second reading, however, it
becomes clear that certain of Frye's points bear noting. For
example, it is useful to distinguish what happens when a single
author revises or re-edits his or her own work from what happens when an author adapts or edits an earlier work or works
by a different author or authors. Certainly, the Synoptic Problem
finds its primary literary analogies in cases where it is envisioned that different authors are at work. And here, as Frye
confirms on the basis of a lifetime of work in the history of literature, there is no evidence that secondary authors characteristically tend to produce longer narratives. What is most significant
in Frye's presentation is the point that biographers and historians who are using sources often make "what appear to us to be
strange omissions" (p. 274). This is relevant to the Synoptic
Problem, because, as Frye notes, Mark's omission of the birth
narratives, for example, is often cited as an argument against
the Griesbach Hypothesis.

Frye's quotation from Plutarch, in which this near contemporary of the Evangelists asks his readers not to criticize him for
making omissions, because he was "writing biography, not history" (p. 274), seems to me appropriate. Not only does the quota-   306

tion make it easier to understand Mark's omissions from Matthew and Luke according to the Griesbach Hypothesis; it also aids us in our search for a more satisfactory answer to the question of the literary genre of Mark by suggesting that we view this Gospel as related to popular Hellenistic religious biography rather than as a crude and unsophisticated attempt to write history.[2]

The Criterion of Conflation. In my opinion, it is what Frye has written about "conflation" that constitutes his most enduring contribution to the solution of the Synoptic Problem. Of particular importance here is his observation that an author who conflates two or more sources will sometimes, by the literary license of omission, compose a work whose overall length is considerably less than the combined lengths of the sources, while at the same time producing a text that at many points is more wordy and is characterized by added details. Of course, none of the analogies cited by Frye is exact. The point is that they are the best examples of literary conflation he could find. Each example is worthy of discussion, and the discussion of each leads Frye to the same conclusion: the Griesbach Hypothesis is credible.

Those who are already favorably disposed toward the Griesbach Hypothesis will justly welcome this further evidence of its viability. The critic who hopes to find support for Marcan priority (or for the view that Mark was written second) and who wishes to give serious consideration to literary analogues will now be challenged to find evidence of equal weight supporting his or her view. Perhaps such evidence will be found, and the search for it should be welcomed and encouraged. In the meantime, however, Frye's discussion of this topic holds the field, and advocates of alternate views will need to bear the burden of proof.

Thomas R. W. Longstaff's study of conflation was published only after the completion of Frye's essay.[3] Like Frye, Longstaff concludes that writers who are known to be combining sources have in fact behaved as the Griesbach Hypothesis imagines Mark to have behaved in combining Matthew and Luke. The fact that both Frye and Longstaff independently arrive at the same general conclusion is bound to give added weight to the separate

---

[2] See Philip L. Shuler, Jr., "The Synoptic Gospels and the Problem of Genre" (Ph.D. diss., McMaster University, 1975).

[3] Thomas R. W. Longstaff, *Evidence of Conflation in Mark? A Study in the Synoptic Problem*, Society of Biblical Literature Dissertation Series 28 (Missoula, Mont.: Scholars Press for The Society of Biblical Literature, 1977).

witness of each. Taken together, the carefully wrought dissertation by Longstaff, originally prepared under the direction of a distinguished doctoral committee, and the essay under present discussion, written by a noted and well-established literary critic, will constitute a broadly based and detailed literary testing of the Griesbach Hypothesis quite unparalleled for any other proposed solution to the Synoptic Problem. Even before Frye's essay, it was possible to claim that no hypothesis had undergone the rigorous testing to which the Griesbach Hypothesis had been subjected during the past decade;[4] now this statement can be made with even greater justification.

Canons of Criticism. At the first meeting of the Society of Biblical Literature's task group on "The Sequence of the Gospels" in 1968, Charles H. Talbert accepted the assignment of attempting to falsify the Griesbach Hypothesis, and George Wesley Buchanan agreed to analyze Talbert's paper and prepare a critical response. Talbert was later joined by Edgar V. McKnight. A discussion of their paper and of Buchanan's response took place at the next meeting of the task group in 1969. The Talbert-McKnight paper and Buchanan's response have subsequently been published,[5] but neither article explains that both were written at the request of a research task group of the Society of Biblical Literature as part of a systematic attempt to test the Griesbach Hypothesis.

I participated in the group that commissioned and discussed both papers, and I am satisfied with the outcome of the discussions that took place within this group. I am also satisfied with the subsequent decision to make both papers available to a wider reading public. Thus, I have felt no need to comment publicly on either paper, although privately I have expressed to Talbert the hope that some day the discussion can be taken up where it was left off with Buchanan's reasons for concluding that the Talbert-McKnight effort to falsify the Griesbach Hypothesis did not succeed.

My reason for mentioning this in a response to Frye's essay has to do with what Frye says about certain "canons of criticism"

[4] William R. Farmer, "Modern Developments of Griesbach's Hypothesis," *New Testament Studies*, 23 (1977), 279.

[5] Charles H. Talbert and Edgar V. McKnight, "Can the Griesbach Hypothesis Be Falsified?," *Journal of Biblical Literature*, 91 (1972), 338–368; George Wesley Buchanan, "Has the Griesbach Hypothesis Been Falsified?," *Journal of Biblical Literature*, 93 (1974), 550–572.

that I proposed for recognizing a secondary or derivative form of a tradition (p. 283):[6]

> Before summarizing my own appraisal of the Griesbach Hypothesis, it is necessary to consider one issue in the scholarly debate that seems to me to have been a "red herring." This concerns the "canons of criticism" that Farmer proposed for recognizing a secondary or derivative form of a tradition. Whereas Reginald H. Fuller regarded the formulation of these canons as "a notable contribution," I have always seen them as an unnecessary weakness that could divert attention from Farmer's major argument and achievement. They are a weak link, but as a link they are not really a part of the chain of his argument but rather an attachment to it.

In order to appreciate Frye's point that these "canons of criticism" can become a "red herring" that draws us off the right course, it will be helpful to examine Fuller's discussion of the matter in greater detail.[7]

Fuller summarizes Talbert's and McKnight's use of certain of the canons in such a way as to detect "instances where Mark seems prior to Matthew, where Mark seems prior to Luke, where Luke seems prior to Matthew, and where Luke and Matthew seem independent of one another," and thus, in their judgment, to "falsify" the Griesbach Hypothesis.[8] Fuller then points out certain fallacies that he finds in the Talbert-McKnight paper but concludes:

> Although they set out to refute Farmer, Talbert and McKnight have, in my opinion, highlighted the abiding significance of Farmer's work. Farmer has compelled those who accept the two-document hypothesis to demonstrate its tenability pericope by pericope. Too often, what was at the outset adopted as a working hypothesis became an assured result. Second, these two authors have demonstrated the importance of Farmer's canons of criticism and those of Burton which Farmer resurrected from oblivion. Henceforth, when we work on the synoptic tradition, all the available direction indicators must be applied afresh to every pericope. We must even be prepared to find them working in opposite

---

[6] William R. Farmer, *The Synoptic Problem: A Critical Analysis* (New York: The Macmillan Company/London: Collier-Macmillan Limited, 1964), 227–229; this book has now appeared in a very slightly revised edition (Dillsboro, N.C.: Western North Carolina Press, 1976), but, unless otherwise indicated, all references will be to the first edition.

[7] Reginald H. Fuller, "The Synoptic Problem: After Ten Years," *The Perkins School of Theology Journal*, 28 (1975), 67.

[8] Talbert and McKnight, "Can the Griesbach Hypothesis Be Falsified?," 368.

directions, without committing ourselves in advance to one synoptic theory.[9]

My observations are as follows: In the first place, I agree with Frye that it is possible to use the canons of criticism in a way that can throw us off the track in our efforts to make progress toward a more adequate and reliable consensus regarding the relationships among the gospels. As Frye points out, Talbert and McKnight were able to turn these canons against the Griesbach Hypothesis and to use them at certain points in support of Marcan priority, thus demonstrating that they "can be cited to support conflicting answers to . . . many questions" (p. 284). Then, when Fuller singles out these canons as constituting "a notable contribution"[10] and goes on to say that "those who accept the two-document hypothesis" are now "compelled" to demonstrate the tenability of this hypothesis "pericope by pericope,"[11] he has, in my view, completed the act (no doubt inadvertently) of drawing a "red herring" across our path. For one thing, such a demonstration is not likely ever to be completed; the time and energy required would be virtually prohibitive. For another, there is no consensus among scholars that demonstrating the tenability of any particular hypothesis "pericope by pericope" will ever solve the Synoptic Problem. Those who have abandoned Marcan priority or belief in the "Q" hypothesis, for example, are not impressed by this approach to the problem, for they know that it is at least equally possible to demonstrate the tenability of other solutions "pericope by pericope." Some have been led to their views because of other considerations, such as the argument from order, the weight of external evidence, or compositional and redactional factors—all considerations that call for something more than a "pericope by pericope" demonstration.

In the second place, however, I agree with Fuller in recognizing the need for "canons of criticism" and in emphasizing the importance of being able to give a detailed demonstration of the tenability of whichever solution one holds, on the basis of larger considerations, as most adequate to explain the data. I note that Frye himself argues his case in terms of certain "criteria" (i.e., those of language, comparative length, and conflation). Where does one draw the line between literary "criteria" and "canons

[9] Fuller, "The Synoptic Problem," 67.
[10] Fuller, "The Synoptic Problem," 64.
[11] Fuller, "The Synoptic Problem," 67.

of literary criticism"? I think that the way out of the difficulty recognized by Frye is not to abandon the search for and use of reliable canons of criticism. Rather, I would urge a refining and developing of these canons on the one hand and more careful use of them on the other. As examples of how these canons can be refined and developed, I mention the following: The very canon that Frye has found wanting in terms of his own work (that of specificity) has already been eliminated from the second edition of *The Synoptic Problem*,[12] an indication that there is some objective ground for deciding what is or is not a reliable "canon of criticism," and the canon concerning redactional characteristics has been developed in a position paper by William O. Walker, Jr.[13]

As an example of the need for a more careful application of these canons, we can take Fuller's observation that Talbert and McKnight had in one instance assumed Marcan priority in determining what was redactional, so that their application of a particular canon in demonstrating Marcan priority was at this point circular and thereby flawed.[14] The point that Fuller would make to Frye, I should imagine, is that there is nothing wrong with the canon; it was simply wrongly applied. At least, this is the point that I would make in agreement with Fuller's general recognition of the importance of developing and then *carefully* using "canons of criticism" as "direction indicators." The Seminar on the Synoptic Problem of *Studiorum Novi Testamenti Societas* has recognized the need for objective methods and tools to distinguish redactional from source materials in the Synoptic Gospels and, to this end, has called for the compilation of the literary characteristics of Matthew, Mark, and Luke. This work is now well underway in three Ph.D. dissertations at Southern Methodist University.[15]

In the third place, my agreement in this way with Fuller's position should not obscure my fundamental concurrence with Frye's general point, which I take to be that we must give prior

[12] Farmer, *The Synoptic Problem*, rev. ed., 228.

[13] William O. Walker, Jr., "A Method for Identifying Redactional Passages in Matthew on Functional and Linguistic Grounds," *The Catholic Biblical Quarterly*, 39 (1977), 76–93.

[14] Fuller, "The Synoptic Problem," 67.

[15] One of these dissertations has now been completed: Franklyn J. G. Collison, "Linguistic Usages in the Gospel of Luke" (Ph.D. diss., Southern Methodist University, 1977).

consideration to the gospels as literary wholes and not build false hopes on what can be accomplished by a detailed analysis of component parts of the gospels. Thus, I also agree with Frye's perception that the "canons of criticism" are an attachment to the chain of the argument for the Griesbach Hypothesis and not an indispensable link in the chain. This should be obvious in the construction of my book, where these "canons of criticism" are only listed for the benefit of the reader as a part of the discussion of one step in the argument, a step which in and by itself is not even essential to the argument as a whole, as I clearly state. When the canons are thus seen in proper perspective, i.e., within the context of the whole book, there is no need to conclude, as Frye does, that they are an "unnecessary weakness," although I readily admit that they can and should be further strengthened (for example, some seem to be too succinct as they now stand).

Having taken exception to this small point in Frye's essay, I wish to thank him for the larger point he has made and, of course, for the whole of what he has written concerning the Griesbach Hypothesis. This first part of Frye's essay is a learned piece of work, artfully put together, and delightful to read. I do not doubt that it will eventually, like Austin Farrer's classic essay, "On Dispensing With Q",[16] find its place among the works that all experts on the Synoptic Problem will need and want to read.

On Disintegrating the Gospels

Basically, what Frye seems to be saying in the second half of his essay is this: "For goodness sake, once we get the question of sequence settled (if we do), let us not turn around and make the same old mistake of trying to get back behind the texts of the gospels as we have them to earlier stages of the tradition. We do not have the controls for this task, and anyway there is a better way to proceed. Granted that the actual Jesus, or the Jesus of history, is important and that it is a desirable goal of criticism to see whether we can get back to him, we shall be far better off if we apply readily available techniques of literary study to the gospel texts as they stand (without attempting to analyze these texts for earlier stages of the tradition) and thus bring to life the character of Jesus literarily. Then we can compare the figure

[16]A. M. Farrer, "On Dispensing with Q," in *Studies in the Gospels: Essays in Memory of R. H. Lightfoot*, ed. D. E. Nineham (Oxford: Basil Blackwell, 1955), 55–88.

(or figures) of Jesus emerging from the four gospels (each with its distinctive presentations and emphases), and this comparison will better prepare us "to assess the historical figure who lies behind the four characterizations and his relevance to us" (p. 302).

This is a healthy admonition, and it should be taken seriously. Frye has not actually denied that once the question of sequence is settled, we might be better able to tell how the later Evangelists used or modified the work of their predecessors and thus establish more reliable source critical and redaction critical results than have been obtained by working on a hypothesis where the true sequence may have been reversed. He simply ignores this possibility. I think he may be justified in so doing, on the grounds that until the sequence question has been settled, we need an interim method of working with the gospels. Critics who continue to work within the critical tradition set by adherence to the Two-Document Hypothesis, as well as those who accept the Griesbach Hypothesis, can only benefit from taking seriously Frye's observations about disintegrating criticisms.

I fully concur in Frye's citation of E. P. Sanders' trenchant question, "why is synoptic research not being redone from top to bottom?" (p. 286). I agree that the need for reappraisal and redirection is pressing and even urgent, and I also agree that the conclusions provided by the popular methodologies now being employed do little to carry us beyond subjective satisfaction. This seems to me to be particularly true in the case of Marcan studies, but it is also true to a large extent of Lucan and Matthean studies as well.

I find it singularly instructive to learn that in the nineteenth century and the first decades of the twentieth it was fashionable among some critics to identify and correct or reject those passages in the Shakespeare corpus that they did not wish to accept as authentically Shakespearean. This is precisely what the Two-Document Hypothesis facilitated in gospel studies. If behind the canonical gospels there was a common *Grundschrift*, as Heinrich Julius Holtzmann held, made up largely of two foundational apostolic sources, *Ur-Markus* and a collection of the sayings of Jesus, then every liberal theologian had the perfect exegetical paradigm he needed. He could pick and choose gospel texts at will, so long as he was careful not to base any doctrinal point on a text for which there was only one witness (i.e., only Matthew or only Luke). In the short run this enabled liberal theology to develop

313

viable alternatives to Protestant Orthodoxy. But the effect of this procedure was devastating for theology in the long run, because some of the most important texts, especially those grounding the gospel in the historical preaching of Jesus, are found only in Matthew or only in Luke. The parable of the Prodigal Son is the most famous case in point. Holtzmann and his generation held that such parables of Jesus had originally been included in the sayings source copied by both Matthew and Luke, but by the end of the century, those who wanted to be scientifically rigorous in their methodology regarded it as historically unsound to base anything important on such texts (especially the Lucan parables), because the texts were not in Mark and could not be attested from Matthew as belonging to "Q," and because, on the basis of their kinship to Pauline theology, they could be explained away as "Lucan" constructions.

In the Anglo-Saxon world it was Burnett Hillman Streeter's Four-Document Hypothesis that best met the exegetical impasse thus created by the Two-Document Hypothesis. It did this by positing two additional sources, "M," and "L," used respectively by Matthew and Luke, and assuming that these sources, like Mark and "Q," also contained "a large part of the most obviously genuine, original, and characteristic teaching" of Jesus.[17] As a result, much of the material unique to Matthew or Luke could be rescued for Christian theology.

On the continent it was form criticism, with its aim of reconstructing the pre-literary history of separate pericopes without reference to their inclusion or non-inclusion in either Mark or "Q," that could have offered a way out of the *Sackgasse* but for the rise of Dialectical Theology under the banner of Karl Barth's *Römerbrief*[18] and the subsequent decline of interest in matters of critical history.

Not until the mid-twentieth century, with Joachim Jeremias building on the parable research of C. H. Dodd,[19] and Friedrich Gogarten presupposing the form critical results of Rudolf Bult-

---

[17] Burnett Hillman Streeter, *The Four Gospels: A Study of Origins Treating of the Manuscript Tradition, Sources, Authorship, & Dates*, rev. ed. (London: Macmillan and Co., Limited, 1936), 228; cf. also 223–270.

[18] Karl Barth, *Der Römerbrief* (Zollikon and Zürich: Evangelischer Verlag, 1918); English translation of 6th ed. (1928): *The Epistle to the Romans*, trans. Edwyn C. Hoskyns, rev. ed. (London and New York: Oxford University Press, 1953).

[19] Joachim Jeremias, *Die Gleichnisse Jesu* (Zürich: Zwingli Verlag, 1947); English translation of 6th ed. (1962): *The Parables of Jesus*, trans. S. H. Hooke,

mann,[20] was the way opened anew to find an adequate basis for Christian theology in the earliest stratum of the Synoptic tradition or in the life and preaching of Jesus, and since that time the Two-Document Hypothesis has only hung as an albatross around the neck of the exegete. At the same time, except for the ambiguous renaissance in parable research, the scientific gulf between the theologians on the one hand and the gospel critics on the other only continues to widen, until it has become difficult to see any convincing link between the two. Nevertheless, theologians continue to swear by Mark and "Q" as by the gospel itself, and no wonder, for in nineteenth-century liberal German Protestantism it was by the use of this "scientific" paradigm that the gospel was freed from such embarrassing "encumbrances" as the virgin birth and the physical resurrection of Jesus.

Thus, I am basically positive about most of what I understand to be Frye's primary concern in the second half of his essay. He is not content, however, merely to challenge the results to date of conventional gospel criticism with its dependence upon the Two-Document Hypothesis; his is a more radical critique that covers the full range of research procedures in contemporary gospel studies:

---

rev. ed. (New York: Charles Scribner's Sons, 1963); cf. C. H. Dodd, *The Parables of the Kingdom* (London: Nisbet & Co. Ltd., 1935), rev. ed. (New York: Charles Scribner's Sons, 1961).

[20]See, e.g., Friedrich Gogarten, *Die Verkündigung Jesu Christi. Grundlagen und Aufgabe* (Heidelberg: Verlag Lambert Schneider, 1948); 2d ed., Hermeneutische Untersuchungen zur Theologie 3 (Tübingen: J. C. B. Mohr [Paul Siebeck], 1965); "Theologie und Geschichte," *Zeitschrift für Theologie und Kirche*, 50 (1953), 339–394; English translation: "Theology and History," trans. Louis De Grazia, in *History and Hermeneutic*, ed. Robert W. Funk, Journal for Theology and the Church 4 (Tübingen: J. C. B. Mohr [Paul Siebeck] and New York: Harper & Row, Publishers, Inc., 1967), 35–81; *Jesus Christus, Wende der Welt. Grundfragen zur Christologie* (Tübingen: J. C. B. Mohr [Paul Siebeck], 1966); English translation: *Christ the Crisis*, trans. R. A. Wilson (Richmond, Va.: John Knox Press, 1970); cf. Rudolf Bultmann, *Die Geschichte der synoptischen Tradition*, Forschungen zur Religion und Literatur des Alten und Neuen Testaments, n. F. 12 (Göttingen: Vandenhoeck & Ruprecht, 1921); English translation of 2d ed (1931) with corrections and additions from 1962 supplement: *The History of the Synoptic Tradition*, trans. John Marsh, rev. ed. (New York and Evanston: Harper & Row, Publishers, Inc., 1968); *Jesus*, Die Unsterblichen. Die geistigen Heroen der Menschheit in ihrem Leben und Wirken 1 (Berlin: Deutsche Bibliothek, 1926); English translation: *Jesus and the Word*, trans. Louise Pettibone Smith and Erminie Huntress Lantero, new ed. (New York: Charles Scribner's Sons, 1958).

I must observe that few if any of the leading literary historians in secular fields would be comfortable with the widespread assumption among New Testament critics that it is possible, in the present state of the evidence, to move backwards in time from passages in the extant gospel texts in such a way as to identify previous stages or forms through which the tradition has supposedly developed and, ultimately, to arrive at or near the original life and teachings of Jesus; or that it is possible, through a similar procedure, to explain the Synoptic redactions as we now have them. (p. 287)

Lest Frye's strictures against conventional gospel criticism lead beyond skepticism regarding many of the results achieved on the basis of the Two-Document Hypothesis, a skepticism that I take to be fully deserved, to skepticism regarding contemporary gospel criticism as a whole, which I take not to be fully deserved, I shall comment first on his overall critique of form and redaction criticism and then on certain specific details in his discussion of parables and aphorisms.

Form and Redaction Criticism. Two points should be made about Frye's overall approach, and these go a long way, in my opinion, toward robbing his conclusions in this second part of his essay of much of their probative value: (1) At points Frye appears to write about the aim of the Shakespearean scholar who wishes to recover the real Shakespeare as though this aim were analogous to that of the gospel critic who wishes to recover the real Jesus. Actually, recovering the real Shakespeare is more like finding the real Evangelist or the original text of the work of the Evangelist, like deciding whether the original text of Mark, for example, did or did not contain the last twelve verses found at the end of most extant manuscripts. (2) Frye does not seem to take into sufficient account the fact that the attempt to recover the real Shakespeare presupposes a textual development within a more or less constant or continuous cultural environment, i.e., British if not English, whereas the attempt to recover the real Jesus presupposes major cultural, geographical, and religious changes that offer the gospel critic more control than is available to the Shakespeare scholar. This second point requires further explication.

The environment of Jesus was that of pre-Pauline Jewish Palestine. Presumably, his words and actions, however distinctive or even unique, would have been intelligible within the context of this environment, and traditions regarding these words and actions that achieved a stable form at a very early date would

316

tend to reflect the same environment. On the other hand, the environment of the Evangelists is generally regarded as having been post-Pauline, extra-Palestinian, and primarily Gentile. Therefore, the work of the Evangelists would presumably reflect this latter environment. It is clear from other New Testament literature, such as the letters of Paul and Acts of the Apostles, that the Christian movement spread beyond its original Palestinian-Jewish matrix within a very few years.

Fortunately, the historian is not limited to the New Testament in attempting to reconstruct the environment of Jesus. Jewish writings from the same general period (including the Dead Sea Scrolls, some of the intertestamental literature, certain of the rabbinic materials, and the historical works of Josephus), together with modern archaeological and topographical study of Palestine, not only illuminate the background of the New Testament documents but also provide a basis for understanding the contrast between the environment of Jesus and that of the Evangelists by affording access to first-century Palestinian Judaism unaffected by Christian belief.

When a tradition about Jesus "comes alive" in the context of his environment as thus reconstructed, this may be an indication that the tradition is early. If the tradition would be unintelligible in a non-Palestinian context or unfamiliar among Gentiles, this is an even stronger indication that the tradition may be early. On the other hand, materials that seem to presuppose Jesus' death and resurrection and reflect a situation in which he is worshipped as a transcendent being can be seen as traditions that likely originated in a post-Easter Christian environment.

Once a tradition has thus been identified as early, it is then possible with some confidence, on the basis of such traditions, to speak in specific terms about Jesus himself. How this is to be done is best understood from a consideration of the parables, for within the body of traditions that originated with the historical Jesus it is the parables that afford the best key for understanding both his career and his character.[21] The argument for this view can only be summarized here as follows: Once it becomes

---

[21] The material in the previous three and one-half paragraphs is presented in basically the same form in my two articles: William R. Farmer, "Jesus and the Gospels: A Form-critical and Theological Essay," *The Perkins School of Theology Journal*, 28 (1975), 3–4; "Teaching of Jesus," in *The Interpreter's Dictionary of the Bible: An Illustrated Encyclopedia*, supplementary vol., ed. Keith Crim et al. (Nashville: Abingdon Press, 1976), 863.

clear that the parables are not to be interpreted allegorically (Adolf Jülicher), that in his parables Jesus proclaims that the eschatological Kingdom of God has already broken into reality (Dodd), and that form criticism enables the critic both to identify the parables of Jesus as belonging to the genre of rabbinic parables, while as a whole presenting theologically distinctive content (Jeremias), and to distinguish the original form of Jesus' parables from the additions that were made in the early church (Jeremias), it is then possible to recapture the most adequate possible image of Jesus' career and character.[22]

Parables and Aphorisms. Frye begins his treatment of parables and aphorisms by taking up Jeremias' claim that certain "generalizing logia" or aphorisms have been added to parables attributed to Jesus in the gospels. Noting that such a claim rests on two apparent rationales, Frye gives his reasons for denying the validity of each. The first rationale is that of mere repetition, and here I think we should grant Frye's point that more than one occurrence of the same aphorism is not an adequate basis for

[22] I have addressed myself in some detail to various methodological questions in the following works: William R. Farmer, "On the New Interest in Jesus," *The Perkins School of Theology Journal*, 14 (1960), 5–10; "Notes on a Literary and Form-Critical Analysis of Some of the Synoptic Material Peculiar to Luke," *New Testament Studies*, 8 (1962), 301–316; "The Provenance of Matthew," in *The Teacher's Yoke: Studies in Memory of Henry Trantham*, ed. E. Jerry Vardaman and James Leo Garrett; assoc. ed. J. B. Adair (Waco, Tex.: Baylor University Press, 1964), 109–116; "The Two-Document Hypothesis as a Methodological Criterion in Synoptic Research," *Anglican Theological Review*, 48 (1966), 380–396; "The Problem of Christian Origins: A Programmatic Essay," in *Studies in the History and Text of the New Testament in Honor of Kenneth Willis Clark*, ed. Boyd L. Daniels and M. Jack Suggs, Studies and Documents 29 (Salt Lake City: University of Utah Press, 1967), 81–88; "An Historical Essay on the Humanity of Jesus Christ," in *Christian History and Interpretation: Studies Presented to John Knox*, ed. W. R. Farmer, C. F. D. Moule, and R. R. Niebuhr (Cambridge: Cambridge University Press, 1967), 101–126; "The Dynamic of Christianity: The Question of Development Between Jesus and Paul," *Religion in Life*, 38 (1969), 570–577; "Redaction Criticism and the Synoptic Problem," in *The Society of Biblical Literature One Hundred Seventh Annual Meeting Seminar Papers*, 2 vols. (The Society of Biblical Literature, 1971), 1:239–250; "A Fresh Approach to Q," in *Christianity, Judaism and Other Greco-Roman Cults: Studies for Morton Smith at Sixty*, ed. Jacob Neusner, 4 parts, Studies in Judaism in Late Antiquity 12 (Leiden: E. J. Brill, 1975), 1:39–50; "Jesus and the Gospels: A Form-critical and Theological Essay," *The Perkins School of Theology Journal*, 28 (1975), 1–62; "The Post-Sectarian Character of Matthew and Its Post-War Setting in Antioch of Syria," *Perspectives in Religious Studies*, 3 (1976), 235–247; and "Teaching of Jesus," in *The Interpreter's Dictionary of the Bible*, supplementary vol., 863–868.

concluding that it is a later addition. The second rationale is another matter, however. It has to do with the parable as a form. Frye specifically discusses the case of the parable of the Pharisee and the tax collector in the Temple (Luke 18:10–14) and asks whether the independence of this parable as a literary form precludes the possibility or likelihood that the generalizing or moralizing words, "He who exalts himself will be humbled and he who humbles himself will be exalted," were original rather than secondary. Recognizing that Jesus could have told essentially the same parable on different occasions under varying circumstances, why must we assume that the concluding aphorism could not have been included in at least one version of the parable as Jesus originally told it or possibly added by Jesus himself as a comment at the end of the parable?

In response, I would say two things: (1) As a good teacher, Jesus certainly would have felt free to vary his use of the parable form. (2) He would not have been likely, however, to blunt the point of his parable. We know from a study of the nearest literary parallels, i.e., rabbinic parables, that Jewish teachers used parables to clarify, much as public speakers use illustrations. No good speaker tells a story in order to illustrate a point in his speech, only to add an aphorism that confuses or blunts the point he is trying to make. As Jeremias shows to my satisfaction, the introduction of this parable properly indicates the life situation that is addressed by Jesus in the parable: there are people who put their trust in their own righteousness.[23] The story Jesus tells makes it clear that such persons exist in a wrong relationship to God, while surprisingly enough, the unrighteous person who confesses his sin and casts himself sincerely upon the mercy of God goes to his home in a right relationship to God. To be sure, this parable can also be seen as affording another example of an instance where a person who exalts himself is humbled, but such an interpretation of it is platitudinous by comparison with the earth-shattering point Jesus has just made. How the aphorism came to be joined to the parable, whether by the Evangelist who had his own reasons or as a later marginal gloss serving as a cross reference to Luke 14:11 where it may be original, can involve one in subjective judgment. It is not subjective, however, to say that the aphorism is a separable saying, as is the parable that precedes it. Thus, the question as to whether Jesus joined

[23]Jeremias, *The Parables of Jesus*, 139–144.

the two sayings or they were joined by someone else reduces itself to a question of how Jesus used his parables and what it is reasonable to think an intelligent and effective teacher or speaker would have done. In this instance, I regard the recognition of the secondary character of the aphorism in the development of the Synoptic tradition from Jesus to the text of the Gospel of Luke as a sound critical judgment resting on objective criteria that can be tested (assuming, of course, that there is not all that great a difference between Jesus and other Jewish rabbis or contemporary public speakers).

Of course, to conclude that an aphorism has been added secondarily to a parable does not settle the question about the authenticity of the aphorism as a saying of Jesus. Certainly, there are many originally separate authentic sayings of Jesus in the Sermon on the Mount, for example, that have been joined together at some stage in their compilation. Thus, if Frye's concern about this matter of declaring certain words as secondary is rooted in a deeper concern about whether such words are thereby automatically to be considered inauthentic, we must grant that he has a point and hereafter be careful to observe the distinction I have just noted.

Frye's point regarding the parable of the great supper in Luke 14:16–24 and the parable of the wedding feast in Matthew 22:1–10 (as will be noted below, 22:11–14 is another parable that has been joined to 22:1–10) is also well taken: Jesus may have cast the same story into two shapes, or these two parables may represent different ways in which an original parable was developed in separate Christian communities prior to the time the gospels were written. Exception should be taken, however, to Frye's statement that there is no literary-historical method that can perform the separation of what Jesus actually said from redactional additions ascribed to him (p. 299). In particular instances this may be the case, as for example with Matthew 22:7. I agree that this does not necessarily refer to the destruction of Jerusalem in A.D. 70 and it could be original to Jesus. Nevertheless, in certain other instances form critical considerations are decisive. Thus, we can be reasonably certain that Matthew 22:11–14 was originally a separate parable and has been attached to 22:1–10 only secondarily: first, because rabbinic parallels to 22:11–14 as a complete and independent parable exist and second, because the parallel to 22:1–10 in Luke 14:16–24 serves as a "control" to suggest that Matthew's parable of the wedding feast originally ended with 22:10. Of course, it is still possible that Jesus at some point in his preaching utilized the rabbinic parable preserved in Matthew 22:11–14, for he need not have created all his materials *de novo*. No great teacher does this.

More than three hundred rabbinic parables have been collected over the years at Southern Methodist University. It seems likely to me that Jeremias had access to a similar collection. We know that the first draft of his famous work on the parables of Jesus was done in Germany in a relatively short period of time during the last phase of World War II, and it is possible that, under the pressures of the situation, he did not sufficiently emphasize the great importance of the methodological control that is afforded the form critic by the vast corpus of rabbinic parables now available. By studying Jesus' parables in relation to this corpus we know what parables looked like in the first century, and we can see objective grounds for saying that Matthew 22:1–14, for example, represents two parables joined together. Both parables relate to the theme of repentance, and this helps to explain the grounds for their being joined by some editor. They are separable parables, however, and they make separable if related points.

When Frye concludes that "efforts to move backwards from the written records of the gospels . . . so as to arrive at earlier phases of the traditions about Jesus . . . are not recognizable as literary history to one who represents this field in secular scholarship" (p. 301), I can only ask whether he has not circumscribed secular scholarship unnecessarily. It should include the study of rabbinic parables.

Conclusion. Let this be said for Frye: Redaction criticism, especially when applied to the final form of the gospels as literary wholes, cannot at the present time be pursued with assurance. There is one simple reason for this: We do not possess reliable and comprehensive lists of the special vocabularies and literary usages of the final redactors. The best we have is Henry J. Cadbury's *The Style and Literary Method of Luke*,[24] and it needs improving. There is nothing comparable for either Matthew or Mark. It says something about the guild of New Testament scholars that we could allow this scandalous state of affairs to exist.

[24] Henry J. Cadbury, *The Style and Literary Method of Luke*, Harvard Theological Studies 6 (Cambridge, Mass.: Harvard University Press/London: H. Milford, Oxford University Press, 1920). Collison's dissertation, "Linguistic Usages in the Gospel of Luke," was not generally available when my response was written.

And we do ourselves a disservice if we take umbrage at the challenge of a literary critic like Frye, who sees reasons to doubt the objectivity of much of our work.

As for Frye's positive proposal that the gospels be analyzed with the standard techniques used in reading other literature, I can only wonder why we have not done this before. It seems such an eminently intelligent thing to do. Frye has helped us to get started. Let us hope that he will continue to help. We need all the assistance our colleagues in related disciplines are willing and able to give us.

Literary Criticism and the Gospels: The Seminar

Joseph B. Tyson

In the other seminars of the Colloquy on the Relationships among the Gospels—seminars dealing with oral traditional literature, classics, and Judaic studies—participants were repeatedly reminded that the relationships among the gospels are most likely not simply literary but, at least partly, also oral. On the other hand, whatever else it may be, literary criticism includes the process of making judgments about written materials. Thus, the Seminar on Literary Criticism, by definition, was under obligation to take seriously certain phenomena, such as verbal agreements and sequential similarities among the gospels, phenomena that indicate to most modern critics the near certainty of some type of literary relationship, at least among the three Synoptic Gospels.

Members of the seminar, and indeed participants in the Colloquy as a whole, were anxious to ask Roland Mushat Frye to offer sage advice regarding the practice of the art of literary criticism and in particular to select materials from his field, the analysis of which might serve to shed some light on the literary relationships among the Christian gospels. As expected, Frye fulfilled the assignment with competence and grace and, in fact, did a good deal more.

Frye's essay is divided into two major sections, and it seems best to follow the same kind of division in this report and commentary on the discussion of his essay and of William R. Farmer's response. To the two sections dealing with the major parts of Frye's essay, a short third section is added, containing some suggestions regarding a future agenda for studies of the relationships among the gospels.

On Sequence and Dependence: The Griesbach Hypothesis

In the first part of his essay, Frye devotes attention to certain literary processes and examines the way these processes have worked among documents whose literary relationships are known. The three processes are dealt with under the headings, language, comparative length, and conflation.

With respect to language, Frye suggests that creolization may take place late in the game rather than early, but he would also suggest submitting the limited evidence that he has been able to observe to the broader judgment of historical linguists. He does show that, in general, colonized people who wish to attract the attention of the dominant culture will initially take pains to write in the language of this culture. Only much later do such persons introduce idiomatic expressions from their own language. In applying this to the question of gospel relationships, Frye asks: "When a conquered or colonized people begin to *write* in the language of colonization, do they *typically* show care to observe the standard forms of this language, as Matthew and Luke do with Greek, or do they *typically* introduce into their writings the type of creolized forms that have been noted in Mark?" (p. 266). His answer is that Mark's Aramaicized Greek does not represent "the most typical early form in which a colonized or conquered people would *write* the language of colonization" (p. 271).

With respect to comparative length, Frye observes that when a single text is being revised, particularly by the same author, there is a tendency toward increased length. This observation does not apply to the gospels, however, because they do not represent successive revisions of a single text by the same author. "When the Griesbach progression places the two longer Synoptics first and sees Mark as a kind of independent abridgment of the fuller and earlier treatments, this accords with a progression that we can identify elsewhere" (p. 273). According to Frye, Mark can be perceived as an abridgment of longer gospels, and

324

in this respect it is similar to the epitomies of Aristotle, Strabo, and others and to the compends of John Calvin.

In examining the process of conflation, Frye cites examples from Old English literature and from Shakespeare. In general, the procedure he finds is one that swings back and forth from one source to another. The conflator will omit some things, abbreviate others, and enlarge selected sections, but his overall product will be shorter than the combined length of his sources. Frye also notes examples in which the product of the conflator is more vivid than any of his sources. Shakespeare's use of three biographies by Plutarch in his dramatic history of *Julius Caesar* receives special attention. In writing the play, Shakespeare shifted back and forth among the biographies and produced a work that is shorter than the three sources combined but longer in the passages he selected to use. Frye notes that the length of *Julius Caesar*, relative to the sources, is very close to the length of Mark relative to Matthew and Luke together. The conclusion is stated as follows: "In terms of conflation, the procedure postulated for Mark in the Griesbach Hypothesis conforms closely to what can be seen wherever I have found a literary work in which conflation is demonstrable beyond a shadow of doubt" (p. 285).

Admitting that there is not sufficient evidence to prove either Matthean or Marcan priority, Frye is appropriately modest in stating his conclusion and is quite willing to regard the Griesbach Hypothesis as *non liquet*. Nevertheless, he believes that this hypothesis presents a more credible explanation of the relationships among the Synoptic Gospels than do any of the other linear or "diachronic" hypotheses. But discussion in the seminar suggested that the force of Frye's argument is not what he claims for it.

Frye maintains that the Griesbach Hypothesis is in agreement with phenomena of language, comparative length, and conflation that he has observed elsewhere in the history of literature; but otherwise he does not expose us to the grounds on which he judges this hypothesis to be preferable, except in his reference to "Ockham's razor." A basic corollary of Ockham's law of parsimony is that one does not continue to engage in the formulation of hypotheses after the problem has been solved, but as Frye apparently understands it, the principle involves an inevitable preference for the simpler solution. At least in the case of the Synoptic Problem, there are substantial reasons for suspecting this preference for simplicity. As we were frequently reminded in the course of the Colloquy, the simpler explanation is not inherently better than the more complex in literary and historical matters. Frye himself stressed the extraordinary complexity of any attempt to search for literary sources, and various participants in the Colloquy pointed out that the situation with respect to the gospels is complicated by such factors as textual problems, the use of the gospels by believing communities, and the continued influence of oral tradition.

E. P. Sanders is one whose research has led him to wonder whether the simpler solution is the better one:

I rather suspect that when and if a new view of the Synoptic problem becomes accepted, it will be more flexible and complicated than the tidy two-document hypothesis. With all due respect for scientific preference for the simpler view, the evidence seems to require a more complicated one.[1]

Farmer raised an objection to Sanders' viewpoint, claiming that however complex the correct hypothesis may be, it is no more complex than necessary. But since we have no way at present of knowing when we have arrived at the correct view, we cannot know how complex it is. In a sense Farmer has rightly perceived the meaning of Ockham's razor, but at the same time, he has inadvertently pointed to its inappropriateness to the study of gospel relationships.

Nevertheless, as Frye understands it, the principle is as follows: If we have two or more hypotheses, all of which adequately account for the phenomena and none of which has a disadvantage in respect to unresolved problems, then we should choose the least complicated hypothesis. On this principle, it is necessary for Frye to show that the Griesbach Hypothesis is fully as adequate as any other linear hypothesis and also that it is the simplest. Although he does not approach the matter in quite this

[1] E. P. Sanders, *The Tendencies of the Synoptic Tradition*, Society for New Testament Studies Monograph Series 9 (Cambridge: Cambridge University Press, 1969), 279. During the seminar discussion, Sanders pointed out that his reference to a "more flexible and complicated" view had in mind not so much the possible existence of hypothetical sources as the probability of "cross-fertilization" among the gospels after their original composition and the continuing influence of oral tradition.

Subsequent references to the seminar discussion will not be documented. In the preparation of this paper I used audio tapes of the discussion, and these tapes will be retained by the editor of this volume.

way, it is nevertheless important for us to apply these tests to his argument.

On the matter of simplicity, Frye is convinced that the Griesbach Hypothesis is the least complicated, but he offers no comparative analysis of the various hypotheses in order to demonstrate this belief. One may suspect that, in this respect, he agrees with Farmer, who stated his preference for simplicity as follows:

. . . a critic should not posit the existence of hypothetical documents until he has made an attempt to solve the problem without appeal to hypothetical documents. Only after the investigator has been unable to understand the relationship between Matthew, Mark, and Luke without appealing to unknown sources is he justified in hypothecating the existence of such sources, in order to explain phenomena otherwise inexplicable.[2]

Surely, both Farmer and Frye are referring to "Q," an essential hypothetical source for the Two-Document Hypothesis which is not operational in the Griesbach view.

On the matter of adequacy, Frye is convinced that the Griesbach Hypothesis is as adequate as the Two-Document Hypothesis: "If we operate within an assumption of sequential source relationships, Matthean priority and the Griesbach Hypothesis cover the data we have in the three Synoptics at least as adequately as does Marcan priority, but with greater simplicity and elegance" (pp. 285–86). Support for this conclusion is apparently to be found in the discussions of the various criteria: language, comparative length, and conflation. When we examine these discussions carefully, however, we find that they do not provide grounds for Frye's conclusion. As he himself acknowledges in effect, his contributions at these points are presented not as positive arguments for the Griesbach Hypothesis but rather as counterarguments to the hypothesis of Marcan priority and as answers to those who reject the Griesbach Hypothesis (p. 263).

Frye's discussion of the criterion of language proceeds from the assumption that Mark contains more Aramaisms than do Matthew or Luke. It then questions the argument that Arama-

---

[2] William R. Farmer, *The Synoptic Problem: A Critical Analysis* (New York: The Macmillan Company/London: Collier-Macmillan Limited, 1964), 209; this book has now appeared in a very slightly revised edition (Dillsboro, N.C.: Western North Carolina Press, Inc., 1976), but, unless otherwise indicated, all references will be to the first edition.

isms are signs of early date by maintaining to the contrary that, in some historical situations, creolization is characteristically a sign of late date. Reuben J. Swanson questioned the relevance of Frye's analysis of creolization, however, suggesting that the time frame within which the Gospels were written was far too short to allow for the kind of process that Frye described. Swanson also observed that the earliest extant Christian writings, the letters of Paul, do in fact contain Aramaic words: *Maranatha* (1 Corinthians 16:22), *Abba* (Romans 8:15; Galatians 4:6), and *Cephas* as the name of Peter (1 Corinthians 1:12; 3:22; 9:5; 15:5; Galatians 1:18; 2:9, 11, 14).

In addition, it is probable that Frye has not correctly perceived the nature of the argument about Aramaisms in Mark. Burnett Hillman Streeter's discussion of this matter, for example, is confined to a half paragraph, which forms the last point in his fourth argument for Marcan priority, namely, the argument that the use of more primitive language is evidence of priority. Streeter says:

> ... there are eight instances in which Mark preserves the original Aramaic words used by our Lord. Of these Luke has none, while Matthew retains only one, the name Golgotha (xxvii. 33); though he substitutes for the Marcan wording of the cry from the cross, 'Eloi, Eloi . . .' the Hebrew equivalent 'Eli, Eli . . .' as it reads in the Psalm (Mk. xv. 34 = Mt. xxvii. 46 = Ps. xxii. 1).[3]

Streeter is drawing on the work of Sir John C. Hawkins, who lists seven [sic] instances of Aramaic or Hebrew words or phrases in Mark: *Boanerges* (3:17), *Talitha cumi* (5:41), *Corban* (7:11), *Ephphatha* (7:34), *Abba* (14:36), *Golgotha* (15:22), and *Eloi, Eloi, lama sabachthani* (15:34).[4] What Streeter and others are arguing is not that Mark represented an Aramaic-speaking minority in a society dominated by Greek language and culture, but that the presence of Aramaisms in Mark is a sign of contact with an oral tradition that originally circulated in the Aramaic language and indeed went back to Jesus himself. Thus, it is doubtful that the examples of creolization cited by Frye are really analogous to the alleged Aramaic characteristics of Mark.

An even more serious problem in Frye's discussion of the

[3] Burnett Hillman Streeter, *The Four Gospels: A Study of Origins Treating of the Manuscript Tradition, Sources, Authorship, & Dates*, rev. ed. (London: Macmillan and Co., Limited, 1936), 164.

[4] John C. Hawkins, *Horae Synopticae: Contributions to the Study of the Synoptic Problem*, 2d ed. (Oxford: The Clarendon Press, 1909), 130.

criterion of language, however, is that the Aramaic character of Mark has itself been frequently challenged, and many scholars have called attention to the Semitic character of Matthew. Wayne A. Meeks, for example, says that "Matthew's language abounds with Semitisms, perhaps more than any other New Testament document" (p. 166), and Farmer points to such Aramaic terms in Matthew as *hraka* (5:22) and *korbanas* (27:6).[5] Farmer also minimizes the significance of Aramaic in Mark as a sign of its Semitic character by pointing out: (1) that Mark always translates the Aramaic words while Matthew does not; (2) that foreign words were sometimes used in Hellenistic healing stories; and (3) that Aramaic was used as a literary device in Christian literature as late as the *Acts of Pilate*.[6] During the course of the discussion, Frye acknowledged that he had simply assumed that Mark contained more Aramaisms than the others, and he recognized that if this is not the case, his argument from the criterion of language clearly loses its validity.

What then has Frye's discussion of language done? It has challenged the view that Aramaisms in Mark are necessarily a sign of early date. It has also shown the need for consultation between New Testament scholars and linguistic historians. What has it not done? It has not shown that Aramaisms in Mark are necessarily a sign of late date. For this latter point to be established in accordance with Frye's own analogies, the following conditions would be requisite: (1) Mark must use more Aramaic phrases than Matthew or Luke; (2) Mark must be using Greek as a second language; (3) Mark must represent a people subdued by Greek culture; and (4) Mark must represent a stage of the Christian tradition later than the earliest gospels by at least a century. None of these conditions seems likely. Although Frye acknowledged that he may have misjudged the first, he did not address himself to the other three. Thus, Farmer's judgment on the value of Frye's argument regarding language hits the point: the value "is mainly rhetorical" (p. 305).

Frye's discussion of the criterion of comparative length can be dealt with more briefly, because there is no disagreement regard-

---

[5] Farmer, *The Synoptic Problem*, 173. For a thorough study of Semitic features in the Synoptic Gospels, see Sanders, *The Tendencies of the Synoptic Tradition*, 232–255. Sanders finds that Mark has more constructions that are usually regarded as Semitic than do Matthew or Luke, but he shows that this is not necessarily a sign of an earlier date.

[6] Farmer, *The Synoptic Problem*, 172–173.

ing the facts involved. His discussion is intended to answer the claim that the longer documents (Matthew and Luke) are later than the shorter (Mark). Frye claims that such is the case only when we are dealing with a single author or with revisions of a single text and that this criterion of length thus does not apply in the case of the Synoptic Gospels. Although some may feel that we have in these gospels something like revisions of a single text, this point was not pressed in the discussion. Clearly, Frye's purpose in discussing the criterion of length was to nullify an argument for Marcan priority.

In the discussion of conflation, the shoe is on the other foot. Here, Frye has selected the best examples of conflation he could find and has shown that in these examples there is a clear tendency to conflate in precisely the way Griesbach imagines for Mark. It is worthy of note that Thomas R. W. Longstaff has applied the same kind of test to other documents in which conflation is known to have occurred and that he has independently come to the same conclusion as did Frye.[7] This is not to say that counter examples cannot be found, but until and unless they are, Frye's and Longstaff's treatments of conflation must stand. Still, we must be clear that what Frye's argument has done is to show that where conflation occurs, it occurs in a certain way. Frye has not shown that Mark's Gospel is in fact a conflation of Matthew and Luke.

In conclusion, it appears that the logical force of Frye's arguments in the first part of his essay does not fully support his tentatively expressed contention that the Griesbach Hypothesis explains the data in the Synoptic Gospels at least as adequately as does the theory of Marcan priority. This sentiment was expressed by Lonnie D. Kliever, who pointed out that Frye had undermined the self-evidence of the criteria of language and comparative length as supports for Marcan priority by challenging the notions that creolization is necessarily early and that derivative documents are necessarily longer. In other words, these criteria do not simply and automatically support Marcan priority, and Frye has in effect issued a challenge to Marcan priorists to show that their position can be strengthened by the use of the criteria. This does not mean, however, that Matthean priority now becomes more likely. On the matter of conflation, Frye has

[7] Thomas R. W. Longstaff, *Evidence of Conflation in Mark? A Study in the Synoptic Problem*, Society of Biblical Literature Dissertation Series 28 (Missoula, Mont.: Scholars Press for The Society of Biblical Literature, 1977).

succeeded in showing that the Griesbach theory is possible. If we have grounds for believing that Mark conflated Matthew and Luke, we need not reject this possibility because his procedure appears strange. When writers conflate, they do it approximately as the Griesbach Hypothesis says Mark did it. Nevertheless, Kliever's judgment rings true: Frye has undermined the self-evidence of certain arguments for Marcan priority and has shown that, in respect to Marcan conflation, the Griesbach Hypothesis is not impossible. This is not the same, however, as showing that the Griesbach theory explains the data as adequately as the theory of Marcan priority.

On Disintegrating the Gospels

The second part of Frye's essay, originally entitled, "Beyond the Griesbach Hypothesis," received a good deal of attention at the Colloquy.[8] In this section, Frye began by questioning the methods of source, form, and redaction criticism:

At this point, coming from outside the "system," as a representative of literary history in the secular fields, I must observe that few if any of the leading literary historians in secular fields would be comfortable with the widespread assumption among New Testament critics that it is possible, in the present state of the evidence, to move backwards in time from passages in the extant gospel texts in such a way as to identify previous stages or forms through which the tradition has supposedly developed and, ultimately, to arrive at or near the original life and teachings of Jesus; or that it is possible, through a similar procedure, to explain the Synoptic redactions as we now have them. (p. 287)

Frye then compares the methods in question with a particular approach to Shakespearean studies known as "disintegration," which was widely practiced in the nineteenth and early twentieth centuries. This method attempted to separate Shakespearean from non-Shakespearean materials in the plays. The efforts of the disintegrators are now thoroughly discredited, and it is "universally recognized that their detailed and impressive analyses

---

[8] The first version of Frye's paper, prepared and distributed prior to the Colloquy on the Relationships among the Gospels and discussed during the Colloquy, was entitled, "The Synoptic Problem: A Literary Historical Approach." The two major parts of the paper were "Concerning the Griesbach Hypothesis" and "Beyond the Griesbach Hypothesis." After the Colloquy, Frye's paper, like the others, was revised for publication, and in this revision he changed the titles of the entire essay and of both parts.

moved from equivocal uses of evidence to subjective conclusions" (p. 288). Quoting and agreeing with Paul Gottschalk, Frye says that the result of the disintegrating approach to Shakespeare was "the almost total divorce of character from plot, of Hamlet from *Hamlet*, and indeed, of Hamlet at one moment from Hamlet at another" (p. 289).[9]

Next, Frye questions the tendency of New Testament critics to separate parable from aphorism and to treat the aphorism as a secondary interpretation of the parable rather than as a word of Jesus. He refers to a saying that appears in Luke 14:11 and 18:14b, as the conclusion to two quite different parables, and in Matthew 23:12, as an independent saying. Supposing that one rationale for the exclusion of an aphorism is that some are found more than once and in different contexts, Frye questions the judgment that such aphorisms are not authentic to Jesus on two grounds: (1) it is not unlikely that Jesus repeated himself; and (2) sayings might be used in the gospels to signal thematic developments. Another possible reason for excluding an aphorism depends on the understanding of the parabolic form, which includes no moralizing comments or conclusions. Frye observes, however, that every form is subject to alteration and development, and he cites the example of the sonnet form to show that "a literary form is highly flexible" (p. 293). He is willing to entertain the possibility that a particular aphorism is secondary, but only when this possibility can be supported by such evidence as changes within a text, the existence of objective external data, or the correlation of internal and external data. Frye then shows how an aphorism can legitimately be disassociated from an alleged speaker by showing how Wellington's laconic about the playing fields of Eton was shown to be inauthentic. With regard to the great supper/wedding feast parable, however, he says: "There are no convincing literary-historical reasons for denying to Jesus, as narrator, the two divergent recountings of this story" (p. 298). He cites Shakespeare's triple use of the same incident in his English historical dramas and William Faulkner's presentation of different accounts of the same situation as analogies.

Frye then suggests that Shakespeare's use of sources constitutes an analogy to the use of sources by the Evangelists. It must

[9]Cf. Frye's paper for the Pittsburgh Festival on the Gospels: Roland Mushat Frye, "A Literary Perspective for the Criticism of the Gospels," in *Jesus and Man's Hope*, vol. 2, ed. Donald G. Miller and Dikran Y. Hadidian, A Perspective Book (Pittsburgh: Pittsburgh Theological Seminary, 1971), 193–221.

be noted here, however, that Frye seems to be less interested in the use of one gospel by another (i.e., the literary inter-relationships of the gospels) than in the various authors' use of pregospel material. If, Frye says, we wish to test the validity of the methods of form and redaction criticism, we can do so by applying them to Shakespeare. Presumably, if we are thus able to reproduce accurately the stages through which the tradition about Julius Caesar developed (various editions of Plutarch), or if we are able to reproduce Raphael Holinshed's *Chronicles of England, Scotland and Ireland* from an analysis of Shakespeare's cycle of English historical dramas, then the methods would be validated. But Frye seems convinced that the process would result in more erroneous than accurate hypotheses. With the example from Shakespeare we have the proper controls that will allow us to distinguish between good and bad hypotheses, but with the gospels such controls are lacking, and so there is no way to validate the results.

In his conclusion Frye calls upon New Testament scholars to apply the methods of literary criticism to the gospels, and this means to examine the literary characterizations of Jesus. If we first bring "the character of Jesus to life literarily . . ., we may be able better to assess the historical figure who lies behind the four characterizations [in the four canonical gospels] and his relevance to us: we can only get back to the Jesus of history through the Jesus of literature" (p. 302).

Many of the participants in the Colloquy wondered aloud about the purpose of this second section of Frye's essay, about its relationship to the first section, and about its relevance to the announced topic for the Colloquy. Meeks, for example, expressed "mystification" in particular at the concluding paragraph. He felt that the reference to the complaint of E. Bolaji Idowu, "They have taken my Lord away, and I know not where they have laid him" (p. 302), was intended to imply that we ought not to use certain methods of study because they might lead to a corruption of piety. Meeks maintained that questions about Jesus as the object of Christian devotion are of a completely different order from those about the historical Jesus. He was further mystified about the proposition that a study of the gospels as literary wholes is the only way to arrive at the historical Jesus. In reply to Meeks, Frye denied that his concern was with the destruction of faith but rather with the failure to employ adequate methods of literary-historical scholarship. Nevertheless, it is the case, as

333

Meeks observed, that Frye has not shown us how the understanding of the literary characterizations of Jesus in the gospels relates to the search for the Jesus of history, although he acknowledges that the two are not the same.

In his initial response to Frye's essay, Farmer questioned the relevance of this second section, "Beyond the Griesbach Hypothesis," to the announced topic for the Colloquy, as well as to the first part of the essay:

The second half raises very important questions that Frye can justly "piggy back" into the consciousness of N. T. critics who read his paper. But on procedural grounds I think these questions deserve another colloquy, and are not directly relevant to the stated purpose of this Colloquy.

But Farmer then qualified his comments by asking, "Or have I missed something?"[10] Several members of the seminar felt that Farmer had indeed missed something and that Frye's comments did bear on the subject of the relationships among the gospels. There was no general agreement regarding the relevance of part two, but participants in the Colloquy found the issues raised in it worthy of attention and provocative of heated discussion.

In defining the relationship between the two parts of his essay, Frye set up two alternative suppositions. If, he said, our work on the relationships among the gospels issues in a new consensus but we continue to use the same old methods of critical study, then our overall situation has not improved. If we do not arrive at a new consensus, then we should be challenged to use more fruitful methods than we have used in the past. Since Frye did not state what he takes to be the goal of these "more fruitful methods," there remains some perplexity at this point.

Charles Thomas Davis was among the more outspoken supporters of Frye within the seminar. He pointed out that there was strong agreement among the other principal participants in the Colloquy—Albert B. Lord, George Kennedy, and Lou H. Silberman—that the influence of oral tradition must be treated more seriously and that a greater degree of trust in the accuracy

[10]William R. Farmer, "A Response to Professor Roland Mushat Frye's paper prepared for the Colloquy on 'The Relationships of the Gospels,' "14. Like Frye, Farmer revised his paper subsequent to the Colloquy, and, in the process, he both deleted from and added to the original version. The material quoted above is missing from the published version, in which Farmer expresses a more positive appreciation for much of Frye's basic intent in the second part of his essay.

of the primary sources and of the external evidence is justified. Davis also suggested that it is now time to raise the question of the relationships among the gospels in a different way, in view of the fact that the older methods of research have failed to produce a consensus. He warned against the over-extension of the historical-critical method and its application to problems that it is not equipped to answer. For him, the key issue was whether to retain the old methods and disagree only about answers or to raise the pertinent questions in completely new ways.

The discussion of the disintegrating approach to Shakespeare clearly supports Frye's call to treat the gospels as literary wholes. Some members of the seminar, however, questioned the appropriateness of comparing this approach with form and redaction criticism on the grounds that the aims of Shakespearean studies and of gospel studies are not really comparable. One kind of study includes a search for a historical phenomenon (person or tradition), while the other constitutes an attempt to trace the hand of an artist. Nevertheless, Frye maintained that disintegrating approaches by New Testament critics bypass the first essential step in historical scholarship, namely, the understanding of the relevant documents in their integrity. It is probable that modern New Testament scholars would find little to object to in this phrasing of Frye's proposed methodology. One can delineate the stages in gospel research as including, even beginning with, the attempt to understand the gospels in their entirety and integrity. It is the exclusion of the other approaches—redaction, source, and form criticism—that will worry the guild, and it is by no means clear that Frye advocates their total exclusion.

To be sure, Frye found support for his proposal to approach the gospels "holistically." Davis argued that it is time for us to "take the documents to heart," to "let them lie before us undissected." Pointing out that we cannot anticipate where this will lead, he maintained that we should have confidence that an intrinsic and more adequate understanding will result. In an effort to explore the meaning of such a "holistic" approach, Elizabeth Carey asked if it was similar to the way the gospels were read prior to the rise of modern biblical criticism. Frye's answer was that it was not radically different. There is, however, a significant difference that was not noted at the time. The usual precritical method of reading the gospels appears to have been one that conflated them, i.e., brought the four together within some related framework. What Frye is advocating, on the other hand, is a comparative look at each gospel in its enclosed entirety. As Kliever pointed out, this constitutes a "disciplined" approach to the gospels that could parallel rather than replace the historical-critical approach.

The treatment of the relation between parable and aphorism may turn out to be a reasonably concrete illustration of Frye's proposed method of study. It clearly harmonizes with his call to treat the gospels as wholes and with his warning against disintegration. He appears to be on the strongest ground when he cautions us not to treat forms too rigidly. The supposition that a parable cannot have an aphorism or moralizing conclusion is surely questionable. But one wonders if New Testament scholars actually adhere to this position. Joachim Jeremias, who is cited disapprovingly by Frye, does not think that the form of the parable excludes the possibility of a conclusion, and he discusses some parables that, in his view, probably retained the conclusion that Jesus spoke. In general, it is the changed setting of the parable that makes a conclusion suspect for Jeremias. The parables have a double historical setting: that within the life of Jesus and that within the primitive church. The altered setting means that embellishments may have been added to the parables that do not fit the original setting and that may reflect an understanding which is inconsistent with the parable itself. In the main, it is this last point that Jeremias uses to identify the added conclusions. Indeed, in commenting on the aphorism used by Frye as an illustration (Luke 14:11; 18:14b; Matthew 23:12), Jeremias approaches Frye's position:

With regard to such cases of divergent applications it may often remain uncertain whether Jesus himself used the same simile on different occasions with a different application, or whether only one of the applications is original, or whether the simile was transmitted without an interpretation and all the applications are secondary.[11]

While it is true that Rudolf Bultmann displays a stronger tendency than does Jeremias to suspect the authenticity of such applications, he does not reject them on stylistic grounds. Indeed, he does not regard all applications in the gospels as necessarily secondary.[12]

There is yet another point in Frye's treatment of parables and

[11]Joachim Jeremias, *The Parables of Jesus*, trans. S. H. Hooke, rev. ed. (New York: Charles Scribner's Sons, 1963), 107–108; cf. also 96–113.

[12]Rudolf Bultmann, *The History of the Synoptic Tradition*, trans. John Marsh,   336

aphorisms that lacks clarity. He says that repetition is frequently used in literature as a signal of thematic development. One might not quarrel with this and may find that the repetition of the aphorism in Luke 14:11 and 18:14b functions as such a signal. But to say that Jesus repeated himself and to say that Luke used repetition as a literary device is to say two quite different and unrelated things. Luke's use of repetition does not provide evidence that the repeated statement did or did not stem from Jesus.

On closer examination, then, Frye's discussion of parable and aphorism is less helpful than it might be. In one respect, he turns out to be closer to New Testament scholarship than he seems to think. But in another respect it is not clear whether he wants us to understand repeated aphorisms as signals of literary thematic development or as authentic words of Jesus.

As might be expected, a good deal of attention was given to the discussion of Shakespeare's sources. In his essay, Frye had proposed a test in which New Testament scholarly tools would be used without the knowledge of Shakespeare's sources in an attempt to reconstruct them. Joseph A. Fitzmyer was particularly interested in the test, but he suggested that the analogy between Shakespeare and the gospels was not pertinent at this point: "If we had a New Testament Holinshed, I don't think we would be doing what we are doing." Frye replied to Fitzmyer that he was suggesting a way to test the validity of New Testament scholarly methods. If they are sound, one should be able to apply them to Shakespeare's plays and move back to the sources. Frye also indicated, however, that because of the extraordinary complexity of the situation, he would not try to reconstruct Holinshed if it were not extant, and in his essay he had revealed his belief that the proposed test would succeed *only* in a case where we have a control document.

Lou H. Silberman cited an example that illustrated yet another danger in the effort to reconstruct no longer extant sources. Early in the twentieth century, David Hoffmann attempted to use available rabbinic literature to reconstruct a lost midrash on Exodus, the Mekilta of Rabbi Simon ben Yochai.[13] Within the

---

rev. ed. (New York and Evanston: Harper & Row, Publishers, Inc., 1968), 182–187.

[13] D. Hoffmann, *Mechilta de-Rabbi Simon b. Jochai. Ein halachischer und haggadischer Midrasch zu Exodus nach handschriftlichen und gedruckten Quellen reconstruirt und mit erklärenden Anmerkungen und einer Einleitung versehen* (Frankfurt a. M.: J. Kauffmann, 1905).

last twenty years, a medieval manuscript of the Mekilta turned up, and it was found to be nearly the same as Hoffmann's reconstruction. Silberman suggested that it is altogether possible that the medieval manuscript was produced by a scholar as intelligent as Hoffmann, one who used the data then available to reconstruct the Mekilta. In this event, Hoffmann's work of reconstruction would be simply a second scholarly attempt, not at all verified by the subsequent discovery.

The discussion of Shakespearean sources concluded with an exchange between Frye and William S. Babcock. Babcock observed that, if Holinshed were not extant, the decision to attempt its reconstruction would be made on the basis of one's interest. If a person is interested in the history of English chronicles, for example, he or she might very well attempt to reconstruct Shakespeare's sources. But one whose interest is in characterization in Elizabethan drama will probably find no good reason for such an attempt. This observation is particularly germane, for Babcock implied that one's interest in the historical Jesus would require a different method of scholarship from that required to investigate the character of Jesus in the gospels. Frye agreed with Babcock on this point but warned, "We cannot allow what seems to us to be interesting to lead us to think that things are possible historically that are not in fact historically sound." Frye's position is that methods of scholarship that are alleged to be fruitful can be tested within the context of a group of documents whose relationship is known. If successful there, then they can be applied in areas of greater uncertainty. In the final analysis, however, the test of the validity of these scholarly tools would await the discovery of hard evidence, which by the nature of the case must come from archaeology.

Notes for a Future Agenda

The Seminar on Literary Criticism devoted a good deal of its attention to a discussion of the present and future state of research on gospel relationships. It was generally agreed that, with respect to the criteria of language and comparative length, Frye's paper had undermined the self-evidence of the hypothesis of Marcan priority and that the discussion of conflation had made the Griesbach Hypothesis appear possible. If this consensus can be said to represent the current state of the question, what does it imply regarding a future agenda for scholars who are interested in gospel relationships? A number of suggestions were made.

J. D. Thomas cited the work he had done in his doctoral dissertation.[14] Working with two Greek texts of Tobit, between which there was evidence of literary dependence, he found that the older text was a translation of a Hebrew original, while the other was an abbreviation, in which no significant parts of the story were omitted. There is, said Thomas, a third Greek text, which shows evidence of conflation. One could study these documents in an effort to find certain principles of conflation. Such a study would be a notable addition to the work of Longstaff and Frye. It was suggested that a study of other documents showing evidence of conflation would also be useful in ascertaining whether the type of conflation envisioned by the Griesbach Hypothesis is typical. Frye observed that he knew of no study of the principles involved in the production of literary epitomes, condensations, or abbreviations but that such a study would be helpful.

Several persons suggested that it is now necessary to give attention to concrete problems that relate to particular hypotheses. An illustration of such a problem relating to the Griesbach Hypothesis is Mark's omission of the stories of the birth and precocious childhood of Jesus. Kliever noted that such stories frequently occupied a central position in mythic narratives and that their deliberate omission by Mark would be difficult to explain. Daniel Wm. O'Connor also found difficulty in the Griesbach Hypothesis at this point and suggested that literary analogies would not be relevant unless they are found in materials that function in the way gospels do. Farmer called attention to the work of David L. Dungan, who, in a paper on the gospel-producing activity in early Christianity, had addressed himself to the problem of the omission of birth stories in Mark.[15] Nevertheless, it was evident that further work is needed on such concrete problems relating to various hypotheses.

One suggestion seemed to arise directly out of the discussion

[14]James David Thomas, "The Greek Text of Tobit" (Ph.D. diss., The University of Chicago, 1957); cf. J. D. Thomas, "The Greek Text of Tobit," *Journal of Biblical Literature*, 91 (1972), 463–471.

[15]David Laird Dungan, "Reactionary Trends in the Gospel-Producing Activity of the Early Church? Marcion, Tatian, Mark," in *L'Evangile selon Marc. Tradition et Rédaction*, ed. M. Sabbe, Bibliotheca Ephemeridum Theologicarum Lovaniensium 34 (Gembloux: Editions J. Duculot/Louvain: Louvain University Press, 1974), 188–194.

of the second part of Frye's paper, namely, to compare the gospels "macroscopically" rather than "microscopically." Mention has already been made of Davis' call to "let [the gospels] lie before us undissected." Although no one could anticipate the possible results, it was generally felt that this approach might be a significant agenda item that has merit as an addition to, but not as a replacement for, the more traditional analytic approaches.

Farmer called attention to work that is presently being pursued in an effort to identify redactional characteristics in each gospel without presupposing any particular source theory. He suggested that redactional characteristics of one gospel that occur also in parallel passages of another might serve to establish the direction of literary relationship between the two gospels.[16] Swanson sounded a note of caution at this point, however, reminding participants that the type of note-taking proposed by George Kennedy and the phenomenon of textual harmonization might go a long way toward accounting for such occurrences.

Several members of the seminar were interested in extending the scope of the search for materials that might shed light on the relationships among the gospels. The Fourth Gospel and the non-canonical gospels, as well as the Apostolic Fathers and the Apologists, were mentioned as candidates for analysis in this light. The role of Marcion as a "catalyst" in the stabilization of the gospel traditions could be significant. Swanson suggested that the field of the history of religions—for example, Islamic studies —might provide relevant analogies to New Testament problems, particularly in showing how religious traditions develop.

At several points in the discussion, Farmer stated that there is sufficient evidence to show that the Griesbach Hypothesis is the most probable solution to the problem of the relationships among the gospels. He described this evidence as hard but tacit. He felt, however, that it is adequate to convince scholars, provided that an effective way to present it can be found and provided that prejudice against the Griesbach Hypothesis can be further reduced. Most participants in the seminar concluded that the Griesbach theory had now achieved a position of respectabil-

[16] William R. Farmer, "Redaction Criticism and the Synoptic Problem," in *The Society of Biblical Literature One Hundred Seventh Annual Meeting Seminar Papers*, 2 vols. (The Society of Biblical Literature, 1971), 1:239–250; William O. Walker, Jr., "A Method for Identifying Redactional Passages in Matthew on Functional and Linguistic Grounds," *The Catholic Biblical Quarterly*, 39 (1977), 76–93.

ity, that it is at least a possible solution. The seminar was not interested in making suggestions about an effective method of presenting the evidence for any particular hypothesis, but it appears that the time has now come for the explicit presentation of evidence that is thought to be hard but tacit. Surely, at some point, a thorough discussion of the nature of evidence and of the use of criteria for sorting out relationships is in order.[17] The history of scholarship shows, however, that such discussions are best carried on in connection with the presentation of alleged evidence and in response to it. The situation now appears to be one in which there are no certainties and few probabilities regarding relationships among the gospels. Thus, those who hold particular views on this matter should be encouraged to present the evidence in open forum and as fully and clearly as possible.

[17] Progress was made in the Colloquy as a result of Frye's objection to the "canons of criticism" earlier proposed by Farmer (see *The Synoptic Problem*, 227–229). It turned out that the difference was largely semantic. Frye objected to the term "canons" because the word carries implications of authority and inflexibility that are inappropriate in the context of literary history. Farmer said that, under the circumstances, he would henceforth use the word "criteria" rather than "canons," with the understanding that "criteria" means something like "rules of thumb or general principles that tend to apply most of the time." Frye then noted that he would have to reanalyze his claim that the "canons" were "an unnecessary weakness" in Farmer's position. The way is now open for a discussion of the appropriateness of these and other proposed criteria and of their proper use in attempting to clarify the relationships among the gospels.

INDEX OF NAMES

Index

Douglass, Frederick, 270–71
Douris, 138
Duckworth, George E., 98 n. 8
Dundes, Alan, 99
Dungan, David L., 19, 24 n. 18, 262, 339
Einhard, 274
Eissfeldt, O., 221 n. 4
Eliade, Mircea, 35
Elliger, Karl, 221 n. 5, 224 n. 15
Emmelius, Johann-Christoph, 112 n. 20
Empiricus, Marcellus. *See* Marcellus Empiricus
Ennius, 128, 145
Ephoros, 138
Ephraem Syrus, 277
Epictetus, 129, 129 n. 3, 131
Epicurus, 145
Ernesti, Johann August, 20, 20–21, 21 n. 13, 28
Eusebius, 13, 27 n. 24, 135, 136, 137, 138, 147–52, 165, 165–66, 165–66 n. 17, 167–71, 167 n. 22, 176–82, 183
Fackenheim, Emil, 208
Farmer, William R., 2 n. 2, 3 n. 4, 5, 5 n. 6, 7 n. 8, 12, 19, 19 n. 4, 24 n. 18, 147 n. 36, 174, 174, 176, 187, 192, 257 n. 20, 262, 262–63 n. 2, 264, 283–84, 308–310, 308 n. 4, 311, 312, 317 n. 21, 318 n. 22, 323–341 *passim*, 327, 329, 334, 340 n. 16
Farrer, Austin M., 312
Faulkner, William, 297, 298, 332
Feldman, Louis H., 146 n. 34
Feuerbach, Ludwig, 20
Finkelstein, Louis, 196
Fitzmyer, Joseph A., 11, 164 n. 10, 165 n. 12, 165 n. 14, 247 n. 9, 255 n. 18, 257 n. 20, 337
Fleay, F. G., 288
Foakes Jackson, F. J. *See* Jackson, F. J. Foakes
Fontenrose, Joseph E., 54 n. 37, 57 n. 48
Frazer, Sir James George, 55 n. 40
Frend, W. H. C., 26 n. 21
Froude, James Anthony, 270
Frye, Roland Mushat, 9, 9–10, 10, 11–12, 13, 294 n. 57, 301, 303–322

passim, 304 n. 1, 323–341 *passim*, 332 n. 9
Fuller, Reginald H., 9, 10, 11, 12, 13–14, 174–75, 175, 281 n. 35, 283, 309–11
Galdi, Marco, 274
Gallie, W. B., 23 n. 16
Gaster, Theodor H., 55 n. 40, 55 n. 41
Gaynor, Frank, 266 n. 6
Gennep, Arnold van, 40 n. 15
Gerhardsson, Birger, 106, 158–59, 159 n. 2, 191, 232, 250–51, 255
Gerould, Gordon Hall, 51–52 n. 36
Gertner, M., 228 n. 26
Ginsberg, H. L., 253
Ginzberg, Louis, 206, 215 n. 54
Gogarten, Friedrich, 314
Goldin, Judah, 208 n. 34, 208–9, 213 n. 45
Gomme, A. W., 138
Goodspeed, Edgar J., 152 n. 42
Gordon, Robert K., 278 n. 33
Goshen-Gottstein, Moshe H., 222, 222 n. 9, 227 n. 24
Gossage, A. J., 141 n. 27
Gottschalk, Paul, 289 n. 49, 302 n. 64, 332
Goulder, M. D., 188
Grant, Robert M., 152 n. 41, 258 n. 22
Greenberg, Moshe, 222
Gregory, 277
Griesbach, Johann Jakob, 3 n. 4, 20, 27 n. 24. *See also* Griesbach Hypothesis *in* Subject Index
Griffith, G.T., 139 n. 22
Grimal, Pierre, 55 n. 41
Gryson, R., 137 n. 18
Guilding, Aileen, 188–89 n. 24
Gunkel, Hermann, 108 n. 13, 111, 220, 220 n. 1
Guthrie, W. K. C., 129 n. 4, 132, 133
Güttgemanns, Erhardt, 105, 109, 111–13, 112 n. 18, 112 n. 20, 113 n. 21, 113 n. 22, 115
Gutwenger, E., 152 n. 41
Hadas, Moses, 243 n. 5
Hanson, R. P. C., 27 n. 24
Harnack, Adolf (Adolph), 22, 24 n. 19
Harrington, Daniel J., 213 n. 47

345

INDEX OF SUBJECTS

Index

Trinity University Monograph Series in Religion